W9-CFO-250

An African Experiment in Nation Building: The Bilingual Cameroon Republic Since Reunification

Other Titles in This Series

Apartheid and International Organizations, Richard E. Bissell

Ethnicity in Modern Africa, edited by Brian M. du Toit

Botswana: An African Growth Economy, Penelope Hartland-Thunberg

Zambia's Foreign Policy: Studies in Diplomacy and Dependence, Douglas G. Anglin and Timothy Shaw

South Africa into the 1980s, edited by Richard E. Bissell and Chester A. Crocker

Crisis in Zimbabwe, edited by Boniface Obichere

The Arab-African Connection: Political and Economic Realities, Victor T. Le Vine and Timothy W. Luke

African Upheavals Since Independence, Grace Stuart Ibingira

Regionalism Reconsidered: The Economic Commission for Africa, Isebill V. Gruhn

Bibliography of African International Relations, Mark W. DeLancey

Westview Special Studies on Africa

An African Experiment in Nation Building:
The Bilingual Cameroon Republic Since Reunification
edited by Ndiva Kofele-Kale

The Federal Republic of Cameroon was created October 1,
1961, when the former British Trusteeship Territory of the
Southern Cameroons and the newly independent Republic of
Cameroun (formerly the French Trusteeship Territory of Cameroun)
joined together in a highly creative venture in nation building.
This volume attempts a critical evaluation of the Cameroon experiment, underscoring both its achievements and failures.

The first chapters, devoted to the search for a Cameroonian identity, chronicle the rise and evolution of Cameroon
nationalism. Parts 2 and 3 examine the nation's major political and economic institutions, focusing on the distribution of
political power and tracing efforts at shaping an equitable
economic order through integration of the federated states'
economies and reduction of economic disparities among the
various regions. The final section, on various aspects of
social development, reflects a concern for bridging gaps between
French- and English-speaking, as well as between rural and
urban Cameroonians.

Ndiva Kofele-Kale is professor of comparative international
politics at Governors State University, Park Forest South,
Illinois.

An African Experiment in Nation Building: The Bilingual Cameroon Republic Since Reunification

edited by Ndiva Kofele-Kale

Westview Press / Boulder, Colorado

Westview Special Studies on Africa

Published in 1980 in the United States of America by
    Westview Press, Inc.
    5500 Central Avenue
    Boulder, Colorado 80301
    Frederick A. Praeger, Publisher

Library of Congress Catalog Card Number: 79-5356
ISBN: 0-89158-685-7

Composition for this book was provided by the author.
Printed and bound in the United States of America.

For Yoti, Meano, Ewenye, and
to the memory of my parents

Contents

Tables and Figures

Figures

Foreword

Willard R. Johnson

THE POLITICAL ACHIEVEMENT

Cameroon is often called "the African continent
in microcosm." It is one of the most diverse and
most beautiful countries in a continent whose
social intricacies and geographical variations
attain a scale matched only by the industrial
world's capacity to stereotype them. There are more
language/cultural groups among Africans than any
other collection of people of comparable size, yet,
to the Western World, "they all look alike." In
this vast region of every geographic and geological
machination the Mind of God has wrought, the
Western eye sees only "jungle." Among the political
traditions of these humanity-oriented peoples, who
created and have maintained the oldest experience in
statecraft, the leaders of the modern imperialist
states concern themselves only with the "fragile new
states" that their own interventions provoked into
being. But, that is today's Africa in context.
And in that context, almost all the many questions
outsiders may pose about the continent may be
answered, in some way, based on the experience of
Cameroonians.

Of course, the questions always reflect one's
own preoccupations as much as the object of concern.
Western intellectuals and policy-makers are just
beginning to appreciate Africa for itself, and not
simply as an open stage on which someone else's
dramas are played out. For too many of them the
good African state is the one that is quiet and
friendly. Cameroon has been that. Old orders have
not crumbled too rapidly, and there are few new
accents to be heard there. But, this was not
always so, and it is remarkable that the fears that
dominated Western officials at the time of
Cameroon's independence have died so quickly.

Cameroon is, with Somalia, Africa's only experience in reconciling the impact of two colonial legacies (actually, for Cameroon, and only potentially for Somalia, it is three). With Kenya, Cameroon was the first colony in "Black Africa" to experience armed rebellion against colonial rule. It created one of Africa's few attempts at federalism. It is one of a handful of states where the identity and authority of the Head of State has not been in doubt for a single day since independence. Next to Sekou Toure, President Ahidjo is Africa's longest ruling political leader. The country has one of Africa's best records of economic growth.

And yet, one of the important questions to pose about this, as any experiment is, "Is it successful?" Proper refinements to this question would include, "successful at what?" and "successful for whom?"

A decade ago I ended my own study of The Cameroon Federation with the following observation: "Cameroon has been remarkably successful in consolidating the state. By doing so it has given itself an even chance for some day becoming the 'One Cameroon Nation'." This present book ably takes up that next issue and argues that the country has made, and had made great strides in achieving a sense of common Cameroonian nationality among its diverse peoples. Both the pre-independence and the more recent experience in consolidating that sense of common history and common destiny is amplified here beyond what has already been published elsewhere. However, one can still ask the important question whether the political success of the state is also the political success of its people? The Cameroonian political order has revealed a high level of centralization and concentrated authority. Indeed, unique among African states, on the day of independence there was only one functioning authoritative institution, the Presidency itself. Since that time the trappings of federalism have been sloughed off, and so also the trappings of competitive political parties. Governmental affairs are mostly technical; the realm of politics is small.

Another open question is whether the Cameroon experience contains useful lessons for the partisans of African unity more generally, and for fragmentary societies elsewhere. President Ahidjo clearly opted to emphasize the structural dimensions of integration over the ideological ones. A firmly established and essentially coercive order preceded the growth of social, cultural and economic

interchanges among the Cameroonian peoples. It is
not clear that reliance on such functional transactions would have, or could have led gradually to
the political and structural unity that the
Cameroon state represents today. Perhaps it is the
same for regional or continental unities. But the
conditions which allowed Cameroon to put these
structures of unity into place may be unique, or
nearly so, involving as they did such a large role
for the United Nations. Perhaps there is little
guidance in this experience for efforts such as the
Customs Union of Central African States or the
Economic Community of West African States. We have
already seen the East African Community fall apart;
it did have some common institutions to manage
functional interaction, but lacked the supranational
political authority that the Cameroon experience
would suggest may be necessary. On the other hand,
this experience may hold a rationale for optimism
regarding the viability of the "bi-communal" state
of Sudan, which despite considerable autonomy for
the Southern Region, preserves a single structure
of national authority. Cameroon has never taken up
the mission a few of its political leadership have
entertained for it, to be a spokesman if not a
"pilot" for African unity. The country has been a
frequent but never a staring participant in the
institutions and special missions of African
diplomacy. The present book does not yet provide
us with the study one wishes to see on Cameroon's
role in African and broader international relations.
      A final question of signal significance is,
"has Cameroon's success in state-building been
translated into economic success? and for whom?"
Kwame Nkrumah is often quoted as having summed up
the modern priorities of African nationalism by
saying, "Seek ye first the political kingdom, and
all things else shall be added unto you." Now
Africans are waiting to judge the truth of that
dictum. The present volume contributes importantly
to our understanding of the forces at work that
shape the country's economic order. We have still
to determine the significance of that order, and my
remaining comments are a preliminary exploration of
that issue.

THE ECONOMIC ACHIEVEMENT

      "Has Cameroon been successful in its efforts to
develop?" This is a deceptively simple question.

No doubt the governmental leadership feels that it
has been successful, and popular attitudes generally
seem to reflect basic satisfaction and optimism.
Admittedly, the hard evidence describing public
opinion on the matter is not available for the
whole country. This volume explores some aspects
of popular attitudes among the West Cameroonians.
Nonetheless, the superficial data available reflects well on Cameroon.

Nonetheless, it is not clear that Cameroon is
successful, if we consider development to require
the transformation of the colonial economy to permit a sustaining pattern of growth away from dependency on factors of production and decisions
made outside the country, a pattern of growth based
on factors of production under the country's own
ownership and/or control. Such a pattern is necessary if the economy is not to stagnate before real
development is achieved. In these respects, while
not yet clearly a failure, Cameroon seems not to
have made the necessary changes, and is therefore
likely to be more like than unlike its neighbors in
terms of its economic future. The picture is a
mixed one, however, with positive and negative
features.

The Positive Features

With respect to the announced goals of the
Government, it is hard to fault the rhetoric used in
Cameroon's documents that represent and guide the
economic planning process. The general themes
appear in President Ahidjo's speech presenting the
Fourth Five Year Plan to the National Assembly in
September 1976. He claimed that Cameroon was being
guided in its development efforts by four broad
principles: 1) "le developpement auto-centre," for
which "self-oriented" or even "self-reliant" might
be a better translation than the litteral one; 2)
"liberalisme plainfie," or a liberal economy that
mixes planning and state participation with private
enterprise; 3) "developpement equilibre," or with
equity not only as between city and countryside, but
the regions of the country and the sectors of the
economy; and 4) "la justice sociale," or a humanis-
tic approach to improving the social welfare of the
people. These guiding principles would find widespread support among the leaders and intellectuals
of Africa. The more socialistic minded persons
might assert that a large role for private enterprise, especially if it involves international

capital, would undermine satisfaction of the other goals, and those with a more capitalistic bent might argue that substantial state planning and control would stifle initiative and bog development efforts down in bureaucratic bumbling, and thus also undermine the achievement of the other goals.

President Ahidjo's elaboration of his meaning for the characterization "auto-centre" tilts his rhetoric towards the more "progressive" formulations for the development approaches of African regimes with quite a different character from that of Cameroon:

> Le developpement auto-centre, qui pour nous signifie d'abord developpement du peuple par le peuple, respond a la necessite de mobiliser toutes les ressources et toutes les energie nationales en vue du developpement, car nous sommes profondement convaincus qu'il n'est de developpement authentique que celui qui repose sur l'effort productif et createur du peuple.

> Self oriented development, which for us signifies primarily the development of the people by the people, responds to the necessity to mobilize all the national resources and the whole of the national energy in the development effort, because we are profoundly convinced that the only authentic development is that which is based on the productive and creative effort of the people themselves.

However, Ahidjo explains that the liberal part of the program reflects a conviction that "private initiative remains the best motor for development, although the state, being responsible for protecting the general interest, should mobilize, coordinate, and guide all development efforts." It was President Nyerere who pointed out that, with so little capital and managerial strength of their own, Africans who promote a system of private enterprise are really promoting a system dominated by foreign enterprises. What may be true for Tanzania may also be true for Cameroon.

On the performance side, however, Cameroon has done well. Throughout the 1960s it enjoyed one of Africa's highest rates of growth in gross national product, with annual average rates of increase during the second half of the decade nearly 7%. Planned targets for growth during the 1970s were even higher, and despite stagnation in mid-decade as

Cameroon also reflected the energy crisis and the general pattern of world inflation, it was among the first African states to recover and at decade's end was booming. Although the goals of the Third Five Year Plan, 1971-76, gave prominence to the satisfaction of basic social needs and to infrastructure, it had an important place for agriculture, in an effort at a "Green Revolution" that has been proclaimed successful. Although the Fourth Plan is styled one that will emphasize industrial development, the figure for investment in agriculture raises the rate from the 9% of the Third Plan to 15%.

Cameroon also had plans to diversify its production for export, in order to protect itself from the rapid fluctuations in prices that bedevil African products in the world markets. This diversification would come by increasing the role of the industrial sector, basically, but also by increasing production of strong agricultural products such as Arabica and Robusta coffee. They also desired to find new customers for their products and expected to gain markets as Cameroon participated in the expansion and trade unification of the European Common Market.

Exploration for petroleum has been proceeding, and discoveries of unannounced dimensions have been made. An air of cautious optimism pervades Yaounde, as work proceeds frantically to build their own refinery, and the basis for an integrated petrochemical industry. The country is not yet to be compared with Nigeria, or even with Angola, in terms of what oil might do for its economic future, but there is at least reasonable expectation that it may be self sufficient in energy resources. Part of the reason Cameroonian officials are so guarded in talking about their petroleum resources is reported to be to avoid arousing popular expectations that might later be disappointed, but part may be due to the location, West Cameroon, which may therefore find its nationalist commitment to the "Kamerun Idea" tested as never before.

The Negative Features

Despite the goals we have described and the efforts made toward reaching them, Cameroon has not made dramatic progress in lessening its dependency on its traditional partners, or in establishing a pattern of growth that might avoid blacked development paths in the future.

Weak Exports. The pattern persists, at least
through the mid-1970s, of prominence among the exports of crops that are bulky and that provide a
portion of the total value of exports lower than
their proportion of the total volume, In 1965, the
most prominent of these exports were palm kernels
and palm products, fresh bananas, and all the products of wood, especially logs and unprocessed wood.
These items remained a prominent feature of the export pattern in 1975. In fact, the proportion of
total exports that raw wood represented actually
increased. Bananas were no less prominent, and
cocoa, which is a favorable product in this regard
had decreased as a proportion of exports. The only
two products with a very favorable position in terms
of value versus volume of exports which actually
gained in their importance among the country's exports was Arabica coffee and rubber products.

Although industrial production has increased
in the country, these products do not figure importantly among exports, and of those which do,
especially to the central African region, many are
products that simply have passed through Cameroon
with virtually no value added there. Exports from
the secondary sector have fluctuated substantially
but tend to amount to about 16-18% of the total
exports, in value, with highs of 23% in 1969 and
33% in 1974. In the latter case, the value of exports rose due, in part, to the inflation caused by
the rises in petroleum prices. Cameroon has not
achieved much diversification of production.

Future plans for the agricultural and primary
sectors may change the pattern slightly, as the
country not only continues to emphasize production
of basic foodstuffs for local consumption, but also
emphasizes those export agricultural crops that
generally have returned more money than the average
in relation to their volume and products whose
prices are likely to remain strong--such as cocoa,
coffee, cotton, rice, sugar, rubber. But there has
also continued to be an emphasis placed on export
of wood which has not been a strong export earner
in relation to other products.

Poor Articulation of Sectors. Cameroon continues to have a very poor indigenous capital goods
sector. Some indication of the build-up in this
sector is seen in the items that the country exports in substantial quantities--hand tools, farm
tools for hand and for use with animals, and
electric batteries. But these products do not

XIX

represent sufficient development of the intermediate
capital goods sector, and some of these items, along
with many other industrial items, are apparently
imported and then exported, with little value-added
in the real sense (although there may be a substantial price increase in some cases). Cameroon now
manufactures electric batteries, for example, but
also continues to import a substantial number of
them. A number of other items that would appear to
be amenable to local manufacture continue to
figure prominently among Cameroon's imports--saws,
pliers, domestic utensils and tools, tongs and
other forge materials, and miscellaneous agricultural tools. So here also Cameroon has not yet suffi-
cently diversified its production.

In its Third Five Year Plan indications are
given of an intention to develop a number of important local capital goods industries, such as a
fertilizer plant, expansion of cement production
capacity, processing plants for metal products
such as structural iron bars and beams, scrap iron
processing, rolled sheet metal, and a petroleum
refinery, as well as plants for making electrical
batteries, tires and inner tubes, paper pulp,
ceramics, and tanning. But, all of these items are
also repeated in the Fourth Plan, and although it
is not obvious that nothing was accomplished on
them in the previous plan, they are most likely
either a continuation or even the initiation of the
project, rather than a further expansion or duplica-
tion of them. There are additional industrial projects in the Fourth Plan, which includes provision
for a plant to make nails and spikes, brick making
plants in rural locations, electric cable making,
an extrusion plant for aluminum sheets and beams,
plants for making hardware, one for making electric
motor parts, and a plant for processing wood, including milling, rolling, and veneering. In all,
the investment in the industrial-mining-and energy
sector, which goes far beyond the intermediate
capital goods category, of course, is planned to
amount to nearly 290 million francs CFA, or about
29% of the total investment program. However, the
projects I have mentioned above, including those
that seem to repeat ones in the previous plan, only
amount to about 50 million francs, or less than
seven percent (7%) of the total. So, the great
bulk of the secondary industry investment seems to
be going into the basic industries for export and
extraction.

Already relatively industrialized in comparison to the other states in the region, much of Cameroon's industrial export strength is based on trans-shipping. The country's industrial "strength" more generally is based on cheaply processing imported bauxite for the European market or import substitution for consumer items. The aluminum smelting plant the French firm Pechiney-Ugine built at Edea in the early 1950s has depended until now on ores owned by the same and other French companies operating in Guinea and elsewhere. Recent plans repeat the often mentioned Cameroonian hope to open up its own deposits of bauxite for exploitation. The aluminum produced in Cameroon has not been oriented to local markets, but there has been some slight spill-over to them, in items such as roofing and other building materials, kitchen ware and other small utensils. Mostly what Cameroon produces in manufactures are luxury or general consumption goods, such as cloth and clothing, shoes, cigarettes, and bottled drinks, especially beer.

The structure of Cameroonian imports has shifted slightly but has not been transformed. It has lessened somewhat its dependency on basic foodstuffs, lowering the proportion of total value of imports represented by food from 12.5% in 1965 to less than 6% in 1975. There was a modest increase in the proportion represented by capital goods, which rose from 21% to about 25%. And there was a surprisingly modest increase in the costs of energy resources, which went from 4.5% to 7.3% of the total. The rest of the import structure remained basically the same as before.

It is safe to say that Cameroon remains far from achieving the structural transformation of imports or of domestic production one normally would associate with real development.

Dependency on Foreign Capital. Cameroon also has yet to lessen its dependency on outside capital. The Government has taken pride repeatedly in being able to balance its operational budget from its own resources, which has happened in a good many years since independence. Its own fiscal and productive resources have also been used to make substantial contributions to the total (national level and provincial level) development budgets. Such contributions will amount to about 22% of the financing for the Fourth Plan. Nevertheless, Cameroon remains dependent on foreign sources for the great bulk of its development financing. Direct foreign subsidies

will cover about 4% of the current Plan, and foreign
borrowing an additional 45%. The private sector,
also almost all foreign, is expected to provide
about 29% of the total funds needed. Thus foreign
sources account for nearly three quarters of the
total funds.

The foreign sources account for about the same
proportion of financing for the Fourth Plan as for
the Third. In the previous plan direct subventions
were up to 10%, loans another 16% and private investment an additional 48%. For the plan prior to
that one, the Second Plan, the foreign component
was probably even higher, inasmuch as the proportion of foreign funding for just the publicly
supported components was about 65%.

Foreign capital is readily welcomed in
Cameroon, which has a very liberal investment code
that is ably discussed in Dr. Ndongko's chapter in
this work. It is also plainly evident from the
material in that chapter, as well as that in Dr.
Clignet's chapter, that foreign investment has not
reduced the income and employment disparities among
Cameroonians or among the regions of the country.

It appears that Cameroon is more generous to
foreign capital than normal business practices
require. This may be due to lack of experience, a
deliberate leniency, or pressures from its aid and
diplomatic partners (especially France). Whatever
the reason, the dimensions of the problem are hinted
at by the following discussion of a single case
study.

Recently several international investors
(including a multilateral lender) joined with the
Cameroon Government in sponsoring a project to cut,
process and ship timber and timber products, in
which industry Cameroon has long been active. The
project was developed and was to be managed by a
foreign partnership that was formed explicitly for
the purpose by a well established French firm. The
Partnership will own forty percent of the share
holdings, the same as the Cameroonian Government
agency. According to investment proposals for the
project, the international public investor would
provide (through an intermediary) a loan that would
amount to nearly twice the equity inputs of the
French Partnership, but would receive only half the
equity shares. Additionally, the intermediary
itself was to match the first loan, but for no
equity shares. Other banks would also loan to the
project an even greater amount, to produce a debt
to equity ratio of about three to one. This is a

level that is higher than what most lenders grant directly to private firms in developing countries. Indeed, one must wonder if the French firm would have been able to mobilize that amount of capital on its own, and this is all guaranteed by the Cameroonian Government.

The story continues, however. The French firm was engaged to provide the preliminary organization of the project, for which it was guaranteed a lump sum payment of at least $704,000 (with increases for inflation). This for a project in which it is a 40% equity owner. The firm was also to receive an exclusive right to market the project's output outside the local region, some 87% of the total output. For this "service" the firm was to receive a commission amounting to 8% of the f.o.b. price, despite the fact that it would be marketing the product to itself and would thus also make additional profits from its resale. These commissions alone were estimated to amount to some $8m over the first ten years. Additionally, the firm was projected to receive $576,000 in distributed profits (the Government would receive an equal amount) and rights to $682,000 in undistributed profits over the first nine years. Were all these profits to be spread evenly over the nine years they would represent an annual return on the equity investment of 29%, an unusually high rate for non-petroleum projects even in the underdeveloped world.

Of course, this project was to generate employment--about six hundred fifty jobs for local people. But despite a built-in training program, the number of expatriate staff in top management positions was to fall only from fifteen to eleven during the first three years, which was as long as there were any specific plans spelled out for a training program.

Perhaps it is the making of arrangements such as the above that keeps Cameroon and other countries like it, which so aggressively pursue foreign capital, underdeveloped.

XXIII

Preface

In the summer of 1977, the Cameroon Students'
Union in the United States of America invited me to
chair a panel discussion during its 15th annual
general meeting in Bloomington, Indiana. The topic
selected for mooting was quite appropriately:
"Cameroon Reunification, Sixteen Years After:
Challenges and Prospects." At the close of that
meeting and in subsequent encounters, the President
of the Students' Union, Dr. Louis Jackai (now a
research scientist at the International Institute
of Tropical Agriculture, Ibadan, Nigeria) and his
able secretary, Mr. Tagne Tantse (currently working
toward an advanced degree in Agriculture Economics
at Southern Illinois University, Carbondale) urged
me to undertake the task of addressing the issue of
Cameroon's unequal union from my dual vantage point
as an Anglophone Cameroonian and a student of
Cameroon politics.

Encouraged by their persistence and finding
the idea itself sufficiently appealing, I agreed to
put together this volume drawing upon the collective wisdom of eminent students of Cameroon affairs.
In inviting contributions from authors, I was guided
by the firm belief that the time has come for
Africans to seize control of their history--as well
as their politics, economy and culture--in order to
effectively counteract the insidious ethnocentricism
that has characterised so much of Euro-American
scholarship on Africa. And that the Cameroon story
in particular, the story of a people's struggle to
throw off the yoke of Anglo-French colonial domination and to develop a national community out of the
messy legacy of political chaos, ethnic and
regional rivalry and economic underdevelopment must
now be told by Cameroonians themselves. This volume
represents a modest first step in this direction.
The majority of the fourteen contributing authors
are Cameroonian scholars. In addition, all of the
six non-Cameroonian contributors have had extensive

field experience in Cameroon and are a far cry from
the pontificating arm chair theorists of very recent
memory.

Although I set out to do a comprehensive
assessment of the reunification story, the reader
will notice quite a few gaps in this collection.
In this respect then, the book does not pretend to
have answered all the questions that have been
raised about the Cameroon experiment. It does,
however, attempt to raise and confront some very
fundamental social, political, and economic issues
about this most critical and significant phase in
Cameroon's modern history; the phase when Cameroonians ostensibly took charge of their destiny. While
the focus is on Cameroon, the issues and problems
raised are not unique to this country. They are
quite properly African. The book should therefore
be of interest to Africanists in several disci-
plines, to statesmen interested in comprehending the
practical problems associated with the search for
pan-African unity, and to students and generalists
who desire a handy reference book--not available
before--that updates earlier studies on the
Cameroon federation.

ACKNOWLEDGEMENTS

I am grateful to a number of colleagues who
generously contributed their time to read portions
of this manuscript and to provide valuable insights.
I would like to mention in particular, Dr. Mudiayi
Ngandu of the World Bank and Dr. Meddi Mugyenyi of
the University of Nairobi, two very promising
scholars whose careers bear watching. Professor
Willard R. Johnson of the Massachusetts Institute
of Technology graciously agreed to contribute the
foreword to this volume. His own writings on
Cameroon stand as a model to which this writer and
all students of Cameroon studies would do well to
aspire. I am grateful to him. Special thanks to
my graduate assistants, Mukaila Kadiri and Semei
Tamukedde Zake, for painstakingly compiling the
index and to Mrs. Lynne Hostetter for assisting in
the typing of the draft of this manuscript. I
should also like to acknowledge the kind assistance
of Ms. Diane Salazar. Ms. Marsha Doyle helped
turned the final draft into a finished product,
quickly and expertly. I acknowledge with deep
graditude her contribution to this project which was

definitely above and beyond professional expectations.

No collection of essays can be better than the
material on which it is based for in a very real
sense the whole is indeed the sum of its parts. I
was extremely fortunate to secure the cooperation
of a fine and dedicated group of scholars who
embraced this project with unbounded enthusiasm.
To the extent that their papers hopefully will
contribute to our appreciation of the challenge and
promise of the Cameroon experiment and help us
toward a better understanding of the dynamics of
national integration in post-colonial Africa, we
owe a heavy debt of gratitude to these contributors.

Finally, grateful acknowledgement is made to
the following for permission to reprint previously
published material: The Royal African Society for
"One-Party Government and Political Development in
Cameroun," by J.-F. Bayart, reprinted from African
Affairs, vol. 13, no. 287, April 1973. The
Canadian Journal of African Studies (CJAS) for
"Le federalisme Camerounias," by Jacques Benjamin
reprinted from CJAS, vol. V, no. 3, 1971 and
"Federalism in Cameroon: The Shadow and the
Reality," by Frank M. Stark, reprinted from CJAS,
vol. X, no. 3, 1976. The Institute of African
Studies, University of Zambia for "Patterns of
Political Orientations Toward the Nation: A Com-
parison of Rural-Urban Residents in Anglophone
Cameroon," by N. Kofele-Kale, reprinted from
African Social Research, 26 December 1978.

Ndiva Kofele-Kale
Park Forest, Illinois

Introduction

The new born nation seeks as its first order of business the establishment of its identity. As Seymour Martin Lipset persuasively argued in The First New Nation, countries, like people, are not handed identities at birth "but acquire them through the arduous process of 'growing,' a process which is a notoriously painful affair."[1] On October 1, 1961, a new nation was born in Africa--the bi-lingual Federal Republic of Cameroon--signalling the culmination of a long and heroic struggle to reunify the former German Kamerun which was partitioned into French and British dependencies at the end of the European War of 1914-18. It is to the history, the peoples, and institutions of this unusual nation that these essays speak. All are dedicated to examining, analysing, and explicating this union, as it struggles through the notoriously painful process of growing up.

The essays are grouped into four major parts. The first part is devoted to the search for a Cameroonian identity. These papers chronicle the rise and evolution of Cameroon nationalism, the ideology that sustained the movement for reunification and the valiant efforts by Cameroonians to internalize the idea of belonging to one nation. Part II of the volume examines the major political institutions of the nation focusing attention on the distribution of political power, one of the key elements in balancing pluralistic pressures militating against national unity. In Part III, the focus shifts to an examination of economic institutions. The articles trace the efforts at shaping an equitable economic order through attempts at integrating the economies of the federated states and reducing economic disparities among the various regions. The final part of the volume draws together a series of essays which address various aspects of the social development front. They share a common denominator

in their concern with bridging the gap between
French and English-speaking, as well as between
rural and urban, Cameroonians. The essays draw our
attention to the formidable obstacles to effective
national communication and consensus formation
posed by extreme linguistic diversity and the unequal distribution of educational facilities and
opportunities for participation in the labor market.

THE SEARCH FOR IDENTITY

     The short introductory chapter in Part I by
Kofele-Kale is a series of reflections on the
Kamerun Idea. This ideological prop for the Pan-
Kamerun Movement has undergone detailed examination
by many Cameroonophiles who, in spite of their expressed verstehen approach, seem bent on stripping
it of its mystique by subjecting it to an unnecessary process of intellectualization. While we agree
that Cameroonian nationalism is not sui generis and
should as such not be spared the rigor in analysis
that scholars employ as they confront social
phenomena; I take the position, nevertheless, that
the significance of the Kamerun Idea lies in the
real impact it had on the lives of Cameroonian men
and women, not on whether it rests on a mythical
foundation of a once unified German Kamerun or
whether the content of its symbols are factual or
not. Arguments that view it in this light are not
only misleading but, quite frankly, detracting.
Misleading in that they fail to acknowledge the
place of myth and mythology in all political movements throughout history and detracting because of
the misplaced emphasis on historical precision.
The Idea must be evaluated not so much in terms of
the factual content of its rhetoric but on the
effects it had on the Cameroonian national psyche.
     This approach at explaining our nationalist
symbols remains the only legitimate one for the
Cameroonian political historian qua nationalist.
For his role is not simply that of a detached
scholar who interprets history from some calculated
vantage point of non-involvement but one whose interpretations of history must serve as the basis for
change. Thus the history of the ideas that gave his
nation the semblance of form and shape must be interpreted (this, after all, is what history is
about) in terms of the effect they had in mobilizing
people and challenging them to reach for new
heights.

The chapter by Njeuma and Chem-Langhee, "The Pan-Kamerun Movement 1949-1961" should be considered a definitive study of the origins of modern Cameroon nationalism. The paper traces the rise and evolution of the Pan-Kamerun Movement in the three Cameroons with particular emphasis on the section under British trusteeship. The paper identifies four major causes that gave rise to this movement: (1) political and administrative reorganization of French Cameroon found it gradually becoming a part of French Equatorial Africa which could have meant losing its special status within the United Nations; (2) the artificiality of the intra-Western Cameroon boundary which proved a wellspring for irredentist sentiments; (3) dissatisfaction at the slow pace of socio-economic development in the British administered section and what was perceived as benign neglect on the part of the British in maintaining the status quo; and (4) the prominent and highly visible positions held by non-Cameroonians in both the civil service and private sector unleashed an avalanche of xenophobia which drained into the nationalist movement.

The realization of the goals of the Pan-Kamerun Movement were postponed, at times unnecessarily, as a result of set-backs it encountered both at home and abroad. And it is in the isolation of the factors that impeded this movement that the Njeuma and Chem-Langhee paper is an improvement over many existing evaluations. At the international level the Pan-Kamerun Movement encountered opposition from the concert of European colonial powers who preferred the status quo and saw in this movement a potential threat which if allowed to succeed would have torpedoed their grand design to keep Africa forever under European domination. The movement also ran into unexpected obstacles at the domestic level; obstacles brought in part by the differences in political outlook and party organization of the various contending ruling elites. The authors' point that these differences in political outlook were the inevitable consequence of the divisive feelings of regionalism actively encouraged by colonial administrative policies is well taken. However, their contention that the political fragmentation of the territory, which was followed by decades of separate development, made it difficult for Cameroonians to see themselves as sharing a common destiny is a potential source of criticism. The thrust of my article: "Reflections on the Kamerun Idea" suggests that Cameroonian

XXIX

consciousness derived its raison d'être from the fact of fragmentation; this was the crucible from which was forged a sense of oneness and a feeling of "Kamerunianness."

The Pan-Kamerun movement was by no means an organizational or ideological monolith. It embraced many political groupings with competing notions of what the end product would look like and how it could be attained. In a very refreshing typology of political postures vis-à-vis the issue of reunification, the authors identify four major schools: (1) the Autonomist/Integrationatist/Associationist who saw the future of British Cameroons as inextricably bound to that of Nigeria; (2) the Secessionists for whom severance of all ties with Nigeria and the establishment of a sovereign independent Southern Cameroons state was the battle cry of the faithful; (3) the Reunificationists who wanted separation from Nigeria followed by immediate reunification with the French-speaking Cameroons; and (4) the Expedientists/Foncharians who were committed to all of the above goals but selectively and vigorously pursued any one at any given time only when it was in their political interest to do so. Even where there was general agreement among the political elite on the intrinsic merits of the idea of reunification, differences arose in translating this idea into practice. For some reunification was a means to an end; an instrument for terminating European colonialism in the Cameroons and the attainment of immediate independence.

Reunification, for this group, was approached with a sense of urgency and immediacy. The alternative view saw reunification as a desirable end but one which should be approached with caution and in stages. Their espousal of reunification was not accompanied by any burning sense of urgency since it was viewed as a long range possibility, an ultimate goal.

In moving from the paper by Njeuma and Chem-Langhee to Kofele-Kale's "The Political Culture of Anglophone Cameroon," we are making an important transition both in terms of focus and methodology. We shift from an historical narrative of the genesis of the identity question to a quantitative analysis of how the concept of "We are all Cameroonians" has taken firm root. The article focuses on Anglophone Cameroonians, the overwhelming majority of whom, as Njeuma and Chem-Langhee have already pointed out, opted for Cameroon citizenship in February of 1961.

The central thrust of Kofele-Kale's paper is
an exploration of the relationship between environment and political orientations toward the nation.
His umbrella hypothesis is that variations in environmental location are accompanied by parallel
contrasts in political orientations, such that urban
and rural residents will subscribe to different
patterns of political attitudes toward the Cameroon
nation. In this vein, rural and urban residents
are compared along two major political culture
dimensions: sense of national identity and feelings
of community. These two types of identity are considered critical factors in the determination of
how well integrated a nation is.

The paper draws attention to some very interesting and ervealing aspects of the Anglophone political culture. It reveals, for instance, that
Cameroonians generally have a low level of political
knowledge mainfestly expressed in their inability to
identify their political leaders, especially the
party leadership. This finding is of some significance precisely because Cameroon is a one-party
state and official party rhetoric unequivocally
asserts that the Cameroon National Union has succeeded in penetrating the masses. Interestingly
enough, Cameroonians seem to express a high level of
national pride. They are attached to their country
and hold their President in very high regard. An
equally significant finding in the Kofele-Kale
paper is the sense of community, of oneness which
was found to be fairly widespread among the sampled
population. Although this sentiment does vary in
intensity and geographic location, the author
nevertheless concludes that on the whole Anglophone
Cameroonians have certainly internalized their
"Cameroonianness" and do not contest the basic
aspects of their citizenship.

THE DISTRIBUTION OF POLITICAL POWER

The first paper in Part II by Stark traces the
life and death of the Cameroon federation which for
him was, from its inception, not a real federalism
but the shadow of one. He argues that federalism
as a concept was interpreted differently by political elites from both sides of the border. The
Francophone elites were in principle opposed to any
form of federation, preferring instead a very centralized unitary state. But for tactical reasons
were prepared to concede to a temporary federation

with Southern Cameroons. Anglophone politicians, on the other hand, wanted a loose federation and saw this as the best arrangement under existing circumstances for preserving the individuality of the Southern Cameroons political persona.

The federal constitutional arrangement that was agreed upon was lopsided since it gave the Francophone partner a clear and decisive superiority. Stark attributes a number of reasons to this unequal union. To begin with, the plebiscite questions, as defined by the United Nations, were virtually forced on the Anglophone leaders. Enjoying very little latitude of choice, Anglophone politicians found their bargaining position severely compromised even before negotiations had commenced. Worse yet, the Anglophone politicians who negotiated for federation were no match for the Francophones advised by a battery of French legal experts who came prepared with well thought-out proposals for the constitutional document. Anglophone politicians were in the main badly advised, had little experience in negotiating on this level and lacked political savvy. The fact that their territory was being incorporated into an already independent and sovereign Cameroon Republic set the stage and prescribed the conditions for the creation of an unequal union. The inequality was further compounded by the triumphant insistence of the Francophone team that its proposals (which were to its advantage) serve as the basis for discussion, and its leader, Ahidjo, act as the arbiter. This in effect amounted to a halo being drawn over Ahidjo's head which was to later give rise to the pervasive belief that he is the deus ex machina in contemporary Cameroon politics. It is therefore no surprise that Ahidjo's presidency has subsequently taken on the trappings of a bonapartist regime (see the Etonga article).

Stark convincingly argues that federalism in Cameroon was primarily an "elite" symbol and concept whose popular appeal had been deliberately suppressed by the present regime. Although it took its public form in the Foumban Conference, its reality had already been shaped in private talks between Ahidjo and Foncha--the two major dramatis personae. When in the course of time, Ahidjo succeeded in eliminating "federalism" from the political vocabulary of the Anglophone elite its end was only a matter of time.

The reunification idea drew a large following-- witness the massive vote for it during the

plebiscite--from the rank-and-file. And although
it received strong support from the Anglophone
political elite, it is unlikely that more than a
very few (and one is being quite charitable here)
had any but the haziest notions as to what reunification could mean or what kind of a society might
lie over the horizon. It is still unclear--and
further study is needed--whether the massive pro-
reunification vote was for an idea (restoration of
the Kamerun volk) and/or for a particular kind of
constitutional set-up (federalism or unitarism).
The absence of a definitive answer to this question
should serve as a restraint to those who insist on
invoking the positive results of the 1961 plebiscite
as an imprimatur from the people to indulge in
radical constitutional rearrangements whenever these
become expedient.

Moving from the macro to the micro level of
analysis, Etonga examines the Cameroon presidency
in the light of the American experience. His reliance on this experience as a comparative base is
useful and highly instructive because Americans, as
the framers of the first modern presidential constitution, created a system of government which has
served as a model for subsequent new nations. But,
as it is often the case, the adaptation of western
institutions and ideas in Africa has almost always
been accompanied by vulgarisations and major per-
versions. Etonga points out in his essay that the
framers of Cameroon's constitution selectively incorporated certain features of American presidentialism into their system of jurisprudence. The
result is a uniquely Cameroonian presidency which
is both imperial and totalitarian, and whose formal
powers exceed those of the American prototype.

Etonga examines the sources (both formal and
informal) of presidential power in Cameroon and the
extent to which its imperial and caesarist features
are manifested in practice. Presidential power in
Cameroon, he shows, is vested in a single individual, a veritable pontifex maximus who in addition
to being the President, is also Head of State and
Government, Commander-in-Chief of the Armed Forces,
and Leader of the only party in the country. The
unitary constitution provides that "State authority
shall be exercised by the President of the Republic,
and the National Assembly" (my emphasis). In practice, however, it is the President and not parliament who exercises effective powers (to appoint and
dismiss all ministers, to enact ordinances that have
the force of law and to execute residual powers of

the constitution where these are not specifically
stated). This individual is independent of the
legislature and judiciary and is accountable to no
one, except, theoretically, the people. The
imperial presidency derives its powers from several
sources: the constitution; traditional political
culture; conditions and circumstances peculiar to
nations in the grip of economic underdevelopment;
and by the sheer and overwhelming ambition for
power.

Etonga believes that the federal arrangement
under the 1961 constitution successfully limited
presidential power and argues that Federalism was
an effective restraint in this relatively brief
period of Cameroon constitutionalism because it
provided for the separation of powers at a functional level (i.e., legislative, executive, and
judicial) as well as at the territorial level (i.e.,
eastern and western states). Because this structure
imposed severe restraints on a leadership thirsty
for far-reaching command powers, is, for Etonga,
probably one of the major reasons for the shift from
federalism to unitarism. The creation of a unitary
state only sanctioned what was already de facto;
the devolution of all powers on the President
served by a passive, decorative, patronage-packed
National Assembly. But this subordination of parliament to the will of the executive and the emascu-
lation of its lawmaking power strikes Etonga, the
jurist, as a serious qualification upon the legislature's autonomy and one which is difficult to justify in a republican constitution such as Cameroon's

The shift to a strong centralized government
brought in its wake a parallel decline in the en-
joyment of human rights. As Etonga points out,
concentrated power is very suspicious and sensitive
to criticism, and intolerant of opposition or competition. The security of the state becomes an
overriding concern under these circumstances, and in
the process of evoking the government's extraordinary powers to preserve the nation, individual
rights and freedoms are usually suspended. Cameroon
constitutional jurisprudence, in reproducing the
specific features of American presidentialism,
failed to include its correlation of federalism and
judicial protection of human rights. A very unfortunate omission indeed.

Etonga concludes his trenchant analysis of
Cameroon presidentialism by suggesting two factors
responsible for its tendency towards dictatorship
and tyranny: first, the absence of

institutionalized restraints to check on presidential power and secondly, the presence of a political culture that is particularly favorable to the growth of dictatorship.[2]

The shift from multipartism to one-party states in Africa was hailed everywhere as the fulfillment of liberal democracy in that continent. As Etonga points out in the preceding essay, the most forceful argument advanced to justify this shift was that only a powerful, broadly based, national party was capable of achieving national unity, stability, and economic development, as well as diffuse ethnic divisions and conflicts. However, with the fossilization of the single-party and the emergence of neofascist totalitarian states, the effusive roars of approval that first greeted its appearance have not quieted down. It is against this backdrop that Bayart examines one-party government in Cameroon. Bayart argues that the Cameroon National Union's (CNU) ideology of nation-building, which he refers to as the "ethnic of unity," sees a contradiction between modernity (read: CNU, national unity) on the one hand, and the political tradition inherited from pre-colonial and colonial periods (read: UPC, multi-parties) on the other. The ethnic of unity approaches the relationship between modernity and ethnic attachments--tribalism so called--in terms of a zero sum game; an either/or situation in which one, for instance, cannot be a Bamileke and a Cameroonian at the same time.[3] Because it rests on this fallacious and myopic interpretation of African social reality, Bayart contends that the ideology is inherently incapable of promoting genuine political development in Cameroon.

Broadly defining development as the degree to which an established society and culture prove themselves capable of traditionalizing and assimilating change, Bayart proceeds to critically evaluate the CNU's role in this process in terms of the degree to which the party has succeeded in (1) promoting group integration; (2) generating a sense of Cameroonian identity; (3) providing for the expression of diverse interests; and (4) allowing citizen participation in the management of the affairs that most closely concern them. He argues that as a result of the rapid and far-reaching economic, social, and political changes Cameroon has experienced in the last decade, the established modes of meeting the above four functional requirements of political development have completely broken down. It is Bayart's view that the CNU

regime has not succeeded in filling the vacuum
created by this dislocative social change. He
finds that one-party rule in Cameroon has: (1)
spawned a climate of ideological monism, destroyed
all opposition, and blocked all forms of competition
at the political market place; (2) minimized, where
it has not outright eliminated, all channels for
popular participation in government. In the same
vein, it has clogged all channels of communication
such that the mass of workers and peasants no longer
have available specific avenues through which to
articulate their demands; (3) succeeded in slowly
generating a sense of national consciousness, but
one which regrettably is being achieved through the
suppression of ethnic identifications and an acculturation forcible imposed from above. The party, it
seems, has rejected completely the notion that the
people of Cameroon can be held together, their sense
of community strangthened and deepened not by homogeneity but by diversity; and (4) not opposed but
encouraged the concentration of power in the hands
of the state which has led to the emergence of a
regime with strong bonarpartist tendencies.

THE SEARCH FOR AN ECONOMIC ORDER

From its birth, the union of the two Cameroons
was an unequal one, not only in terms of the distribution of political power but also in the
economic resources at their disposal. It is the
latter aspect and the role the federal government
exercised in correcting the imbalance that is the
subject of Benjamin's lead essay in Part III. Although the paper was written during the federalist
phase, it does raise some very fundamental issues
about the economic relations between the federal
government and the federated states and thus provides a necessary background for an appreciation of
the birth and death of Cameroon federalism. The
essay begins by pointing out the salient differences
between the two Cameroons. In the former East
Cameroon priority has always been accorded to industrialization, while for former West Cameroon the
emphasis has been on the primary sector. Parallel
differences are also registered in the standard and
cost of living between the two regions; the East has
historically been more affluent and better endowed
than the West. Faced with these contradictions the
challenge of federalism became one of devising ways

to integrate the weaker economy of the West into the more virile Eastern economy.

Benjamin examines the several steps that were taken by federal authorities to incorporate the Western economy into the broader framework of the national economy. One step was the maintenance of an internal customs wall during the first five years of reunification to check and regulate inter-state trade and the flow of consumer goods between the federated states. Although the erection of this border was contrary to the principle of free movement of goods and people which is so central to federalist theory, it was considered politically and economically desirable; a gesture, as it were, of the federal government's commitment to a program of economic equalization. A second step in bringing West Cameroon's economy into the national mainstream was through the harmonization of the customs' systems. Towards this end a common external customs tariff for Cameroon and the other member states of UDEAC (Central African Empire, Chad, Congo-Brazzaville, and Gabon) was established in the Federal Republic.

The effects of the harmonization of customs systems were disastrous for the West Cameroon state which found itself deprived of its most important source of revenues--custom taxes. To offset this loss, the West Cameroon government tried to set-up several self-financing schemes--such as the Cameroon Commercial Corporation (CCC), Cameroon Bank Ltd. (Cambank)--to provide it with an inde-pendent financial base. As it turned out, not only were these institutions founded on questionable business practices but they were managed along lines that left much to be desired. The Cameroon Bank Ltd., which received heavy financial backing from the West Cameroon government, was saved from certain ruin only by the timely intervention of the federal government.

The federalization of key institutions in West Cameroon was interpreted by many Anglophones as part of a sinister plot hatched in Yaounde designed to subjugate the "independentist" tendencies of the Anglophone ruling elite. However, in the instance of the federal take-over of Cambank, the intent was not the assertion of Yaounde "imperialism" but an embarrassing admission that, left on its own, the West Cameroon government was incapable of maintain-ing a viable economy without federal government assistance.

Benjamin contends that the process of integration was one-sided and consistently applied to the disadvantage of West Cameroon. However, his own evidence demonstrates that the failure of West Cameroon government to establish financial autonomy (a necessary condition if it had to break away from financial dependence on Yaounde) was due to lack of economic foresight and poor fiscal management. West Cameroon's dependence on the federal government was an inevitable, albeit unfortunate, consequence of the integration process as much as it was the failure of its leadership to demonstrate sound judgement, a sense of purpose, and a commitment to the public good, at a very challenging period in the territory's history.

In describing the impact of federal institutions on West Cameroon's economic activity, Benjamin very skillfully draws our attention to the difficulties the new republic faced in trying to reconcile the political rhetoric of federalism and its economic philosophy of centralized planning: where the former with its multiple levels of government and centers of decision-making, each sovereign in its own areas of jurisdiction, insisted on making decisions bearing on economic development in their areas of jurisdiction, i.e., the state level. This contrasted sharply with the imperatives of centralized planning which approached economic development through an integrated process animated and monitored from one point, the national center. The implementation of development under this philosophy meant by-passing the states and subordinating their "sovereignty" to the national center in Yaounde. It was either federalism (political and economic decentralization) or unitarism and centralized planning and, as the essays in Part II indicate, the latter won out in the long run.

Ndongko's essay is concerned with the activities promoted by the National Investment Code and its auxiliary institutions, the Cameroon Development Bank (CDB) and the National Investment Corporation (NIC). He examines the role of the NIC—especially in the granting of investment incentives—as a first step towards redressing the adverse effects of economic and social disparities and the uneven development of the major economic/administrative regions in the country.

The problem of regional economic disparities is viewed from a broader framework and analyzed from a perspective quite different from Benjamin's who saw the fundamental economic contradiction as one between Anglophone and Francophone Cameroon. Ndongko correctly points out that, in the main, regional disparities in Cameroon have existed between the northern and southern parts of the country; and these economic disparities were spawned by preferential colonial policies which favored certain areas over others. This inherited framework of uneven distribution of developmental resources has survived into the post-colonial period; as examination reveals that the Littoral and Central South provinces have received the largest share of investments approved under the Code, despite the fact that these two provinces were before independence the more developed ones.

The central thesis of Ndongko's paper is that the overall government activities, the provisions of the National Investment Code and investment policies of public financial institutions, like the CDB and NIC, have failed to reflect the much talked about objectives of balanced regional economic development. The most compelling evidence to support this position is the persistence of wide economic and social disparities between the different regions and provinces of the United Republic a decade after planned development was introduced.

The failure of the National Investment Policy is attributed to several factors. To begin with, social and economic change cannot be achieved overnight. While conceding this point, Ndongko still makes a forceful argument that the provisions of the National Investment Code as well as those of such public institutions like the CDB and NIC have failed to grasp the compelling need to provide the more backward provinces with greater investment incentives in order to attract both foreign and domestic capital. Rather than decentralize economic activities, application of investment legislation has resulted instead in the concentration of industrial activities in the more economically endowed regions. In addition, foreign and private beneficiaries of investment incentives have interpreted their mission within the framework of national development as one of maximizing profits and not in achieving a rationally distributed pattern of economic activities among the seven provinces. So, for instance, foreign capital and investment have tended to remain in the Littoral and Center-South because they enjoy locational advantages over the other provinces.

The failure of the National Investment Policy has much to do with the shortsightedness of economic planners who insist on approaching the question of economic justice as one that can be resolved exclusively within the framework and on the strength of rational economic logic. The problem has far-reaching social and political consequences to be subjected entirely to economic calculus. A balanced approach to economic development, particularly in a country like Cameroon with its diverse cultures, ethnic, and historical background, in order for it to succeed must include these particularistic structures and conditions into the calculus for change. That is, an affirmative effort must be made to provide extra incentives to those regions that consider themselves the neglected stepchildren of the republic if they are expected to catch-up with the more developed regions.

In the final analysis, Ndongko argues that only an investment policy which places greater emphasis on the spatial dimension of economic activities can redress the adverse effects of economic and social disparities and the uneven development of the various regions of Cameroon.

As Benjamin notes in the lead essay in Part III, the C.D.C. began to feel increasingly the weight of centralization emanating from the federal capital. As an important producer with a long and distinguished history of involvement in the economic development of Southern Cameroons, the position of the C.D.C. in the new emerging federal economic framework was eagerly anticipated. Would the corporation remain under the jurisdiction of the West Cameroon as had been the case since its inception in 1946? Or would it become federal property? Would the wide range of activities it had traditionally been associated with--medical services, ports, roads, schools--be assumed by the federal government since these coincided with domains reserved for federal jurisdiction under article 6 of the federal constitution? What role would the Commonwealth Development Corporation play in the new C.D.C. set-up? At what pace would Cameroonisation of the management personnel be followed?

Students of plantation agriculture have blamed the persistent poverty and underdevelopment of Third World economies on this mode of production.[4] However, in the case of the C.D.C. this thesis finds little support, for the corporation has been a major instrument of modernization and largely credited for the social and economic development-- wherever this was evidenced--in former West Cameroon. Bederman and DeLancey trace the turbulent history of plantation agriculture in Cameroon, in particular the events that led to the founding of the Cameroon Development Corporation in 1946 and the subsequent experiences of its three decades of existence.

Beginning its official life as a statutory corporation to serve the people of the Southern Cameroons, the C.D.C. has since then been managed as a commercial operation with unusual social responsibilities. It gradually grew into a leviathan ranking only second to the central government in the number of employees on its payroll. With its activities no longer confined to English-speaking Cameroon, its management completely indigenised, C.D.C. has become a truly national institution and a major partner with the government in economic development of the country.[5] Bederman and DeLancey conclude their excellent analysis with a word of caution on the additional responsibilities C.D.C. has been shouldering in keeping with its new profile as a national institution. These operations, the authors point out, have not always been well thought out in advance and the corporation has found itself yielding to pressure from the national center to expand its activities even when these cannot be economically justified. An institution of such importance as the C.D.C. can be expected to engage in projects from time to time that are necessary from the point of view of political logic; but the premature death of many state corporations in the emerging nations has had to do with the failure of the managers of modernization to strike a happy balance between political requirements and economic good sense. It is hoped that the C.D.C. will learn a lesson or two from the experience of parastatals in other African countries and not fall victim to their shortsightedness.

ASPECTS OF SOCIAL DEVELOPMENT

Given the extreme linguistic fragmentation in the majority of African countries, language policy becomes a critical factor in a country's struggle to achieve national unity. This is especially true for a country like Cameroon with an estimated 250 indigenous and two foreign languages. Chumbow's paper in Part IV "Language and Language Policy in Cameroon" draws attention to this complex linguistic reality with which Cameroon's leaders have had to cope since reunification. Although English and

French are the country's official languages, this choice was not dictated by any elaborate linguistic or paralinguistic considerations. Official bilingualism was simply a pragmatic and politically expedient choice in response to the immediate challenge posed by reunification.

Chumbow correctly points out that Cameroon does not enjoy a language policy as such. That is, a policy which, from the sociolinguistic perspective, is based on an exhaustive study of a wide range of social, economic, and political variables relevant to the country's long as well as short term developmental needs. Chumbow has painstakingly documented the explosive contradiction between the official English-French bilingualism fiction and the everyday world of French monolingualism in which official Cameroon lives. The limited achievements in bilingualism are attributable to several factors: (1) the unconstitutional ascendancy of French over English as result of the demographic factor which heavily favors French-speaking Cameroonians, as a consequence; (2) only an enlightened few in the Francophone population see a strong need to learn English; this contrasts with the minority Anglophones, almost all of whom see the necessity of achieving proficiency in French--if only to survive in a predominantly "frenchified" Cameroon. Perhaps the most critical factor in explaining the limited success of English-French bilingualism in Cameroon is the absence of clear cut goals with respect to the implementation of this desirable objective. More precisely, the failure of government to evolve a meaningful language policy. Chumbow warns that in the evolution of such a policy, careful consideration must be given to the role of indigenous languages. As he points out, linguists are agreed that the mother tongue as a medium of instruction in the first few years of schooling has favorable psycholinguistic implications for the overall intellectual formation of a child. It is well to heed Chumbow's timely warning that no viable language policy can be evolved in Cameroon which fails to recognize and involve vernacular languages.

One of the fundamental challenges confronting African educators is that of adapting the inherited European educational systems to the practical requirements and exigencies of their societies. For we find that one of the greatest shortcomings of the European legacy has been the uneven distribution of educational facilities with a heavy concentration in the coastal and urban areas to the neglect of the

rural regions where, incidentally, the vast majority
of Africans are domiciled. This uneven distribution
of educational resources has persisted long after
the colonialists have departed and is still very
much evident in Cameroon. In 1970, 64 percent of
the population aged between six and thirteen years
in the more developed Francophone Cameroon were enrolled in primary schools as opposed to 46 percent
in the Anglophone sector. And even in the Francophone sector considerable regional disparities
exist; to take one example, only 22 percent of
school-age children are enrolled in schools in the
Islamized North against 94 percent in the Center
South provinces.[6]

These profound disparities in the distribution
of educational resources have not been lost on
Cameroonian policy-makers as the paper by Kale and
Yembe indicate. Their paper examines government's
efforts to redress the problem of maldistribution
of educational facilities in general and the adaptation or "ruralization" of the primary school
curriculum to the conditions of rural village life
in Cameroon in particular.[7] The instrument for
planning and implementing these reform efforts is
IPAR (Institut de Pédagogie Appliquée à vocation
Rurale) a research and training institute jointly
founded and funded by the Cameroon government and
UNESCO. IPAR came into existence in 1965 and
since then its innovative strides have met with
vigorous opposition from a cross-section of the
Cameroon public. This resistance to change, as Kale
and Yembe point out, owes its origin to what they
refer to as the powerful saga the school has built
into the Cameroon social system. Since the society
is largely agriculturally based, the school has
always been viewed as the only escape from manual
labor, the avenue to a white collar job and a more
comfortable life in the urban areas. The IPAR
reforms on the other hand, with their emphasis on
ruralizing the curriculum so that pupils processed
through this system can remain on the land, were
seen everywhere as a negation of the whole idea of
the school as the avenue for upward mobility. Since
the system of rewards is generally more favorable
toward pupils who have benefited from a traditional
curriculum than ones processed through a "ruralized"
curriculum, few can understand or see the need to
change the curriculum. Clearly then for IPAR to
succeed, not only must government seek to change
traditional values and dispositions toward agriculture but it must introduce a new system of rewards

which reflects the importance and high priority the
government attaches to its reformed primary school
curriculum.

We close this volume with a paper by Professor
Clignet: "The Multiplicity of Times Operating in
the Cameroonian Modern Labor Force." Although his
paper is articulated around the notion of time as
it affects the analysis of labor economics in
Cameroon, his conclusions and insights have wide
theoretical implications for the study of African
labor markets.[8]

Four major factors or times for Clignet explain the discontinuity in the structure of
Cameroonian labor markets and labor force in the
advanced sector of the economy. Historical developments in the political economy of the country,
the increasing technological scale of economic
organizations and the interaction between workers'
and job characteristics have divided the labor
force into segments i.e., the labor markets of the
manual and non-manual worker (employé de bureau).

Three time periods mark the development of
the structure of Cameroonian labor markets; the
pre-WW II period, the post-WW II period up until
1960, and the post-independent period. In the
early period, international scrutiny as a result of
the U.N. mandate has important implications for the
structure of labor markets. The inability of the
French colonial authorities to control European
immigration and the greater availability of schooling to the Cameroonian elite relative to elites in
other colonies account for the early rise of a
local commercial elite competing with marginal expatriate concerns and the initial large size of the
public sector.

The intermediate period is characterized by
the increasing dependency linkages between the national economy and the metropolitan economy.
Clignet astutely sees these linkages as multidimensional, involving not only economic institutions but political, educational, and legal institutions as well. Despite the political and economic
directives emanating from the center to the periphery, a local political and commercial elite is
allowed some room to maneuver within these centralized structures.

The third or late period is characterized by
the opening up of the Cameroonian economy to multinational corporations, the emergence of state-owned
enterprises and the burgeoning of indigenous-owned
firms. These developments take place within

centralized political structures and a more diversified national economy. Economic dependency is
increased, though its impact may be cushioned or
exacerbated by policies of the ruling elite in its
efforts to adjust to the vagaries of international
markets.

The changing scale of Cameroonian economic
organizations is associated with the spatial development in the national economy. The structure of
economic units varies according to the age of the
firm, the state of development of its geographical
location, the referrent historical time period, and
the firm's own internal policies. These variables
explain firms' differential access to labor of
varying characteristics i.e., education, skill
level, ethnic affiliation.

Lines of segmentation are thus product of the
functioning of labor markets within the regionally
concentrated pattern of colonial development. Neoclassical assumptions of one theoretically homo-
genous labor market where effort is competitively
rewarded according to one's contribution to output
(proxied by the level of skill and education) are
questioned. Since labor markets are balkanized,
norms of reward, i.e., hiring, promotion, pay,
status differ across segments of the labor market
at various stages in its development.

Underlying Clignet's analysis of labor market
experiences of cohorts of workers in the intermediate and the late periods are the changing conditions
in supply and demand. For Clignet, these are reflected in the rates of workers' educational attainment and the region's economic development. The
mismatching between job and workers' characteristics
or the degree of imbalance partially explains the
distribution of differential income and employment
opportunities across submarkets i.e., manual versus
non-manual workers. In this regard, Clignet's
analysis is consistent with received but modified
neoclassical theory about the functioning of labor
submarkets. Clignet's findings about higher occupational mobility for non-manual workers and their
age-earnings functions peaking later than those of
manual workers are not peculiar to labor submarkets
in developing economies. The weaker correlations
between on one hand skill and age and between earnings and age on the other hand, if they mean anything at all, simply imply that manual and non-
manual workers embody different amounts of human
capital investments (institutional and on-the-job)
and therefore have different internal mobility

XLV

clusters or time structures of returns on such
investments. The divergence and convergence in
hiring and promotion standards between international
and local firms is the most interesting finding in
Clignet's paper. That international firms, given
their oligopolistic product and labor markets as
well as their high-profit postures, pay manual
workers more than local firms is not surprising
especially those firms with a colonial legacy of
low-wage policy. That this differential has narrowed especially in regard to educational requirements
for non-manual jobs in the post-independent era,
reflects employers' adjustment to larger supplies
of better educated workers but also a gradual
lowering of excessive credentialism in colonial
firms. The latter result undoubtedly flows from
the pressure to Africanize the labor market at the
top of the job hierarchy. Whether Africanization
has been translated into effective participation in
decision-making in international firms is less
certain.

In his paper, Clignet transcends "colonial"
anthropology by examining an important question in
development sociology and economics in an historical
perspective, namely the fragmentation of labor
markets. Indeed, the distribution of employment
and income opportunities in the course of development is closely tied to the segmentation of labor
markets. After all, labor markets, aside from
allocating and pricing labor resources, determine
"who gets what and how."

Moreover, most development and labor economists
would concur with Clignet that labor markets have a
history from which they derive their structure.
Labor markets are not simply abstract textbook con-
structs suddenly thrust upon the economic scene.
They are historical processes with elements of
continuity and discontinuity within the framework of
development. In this sense, the title of Clignet's
paper, "The Multiplicity of Times Operating in the
Cameroonian Modern Labor Force" is unduly restric-
tive. The paper deals with the historical structuring of Cameroonian labor sub-markets.

The historical perspective on labor markets is
commendable. However, it suffers from the fact that
the labor market in the Cameroonian economy is seen
as originating with the U.N. mandate. Pre-colonial
labor market arrangements, their manipulation by
German employers and colonial administrators are
not treated at all. The evolution of the labor
market as to its convergence to and divergence from

the subsequent stages (the second colonization by
the French) is thus truncated. The consequences of
such a lacuna are found in Clignet's distinguishing
features between the stages of the labor market
development. The late period is characterized by
the opening up of the Cameroonian economy to the
multinational corporations, the emergence of state-
owned enterprises, and increasing political centralization. A close examination of the early
colonization process reveals that charter companies
privately financed and/or jointly financed by both
the metropolitan state and private investors were
in the forefront of the rush toward the golden em-
pires. The active role of the colonial administration in "settling the colony," an alias for
creating a "law and order" climate conducive to
political, economic, and cultural domination, better
explains the extensive role of the colonial state
as owner of enterprises and major employer as well
as the increasing political centralization. It is
naive to believe that pre and post-independent
nationalism fully account for these trends, though
it certainly accentuated them. Therefore, it is no
surprise that a large tertiary sector emerged at an
early stage in the pattern of colonial development.
Pacification missions, a euphemism for military
raids for territorial conquest, labor recruiting,
and tax collecting agencies all required a functional administrative apparatus.

The implication for labor markets of this
forced industrialization is that the very nature of
the employment relationship initially approximated
involuntary servitude. The transformation of the
colonial labor market from involuntary to voluntary
servitude or the making of the "fully committed"
Cameroonian industrial worker begs an explanation.
It is this legacy which sheds light on the present
wage policy of international firms established
during the colonial era. The convergence and
divergence, to use Clignet's terminology, in
colonial employers' strategies toward structuring
labor markets and the labor force ought to be
scrutinized more thoroughly. Creating well-
functioning labor markets or insuring adequate and
reliable labor supplies involved labor conflict or
resistance by individual workers and local institutions surrounding pre-colonial labor market arrangements. The labor market transition from the early
to the intermediate periods must be analyzed in this
light.

While recognizing the multidimensional center-periphery relationship, Clignet suggests that colonial institutions did not necessarily pursue goals that were consistent with one another. Disagreements on such issues as methods of subjugating the colonized society and distribution of the ensuing spoils occurred. Nevertheless, adherence to the fundamental objective of domination and control by submerging the local institutions was the norm of the day.[9] Similarly, the analogous educational institutions and French-like protective labor legislation, while benefiting segments of Cameroonian society, also made it an easy prey to colonial shackles. As Clignet would readily admit, French assimilation policies in Cameroon like in other former French colonies resulted in the subordination of indigenous institutions to those of the metropole.

At the level of theory, it is not clear which labor market segmentation framework Clignet has adopted. In his discussion of the history of the Cameroonian political economy and the scale of economic organizations, it appears that Clignet adheres to elements of the radical theory of labor market segmentation as spelled out in D. M. Gordon Theories of Poverty and Unemployment and in D. M. Gordon, et al. Labor Market Segmentation. According to this theory, the labor market is divided in two major segments, the primary labor market and the secondary labor market. Job and workers' stability characteristics differentiate the two segments. Jobs in oligopolistic, high-profit, high-wage, and capital-intensive firms require and foster stable working habits. Jobs in competitive, low-profit, low-wage, and labor-intensive firms discourage stable working habits. The primary sector is segmented into two submarkets; subordinate jobs requiring worker's docility and independent jobs fostering creativity and initiative. Also, race, sex, and geographic location further subdivide the major submarkets into distinct "race-typed" and "sex-typed" jobs. The secondary labor market jobs are mainly filled by minority workers, women, and youth. These processes of segmentation have historical roots in systemic forces in the development of U.S. monopoly capitalism and employers' efforts to break down the unified workers' interests. Systemic forces include the rise of the large corporation replacing the competitive individual entrepreneurs and the divergent rates of growth between firms in different sectors of the

economy with opposing structural characteristics.
Differences in scale, market structure, technology,
and financial positions between firms (the dual
economy) account for contrasting working environments, wage, and mobility patterns. Employers'
deliberate strategies within the firm include the
bureaucratization of the firm, the structuring of
authority relationships through scientific management and creation of segmented internal markets with
different norms of rewards, promotion patterns and
expectations. Externally, employers consciously
manipulated ethnic antagonism, race, and sex.

By contrast in his empirical analysis, Clignet
distinguishes only two major lines of segmentation,
the dichotomy between the local firm and the international firm and the occupational dichotomy between manual and non-manual workers. Without embracing the radical theory of labor market segmentation, Clignet correctly associates the uneven
regional development in the Cameroonian economy
with the age and the employment size (Tables 12.1
and 12.2) of firms thus sketching the theoretical
skeleton of a segmentation theory resembling that of
American radical economists. But profiles of firms
by degree of labor mobility, skill level, and wage
distribution for the two occupational categories
and the stages of labor market development illus-
trate the dualistic structure of labor markets.
The dual structure of labor markets is seen here as
a simple deviation from neoclassical competitive
labor markets rather than a product of historical
segmentation processes. Clignet's profile of local
and international firms implicitly remain in the
mold of the dual labor market analysis as initially
formulated by Piore and Doeringer in, Internal
Labor Markets and Manpower Analysis, while his
analysis of the political economy of Cameroon is
close to that of American radical economists.
Clignet's concept of experience (age), on-the-job
and off-the-job training as well as firm and worker
characteristics are selectively borrowed from
Thurow's early book, Poverty and Discrimination,
and not from Thurow's later book, Generating Inequality in the U.S. Economy, Clignet would have
found Thurow's labor market segmentation valuable,
even though Thurow is by no means a radical econo-
mist. A stronger link between Clignet's analysis
of the Cameroonian political economy and his firm
profiles would have been established. The profile
of firms is incomplete in that factor proportions
of firms by degree of capital or labor intensity,

product and labor market structure, and their profit
situation are not assessed even qualitatively.
Finally, the dual typology of local and international firms conceals the segmentation in other
submarkets i.e., French firms, firms owned by other
European expatriates, state-owned firms, firms
owned by Non-Europeans, local firms, modern, and
non-modern.

Clignet's paper is a welcome addition to
Africanist labor market studies which are few in
number. The use of his insights about Cameroonian
society to interpret micro-data is an example of
scholarship Western and indigenous Africanists
ought to think about seriously.

NOTES

1. Seymour Martin Lipset, The First New
Nation. (N.Y.: Anchor Books, 1967, p. 18).
2. This phenomenon is not uniquely Cameroonian
as I have argued in Ndiva Kofele-Kale, "The Politics
of Development and the Problem of Leadership in
Africa," Cross Currents, vol. XXVIII, No. 4 (Winter
1978-79), pp. 432-552 and Ndiva Kofele-Kale, "The
Problem of Instrumental Leadership in Contemporary
African Political Systems," Journal of Asian &
African Studies, Vol. XIII, No. 1-2 (January-April
1978), pp. 80-94.
3. For an extended critique of this jaundiced
approach to national unity, see my "The Political
Culture of Anglophone Cameroon: A Study of the
Impact of Environment on Ethnic Group Values and
Member Political Orientations," unpublished Ph.D.
dissertation, Northwestern University, 1974; esp.
pp. 12-29.
4. One of the most incisive critiques of
plantation agriculture is George L. Beckford's,
Persistent Poverty: Underdevelopment in Plantation
Economies of the Third World. London: Oxford
University Press, 1972.
5. Joki Manga, "The Role of the CDC in
National Development of the United Republic of
Cameroon," unpublished mss. Harvard University,
Summer 1978.
6. Remi Clignet, The Africanization of the
Labor Market: Educational and Occupational Seg-
mentation in Cameroun. Berkeley & Los Angeles:
University of California Press, 1976, p. 31.
7. The attempts to use the policy of animation
rurale as the engine for development were first
tried out in Senegal and Niger and in these two
countries the theory failed in practice as Jeanne
Marie Moulton has argued with remarkable insight in
Animation Rurale: Education for Rural Development
Amherst, Massachusetts: Center for International
Education, University of Massachusetts, 1978.
8. I am deeply indebted to Mudiayi Ngandu of
the International Bank for Reconstruction and
Development, Washington, D.C., for sharing with me
his vast knowledge of the economics of labor markets. (See Mudiayi Ngandu, "An Indigenous-Based
Employment Strategy for African Economies," Third
World Review Vol. 4, No. 1, 1979, pp. 46-59). His
very perceptive and insightful comments on Professor
Clignet's book length study on the Cameroonian labor
force (see footnote No. 6) have been of immense

help to me in reviewing this chapter.

    9. For example, the affiliated African labor confederations to the French left-of-center Confederation Generale du Travail (C.G.T.) were at best junior partners whose strategies to acquire independence and develop had to be patterned after the P.C.F. (The French Communist Party--C.G.T. model to gain power. Benoit Frachon's book Au Rythme des Jours, Tome 1, Editions Sociales, 1967) is insightful in this regard.

Part 1
The Search for Identity

1
Reconciling the Dual Heritage: Reflections on the "Kamerun Idea"

Ndiva Kofele-Kale

Chrétiennement parlant, tout le monde reconnaîtra
que Dieu a crée un seul Cameroun; c'est là le
point de depart.

---- Um Nyobe

There is one sole historic unity--the Cameroon
Nation, one sole moral unity, the Cameroon Fatherland.

---- Ahmadou Ahidjo

INTRODUCTION

The United Republic of Cameroon is a large
complex territory whose political development has
been shaped by many influences. Strategically
located in the hinge of Africa and covering an
area nearly 178,381 square miles, the country
exhibits marked climatic, ecological, and ethnographic differences. Temperature ranges from 68
degrees Farenheit around the foothills of Mount
Cameroon to well above 90 degrees Farenheit in the
extreme northern section of the country; the arid
lands of the north contrast with the dense forest
of the coast; and the array of ethnic groups is
bewildering in its complexity, making Cameroon, as
many expert observers have noted, the racial and
cultural cross-roads of the African continent.
The natural differences just mentioned are by no
means unique to Cameroon as these are relatively
common features found in the majority of African
nations. It is, however, the contradictions
resulting from four decades of French and British
colonial occupation and the subsequent attempts to
reconcile this dual heritage that makes Cameroon's

experiment in nation-building so fascinating and
instructive.

The Cameroon union, with its many imperfec-
tions as Beti and Eyinga have forcefully and convincingly argued,[1] has endured over fifteen years,
unfazed by the protracted epidemic of fragmentation that its neighbours to all points on the
compass have had to contend with (witness Biafra,
Eriteria, Shaba, to mention only the most celebrated cases). This remarkable feat, at least for
Africa, poses a challenge to students of nation-
building who are not in the habit of running into
this such seeming departure from orthodoxy; for
the Cameroon experiment in nation-building is sui
generis. This introductory essay reflects on the
nature of Cameroon reunification with particular
emphasis on the role the Kamerun Idea played in
this evolutionary process. It is not my intention
to focus attention, except in passing, on the
many forces, factors, and circumstances that went
into defining this collective effort at creating a
viable polity out of the ashes of a burnt down
Anglo-French colonial edifice. My objective here,
and a modest one at that, is to critically re-
examine the many attempts by foreign scholars to
question the validity of the Cameroon volksgeist
as expressed in the Kamerun Idea.

A BRIEF HISTORICAL BACKGROUND

Cameroon has had a long history of contact
with the western world. The coastal areas were the
first sectors to be exposed to European influence
dating back to the 1500's when Portugese traders
sought to establish trading bridge-heads along the
littoral. After the Portuguese came the Dutch,
Spanish, Swedish, and a seemingly endless stream of
European traders who capitalised on the lucrative
trade first in palm nuts and ivory and later in
slaves.[2] Traders were joined by explorers, missionaries, and finally, colonisers; and their influence
spread from the coast into the hinterland, even as
trade and evangelistion gradually made room for
colonisation.

However, the political history of 'modern'
Cameroon only dates back to July 1884 when a series
of treaties and agreements between Gustav Nachtigal,
the accredited representative of the German government, and the chiefs of Duala formally brought the
territory under German control. In the ensuing

4

years, Germany consolidated its hold over Cameroon
by various treaties with the United Kingdom and
France and remained in control until the outbreak
of the European War of 1914-18 when the protectorate was invaded and subsequently conquered by
British and French armies. By the terms of the
Milner-Simon Boundary Declaration of 1916, German
Kamerun was divided between the United Kingdom and
France with the larger area going to France.[3] The
partition of Cameroon received international
recognition and legitimacy in 1922 under the League
of Nations mandate system. In 1946, following the
abolition of the League of Nations, the French and
British mandates over the territory were converted
by the United Nations into trusteeships. In
December 1958 the U.N. General Assembly voted to
end the French trusteeship, thus paving the way
for its eventual independence which was achieved in
January 1, 1960, as the Republic of Cameroun.

In February 1961 a plebiscite was held in
British Cameroons, under U.N. supervision, to
determine whether its people wished union with
Nigeria or with the new Republic of Cameroun.
Northern Cameroons chose the former alternative,
Southern Cameroons, the latter. On June 1, 1961,
Northern Cameroons was attached to Nigeria and
renamed Sardauna province, henceforth to be administered as part of the Northern Region of Nigeria.
The Federal Republic of Cameroon came into
existence on October 1, 1961. For the next eleven
years Cameroon was governed as a Federation with
East (former French) Cameroon and West (former
British/Southern) Cameroon having separate regional
governments, each with a legislature and ministries,
in addition to the Federal Government structure.
In 1972, Cameroon's President Ahmadou Ahidjo proposed abolition of the federal structure on grounds
that it was costly and inefficient (see essays by
Etonga and Stark in this volume). A referendum
held on May 20, 1972, gave massive endorsement to
the proposal for a unitary system. This was
followed by a decree issued on June 2 proclaiming
the United Republic of Cameroon.

The Cameroon Federation was born in apparent
defiance to the prevailing climate in post-colonial
Africa which favoured the balkanisation of old
political unions as opposed to encouraging attempts
at amalgamating several small units into larger
groupings. As new states emerged into independence,
nationalist aspirations began to build up within the
old forms, finally exploding into overt calls for

5

redrawing extant boundaries.[4] So it was that the
reunification of the two Cameroons was being consummated at approximately the same time--to mention
a few prominent examples--the old French Soudan had
already been carved up into a multitude of mini-
states and Senegal was suing for divorce from the
abortive Mali federation. As Cameroonians were
celebrating their reconstituted Fatherland, Ruanda
and Burundi were going their separate ways after
having been administered jointly since the end of
the European War of 1914-18 as the Belgian colony
of Ruanda-Urundi; and in the newly established
Congo Republic, where the departing Belgians
hastily propped up a unitary government (as if it
was only here that amalgamation was desirable),
the intrepid Katangese were busy making a mockery
of Congolese unity as they relentlessly pursued
their autonomy aspirations in the years 1960-63.
The period also witnessed the break-up of the
Central African Federation and the British High
Commission territories into separate national
entities.

Against the background of these fissiparous
pressures, Cameroon reunification must be viewed
not only as a triumph over balkanisation but, more
importantly, as a living expression of the very
essence of pan-Africanism. Thus Cameroon's claim
to the guardianship of the fundamental ideas of the
pan-African dream is historically justified and
supremely deserved.

Its role as the laboratory for continental
unity aside, the reconstituted Cameroon is also of
interest to students concerned with African boundary problems; for the country came into being as a
challenge to the principle of uti possedetis which
has governed intra-African relations and served as
the ultimate authority on all questions with respect
to the definition of successor states since the
fall of the colonial order. The principle,
borrowed from Roman Law and followed in post-
colonial Latin America, holds that the existing
state of affairs should be preserved, whether its
origin was lawful or not.[5] In the African context
uti possedetis translates to mean that all territorial boundaries inherited from the colonial
period are acceptable and immutable geo-political
frames that lend reality to the modern successor
states and as such not subject to modifications.
The O.A.U. embraced this doctrine in its now famous
resolution of July 1964, which "solemnly declares
that all Member States pledge themselves to respect

the borders existing on their achievement of
national independence."[6] Again in Article III,
paragraph 3 of its Charter, the O.A.U. gave further
prominence and legitimacy to this doctrine.
Speaking for the fraternity of African leaders,
former President Tsiranana of the Malagasy Republic,
declared at the 1963 O.A.U. Summit Conference that
"It is no longer possible, nor desirable to modify
the boundaries of Nations, on the pretext of
racial, religious, or linguistic criteria . . .
should we take (these) criteria for settling our
boundaries, a few states of Africa would be blotted
from the map."[7] He should have added also that a
few new states would have appeared to replace those
blotted from the map of Africa.

Cameroon is one such state which found it,
contrary to Tsiranana's admonition, both desirable
and possible to modify its boundaries in response
to compelling historical forces, and in so doing
repudiated the principle of uti possedetis. Had
Cameroon insisted on staying with the rest of the
pack, then the status quo would have meant the
boundaries as delimited and demarcated in 1916 and
reified in 1922. That is, instead of one there
would have been several Cameroons. Some have
confidently advanced the argument that the desire
to recreate the new Cameroon in the image of the
old German Kamerun was in essence a reaffirmation
of colonial uti possedetis.[8] An argument such as
this is premised on the belief that the concept of
"Cameroon" is the creation of a German colonial
deus ex machina. An assumption Cameroonian
nationalists--pre- and post-reunification--would
summarily reject.[9] Um Nyobe, Cameroon's foremost
nationalist and the guiding spirit of the reunification movement, repeatedly reminded his followers
and the world at large that "Chrétiennement parlant,
tout le monde reconnaitra que Dieu a crée un seul
Cameroun."[10] Nyobe was echoing the feelings of his
compatriots who correctly maintained that Germany
did not discover nor invent Cameroon. It was in
existence long before the Woermann boys set up shop
in the coastal ports of the territory. German
colonialism may have been the catalytic generator
setting loose latent feelings of community identity;
in which case, the boundaries of German Kamerun on
the eve of the Allied invasion of the protectorate
were, in the nationalists' imagery, nothing more
than the reification of pre-colonial uti
possedetis.[11] To understand Nyobe's bold assertion
and to also understand how it was possible for

7

Cameroon nationalists to swim against the tide of post-colonial African history, one must turn to the ideology for reunification. It provided the framework and set the stage for the events that were later to culminate in the birth of Africa's first bi-lingual nation.

THE 'KAMERUN IDEA', IDEOLOGY FOR REUNIFICATION

Zolberg states the obvious when he reminds us that political architects who engage in nation-building see in ideology precisely what the construction engineer finds in blue-prints.[12] For the political engineer, an ideology serves as the national plan which identifies the salient political goals and the means for achieving them. The ideology that served as the basis for Cameroon reunification is often referred to as the 'Kamerun Idea'.[13] It was an ideology powerful enough to melt the physical and mental barriers which for forty-five years separated 'French' Cameroonians from 'British' Cameroonians; of such broad popular appeal as to evoke deep psychic attachment from a cross-section of the Cameroonian masses, and yet premised on a logic so compelling as to prove irresistible to even the most reactionary of the political elites. Simply stated, the Kamerun Idea embodied the aspirations of the Cameroon people for a recreation of their nation within the framework of the pre-1916 German protectorate of Kamerun. The movement for reunification for which the Kamerun Idea served as an inspiration cannot be appreciated without reference to this period of German occupation.

The German presence in Cameroon was relatively brief, only thirty years; yet these were important years in the political annals of modern Cameroon. There is some amount of debate, especially among foreign commentators, as to the importance of German colonial rule in the crystallisation of modern day Cameroon nationalism. Three points of controversy seem to have emerged in the numerous attempts to give perspective to Cameroon reunification. For a number of foreign scholars, the nationalist appeal to a once united German Kamerun is nothing more than a fanciful myth; secondly, nationalist claims that the dismemberment of German Kamerun also resulted in the partitioning of many ethnic groups (with substantial numbers on both sides of the French/English divide) have no

foundation in ethnographic reality; and finally,
nationalist claims of strong ethnic solidarity
among the partitioned peoples is equally absurd
from an examination of facts.

The Myth of Partitioned Peoples/Claims of Cultural Solidarity

Implicit in the dream of unity was the belief
that the arbitrary partitioning of German Kamerun
created boundaries that did not correspond to
ethnic frontiers. That is, ethnic groups and
families were split up. The reunification movement popularised this sentiment of a partitioned
peoples. But in his very critical examination of
the nature of Cameroon reunification, Ardener
advances the thesis that there were no great partitioned peoples on the intra-Cameroon boundary to
lend force and weight to the dream of unity based
on ethnicity.[14] While admitting the genuine and
compelling sentiments which reunification expressed,
Ardener, nonetheless, maintains that these were
not "tribal"; unless of course, the term is given
a very special meaning in the Cameroon context.
He goes on to suggest that: (1) "The only extensive group of recognized ethnographic status which
was cut by any boundary was the Ejagham (Ekoi) of
the Upper Cross River, through whose territory ran
the old Nigeria-Kamerun frontier from its very
earliest days" and (2) the few "tribal" units
which were clearly split by the Anglo-French
boundary were generally small groups of minor
political importance in the reunification movement.[15]
Furthermore, the movement for reunification,
according to Ardener, did not derive its inspiration from the same source which provided the spark
that set ablaze the Pan-Ewe or Pan-Somali irredentist movements. That is, the Ewe and Somali prior
to their partition existed as cohesive culture
units with a strong sense of group identity
nurtured over centuries of communal existence. The
fact of partition did not weaken these cultural
ties or dilute the feelings of solidarity; rather
these persisted and subsequently served as the
basis for their respective reunification movements.[16] This, in Ardener's view, was not the case
in Cameroon. First, because only marginal groups
were actually split; and second, the claims of
cultural solidarity were made by groups that were
putatively similar--such as the Tikar in

English-speaking Cameroon and the Bamileke in the French-speaking sector--and even then, the claims were highly exaggerated.

Two points should be made in comment. First, if there were no partitioned peoples in Cameroon, this must be taken to mean that the carving up of the country was done in such a way that the emerging frontiers corresponded with extant ethnic frontiers. A position which admits to a logic that is quite simple: either no ethnic groups were split which would then suggest that, breaking from a tradition established at the Berlin Congress, the Franco-British cartographers took great pains, in this one instance, to ensure that no pencil lines were drawn through culturally homogeneous groups. Or, ethnic groups were partitioned in which case their members would be found on both sides of the intra-Cameroon boundary. The former position is highly improbable, for the same haphazard approach that characterised the European scramble for Africa was employed on a smaller scale in Cameroon.[17] Since the approach was not backed by ethnographic logic the result was that the inter- and intra-Cameroon boundaries it created were quite artificial at several points. A fact well recognised by the colonial authorities themselves.[18] To take one example, Njeuma and Chem-Langhee point out that the northern section of the inter-Kamerun boundary actually split Kanuri, Mandara and Shuwa Arab people placing some in Northern Cameroons and others in French Cameroun (in this volume).

The second point to be made is that the vast majority of Cameroonians (in both the Northern and Southern sectors) had stronger ethnic ties with the peoples of French Cameroun than they did with Nigerians. As Bernard Fonlon has observed:

> During the Franco-British period when the two sections of the country were separated, Cameroonians on both sides never ceased to think of themselves as one. I know this from personal experience. In the 1940's, for example, which I spent entirely as a student in Nigeria, wherever Cameroonians were found they associated as brothers, and it was very seldom that the distinction was made that this one came from the French sector and that one from the English. During that period, and even before then, large communities of Cameroonians from almost every

10

sizable group in the French Cameroons came
to the British Cameroons, and never did it
occur to their brethren indigenous to the
British sector to consider them foreigners.
On the other hand, no Cameroonian from the
British sector, despite our 40 years of
intimate political, administrative, and
cultural association with Nigeria, ever
considered themselves Nigerians.[19] (my
emphasis)

Thus, if, and this is an important if, the
intra-Cameroon boundary did not split major ethnic
groups it at least fragmented groups that were
similar in a number of ways (the Duala, Isubu and
Kpe for example share a myth of common ancestry,
similar historical experiences, and similar
traditional social patterns).

The Myth of a German-created Kamerun Nation

In his highly regarded book, The Cameroon
Federation, Professor Johnson takes the position
that the significance so often attached to the
German occupation of Cameroon is highly exaggerated,
especially by Cameroonian nationalists. In his own
words:

The German colonial period can, nevertheless,
be dismissed because though it created a myth
of some value to Camerounians, it did not
create a durable legacy. Apparently little
appreciated by the nationalist movements
which were rooted in the myth of a German-
created 'Kamerun Nation' is the fact that
the German colonial administration had only
a decade of relatively peaceful administration of the territory--too little time to
elicit a sense of 'national' identity. The
Cameroun nationalists also tend to exaggerate
the German contribution to the economic
development of the territory. Despite greater
material gains during the longer mandate-
trusteeship period . . . Cameroun nationalists
speak better of their German masters than of
those succeeding the Germans.[20]

Approaching the so-called myth of a German-created
Kamerun nation from a slightly different angle,
Edwin Ardener, the social anthropologist, is quick
to point out that the boundaries of the reunified

11

Cameroon are not coterminous with those of the
German protectorate (<u>Schutzgebiet</u>) of Kamerun of
1894 or 1911. As he puts it:

> The political movement of the reconstruction
> of Kamerun was, from the outset, held within
> new boundaries, which were stated after 1922
> by the mandate and (later) trusteeship
> system . . . . The Federal Republic of
> 1 October 1961 therefore came into existence
> within even narrower boundaries than those
> of 1922 . . . . Any picture of the Federal
> Republic as simply reconstituting a previous
> political entity is therefore bound to be
> inadequate.[21]

Both Ardener and Johnson are suggesting, it seems,
that the notion of a reunified Cameroon being a
reincarnation of the destroyed German Kamerun is
a myth on two counts. On the first count, since
Germany failed to detonate a sense of 'national'
identity during its brief period of occupation
one could not accurately speak of contemporary
Cameroon nationalism as simply a rekindling of a
profound feeling once shared by all Cameroonians.
But even if one were to entertain such an absurdity,
then the reality that present day Cameroon is far
from being a geopolitical replica of German Kamerun
makes the earlier pretension all the more absurd.
  The first weakness with this position is the
appearance it gives of questioning the basis for
the Kamerun Idea, stripping it of its mystique,
and in fact substituting other causes in place of
those advanced by Cameroonians <u>themselves</u>.[22] These
efforts directed toward reducing the mystery of
the Cameroon <u>volksgeist</u> to comprehensible terms
fail to take into account Rupert Emerson's trenchant
observation that nationalism like other such profound emotions as love and hate does not easily
lend itself to cold, mechanical and rational
analysis. And as he repeatedly emphasized in his
monumental study of the rise to self-assertion of
the Afro-Asian peoples,[23] "the nation is a
community of people who feel that they belong
together in the double sense that they share deeply
significant elements of a common heritage and that
they have a <u>common</u> <u>destiny</u> for the future."[24]
(My emphasis.) Thus the appeal of the Kamerun
Idea lay in the simple fact that it expressed the
feelings of the Cameroonian people that they are a
nation by <u>choice</u> and long <u>inheritance</u>. To advance

beyond this point, as many non-Cameroonian scholars have done, is to subject the profound emotion of Cameroon nationalism to an overly mechanical process of analysis.

The insistence of interpreting the symbols of Cameroon nationalism as simply myths is equally unfortunate. To begin with, any scholar who fails to recognise the place of myth in the gestation and subsequent birth of a nationalist movement has, quite frankly, read his history badly. For it is out of myths that nations are founded, and as George Sorel, the man who introduced the concept of myth into the language of political science, reminds us "The myth must be judged as a means of acting on the present; any attempt to discuss how far it can be taken literally is devoid of sense."[25] Sorel saw myths as things that may never be fulfilled; but which provide, nonetheless, an indispensable incentive to action since, as he put it, "man would probably never abandon his inertia if he had a perfectly clear view of the future, and if he could calculate exactly the difficulties in the midst of which he ventures."[26] All great national movements in history were based on an elaborate myth structure; such was the case with the French Revolution, the Italian Risorgimento and the assorted waves of nationalism that swept across Europe following the fall of the Napoleonic empire. The invocation of mythology as part of nationalist rhetoric is not peculiarly Cameroonian but one with a distinguished pedigree in human history. If the myth of a once united German Kamerun was able to sustain the momentum of Cameroon nationalism, inject it with an élan vital, then any attempts to take it too literally would be devoid of sense and meaning.

One should therefore not lose sight of the strength of the Kamerun Idea; it is to be found not so much in what it promised or actually attained but rather in the actual effect it had on the Cameroonian people at a challenging period in their history. As such, it should be judged independently of its pretensions of resurrecting a once united German Kamerun. The Idea's achievements derive from the very real effects that it had on the national consciousness; it inspired Cameroonians, fired their imagination, and mobilized them to action. Herein lies the validity of its purpose.

But was the Kamerun Idea all romanticism devoid of any factual content? Was the German

13

contribution towards an emerging Cameroon national
identity a myth? Have nationalists exaggerated
German contribution to the economic development of
their territory despite greater material progress
during the longer mandate-trusteeship period? To
respond in the affirmative is to overstate the
case. In the first place, if the Germans had only
ten years of relatively peaceful administration
against forty-five years for the British and French
trustees, then any reasonable comparison of both
periods must make sufficient allowance for the
discrepancy in time. In which case, one would be
comparing German achievements in ten years against
those of France and Britain during their forty-
five years as administrators of former German
Kamerun. The logical questions that should be
asked are: could France and Britain have done more
for Cameroon had they, like the Germans, enjoyed
only a decade of peaceful occupation? Did they
perform better in the longer period they had the
country under their control? If they did, why
then are their achievements ignored and those of
the Germans extolled by Cameroonian nationalists?

Cameroonian scholars are in agreement that
the legacy of a solid economic infrastructure and
the rudimentary trappings of a modern state system
remain largely the work of German colonial administration in Kamerun.[27] It was on this impressive
foundation, laid down during ten years of peaceful
reign, that the French and British built their own
edifices. When, therefore, Cameroonian nationalists talk nostalgically about German times, they
certainly mean inter alia those concrete legacies
of that period. Admittedly, no self-respecting
nationalists speak admiringly of that pernicious
system called colonialism; Cameroonians are no
exception to this rule. Yet when mention is made
of the durable legacies of German colonialism (and
said with some fondness), a proper interpretation
of that sentiment is not the expressed statement
but the implied, unvoiced thought; for the expressed
statement carries with it a veiled criticism. The
Cameroonian nationalist speaking ex cathedra as a
comparativist compared the achievements of the
relatively few years of peaceful German rule
against the almost five decades of the successor
colonialists and quickly came to the conclusion
that the former was the better of the two. This
was more evident in the British-administered part
of the Cameroon where the nationalists felt the

14

pace of socio-economic development lagged behind the French-administered part.

In terms of the socio-economic development, the nationalists were saying that under the Germans that commitment was arduously pursued which, regrettably, was not the case under the British. A 1958 United Nations Visiting Mission was received by the leaders of the Southern Cameroons Under United Kingdom Trusteeship who expressed their dissatisfaction at the low level of development in their country:

> . . . we need hardly emphasize the fact that the Southern Cameroons is one of the under-developed areas of the west coast of Africa and needs extensive external financial aid if the territory is to keep pace with her neighbours in all fields of human endeavour. The mission will recall that we have repeated-ly laid strong emphasis on this unenviable situation. . . .[28]

Britain was doing precious little to develop the country. In fact, many Cameroonians who studied in Nigeria were made to understand that their country was considered a colonial backwater. French-speaking Cameroonians were even more brutal in driving home the point. To them the Southern Cameroons was ". . . une colonie d'une region d'une colonie."[29] One explanation why Cameroonian nationalists spoke with some admiration for the Germans is precisely because they believed that in the short period their country was under this colonial rulership relatively more was done than during a comparable period under, say, the British. We must see it strictly as a case of choosing the lesser of two evils.

Johnson rightly points out that the short period of German occupation was too brief to elicit a sense of national identity--a factor he feels nationalists have stressed. Caution must be exercised when interpreting this frequent reference to German colonial rule by Cameroonian nationalists as simply a belief that there has existed a sense of national identity all Cameroonians shared created under fiat of German colonialism. It had little to do with that. At issue was the memory of the 1916 dismemberment of what was once a united Kamerun Protectorate administered as a single political and economic unit under a single political authority, albeit a colonial one. Germany did not

create a sense of Cameroonian identity any more
than Lugard and the British did for the Nigerians.
Nor should they have been expected to. After all,
colonial interests and objectives were by nature
diametrically opposed to the idea of national unity
and identity, especially when the objects that
elicited such subjective behavioral attachments
were rooted in areas other than the metropole. The
colonial mission was best pursued within a framework that permitted and promoted mutual antagonisms
among the colonized subject peoples such that the
disunity of the colonized provided the fuel that
kept ablaze the fire of colonial domination and
exploitation. This could not have been lost on
Cameroonian nationalists. So, how did they interpret the German legacy?

What the Germans did for their subject people
was to leave behind three important legacies: a
memory, an idea, and the hope. A memory that at
one time in the not too distant past all of Cameroon
was administered as one unit; an idea that people
from even as disparate ethnic groups as Cameroonians
belong could still be brought together under one
economic and political umbrella. It was in this
idea that lay the hope that if the Germans could do
it then Cameroonians, for whom the stakes were even
higher, could replicate the feat. Germany did not
leave behind a sense of 'Kamerunianness' but a
framework from which, with proper management and
care, this sense of togetherness could re-emerge.[30]
This, I submit, is what Cameroonian nationalists
(whether in the French- or English-speaking sector)
may have seen in the German legacy--an experiment
in national integration rudely interruped by two
occidental wars but which, nevertheless, could be
tried again. This second time under Cameroonian
sponsorship.

The short period of German rule cannot, therefore, be summarily dismissed as inconsequential,
for it was in this period that the country's
international boundaries were drawn and universally
accepted by the commonwealth of nations.[31] Though
these boundaries were somewhat tinkered with after
the Allied defeat of Germany in 1916, they were
reconstituted forty years later only with some
minor modifications. Essentially, the boundaries
of German Kamerun are still the parameters that
distinguish contemporary Cameroon from her
neighbors in Africa. German colonial rule is also
of political significance because this was the
first colonizer and the only external agency under

16

which the nucleus of a Cameroonian nation was created. Against this background, one begins to understand nationalist attachment to the symbols of this epoch in Cameroon's chequered history.

NOTES

1. See Mongo Beti, Main basse sur le Cameroun: Autopsie d'une decolonisation. Paris: editions Maspero, 1972 and Abel Eyinga, Mandat d'Arrêt pour cause d'élections: De la democratie au Cameroun. (1970-1978). Paris: Editions l'Harmattan, 1978.

2. Victor T. Le Vine, The Cameroons from Mandate to Independence (Berkeley & Los Angeles: University of California Press, 1964).

3. Based on 1926 estimates, French Cameroons covered an area of 164,094 square miles with a population of 1,877,113. British Cameroons occupied 34,236 square miles of territory and had a population of 66,841. It should be pointed out that the British mandate consisted of two administrative units, Southern Cameroons and Northern Cameroons both of which were administered as part of Nigeria until 1961. Figures quoted are from Claude E. Welch, Dream of Unity (Ithaca, N.Y.: Cornell University Press, 1966), p. 27.

4. See for example, M. Crawford Young, "Nationalism and Separatism in Africa" in Martin Kilson, ed., New States in the Modern World (Cambridge, Mass.: Harvard University Press, 1975), pp. 57-74.

5. A. Allott, "Boundaries and the Law in Africa," in Carl Gosta Widstrand, ed., African Boundary Problems (Uppsala: The Scandinavian Institute of African Studies, 1969), p. 17.

6. Ibid.

7. Quoted from Samuel Chime, "The Organization of African Unity and African Boundaries," in Widstrand, op. cit., p. 67.

8. In response to Nyobe's celebrated claim that God created one single Cameroon Thomas Hodgkin was quick to point out, with sarcasm intended, that "If God did in fact create a single Cameroon then the Prussian State--as Hegel thought--must have been acting as the divine agent. For the movement for Cameroons unification has as its aim the recreation of the Cameroons state within its pre-1911 German frontiers." In Thomas Hodgkin, "The Cameroons Question," West Africa, no. 1969 (Nov. 20, 1954), p. 1093.

9. Dr. Felix-Roland Moumie drawing from the writings of Ptolemy and John Barbot maintained that Cameroon was already existing as a nation as far back as the sixth century. See his letter to the Editor in rebuttal to Edwin Ardener's series of articles on the "Kamerun Idea," West Africa,

September 13, 1958, p. 876. Ardener's reply
appears in West Africa, October 11, 1958, p. 972.
    10. "Rapport presente par Um Uyobe au 2e
Congres de L'U.P.C." (Eseka, 28-30 Septembre,
1952) p. 76.
    11. See Moumie's comments in footnote #9.
    12. See Aristide Zolberg, Creating Political
Order: The Party-States of West Africa. (Chicago:
Rand McNally, 1966) for further exploration of this
point.
    13. See Edwin Ardener, "The Kamerun Idea," in
West Africa nos. 2147 and 4148.
    14. Ardener, "The Nature of the Reunification
of Cameroon," in Arthur Hazelwood, ed., African
Integration and Disintegration (London: Oxford
University Press, 1967), p. 293.
    15. He lists the following ethnic groups:
Mongo (E. 300; W. 600), Balong (E. 2,406; W. 2,000),
Bakossi (E. 4,257 = Muamenam + Manehas; W. 17,086),
Elung (E. 2,665; W. 1,447), Mbo (E. 7,816;
W. 5,041); as the most notable cases of ethnic
splits.
    16. Welch, op. cit.
    17. The process by which European powers
acquired territories overseas in the 19th century
did not follow any logical pattern; as a conse-
quence, territories were carved out without any
regard for symmetry. Overseas expansion was
generally unpredictable and irrational as Messrs.
Robinson and Gallagher have shown in the case of
the British. See R. Robinson and J. Gallagher with
Alice Denny, Africa and the Victorians: The Climax
of Imperialism. New York: Anchor Books, 1968.
    18. U.N. Trusteeship Council T/486:
Supplement No. 2, 1950, p. 56.
    19. Bernard Fonlon, "The Language Problem in
Cameroon: A Historical Perspective," in David R.
Smock & Kwamena Bentsi-Enchil, eds., The Search for
National Integration in Africa (New York: The
Free Press, 1975), pp. 196-197. The Cameroonian
nationalist, Samson A. George, echoes the same
sentiments: "In answer to these doubts/the success
of reunification/I can only say one thing, that
every event that has surrounded the existence of
our people as a community has contributed in all
ways to maintaining the identity of the people of
Kamerun. When the Germans carved it out and gave
it the political expression which we now know to be
Kamerun, the wars came--two world wars--the country
was torn into two again, and yet in the first act
of partition which was sanctioned by the League

19

of Nations, the country in both Sections was still
called Kamerun, even in the agreement by which they
were administered as mandated territories. In
later years, when the mandate was changed into a
trusteeship system, the two sections are still
called Cameroons/Cameroun in each case. When the
British section was further cut in two, even that
Section which chose to remain in Northern Nigeria
continues to be called Cameroons, and the Southern
Section is still called Cameroons. No matter what
we do, no matter how we have tried, no matter how
our enemies have tried, they have not succeeded in
eliminating that one word that is the symbol of the
unity of the country of Kamerun. It is the
foundation of our existence and it is upon that I
hope and pray that we shall build our nation" in
S. A. George, Kamerun Unification (London: Carey &
Claridge, 1956), pp. 26-27. For a similar view
see Aloys J. Tellen, The Kamerunian's Bedside
Catechism (Ibadan: Starlight Press, 1958).
    20. Willard Johnson, The Cameroon Federation:
Political Integration in a Fragmentary Society
(Princeton, N.J.: Princeton University Press,
1970). For the same line of argument, see also
Victor T. Le Vine, "The Politics of Partition in
Africa: The Cameroons and the Myth of Unification,"
Journal of International Affairs, Vol. 18, No. 1,
1964.
    21. Edwin Ardener, "The Nature of the
Reunification of Cameroon," in Arthur Hazelwood,
ed., op. cit., p. 288.
    22. My somewhat severe criticism of these
scholars should not in any way detract from nor
conceal my genuine admiration for their outstanding
contribution to Cameroon studies through their many
books and articles. Willard Johnson and Victor T.
Le Vine (The Cameroons from Mandate to Independence.
Berkeley and Los Angeles: University of California
Press, 1964, and The Cameroon Federal Republic.
Ithaca: Cornell University Press, 1971.) are
unquestionably the foremost American authorities on
Cameroon political history. Edwin Ardener's
pioneering work on the coastal ethnic groups
(Coastal Bantu of the Cameroons. London: International African Institute, 1956.) and his
investigations on the social and demographic
problems of plantation agriculture (Plantation and
Village in the Cameroons. London: Oxford
University Press, 1960.) are important landmark
studies.

23. Rupert Emerson, From Empire to Nation: The Rise to Self-Assertion of the Asian and African Peoples (Cambridge, Mass.: Harvard University Press, 1960).

24. Ibid., p. 95 and passim.

25. Quoted in Immanuel Wallerstein, Africa: The Politics of Unity. New York: Vintage Press, 1967. See also Rupert Emerson's From Empire to Nation for an extended discussion on the place of myth in the development of national consciousness.

26. Georges Sorel, Reflections on Violence (Paris, 1930), p. 32. Sorel distinguishes between utopia which is the description of a rational scheme of economic or political organization, and a social will based on imagination and expressed in religious or poetical terms--a myth, that is. The former is the product of an intellectual process while the latter is an anti-intellectualist construction. Because it derives part of its dynamic force from faith, Sorel believes that the myth is therefore not amenable to criticism by the ordinary rationalist methods of analysis. I take it then that if nationalism (for Sorel, it was the proletarian movement) draws from myth, it too cannot be explained or understood purely on the basis of scientific method. The reader interested in Sorel's ideas on this subject is referred to the following excellent studies of him: Richard Humphrey, Georges Sorel, Prophet Without Honor: A Study in Anti-Intellectualism (New York: Octagon Books, 1971), pp. 170-172 passim; J. H. Meisel, The Genesis of Georges Sorel (Ann Arbor, Michigan: George Wahr Publishing Company, 1951), pp. 264-265 passim. See also Neil McInnes, "George Sorel," in Paul Edwards, ed., The Encyclopedia of Philosophy, vol. 7 (New York: MacMillan Company & The Free Press, 1967), pp. 497-499.

27. This is the position of scholars such as Thomas Ketchoua, Contributions a l'histoire du Cameroun de 450 avant Jesus-Christus a nos jours. Yaounde: Imprimerie Nationale, 1962; Engelbert Mveng, Historie du Cameroun. Paris: Presence Africaine, 1963.

28. Cited in Johnson, op. cit., p. 104.

29. The following statement by President Ahidjo reveals this same attitude: "The Cameroon Republic and the territory previously under British trusteeship constituted a single historic unit. . . . But on the other hand, they were two distinct political entities: on one side, an independent sovereign state possessing an international legal

21

personality; on the other, a territory <u>without</u> a
political international status." Ahmadou Ahidjo,
<u>Contribution to National Construction</u>. Paris:
Editions Presence Africaine, 1964, p. 23 (my
emphasis). This haughty, condescending attitude
adopted by Francophone <u>ruling</u> elites toward their
Anglophone compatriots has not been very helpful in
the drives toward creating a sense of community.
As a result of such prevailing attitudes the
Anglophones now consider themselves the neglected
step-children of the union. See Jacques Benjamin,
<u>Les Camerounais occidentaux: La minorite dans un</u>
<u>Etat bicommunautaire</u>. Montreal: Les Presses du
l'Universite de Montreal, 1972; and Sammy Kum Buo,
"How United is Cameroon?" <u>Africa Report</u> (November-
December, 1976), pp. 17-20.

30. The point has been made by Apter and
Coleman of the role colonial governments played--
although not intentionally--in providing the
foundations for national consciousness among the
colonized peoples.

> The net effect of European colonialism in
> Africa has been to create--albeit unwittingly--
> embryonic nations coterminous with boundaries
> of the colonial administrative units. Despite
> the brevity of European rule, a variety of
> integrative processes have operated within the
> confines of those boundaries to create, at
> least, among certain strata of the population,
> a sense of national consciousness. The mere
> fact of establishing a common administrative
> and judicial system, common representative
> institutions, a common communication and
> transportation grid, a common educational
> system and acculturative process, and of
> providing a lingua franca, among many other
> things, served to differentiate the peoples
> inhabiting one territory from those in
> another. Territorial differentiation has
> been further strengthened by the consequential-
> ly greater interaction and communication among
> the peoples of one territory against those in
> other territories. All of these factors have
> operated to create a "territorial" as
> distinguished from an "African Personality."

David E. Apter & James S. Coleman, "Pan-Africanism
or Nationalism?" in Society of African Culture, eds.,
<u>Pan-Africanism Reconsidered</u> (Berkeley & Los Angeles,

California: University of California Press, 1962),
pp. 92-93.

    31. Neville Rubin, Cameroun: An African
Federation. London: Pall Mall Publications, 1970,
pp. 48-88.

2
The Pan-Kamerun Movement, 1949–1961

Bongfen Chem-Langhee
Martin Z. Njeuma

In February 1961, the majority of the Southern Kamerunians,[1] according to the number of votes,[2] opted for Cameroun citizenship in a United Nations supervised plebiscite. In October, same year, Southern and Eastern Kamerun were united to form the Federal Republic of Cameroon. The plebiscite itself and the act of union were a function of several nationalist aspirations in Kamerun, one of which was the desire, on the part of some people, for the re-creation of the 1914 boundaries of Kamerun. This article attempts to examine the factors which worked for or against the Pan-Kamerun Movement, its rise, evolution and the problems it faced as it progressed with particular emphasis on the Western Kamerun situation.

Perhaps, the best point from which to begin is the pre-colonial political organization of the territory under study. Before and during the German colonial period, Kamerun was inhabited by a conglomerate of heterogeneous peoples organized in traditional states (Fondoms) and villages.[3] Despite their diversity, these Fondoms shared some common experiences: they had well-organized and highly sophisticated political, cultural and social institutions for the maintenance of law and order; there was a great deal of inter-regional trade among them with the central area acting as an entrepot of the northern and southern areas; some of them had diplomatic and trade relations with one another; and, although the list is by no means complete, each of them was highly jealous and protective of its political independence.[4] Generally, therefore, while the desire and abilities of each Fondom to remain politically independent hindered the emergence of a larger political entity, several factors were con-

ducive to the creation of a modern state in the
territory before the Germans came to the scene.

But the Germans (1884-1914) apparently did
little to instill in the minds of the inhabitants
of their Kamerun Protectorate the spirit of Kamer-
unism, the notion of Kamerun citizenship, or the
idea of a common political destiny. By 1914, the
territorial boundaries of Kamerun had been fairly
well-defined and recognized by the European powers
whose African possessions shared common boundaries
with it, thereby making the territory a political
entity under effective German rule with its inhabitants sharing the same administration. But,
that is about all there was to it. No doubt the
Germans encouraged and redirected the inter-regional
trade through their posts. But, the trade was already in practice before the occupation and colonization. Without question, they encouraged and
facilitated, by a good communication network, the
inter-regional movement of people, particularly from
the northern and central areas to the south for work
in the plantations. But, that movement and mixing
of peoples made more sense to the Germans in so far
as they helped to promote the economic development
and exploitation of the territory. That these two
elements would foster a sense of a common political
destiny among the diverse peoples was hardly any
part of the calculation.

In short, the Germans did very little to exploit some of the requirements of a modern state
which already existed in the territory to make its
inhabitants aware of a shared political experience
and common destiny, personified by the German colonial rule and administration. Ardener and Le Vine
have, individually and convincingly, argued that
there was no such thing as a "Kamerun people" or a
"Kamerun nation" before and during the German colonial period, adding that the political leaders who
proclaimed the existence of such a thing at that
time were fundamentally creating myths.[5] Seen in
this way, although the Germans had built the foundation of a Kamerun State by establishing its boundaries and putting its inhabitants under the same
administration, the partition of Kamerun in 1919
and the re-organization of the territory thereafter
would have meant very little to the Kamerunians had
other things remained equal.

But, they did not. The inter-Kamerun boundary,
which emerged from the Anglo-French partition of the
territory, was artificial at almost every point; it
either divided Fondoms or separated ethnic groups,

families and some people from part of their land.[6]
The problem was further aggravated when the French
in particular and, the British began to enforce
their frontier regulations in the early part of the
trusteeship period. Although many of them would
behave differently during the plebiscite period, a
situation had been created for the frontier dwellers and smugglers on both sides of the boundary
line to agitate for Reunification - the idea that
all the various fragments of Kamerun be brought together administratively to form a single political
entity.

Moreover, some Kamerunians particularly those
attracted to Marxism, would see the very partition
of Kamerun as the evil work of imperialism and
would not rest tranquil until they had undone that
imperialist design and chased the imperialists away
from the territory. The political and administrative reorganization of Eastern Kamerun worried the
anti-imperialists of that region. The French had
constituted Eastern Kamerun into a distinct political entity but administered it in association
with the rest of the so-called French Equatorial
Africa. Worse still, the French applied the policy
of assimilation in Eastern Kamerun in very much the
same way as it was applied elsewhere in France's
African territories.[7] The anti-imperialists, who
were aware not only of the international status of
the region but also of the fact that the mandate
and trusteeship systems aimed at developing the
region to independence could be expected to, and
indeed did, use Reunification as a means to acquire
independence rapidly and end the subjective forms
of the policy of assimilation.[8]

If the political and administrative reorganization of Eastern Kamerun contributed to the rise
of the Pan-Kamerun Movement, the conditions were
more inducive in Western Kamerun. The British
divided the region into two sections, Northern and
Southern Kamerun, each of which had little to do
either with each other or with Eastern Kamerun. A
new boundary, the intra-Western Kamerun boundary,
artificial at some points, had thus been created.
Those frontier dwellers affected by the artificiality of the boundary could be expected to register
their opposition to it when and if the opportunity
offered itself. The very fact that the region
constituted a single trusteeship territory would
not be lost to some Western Kamerunians and many
members of the United Nations, all of whom would

27

demand Unification - the idea that Northern and
Southern Kamerun should form a single and distinct
political and administrative unit whether or not
within Nigeria. Northern Kamerun was further fragmented into three separate units, each of which was
integrated with its nearest Northern Nigerian administrative sub-unit and had little to do with the
others. This arrangement brought the non-Fulani
Northern Kamerunians under Fulani rule and therefore
closer to the source of Islam which they had seen as
a threat to their lives and cultural identity since
the beginning of the nineteenth century when Modibbo
Adama of Yola declared jihad against them. Opposition to this arrangement could, therefore, be expected from this group of Northern Kamerunians. Unlike Northern Kamerun, Southern Kamerun, for the
most part, was unsegmented. But, until 1954, it
formed an integral part of the Eastern Region of
Nigeria. This arrangement obliterated the true
identity of the area and that of its inhabitants.[9]
The Southern Kamerunians who were aware of the international status of the region and the anti-imperialists members of the United Nations could be
expected to oppose the arrangement and in their
various ways press to regain Southern Kamerun's
identity.

Other factors, connected with subsequent British activities, also contributed greatly to the
rise of the Pan-Kamerun Movement in Western Kamerun.
Because of the administrative arrangements, the
British almost completely neglected the economic,
educational, political and social development of
Western Kamerun, Northern Kamerun in particular.[10]
Dissatisfaction with this situation, particularly
among the Western-educated elite, contributed to the
demand for Separation--the idea that the various
segments of Western Kamerun be separated from the
Nigerian administrative units with which they had
been integrated. From this base, would come the demand for Unification, Reunification and Secession--
the idea that either Northern, Southern or Western
Kamerun be constituted into a separate and distinct
political entity without any reference to either
Nigeria or Eastern Kamerun. In Northern Kamerun,
the British deposed some of the German-time Fulani
rulers on charges of corruption and abuse of power,
thereby making enemies of them and their descendants.
In order to avenge themselves on the British, these
people opposed whatever the British stood for in
Northern Kamerun. Moreover, many of the senior jobs
in administration in the area were controlled by

28

Nigerians proper with the result that the majority of the Western-educated Northern Kamerunians saw the alternatives, Reunification and Secession or at least Separation, as the best means of securing higher positions for themselves in the Civil Service.

The job situation in Northern Kamerun was replicated in Southern Kamerun and with the same expectations.[11] After the Second World War, the Ibo of Eastern Nigeria moved into Southern Kamerun in large numbers and, they not only proved better competitors of the local traders,[12] but also violated, whether or not consciously, many local traditions and customs. Such behaviour led local traders and the a-Fon with their subjects, who had equated the Ibo with Nigeria, to determine to have Secession.[13] It seems, therefore, that many factors, connected with the Anglo-French presence and behaviour in Kamerun and the international status of the territory were very conducive to the rise of the Pan-Kamerun Movement, particularly in Western Kamerun.

Nevertheless, there were other factors which militated against the Movement's developments. The partition of Kamerun was a product of the agreement between France and Britain, and between the United Nations, on the one hand, and France and Britain, on the other. The British and the French could not, therefore, be expected to support the movement which aimed at the destruction of what they themselves had created and found otherwise convenient. Nor could some members of the United Nations, those who administered trust territories or had their own colonies in particular, be expected to challenge their co-colonialists. The British and French Trusteeship Agreements clearly indicated that Eastern and Western Kamerun would be administered as integral parts of their respective neighbouring colonial territories. The United Nations, itself, was composed for the most part of two major groupings: the imperialists who, for the most part, were the Western Democracies and their supporters, and the anti-imperialists who were Socialists, in the main, and their supporters. It is, therefore, not surprising that the advocacy of Reunification became encumbered by the tentacles of the Cold War octopus.[14]

Even at the local level, the Pan-Kamerun Movement had to face several problems. The fragmentation of Kamerun and the development of the various segments in different directions made it difficult for the Kamerunians to develop any sense of oneness or of a common political destiny. The Western Kam-

29

erunians became accustomed to the Anglo-Saxon customs, systems and traditions with no real acquaint-
ance with the Gallic situations. Nevertheless by
the time the nationalist movement was at its zenith,
it was common knowledge that there was a big difference between the British way of life and that of
the French, which obtained in Eastern Kamerun, although the majority of the Southern Kamerunians
could not say exactly what that difference was. It
was, therefore, natural for them to find themselves
alienated from the Eastern Kamerunians and attached
to the idea of a Southern or Western Kamerun State,
Member of the Commonwealth.[15] Generally unaware of
the British systems, and accustomed to those of the
French, it was difficult for the Eastern Kamerunians
to take Reunification very seriously for the most
part. As late as 1957, the most prominent politicians of Eastern Kamerun, Andre-Marie Mbida for example, were not inclined to Reunification.[16] As
will be seen later, it was not until 1958 that the
Ahidjo Government and the Eastern Kamerun parlia-
mentarians unanimously declared for Reunification.

Finally, although the list is by no means complete, the way the Eastern and Western Kamerunians
perceived of themselves and the way their political
parties were organized were not conducive to the
Pan-Kamerun Movement. During the trusteeship period,
except during the last days of the plebiscite, nearly all the Southern Kamerun political parties,
judged from their political programmes, spoke a
national language and were national in character,
where the nation meant Southern or Western Kamerun,
and, in the case of the One Kamerun Party (OK),
Kamerun. Essentially, the Southern Kamerunians had
come to recognize themselves as a people with a
common destiny, an eventuality fostered by shared
experiences during the mandate and trusteeship
periods. Likewise, the only two indigenous political parties in Northern Kamerun were national in
character, where the nation meant Western Kamerun or
Kamerun.[17]

On the contrary, except perhaps, for the Union
des Populations du Cameroun (UPC), because of its
very strong commitment to Reunification, Eastern
Kamerun political parties or organizations were
either ethnic or locally based.[18] In time, these
numerous political organizations coalesced to produce four prominent ones: "Union Camerounaise,"
including mainly the Muslim populations of the
North; "Cameroun Democrats", comprising largely the

Ewondo in the central area; "Paysans Independants"
embracing the grasslanders of the west; and, "Action
Nationale du Cameroun", composed mainly of the Edea
and Douala peoples of the coastal region.[19] Unlike
Western Kamerunians, the Eastern Kamerunians had not
therefore developed an all-Eastern Kamerun national
consciousness.

These differences in outlook and party organization were significant in several respects. The
already self-conscious and self-recognizing Southern
Kamerunians would not easily want to loose their
identity in a larger political entity. Aware of the
regionalism in Eastern Kamerun, the Western Kamerunians would not want to join a political system
in which they would not operate effectively. Without even developing an all-Eastern Kamerun national
consciousness, it is doubtful that the Eastern Kamerunians would support the Pan-Kamerun Movement.
Indeed, the Bloc Democratique Camerounaise, which
embraced the most important political leaders of the
region at the time, could hardly see the practica-
bility of the idea of Pan-Kamerun unity and so were
opposed to it.[20] In sum, we have tried so far to
demonstrate that several factors worked for and
against the Pan-Kamerun Movement and, although other
factors would emerge with time, these considerations
form an essential background to a better understanding of the rise of the Movement.

When the nationalist agitation in Southern
Kamerun began in about 1939, it involved a search
for an identity, but by 1948, it had included many
other elements. In late 1939, some of the Western-
educated Southern Kamerunians, under the banner of
the Cameroon Welfare Union (CWU), demanded direct
representation of Southern Kamerun in the Nigerian
central legislature in Lagos.[21] Since the area
was an integral part of Eastern Nigeria, it could
not be represented in Lagos in its own right.
Therefore, fundamental to the request was the assertion of a separate identity for Southern Kamerun and
its peoples. In turning down the request, the British missed the point and argued that "the area did
not enjoy the franchise and its representation in
Lagos was a privilege and not a right."[22] Nevertheless, in 1940, the Cameroons Youth League (CYL)
made a similar request couched in terms of jobocracy,
the idea that jobs and offices in Southern Kamerun
should be controlled by the indigenous inhabitants
of the area and not, as it was, by Nigerians proper.

In fact, the CYL further emphasized this dis-

31

tinction when it demanded, at the same time, autonomy for Southern Kamerun within the Nigerian framework and nationhood or independence for the area outside the Nigerian context. More and better Western education for the area's inhabitants was advocated as the best means for achieving these goals.[23] Between 1940 and 1948, the political leaders continued to demand more and better Western education and autonomy for the Southern Kamerunians. Politically, the stress was on a separate and autonomous Region for Southern Kamerun within Nigeria. This Region was to be equal in status to the other Nigerian Regions. These demans so far were rather limited to a strong desire to develop Southern Kamerun in all aspects of life,[24] so that by 1948, the demand for Reunification had not been officially raised in Southern Kamerun.

But it was not long in coming. In 1949, Dr. E. M. L. Endeley formed a widely representative political organization in Southern Kamerun, the Cameroons National Federation (CNF). In late 1949, the CNF had its first contact with the United Nations Visiting Mission (Mission) in which it made several demands from the United Nations, some of them contradictory. Its leaders requested the United Nations to develop Western Kamerun educationally, economically and socially, all aspects which, they charged, the British had grossly neglected in their treatment of the region as an appendage to Nigeria. Separation, Unification Secession and Reunification could be found among the political demands the CNF made to the United Nations.[25] Reunification as a political programme or idea had thus been discussed for the first time officially in Southern Kamerun. But, the kind of Reunification considered at this time was not to be immediate. As the CNF memorandum, handed to the Mission, indicated, Reunification was to be evolutionary. The intra-Western Kamerun and the inter-Kamerun boundaries and frontier regulations were to be abolished immediately. Both French and English would then be taught in all the schools in Kamerun with equal emphasis. Eastern Kamerunians were all indiscriminately to be granted the human rights which the Western Kamerunians already enjoyed, namely, freedom of speech, of the press, of assembly and of petition. Furthermore, Eastern and Western Kamerunians were to be allowed to form common social, educational, economic and political organizations. All this done, a federal or unitary state of Kamerun would emerge in time,

32

having as its main feature the co-existence of
Anglo-Saxonism, Gallism and the traditional systems
or a fusion of all the three elements.[26]

Three main reasons were given for these aspirations. The existing political arrangements were
not in the best interest of the Western Kamerunians
for they served mainly to retard the development of
Western Kamerun by depriving it of the attention
which its special status as a trust territory demanded of the British. The social, economic and
human problems connected with the Franco-British
boundaries of Kamerun and the frontier regulations
were beyond imagination. The partition of Kamerun
in itself represented the gravest injustice ever
done to a group of people without their consent.[27]
The CNF saw Reunification, not as an ideal in itself, but as a means to an end. As its leader, Dr.
Endeley, put it, Reunification was originally conceived of as an instrument for developing Western
Kamerun and for making Kamerun capable of standing
on its own legs. But, (when it appeared that the
region could be developed without the instrumental-
ity of Reunification), he described the idea as a
"barren political instruction in the hands of ir-
responsible and ambitious people."[28] Nevertheless,
when the present writers interviewed Dr. Endeley,[29]
and Tafoh Ngunjoh,[30] Organizing Secretary of the
Kamerun National Democratic Society (KNDP), both
leaders stated that the members of the CNF were
very sincere when they demanded the evolutionary
form of Reunification in 1949. The very fact that
the CNF had provided concrete suggestions for effecting the idea would seem to support their asser-
tions.

Whatever the case, far from being confused, as
suggested by the contradictory demands made to the
United Nations, the CNF leaders merely served notice
of lines of divergencies within their ranks regarding the future political options of Southern
Kamerun. Some of them emphasized autonomism within
Nigeria. These were the separatists who, later,
transformed into integrationists and, still, later,
metamorphosed into associationists. Dr. Endeley
was at their head. Others stressed Secession.
These were the secessionists. Paul M. Kale was
their leader. Still, others demanded immediate and
almost unconditional Reunification. These were the
reunificationists and diehard anti-imperialists.
Jabea R. Kum Dibonge led them in the earlier stage
and, later, when the idea bore an ultra anti-impe-

rialist imprint, the leadership of the group passed
into the hands of Ndeh Ntumazah. Yet, others remained manifestly committed to Secession, Unification and evolutionary Reunification, but would not
pursue any one of these goals vigorously unless it
was politically in their interest to do so. For
want of a better name, this position is referred to
here as Fonchaism, and its adherents as Foncharians.
John Ngu Foncha was their leader.[31] Considering
all this, it can safely be stated that the Pan-
Kamerun Movement in Southern Kamerun was born in
competition with other nationalist aspirations and,
as will be seen from now onwards, it was to face
that competition as it evolved from year to year.

Indeed, the Movement experienced some encouragement and problems in 1949, the year it became
officially a political issue in Southern Kamerun.
In that year, the CNF and UPC leaders held a conference at Kumba where they agreed to steadfastly
work for the achievement of Reunification.[32] Yet,
there was a glaring difference in the outlook of
the CNF and UPC leaders. The former argued that,
because in social, economic and political development Western Kamerun stood far behind Eastern
Kamerun, any premature Reunification would make
Western Kamerun a Protectorate of Eastern Kamerun.
They felt that the two regions should first become
independent separately before Reunification.[33]
When interviewed, Endeley stated that he and his
colleagues took this position because they did not
want to be rushed into Reunification without adequate safeguards for the interests of Western
Kamerun.[34] Like the CNF leaders, the UPC leaders
saw Reunification as an instrument for acquiring
other goals, a convenient spring-board to terminate
French colonialism in Eastern Kamerun and acquire
immediate independence. For that reason, they
opted for immediate Reunification.[35] The indication is that the UPC brand of Reunification was
both immediate and anti-imperialist in character[36]
whereas that of the Southern Kamerunians carried
with it no such features. In this difference, as
will be seen later, lay the genesis of the problems
of the UPC and Reunification in Southern Kamerun.

In any case, Reunification also experienced
some problems elsewhere in 1949. In Northern
Kamerun the Mission encountered no demand for Re-
unification. The majority of the politically active
Northern Kamerunians, under the leadership of the
Emir of Dikwa, requested Separation and continued

direct British trusteeship administration. The
Kanuri and Shuwa Arabs had a particular idea of
their own couched in ethnocentric terms; they requested that the northern area of Eastern Kamerun
be unified with Northern Kamerun under direct
British administration. Those who made these requests gave two main reasons for them. The northern
section of the inter-Kamerun boundary had split
Kanuri, Mandara and Shuwa Arab peoples who were
culturally closer to each other than they were to
the Northern Nigerian Fulani. The frontier regulations were causing many social, economic and
human problems to the frontier dwellers.[37] But in
Eastern Kamerun, the UPC which advocated Reunification was opposed by Dr. Louis Paul Aujoulat's
Bloc Démocratique Camerounaise (BDC) which embraced
some of the most prominent political leaders of
that region.[38] The BDC and the French local authorities argued that, although the inter-Kamerun
boundary rarely coincided with ethnic boundaries,
it did not constitute a serious obstacle to the
frontier dwellers.[39] This view was also supported
by the British who added that Reunification was not
an active issue in Southern Kamerun.[40] With specific reference to the Kanuri and Shuwa Arabs request, the British remained unconvinced that frontier problems provided sufficient reasons for al-
tering the existing arrangements.[41]

The Mission's recommendations and conclusions
also did little to bolster the Pan-Kamerun Movement.
It recommended not only that frontier regulations
should be eased, a factor which would take off
some heat from the movement, but also that the
British and the Western Kamerunians should carefully examine only "the desirability and practi-
cability of some administrative, legislative and
budgetary autonomy being established for the Trust
Territory".[42] Its conclusions remained uncritical
and virtually supported the territorial demarca-
tions in Western Kamerun. The British and French
pursued their opposition to modifications in the
Anglo-French arrangements in Kamerun at the United
Nations. Against opposition from countries like
Argentina and the Dominican Republic, the British
held that the arrangements did not contravene the
Trusteeship Agreement, and the French warned that
the United Nations "should not give too much stress
to the development of national consciousness in
the Territory which might give rise to an excessive
nationalism contrary to the ideal which governed

the United Nations."[43] It would appear, therefore, that the Pan-Kamerun Movement had more problems than support in the year it was born.

The situation was not very different between 1950 and 1951. During the Ibadan Conference of 1950, Dr. Endeley raised the issue of Reunification, the first time the idea was discussed anywhere, aside from the United Nations, outside Kamerun proper. During the Conference, Endeley spoke forcefully in favour of Reunification.[44] Yet, in the same year, Endeley was opposed to the enfranchisement of the Eastern Kamerunians, resident in Southern Kamerun, for the 1950 general elections. Those CNF members who still believed in Reunification, Dibonge[45] for instance, could not fail to see the internal contradiction between advocating Pan-Kamerunism and excluding some qualified Kamerunians from the voters' list simply because their parents or one of their parents originated from Eastern Kamerun. Suspecting that Endeley was no longer a convinced Reunificationist, Dibonge severed links with the CNF and, with the collaboration of Nerius Namaso Mbile, CNF's Secretary, who was involved in a personal quarrel with Endeley, formed another political organization, the Kamerun United National Congress (KUNC), with Reunification as its primary goal.[46] One other element which contributed to the formation of KUNC was British discrimination against the Eastern Kamerunians who were living in Southern Kamerun. For example, the British would grant them neither passports nor scholarships.[47]

The 1952 situation suggests that the Pan-Kamerun Movement still had more problems than encouragement. In June, the Northern and Southern Kamerun political leaders met in Buea, and discussed, among other things, Unification and all of them supported it in principle.[48] But, when the second Mission came to the region later in the year, only the KUNC seriously advocated Reunification, providing concrete suggestions that would lead to the evolutionary type of Reunification.[49]

The CNF and some non-political and political organizations in Southern Kamerun stressed the need for developing the area in all aspects and then demanded the creation of an autonomous Western Kamerun Region of Nigeria. The local branch of the Northern People's Congress (NPC) in Northern Kamerun complained to the Mission about frontier problems but, surprisingly, demanded regional

autonomy for Northern Kamerun, beginning with
"local government reform in favour of a progressive
Emirate system based on tradition and custom, and
eventual self-government with Dominion status for
Nigeria".[50] When speaking as a group, ten of the
elected Southern Kamerunians demanded Reunification without indicating whether it was to be
evolutionary or immediate. Even more symptomati-
cally, they failed to provide concrete suggestions
for effecting the idea.[51] After some questioning,
the Mission realized that their demand for Reunification was closely associated with the fear that
the interests of Western Kamerun might be subordinated to or prejudiced by those of Nigeria
since, as a minority, they could not significantly
influence any policy.[52] The UPC alone in Eastern
Kamerun advocated Reunification but failed to win
a single seat in the general elections of 1952 to
that region's House of Assembly.[53]

At the international level, the usual pattern
of support and opposition continued to manifest
themselves for the Movement. Using anti-imperialist language, the Soviet Union bitterly criticised
the existing arrangements and then requested the
French and the British to respect the views of the
Kamerunians who were opposed to the status quo.
The Soviet position was supported China, Haiti, El
Salvador, Syria and India.[54] On the other hand,
the United States of America (US) put the debate
within the Cold War context and had nothing but
good word for the Anglo-French arrangements. The
American position received the support of Australia,
New Zealand and Belgium.[55] The British themselves
declared that it was unlikely that Western Kamerun
would become a separate entity from Nigeria and
that their task was to prepare the Western Kamerunians for the public service of Nigeria. Their
position, they added, was based on the wishes of
the Western Kamerunians.[56] France supported and
praised the British arrangements.[57] The Mission
itself informed the rest of the United Nations
that the idea of Reunification was limited to certain areas of Kamerun and was not even popular in
those localities.[58] What all this seems to suggest
is that the Pan-Kamerun Movement had less support
than opposition in 1952.

The situation was not much different in 1953.
During the 1953 Nigerian constitutional crisis,
Endeley, leader of Southern Kamerun, and Mallam
Abba Habib, leader of Northern Kamerun, declared

37

that "they were moving towards a common front for
the formation of a legislature for both Southern
and Northern Cameroons.[59] After this declaration,
Endeley and some elected Southern Kamerunians went
to Kaduna to put their case before the Sardauna of
Sokoto, Ahmadu Bello, the most important leader in
Northern Nigeria in modern politics. The Sardauna
would neither give them audience nor allow them
confer again with Habib. On their way back to
Southern Kamerun, the Land Rover in which they were
travelling was stoned in almost all the Nigerian
cities, towns and villages through which they
passed.[60] Some of the Nigerians had thus registered their opposition to the Kamerunians' aspirations. In any case, when Endeley and his colleagues returned home, they toured Southern Kamerun
and informed its inhabitants about the problems
they faced in the Eastern Nigerian House of Assembly, Ahmadu Bello's behaviour and what happened to
them when they were returning from Kaduna, particularly on Ibo land.

After the tour, the Southern Kamerunians held
a very representative conference, in which the
a-Fon were represented, at Mamfe in May, 1953. The
delegates agreed to merge the CNF and KUNC to form
the first political party of Southern Kamerun, the
Kamerun National Congress (KNC), with Endeley as
its head and Dibonge as its patron. After this,
the KNC addressed a petition to the Secretary of
State for the Colonies "demanding the creation of
a separate and autonomous Legislature for the
Trust Territory".[61] The KNC was thus based on the
principle of Separation. Even the Kamerun People's
Party (KPP), which Paul M. Kale, who was involved
in personal squabbles with his cousin, Dr. Endeley,
formed to oppose the KNC soon after the KNC was
formed, did not include Reunification in its programme. Its programme was evolutionary: it was
first to seek regional autonomy for Southern, if
not Western, Kamerun within Nigeria when Nigeria
became independent, the autonomus region would
separate from it and gain its own independence;
and, thereafter, the independent state of Southern
or Western Kamerun would apply for membership in
the anticipated Federation of West Africa.[62] Thus,
the first two political parties of Southern Kamerun
had failed to make Reunification part of their
programme. Moreover, when the Northern and Southern Kamerun delegates met for the last time in
Buea in June, 1953, Habib, who had been made a

Director of a bank in Northern Nigeria after the
Endeley - Habib declaration,[63] opted out of Unifica-
tion.[64] Another reason for Habib's action was prob-
ably the realization that, if the idea was effected,
Endeley, and not himself, would become the leader of
Western Kamerun.[65]

Habib, however, was not representing the opinion of all the Northern Kamerunians. In the same
year, some Northern Kamerunians, under the banner
of an obscure organization, called the Kamerun
Socialist Convention, with the Emir of Dikwa at its
head, demonstrated against the status quo and demanded Reunification. The local authorities of
Northern Kamerun and Nigeria, including the British,
punished the demonstrators very severely and deposed
the Emir of Dikwa and the other a-Fon who were involved in the demonstration.[66] This harsh treatment had the effect of putting any public opposition
to the status quo in Northern Kamerun at bay until
1958. Indeed, the 1958 Mission was aware that there
was some suppression of political opinion in Northern Kamerun.[67] In any case, despite the demonstration, Habib asserted, during the August 1953 London
Constitutional Conference, that the Northern Kamerunians preferred to remain an integral part of the
Northern Region of Nigeria.[68] Meanwhile, the UPC
alone continued to advocate Reunification in Eastern
Kamerun and, there, it received support mainly from
the Bassa, Sanaga-Maritime, Nkongsamba, Mbalmayo
and Douala areas and, later, from the Bamileke
area.[69]

In 1953, Reunification continued to be a poor
competitor among its rivals. During the 1953
general elections in Southern Kamerun, both the KNC
and the KPP offered the electorate regional autonomy within Nigeria with none of them mentioning
either, Unification or Reunification. The KNC which
enjoyed popular support won all the seats but one
which S. E. Ncha captured for the KPP.[70] With the
end of the elections, the British effected Separation and made Southern Kamerun a quasi-autonomous
region of Nigeria.[71] This eventuality proved a
drawback for the KNC and the Pan-Kamerun Movement
in the area. Endeley and the majority of his
colleagues then began to perceive Southern Kamerun
developing into "a self-governing region within the
independent Federation of Nigeria" and to accept
the permanent integration of Northern Kamerun with
Northern Nigeria as inevitable.[72] The KNC, like
the KPP which had formed a formal alliance with the

National Council of Nigeria and the Cameroons
(NCNC), an Ibo dominated political party of Nigeria, entered a formal alliance with the Action
Group (AG), a Yoruba dominated political party of
Nigeria.[73] The two parties had thus served notice
not only that they intended to involve their
peoples in Nigerian politics, but also that they
would like to have Southern Kamerun remain an
integral part of the Federation of Nigeria (Integration). This was unfortunate for the KNC and
the KPP because, as will be seen later, the majority of the a-Fon and their subjects had decided in
favour of Secession and wished it to remain permanent.

The situation between 1954 and 1955 was somehow modified. The Southern Kamerun electorate,
during that time, was either indifferent to or
supported the ideas of Integration, Unification and
Reunification, interpreting them merely as a
drawing together of peoples separated by incomprehensible European barriers.[74] The attitude of the
electorate also encouraged the sentimentally pro-
Reunificationist Foncha to sever links with the
KNC and, with the collaboration of William P.
Lebaga (King of Youths), Augustin Ngom Jua, Tafoh
Ngunjoh, Angela Lafon, Ndeh Ntumazah, Fon of Nkwen,
Chibikom and P. M. Kemcha, form the KNDP, in 1955,
based on the principles of Secession and Reunification.[75] When the 1955 Mission came to Southern
Kamerun, the KNC and the KPP emphasized full
regional autonomy for the area within Nigeria while
the KNDP stressed Secession. Nevertheless, because
of the attitude of the electorate, the KNC and the
KPP joined with the KNDP in demanding Reunification but the drawback was that none of them, however, provided any concrete proposals for effecting the idea. Nor did they provide any sound
argument in favour of it. Their only argument was
that Kamerun was one before 1914. Yet, when dealing with Unification in which they appeared more
interested, the KNC and the KNDP suggested that
there should be road links between Northern and
Southern Kamerun in order to facilitate Unification and the spread of ideas from the latter to
the former. The KNC even went further and demanded the immediate establishment of a joint
Council of Northern and Southern Kamerun.[76] The
indication appears to be that, although all the
political parties in the area demanded Reunification, the KNC and the KPP were more interested in

regional autonomy and Unification while the KNDP
stressed Secession and Unification. Indeed, after
some probing, the Mission discovered that the
political leaders were using Reunification more as
an instrument for gaining greater constitutional
advancement for Western Kamerun than as a definite
political goal.[77]

Elsewhere in Kamerun, the situation of Reunification was also shrouded in much uncertainty.
Due to the suppression of political opinion, the
Mission encountered no opposition to the status
quo in Northern Kamerun.[78] Similarly, in Eastern
Kamerun, many political parties or semi-political
organizations sprang up to oppose the UPC which
advocated immediate Reunification and independence.[79] And, when the UPC was outlawed by the
French in 1955, Reunification ceased to be an
active political issue in Eastern Kamerun until
1958, although some Eastern Kamerunians who believed in the eventual Reunification of Kamerun
formed committees whose purpose was to study the
problems to be faced when Reunification was finally
achieved.[80] Having been banned in Eastern Kamerun,
the UPC found its way into Southern Kamerun, in the
same year, where it made immediate Reunification
and independence the cornerstone of its program,[81]
thereby laying the groundwork for a clash with the
Southern Kamerunians who preferred the evolutionary type of Reunification. Nevertheless, the KNDP
did welcome the UPC and both parties agreed to work
together,[82] an agreement which, as will be seen
presently, was based on a false premise.

At the international level the situation was
almost identical with that of 1952. As far as the
Mission was concerned, the majority of the Northern Kamerunians desired Integration while the
majority of the Southern Kamerunians opted for
either Unification or Reunification. Even then, it
advised that no precipitate decision be taken on
the issues because the mass of the people, who were
indifferent to them, were unaware of their political implications and because the more enlightened
Kamerunians from all the areas of Kamerun had not
yet come together to examine the ideas.[83] The
majority of the Asian and Latin American countries,
Members of the United Nations, praised the economic,
social and educational advancements in Kamerun,
but doubted whether the existing political arrangements were not destroying the identity of the
Kamerunians and bitterly criticized the French

attempt to assimilate the Eastern Kamerunians. The Soviet bloc at the United Nations, using both anti-imperialist and communist jargon, bitterly criticised what the French and the British had done or were still doing in Kamerun and then demanded that the United Nations unilaterally reunite Kamerun for that was what all the Kamerunians desired. The Administering Authorities, supported by Belgium, praised the British as well as the French for their achievements in Kamerun and pleaded with them to halt further new development and consolidate what had already been achieved. The French in particular sang more praises to the British. As they put it, Western Kamerun's "administrative union with Nigeria presented unquestionable advantages, especially for the Northern Cameroons, the people of which had the closest ethnic, linguistic and religious affinities with those of the neighbouring provinces of Nigeria." British policy took account of culture while preserving Western Kamerun's unity at the same time giving its inhabitants "the benefit of the services of a well-organized administration like that of Nigeria". The United Nations should "take note of those arrangements, the wisdom of which was beyond question".[84] Thus, while the Pan-Kamerun Movement received some boost at the international level, its situation in Kamerun proper remained uncertain.

Indeed, the situation in Southern Kamerun in 1956 suggests very strongly that Reunification as a sound political option was on a decline. When Endeley addressed the Trusteeship Council in 1956, he demanded full regional self-government for Southern Kamerun within the Nigerian framework without saying anything about Reunification. He had even begun to have doubts about Unification; as he put it to the Trusteeship Council himself, "the problem of merging the Northern and Southern Cameroons was identical with that of merging the northern and southern parts of Nigeria. If it was possible to unite parts of Nigeria, it might be possible to unite [Western] Cameroons at a later stage".[85] In Southern Kamerun itself, the KNC, the KPP and some Christian Churches virtually declared war on the UPC, which most rigorously advocated Reunification, describing its leaders and members as violent communists.[86] As a result, the electors then began to associate Reunification with violence and communism, the bogeys of the day. Moreover, the only two reunificationist parties, the UPC and

the KNDP, quarrelled with each other and became
enemies. The quarrel involved two elements: the
UPC insisted on immediate Reunification whereas the
KNDP preferred the evolutionary type; and, the UPC
tacitly demanded the dissolution of the KNDP when
it requested the members of the KNDP to buy and
possess only UPC membership cards. Of all the
founding members of the KNDP, only Ntumazah adhered
to the UPC request.[87] The way the electorate began to perceive Reunification and the quarrel between the UPC and the KNDP not only sealed the fate
of immediate Reunification in Southern Kamerun, but
also gravely harmed the progress of the evolutionary type of Reunification.

This situation was glaringly indicated during
the 1957 general elections. During the elections,
the UPC not only campaigned against the KNDP[88] but
was also "the only significant party that demanded
the recreation of Kamerun as quickly as possible"
and, for that reason, it lost all its deposits.[89]
The KNC and the KPP campaigned in favour of a fully
self-governing region for Southern Kamerun within
the Nigerian context. The KNC claiming to maintain
"useful contacts" with Eastern Kamerun authorities,
it gave the lie that it had not yet abandoned Reunification. In any case, the KPP won two and the
KNC gained six of the thirteen contested seats.
The KNDP called for benevolent neutrality in Nigerian politics, asked for co-operation among the
various groups living in Southern Kamerun, whether
or not indigenous, and then offered the electorate
ultimate Reunification "on the basis of mutual
consent". This programme gave it the remaining
five seats.[90] The electors had thus rejected the
UPC and immediate Reunification or rather violence
and communism.

But, they were not alone in doing so. Six
weeks after the elections, May 30, 1957, the British and the KNC-KPP Government (the KNC and the KPP
formed a formal alliance after the elections) outlawed the UPC and deported thirteen of its leaders
and strong supporters on the grounds that there
existed "a grave possibility that in order to
achieve its political objectives the Party may have
to resort to violence in the Southern Cameroons".[91]
The dissolution of the UPC was greeted with joy by
the majority of the Southern Kamerunians for, as
early as 1956, nearly all the political groups had
come to regard it as an unwanted, troublesome influence in the area.[92] Nevertheless, the diehard

43

immediate reunificationists soon regrouped, under
the leadership of Ntumazah, and produced a dis-
guised UPC, the OK.[93] The position of Reunification, the object of the Pan-Kamerun Movement, was,
therefore, fairly well-defined before the 1958
Mission came to the area.

However, it was in connection with the 1958
Mission that the Southern Kamerun leaders more
clearly defined their policies. The KNC-KPP Alliance, supported by a significant number of the
electors, made it clear to the Mission that its objective was Integration on a federal basis and then
demanded a fully self-governing state of Southern
Kamerun within the Nigerian Federation. It was
against Reunification, it said, because the various
segments of Kamerun had developed in different directions, their inhabitants had become accustomed
to different foreign customs, traditions and systems, and the Eastern Kamerunians were very unlike
the Southern Kamerunians in their political organization and national consciousness. The a-Fon, who
spoke for their subjects, requested that Southern
Kamerun sever all links with Nigeria, continue under trusteeship for a short period and then gain
its independence. Their ultimate goal was, first
and foremost, Secession. A period of trusteeship,
they argued, was necessary for them to gain British
aid in building their smaller Kamerun nations. The
KNDP, which by now was receiving the support of the
a-Fon because it advocated a position closest to
their own and they had no political party of their
own, requested that Southern Kamerun sever all
links with Nigeria, continue under trusteeship for
a short time and then gain independence in its own
right. It would welcome Unification provided the
Northern Kamerunians had first severed all links
with Nigeria. Reunification too would ultimately
be effected provided the "two self-governing states"
were in favour of such a move. Pointedly, it argued not only that a period of trusteeship was necessary for a smooth withdrawal from Nigeria and
careful construction of the Southern Kamerun state
but also that its position was a function of the
wishes and desires of the majority of the Southern
Kamerunians. At the other end of the road, and
with very little support from the electorate, stood
the OK pleading with the United Nations to unilaterally effect Reunification and grant Kamerun
independence immediately. Using authentic, but
misleading evidence, it argued not only that Kame-

44

run was partitioned without the consent of its people but also that all the Kamerunians desired Reunification.[94] What the OK said at home and at the United Nations was iterated by the UPC at the United Nations using the same evidence.[95]

The situation in Eastern Kamerun was also fairly well-defined. The frontier dwellers in Eastern Kamerun, as were those in Western Kamerun,[96] who were more aware and conscious of the differences between the two foreign systems in Kamerun and were more affected by these differences, were ironically for the most part, anti-Reunification.[97] Nevertheless, on October 20, 1958, the Eastern Kamerun Parliament unanimously passed a resolution in favour of Reunification and independence; the independence in particular was not to come later than January 1, 1960.[98] It can, therefore, be safely established that, by 1958, the majority of the Eastern Kamerunians were in favour of Reunification, althought they apparently did not indicate whether it was to be evolutionary or immediate.

Unlike in Eastern and Southern Kamerun, there was no demand for Reunification in Northern Kamerun. Instead, some of the Northern Kamerunians, in particular the local authorities, the indirectly elected representatives to the Nigerian legislatures and the government employees, all of whom were members of the NPC, wanted no modifications in the status quo. Even the leading political figures in Northern Nigeria connected with Northern Kamerun, Ahmadu Bello and the Lamido of Adamawa, Mallam Aliyu Mustafa, could neither perceive a better future for the Northern Kamerunians than that they remained Northern Nigerians nor contemplate any changes in the existing arrangements. Other Northern Kamerunians, the members of the local branches of the AG and the United Middle Belt Congress (UMBC) in particular, requested Separation and continued direct British reformed trusteeship administration until self-government and independence. Their argument was that the status quo had virtually made Northern Kamerun a colony of Northern Nigeria and had destroyed or undermined their traditional institutions. Yet, others, the Mambilla and a substantial number of people from the Tigon-Ndoro-Kentu areas in particular, requested that they be separated from Northern Kamerun itself and included in the Southern Kamerun administration. They argued not only that they were being ruled by people who were both oppressive and culturally unrelated to them but also that they were ethnically a part of the people who inhabited the Southern Kamerun part of the intra-Western Kamerun frontier.[99] A very careful analysis of the situation, however, revealed that the majority of the electors preferred Separation and continued reformed trusteeship administration for an unspecified period of time.[100] The results of the 1959 plebiscite testify to this statement.[101] By the end of 1958, therefore, Reunification was popular only in Eastern Kamerun. The same situation obtained in the early part of 1959 as demonstrated by the statement and behaviour of the leaders at the United Nations and elsewhere.

At the United Nations, in February, 1959, Mallam Abdullahi Dan Buram Jada, Minister for Northern Cameroons Affairs in the Northern Nigerian Regional Government, dissociated Northern Kamerun from Separation, Secession, Unification and Reunification and declared that, for geographical, linguistic, religious and cultural reasons, the Northern Kamerunians unanimously desired to retain the status quo. Iterating the British view,[102] he added that the unanimity in the area would render a plebiscite unnecessary.[103] Yet, the first indigenous political party of Northern Kamerun, the Northern Kamerun Democratic Party (NKDP) formed in February, 1959, but launched in April, made ultimate and evolutionary Reunification its final goal. Aside from its determination to develop the area in all aspects of life and to re-establish or reinvigorate Secession, Unification, independence for Western Kamerun and ultimate Reunification.[104]

The position of the Eastern Kamerunians was clearly stated by their Prime Minister, Ahmadu Ahidjo, and the French authorities at the United Nations. According to Ahidjo, the Eastern Kamerunians were unanimous in the desire for Reunification. But, there was one real problem of a practical nature: how to ascertain the most appropriate means of achieving it. The means, however, would depend, above all, on the position to be taken by the Western Kamerunians. He had taken note of the statement made by the Premier of Southern Kamerun, John Ngu Foncha, at the previous meeting of the Fourth Committee.[105] However, the Eastern Kamerunians did not wish to bring the weight of their population to bear on their brothers of Western Kamerun and, therefore, would not impose integration in disregard of their wishes. If the Western Kam-

erunians desired Reunification, the Eastern Kamerunians were ready to discuss the methods of achieving it with them on a footing of equality.[106]
Significant in this statement is the indication
that Ahidjo preferred a unitary state but would not
press the point too far if Foncha felt otherwise.
Another significant element was added by the French
when they stated that although all the Eastern
Kamerunians unanimously desired Reunification, they
did not want it to delay their independence.[107]
The Eastern Kamerunians, therefore, supported Reunification, although they did not want it to delay their independence.

That was not the case with the majority of the
Southern Kamerunians. Although the OK did not contest the January 23, 1959, elections in its own
right on the excuse that "the pro-Nigerian party
seemed to be gaining ground so that the OK decided
to support the KNDP which opted for reunification,"[108] two of its leaders unsuccessfuly contested as independent candidates, offering the
electorate immediate Reunification. The KNC-KPP
Alliance offered the electors "association" with
Nigeria in a fully self-governing state of Southern
Kamerun, carefully avoiding the word integration
which was repugnant to the electorate. The KNDP
tols its listeners what they wanted to hear: to
some, the offer was Secession with a short period
of trusteeship and ultimate independence; to others,
the teachers in particular, it made Integration
versus Secession the central issues of the elections; and, to the students who were, almost to a
man, reunificationist of the anti-imperialist
type, it made Reunification "a simple matter for a
round-table discussion by the two governments", and
any person who predicated Secession on Reunification was "an enemy working in favour of integration in the Federation of Nigeria". On the whole,
however, the KNDP kept Reunification on the background and stressed Secession.[109] With these
various offers, the results of the elections could
be expected - the KNDP gained 75,326 (55%) of the
votes; the KNC-KPP Alliance claimed 51,425 (37%)
of the votes; and, the independent candidates, two
of whom were OK leaders, got the remaining 10,433
(8%) votes.[110] The electorate had thus once more
shown its dislike for Reunification of the OK or
UPC brand and indicated to the political leaders
what support their policies could muster.

Yet, less than a month later, February, 1959,

the political leaders, more or less, refused to
budge from their positions at the United Nations.
There, the OK and the UPC described the partition
of Kamerun as the work of imperialism, argued that
the Kamerunians were never consulted before the
division and then requested the United Nations to
unilaterally effect Reunification. When they
realized that this request would not be granted,
they demanded a referendum whose only issue would
be Reunification and whose voters were to be all
the Kamerunians at home and abroad. When this too
was not forthcoming, they acquiesced in a plebiscite whose issues would be Integration versus Reunification and whose voters were to be indigenous
Western Kamerunians. The reasons they gave for
these suggestions were that Western Kamerun by itself could not constitute a viable economic and
political entity and that the future of the region
was the exclusive problem of its inhabitants. Arguing also that Northern and Southern Kamerun had
developed separately, they insisted that the votes
of the two areas in the plebiscite be treated
separately.[111] For their part, the KNC-KPP leaders
argued in favour of Integration and then demanded
a plebiscite whose voters were to include every
person resident in Southern Kamerun and whose
issues were to be Integration versus Reunification.
The reasons for their suggestions were exactly the
same as those given by the OK and the UPC, except
for the addition that people who had a stake in the
matter could not be excluded from the plebiscite
simply because they were not indigenes.[112]

On the other hand, the leader of the KNDP laid
before the United Nations a straight forward but
involved programme. Secession was to be effected
not later than the day Nigeria was to gain its independence. After Secession, Southern Kamerun
would go through a short period of trusteeship.
During this short period of trusteeship, the possibility of Reunification on a federal basis would
be explored. Southern Kamerun would then gain independence in its own right before Reunification.
Unification was welcomed at any time provided Northern Kamerun had first severed all links with the
Federation of Nigeria. He based this programme on
the wishes of those who had voted him into power
adding that the policy of the a-Fon represented the
views of the majority of the electorate. He also
asked for a plebiscite whose issues were to be Integration versus Secession and whose voters would

include only indigenous Western Kamerunians. The
argument was that the results of the January 24,
1959, general elections had indicated that the
majority of the Southern Kamerunians preferred
either Integration or Secession and that the plebiscite was exclusively the problem of the indigenous Southern Kamerunians.[113]

To be sure, the policy statements of these
leaders represented their deep feelings and con-
victions. But, their suggestions regarding the
plebiscites's issues and the voters' qualifications were very manipulative. The leaders were
fully aware that Secession would defeat any other
idea if it was involved in the plebiscite. That
is why the Integrationists and the Reunificationists sought to exclude it while the Foncharians
tried to include it in the plebiscite. The Integrationists and the Foncharians were also fully
aware that Reunification was more repugnant to the
electorate than Integration.[114] The Foncharians
therefore saw it as a threat to Secession if it
were matched against Integration while the Integrationists were trying to use it to procure Integration. That is why the Foncharians tried to exclude
it from whereas the integrationists wanted to involve it in the plebiscite. Unaware of the decision of the a-Fon at the Bamenda conference, the
reunificationists mistook the Crowned Princes determination to secede from Nigeria for their desire
for Reunification and, for that reason, they
thought they could use Integration to procure Reunification. What is not understood is why the
Foncharians did not request either that all the
ideas be involved in the plebiscite or that only
Secession and Reunification be involved in it. In
any case, all the leaders were also fully aware
that the Nigerians, particularly the Ibo, constituted the largest number of foreign elements in
Southern Kamerun and that they would more likely
than not vote for Integration and if they were
given the vote. That is why the Integrationists
wished to give the vote to foreign factors in the
area whereas the Foncharians and the Reunificationists sought to exclude them.[115]

In spite of this manipulation, the United
Nations could have used the reults of the general
elections, which Premier Foncha placed before it,
to make its decisions. Instead, it requested the
Southern Kamerun leaders to return home and try to
reach agreement among themselves before the next

session of the General Assembly.[116] The Southern Kamerunians would indicate where the majority stood, but the agreement the United Nations had hoped for was unlikely to be obtainable. Firstly. the differences among the political leaders in general were both ideological, in the Kamerun context, and substantially deeply rooted. Secondly, except for the OK, each political party had substantial support from the electorate and the supporters of each group strongly urged their leaders not to alter their positions.[117] Because of these reasons, Foncha and Endeley, with the knowledge of the British local authorities, made several unsuccessful attempts between April and July, 1959, to reach agreement regarding the plebiscite's questions and the voters' qualifications.[118]

After the collapse of these private negotiations, the Commissioner decided to have a plebiscite conference. The conference which took place at Mamfe on August 10-11, 1959, and which was attended by forty-three delegates, was the most representative of the Southern Kamerun society. The organization of the Conference and the selection of the delegates were discussed and agreed upon by the Acting Commissioner for the Cameroons, Endeley and Foncha. Each group represented selected its own delegate(s). The four Paramount Crowned Princes, the a-Fon of Nso, Kom, Bafut and Bali Nyonga, by dint of their populations, were automatic delegates at the Conference. The remaining six traditional rulers were selected from the six administrative Districts with each District Officer, using population size as the basis for his choice, selecting his own candidate.[119] The KNC-KPP Alliance and the KNDP repeated the same arguments and suggestions they had made at the United Nations and stood firm on their varying positions. The OK wished to support the KNDP but because it could not understand why the Premier dropped the word Reunification from his public utterances only one month after he was voted into office, and because the KNDP programme as it then stood fell far short of what the OK stood for, it could not do so.

The Kamerun United Party (KUP), which Kale formed in early 1959 with Secession as its ultimate goal, stated that the plebiscite would have to involve only Integration and Secession. The students requested that the plebiscite involve only Integration and Reunification.[120] Speaking for the a-Fon, the Fon of Bafut, Achiribi II, made the following statement.

> We believe on two points during a conference
> in Bamenda in which Dr. Endeley and Foncha
> were present. I was chairman of that con-
> ference. We rejected Dr. Endeley because he
> wanted to take us to Nigeria. If Mr. Foncha
> tries to take us to French Cameroons we shall
> also run away from him. To me the French
> Cameroons is 'fire' and Nigeria is 'water'.
> Sir,[121] I support secession without /Re/uni-
> fication.[122]

In these words, the Crowned Princes refused to
budge from their position. The conference had thus
collapsed.

However, although no vote was taken, the
various delegates did indicate where they stood on
each issue. The delegates unanimously agreed that
in order not to confuse the electorate there should
only be two questions at the plebiscite and that
Integration should be one of them. Twenty-nine
(67%) of them, including all the a-Fon, favoured
Secession for the second question while the remaining fourteen (33%) wished to have Reunification. Likewise, thirty-one of them (72%) wished to
give the vote only to indigenous Southern Kamerunians whereas the remaining twelve (23%) favoured
giving it to any person in Southern Kamerun who had
a stake in the matter.[123] Considering these
figures and the representative nature of the conference, one would have expected the United Nations
to make Integration versus Secession the issues at
the plebiscite.

But, that is not what happened. When the
leaders returned to the United Nations in September
1959, Foncha placed the results of the Mamfe
Plebiscite Conference before the United Nations,
carefully described the organization and representative character of the Conference and then
invited the United Nations to use those results as
a guide for its decisions. None of the leaders
contested those results although Ntumazah, mis-
takingly, contended that the results were that way
because the Premier himself had organized the Conference and selected the delegates. A fundamental
problem was that the United Nations itself was already divided in partisan groups on the Kamerun
issue. The Integrationists had been identified as
the friends of the British and non-communists and,

for that reason, they received the support of British friends and anti-communists. Likewise, the Reunificationists had been identified as communists and, for that reason, they were strongly backed by the Soviet block. The Foncharians had no ideological friends or enemies. While the agreement of the Integrationists and Reunificationists on the plebiscite's issues made the work of the United Nations easier, the fact that the Foncharians were in power in Southern Kamerun complicated it. If the United Nations used the principle of democracy to accept Foncha's position, its members would have abandoned their friends when they most needed help. Yet, it could not impose a decision on a democratically elected government in favour of the opposition parties. Faced with this problem, the United Nations decided to ignore the results of the Mamfe Plebiscite Conference and to talk Foncha out of his programme. After some struggle and log-rolling, Foncha, without consulting those who voted him into power and receiving their permission first, agreed to make Reunification the second question of the plebiscite in exchange for a short period of continued trusteeship administration. Consequently, the United Nations made Integration versus Reunification the issues at the plebiscite.[124]

The reaction of the majority of the Southern Kamerunians to the United Nations' decision could be expected. The supporters of Integration who had hoped to use Reunification to procure Integration, greeted it with joy. Likewise, the Reunificationists, who saw the plebiscite as the last chance for at least immediate Reunification to be heard in Southern Kamerun, welcomed the decision, although they were not happy with the one year delay of the plebiscite. Not so for the majority of the Southern Kamerunians whose inclination was for Secession and, at worst, Integration. As soon as the information reached the area, the Concert of the Crowned Princes broke-down and with it the unity of Southern Kamerun. Each Fondom (or groups of Fondoms) began to act separately and individually considering only its interests. However, almost all of them resented the plebiscite questions already provided and demanded a third proposition, namely, Secession. A new political party, the Cameroons Indigenes' Party (CIP), sprang up at the beginning of 1960 to reinforce the Cameroons Commoners' Congress (CCC) formed after the Mamfe plebiscite Conference. Together with the KUP, these two new parties dispatched peti-

52

tions to the United Nations and to well-placed persons all over the world with fairly identical messages. At first, they complained about the two plebiscite's questions describing them as an unwanted and unwelcomed imposition, pleaded that Western Kamerun should be saved from extinction, and then demanded a third plebiscite proposition, namely, Smaller Kamerun State, Member of the Commonwealth. When they realized that this was not forthcoming, they threatened not only Civil war but also the disruption of the plebiscite by either boycotting it or by mutilating the ballot papers. When the threats too failed to work they resigned themselves to cursing the United Nations and the plebiscite, describing both as undemocratic and meaningless.[125] At the same time these parties were writing these petitions, they, and indeed the majority of the Southern Kamerunians, put pressure on the political leaders in general, and on Foncha in particular, to do something to rescue what they perceived as an unfortunate and grave situation.

This pressure forced some of the political leaders to take some initiatives. The leaders of the Cameroon People's National Convention (CPNC), a fusion of the KNC and KPP, suggested that the KNDP and the CPNC abandon the plebiscite and request the United Nations to give Southern Kamerun independence separately, that is, outside Nigeria and Cameroun.[126] Committed to the evolutionary type of Reunification, Foncha ignored the suggestion and instead began negotiations with Ahidjo on the form of the reunified Kamerun State and its relations with both the Commonwealth and the French Community. During the negotiations, Foncha insisted on a Confederation that would not be member of either the Commonwealth or the French Community. When Ahidjo rejected these conditions, the negotiations collapsed.[127]

After that, Foncha arranged for a conference to consider the CPNC's suggestion. The conference duly took place in London in November, 1960. It was attended by the Secretary of State for the Colonies, the Commissioner for the Cameroons--J. O. Field, Foncha, Endeley, Kale, S. T. Muna, A. N. Jua, W. N. O. Effiom, P. N. Motomby-Woleta, J. C. Kangsen, S. E. Ncha, the Fon of Bali--Galega II, and Fon Oben of Mamfe.[128] During the discussions, the Secretary of State for the Colonies and the Commissioner supported the idea and, indeed, were more than prepared to make a case for it before the United Nations.[129]

At one point, it seemed more likely than not that agreement would be reached, "but after some time the atmosphere changed dramatically with a diversity of views and so these other 'round table' talks ended in smoke."[130] When these talks collapsed, Foncha again, unsuccessfully, negotiated the terms of Reunification with Ahidjo and Charles Assale, the Prime Minister of Cameroun, at Douala on December 20-21, 1960.[131] Foncha was, therefore, forced to campaign for Reunification with its terms undefined, a factor which did much to harm the position of Reunification during the campaigns.

However, during the campaigns, no political party or leader accurately interpreted the plebiscite questions to the electorate. The associationists warned against leaping into the dark, substituted the French Community and communism for Cameroun citizenship and pleaded with the electors to retain their British way of life by voting for Nigeria. The anti-imperialists pleaded with the electors not to surrender their Kamerunian identity by voting for Nigeria, substituted the "continuation of the 'imperialistic relationships' with the Commonwealth" for Nigerian citizenship and offered the electorate a United Kamerun Nation whose constitution was to be drawn up after the plebiscite by the representatives of all the political parties aided by constitutional lawyers to be provided by the United Nations. The Foncharians pleaded with voters to retain their Kamerunian nationality, substituted the sale of Southern Kamerun to the Ibo for Nigerian citizenship and offered the electorate a Kamerun Federation in which the Southern Kamerun State would be ruled directly from Buea without necessarily taking instructions from Yaounde. It was this Foncharian offer which converted the majority of the Associationists and a not insignificant number of the intergrationists to Reunification in the end.[132]

The situation in Southern Kamerun was a replica of that in Northern Kamerun. During the November 1959 plebiscite, the Northern Kamerun leaders who supported either the permanent integration of Northern Kamerun with the Northern Region of Nigeria or making a decision at a later date made local administration the central issue of the plebiscite. Despite all the attempts made by the local authorities including the British to procure a pro-Northern Nigerian vote, the majority of the electorate opted for a future decision. But, what they fac-

tually voted for was continued direct British reformed trusteeship administration. After the plebiscite, the British separated Northern Kamerun administratively, but not politically, from the
Northern Region of Nigeria, reformed the administration and ruled the area directly. Because the
new administration gave something lucrative to
every section of the society, it was well-received.
During the campaigns for the February 1961 plebiscite, the parties which favoured the Cameroon proposition counted the advantages to be gained from
Reunification, substituted Yola domination of Northern Kamerun for Nigerian citizenship and offered
the electorate a Federation of Kamerun in which
Northern Kamerun would either be a member in its
own right or a member as part of the Western Kamerun State. Those which favoured the Nigerian alternative substituted the reformed local administration and represented Cameroun as France or alternatively as a country whose government hardly respected its commitments. Due to the uncertain behaviour of the local authorities including the
British who were more than determined to get a pro-
Nigerian vote, and because the voters were about
ninety-seven per cent illiterate and politically
uneducated, the electorate went to the polls thinking that what was at stake was the reformed local
administration. Consequently, the majority of them
voted for Nigerian citizenship believing that they
were choosing continued British trusteeship administration.[133]

NOTES

1. The following names in this article depict the following areas: Kamerun--the total geographic area of the German Protectorate known as Kamerun 1885-1916; Eastern Kamerun--the section of Kamerun under French administration 1919-1960, commonly called Cameroun; Western Kamerun--the portion of Kamerun under British administration 1919-1961, popularly referred to as the Cameroons; Northern Kamerun--the northern segment of Western Kamerun; Southern Kamerun--the southern fragment of Western Kamerun.

2. An analysis of the factual contents of the votes in the plebiscite suggests that the meaning of the votes had little bearing on the questions the electorate had set out to answer. See Bongfen Chem-Langhee, The Kamerun Plebiscites 1959-1961: Perceptions and Strategics. Ph.D. Thesis submitted to the University of British Columbia, Vancouver, British Columbia, August, 1976, pp. 304-333.

3. The word Fondom (Fondoms for plural) is somehow misleading. It is best used to describe the situation in the central grasslands and the greater portion of the northern areas of Kamerun. Here, the head of such a traditional state is referred to as the Fon or any variation of that word. The rest of the northern areas comprised Fulani enclaves, ruled by Lamibbe (equivalent of a-Fon) who paid homage to the Lamido resident in Yola. Except in a few cases where there were Fondoms, the southern areas of Kamerun were composed of several villages, each of which had both a village head and a village council. Despite this diversity, this article will refer to the various situations simply as Fondoms for convenience sake.

4. E. M. Chilver, "Paramountcy and Protection in the Cameroons: The Bali and the Germans 1889-1913," in P. Gifford and W. R. Louis, eds. Britain and Germany in Africa: Imperial Rivalry and Colonial Rule, Yale University Press, New Haven and London, 1967, pp. 479-511; P. M. Kaberry on the Nsaw in Africa, Vol. 29, N°4, October, 1959, pp. 366-383; P. M. Kaberry, Women of the Grassfields, London, 1952, passim; E. M. Chilver and P. M. Kaberry, "The Kingdom of Kom in West Cameroon," in Daryll Fords and P. M. Kaberry, eds., West African Kingdoms in the Nineteenth Century, Oxford University Press, London, 1967, passim; A. H. M. Kirk-Greene, Adamawa: Past and Present, Oxford University Press, London, 1958, passim; M. McCulloch, W.

Littlewood, I. Dugast, "Peoples of the Central Cameroons," Ethnographic Survey of Africa: West Africa, Part IX, Vols. 9-11, 1956, pp. 9-108; R. O. Ardener, "Coastal Bantu of the Cameroons," Ethnographic Survey of Africa: West Africa, Part XI, Vols., 9-11, 1956, passim. For a contrary view, see Victor T. LeVine, "The Politics of Partition in Africa: The Cameroons and the Myth of Unification" in Journal of International Affairs, Vol. 18, N^{O}1, 1964, p. 205 and passim.

5. Edwin Ardener, "The 'Kamerun Idea': I," in West Africa, June 7, 1958, p. 533. Edwin Ardener, "The 'Kamerun Idea': II," in West Africa, June 14, 1958, p. 559; LeVine in the Journal of International Affairs, Vol. 18, N^{O}1, 1964, passim.

6. Using sociological criteria, Edwin Ardener argues that the inter-Kamerun boundary was far from artificial. See Edwin Ardener, "The nature of the Reunification of Cameroon," in Arthur Hazlewood, ed. African Integration and Disintegration: Case Studies in Economic and Political Union. Oxford University Press, London, 1967, pp. 289-298. Ardener's view is misleading. As will be seen later, the Anglo-French local administrators themselves agreed that the frontiers hardly corresponded with ethnic frontiers, and this when they had not considered the separation of people from their land and property.

7. David E. Gardinier, Cameroon: United Nations Challenge to French Policy, Oxford University Press, London, 1963, pp. 9-21; Neville Rubin, Cameroun: An African Federation, Praeger Publishers, London, 1971, p. 44.

8. Martin Z. Njeuma, The Origins of Pan-Cameroonism, Government Printer, Busa, 1964, p. 26.

9. David E. Gardinier, "The British in the Cameroons 1919-1939," in P. Gifford and W. R. Louis, eds. Britain and Germany in Africa: Imperial Rivalry and Colonial Rule, Yale University Press, New Haven and London, 1967, passim; Edwin Ardener, "The Political History of Cameroon," in The World Today, Vol. 18, Oxford University Press, 1962, passim; Claude E. Welch, Jr., Dream of Unity: Pan-Africanism and Political Unification in West Africa, Cornell University Press, Ithaca, 1966, all sections on Cameroon; James H. Vaughan, Jr., "Culture, History and Grassroots Politics in a Northern Cameroon Kingdom," in American Anthropologist, Vol. 66, Menesha, Wisconsin, 1964, pp. 1078-1095.

10. David E. Gardinier, "The British in the Cameroons 1919-1939" in P. Gifford and W. R. Louis,

eds, Britain and Germany in Africa: Imperial Rivalry and Colonial Rule, Yale University Press, New Haven and London, 1967, passim.

11. Ibid., Njeuma, pp. 27-29; Ardener in Hazelwood, p. 299; Edwin Ardener, "Social Change and Demographic Problems of the Southern Cameroons Plantation Area," in Aiden Southeall, ed., Social Change in Modern Africa, Oxford University Press, London, 1961, passim.

12. Njeuma, pp. 27-29.

13. Chem-Langhee, pp. 16-17.

14. Ibid., pp. 137-179.

15. Ibid., pp. 160-179, 201-215, 304-333.

16. Rubin, p. 65.

17. Chem-Langhee, pp. 220-221, 230-236, 248-249, 252-257, 287-303 for more details.

18. Gardinier, 1963, p. 49; Rubin, pp. 63-66.

19. U.N.,T.C., T/1426: Annex 11, January 20, 1959, pp. 2-3.

20. Gardinier, 1963, p. 50; Rubin, p. 65.

21. Paul M. Kale, Political Evolution in the Cameroons, Government Printer, Buea, August, 1967, p. 21.

22. Ibid., pp. 21-22.

23. Ibid., pp. 50-55.

24. Rubin, pp. 77-88; Welch, Jr. all sections on Cameroon.

25. U.N.,T.C., United Nations Bulletin, Vol. 8, March 1, 1950, pp. 204-211; U.N.,T.C., T/708: Supplement N°2, 1950, pp. 14-19; U.N.,T.C., Trusteeship Council: Official Records, Annex Vol. 11, 1950, p. 70; U.N.,T.C., T/PET. 4-T/PET 5/7, December 9, 1949, passim.

26. U.N.,T.C., T/PET. 4-T/PET 5/7, December 9, 1949, passim.

27. Ibid., U.N.,T.C., Trusteeship Council: Official Records, Annex, Vol. 11, 1950, p. 70; UNTC. T/798. Supplement N°2 1950, pp. 14-19; U.N., T.C., United Nations Bulletin, Vol. 18, March, 1950, pp. 204-211.

28. U.N.G.A., A/C. 4/SR. 846, May, 1959, pp. 554-556.

29. Interview with Dr. E. M. L. Endeley held on April 10, 1978 at Buea.

30. Interview with Tafor Ngunjoh held on April 12, 1978 at Buea.

31. Chem-Langhee, pp. 47-62, 90-127, 135-179, 185-198.

32. Njeuma, p. 45

33. Ibid., p. 25.

34. Interview with Dr. E. M. L. Endeley held on April 10, 1978 at Buea.

35. Gardinier, 1963, pp. 62ff. Njeuma, p. 26.

36. Ardener in Hazelwood, p. 303, argues that the UPC brand of Reunification "was a part of an ideological framework of a Marxist type". This view is inaccurate. No doubt, the UPC leaders were inclined to Marxism and, indeed, did use communist jargon when arguing in favour of Reunification. But, they were using Reunification to gain immediate independence which was an expression of anti-imperialism and not of Marxism or communism.

37. U.N.,T.C., T/798: Supplement N°2 1950, all sections on the Northern Cameroons; U.N.,T.C., Trusteeship Council: Official Records, Annex, Vol. II, 1950, all the sections on Northern Cameroons.

38. Gardinier, 1963, pp. 48-50.

39. U.N.,T.C., T/798: Supplement N°2 1950, p. 56.

40. U.N.,T.C., T/486, Trusteeship Council: Official Records, Annex Vol. II, 1950, p. 364.

41. U.N.,T.C., T/517 Trusteeship Council: Official Records, Annex, Vol. II, 1950, pp. 385-386.

42. U.N.,T.C., T/798: Supplement N°2 1950, pp. 17-19.

43. U.N.G.A., A/1306, October 1, 1951, pp. 38-41; U.N.,T.C., T/486, Trusteeship Council: Official Records, Annex, Vol. II, 1950, p. 364.

44. Proceedings of the Conference, pp. 139-140, cited in S. J. Epale, Financial and Fiscal Aspects of the Problems of the Economic Development of West Cameroon 1946-1966, Ph.D. Thesis submitted to Oxford University, Oxford, 1969, p. 365.

45. Dibonge's mother was an Eastern Kamerunian from Douala while his father was a Southern Kamerunian.

46. Rubin, p. 85; Welch, Jr., p. 177; Willard R. Johnson, The Cameroon Federation: Political Integration in a Fragmentary Society, Princeton University Press, Princeton, N.Y., 1970, pp. 122-123.

47. Conversations with Dr. S. J. Epale held on June 15, 1978 in Yaounde. Dr. Epale, who read the first draft of this article and made valuable suggestions and corrections, was one of those discriminated against in terms of scholarship award. He had to apply for British citizenship to travel out of Southern Kamerun in 1951.

48. U.N.,T.C., United Nations Bulletin, Vol. 13, September 1, 1952, pp. 269-270.

49. U.N.,T.C., T/1109, Trusteeship Council: Official Records, Supplement N°4, 1954, pp. 8-10.

50. Ibid.

51. U.N.,T.C., T/1104, March 16, 1953, pp. 25-28.

52. U.N.,T.C., T/1109, Trusteeship Council: Official Records, Supplement N°4, 1954, p. 9.

53. Gardinier, 1963, pp. 49-51.

54. U.N.,T.C., T/SR 490, March, 1954, pp. 32-36, 51-58. The 1952 Mission's Report was discussed at the United Nations either in late 1953 or early 1954.

55. U.N.,T.C., T/SR 488, March, 1954, pp. 33-38.

56. U.N.,T.C., T/SR 491, March, pp. 61-62.

57. U.N.,T.C., T/SR 488, March, 1954, pp. 33-38.

58. U.N.,T.C., T/1042, March 16, 1953, pp. 25-28.

59. U.N.G.A., A/C 4/SR. 1142, July, 1961, p. 304.

60. Interview with Dr. E. M. L. Endeley held on April 10, 1978 at Buea.

61. Kale, pp. 40-41; Tambi Eyongetah and Robert Brain, A History of the Cameroon, Longman Group Limited, London, 1974, p. 134.

62. Kale, pp. 42, 58.

63. Interview with Dr. E. M. L. Endeley held on April 10, 1978 at Beau.

64. U.N.G.A., A/C 4/SR 1142, July, 1961, p. 304.

65. U.N.G.A., A/C 4/SR 1142, July, 1961, p. 304.

66. U.N.,T.C., T/PET 4 and 5/L 42, March 4, 1959, pp. 8-9; U.N.,T.C., T/PET 4/L 15, February 1, 1959, passim; U.N.,T.C., T/PET 4/L 18, September 1, 1959, passim; U.N.,T.C., T/SR 953, April, 1959, passim, particularly p. 80.

67. U.N.,T.C., T/1426, January 20, 1959, pp. 68-70.

68. Kale, pp. 39, 43.

69. Gardinier, 1963, pp. 45-47, 66.

70. Kale, pp. 42-43.

71. Eyongetah and Brain, pp. 135-137.

72. Rubin, p. 87.

73. Ibid.

74. U.N.G.A., A/3170: Supplement N°4, 1956, p. 121.

75. Interview with Tafor Ngunjoh held on April 12, 1978 at Buea.

76. U.N.G.A., A/3170: Supplement N°4, 1956, pp. 119-124.

77. Ibid.

78. Ibid.

79. Rubin, pp. 63-66; Gardinier, 1963, pp. 47ff. 80. Conversations with Dr. S. J. Epale held on June 15, 1978 at Yaounde.

81. U.N.G.A, A/3170: Supplement N°4, 1956, p. 121.

82. Interview with William P. Lebaga held on April 11, 1978 at Buea.

83. U.N.,T.C., T/1239, April, 1956, pp. 8-16.

84. U.N.,T.C., T/SR 677-T/SR 699, April-May, 1956, pp. 188-196, 240-262, 351; U.N.G.A., A/C 4/SR 628-A/C 4/SR.635, April, 1957, pp. 390-420.

85. U.N.,T.C., T/SR 677-T/SR 678, April, 1956, pp. 188-196.

86. The present writers personal experience.

87. Interview with William P. Lebaga held on April 11, 1978 at Buea.

88. Ibid.

89. Welch, Jr., pp. 195-196.

90. Ibid.

91. U.N.,T.C., T/1426, January 20, 1959, p. 45.

92. Ibid.

93. Chem-Langhee, p. 101.

94. U.N.,T.C., T/1426 Annex 11, January 20, 1959, pp. 3-14; U.N.,T.C., T/1426, January 20, 1959, p. 55.

95. U.N.G.A, A/C 4/SR 775, January, 1959, pp. 153-156; U.N.G.A., A/C 4/SR 780, January, 1959, p. 183.

96. See Chem-Langhee, pp. 160-171, 199-206, 287-303, 305-307 and put the information side by side the map of Western Kamerun.

97. Conversations with Dr. S. J. Epale held on June 15, 1978 at Yaounde.

98. U.N.,T.C., T/1426 Annex 11, January 20, 1959, pp. 11-14.

99. Ibid., pp. 1-12, U.N.,T.C., T/1426, January 20, 1959, pp. 67, 82-83; U.N.G.A., A/C 4/400, February 26, 1959, p. 102, U.N.,T.C., T/PET 4/L 15, February 20, 1959, pp. 102; U.N.,T.C., T/PET 4/L 18, September 1, 1959, passim.

100. Chem-Langhee, pp. 72-79.

101. In this plebiscite, the Northern Kamerunians were given a choice between gaining independence as an integral part of the Northern Region of Nigeria when the Federation of Nigeria became independent and making a decision at a later date. During the campaign period, the parties in favour of either proposition made local administration the central issue of the plebiscite. A very substantial majority of the electors chose making a decision in the future.

102. U.N.,T.C., T/SR 953, April, 1959, passim; U.N.,T.C., T/SR 959, May, 1959, pp. 105-107.

103. U.N.,T.C., T/SR 959, May, 1959, p. 197; U.N.G.A., A/C 4SR 847, May, 1959, p. 557; U.N.G.A., A/C 4/400, February 26, 1959, pp. 1-5.

104. U.N.,T.C., T/1491, November 25, 1959, p. 70.

105. Following the 1959 January elections in Southern Kamerun, Foncha became Premier. When addressing the Fourth Committee of the General Assembly in February, 1959, he stated that ultimate Reunification would preferably take the form of a Federation but that the matter was still to be discussed by those concerned.

106. U.N.G.A., A/C 4/SR 849, May, 1959, p. 566.

107. U.N.G.A., A/C 4/SR 849, May, 1959, p. 566.

108. U.N.G.A., A/C 4/SR 889, November, 1959, p. 35.

109. Welch, Jr., pp. 200-206; Chem-Langhee, p. 122.

110. U.N.,T.C., T/PET 4 and 5/L 42, March 4, 1959, p. 8.

111. U.N.G.A., A/C 4/SR 755, January, 1959, pp. 153-156; U.N.G.A., A/C 4/SR 780, January, 1959, p. 183.

112. U.N.G.A., A/C 4/SR 846, May, 1959, pp. 554-556; U.N.G.A., A/C 4/399, February 26, 1959, pp. 1-3.

113. U.N.G.A., A/C 4/SR 846, May, 1959, pp. 553-554; U.N.G.A., A/C 4/SR 848, May, 1959, pp. 561-564; U.N.G.A., A/C4/398, February 26, 1959, pp. 1-8.

114. At a conference of the a-Fon held in Bamenda some time between 1957 and 1958, a conference in which Foncha and Endeley were present, the Crowned Princes made it very clear that while they were for Secession, Reunification was more repugnant to them than Integration.

115. Chem-Langhee, pp. 137-159.

116. U.N.G.A., Year Book of the United Nations 1959, Columbia University Press, 1959, p. 368.

117. For the distribution of support and behaviour of the supporters, see Chem-Langhee, pp. 160ff.

118. U.N.G.A., A/C 4/SR 885, November, 1959, p. 14.

119. See U.N.G.A., A/C 4/SR 885, November, 1959, passim.

120. Document on Cameroun Affairs in Microfilm compiled by the University of Chicago, Illinois, Center for Research Libraries, Circulation Department, Attached to the KNDP Secession Charter as Appendix IV, passim.

121. Sir refers to the Chairman of the Conference, Sir Sydney Phillipson.

122. Cited in Kale, p. 69.

123. U.N.G.A., A/C 4/SR 885, November, 1959, passim.

124. U.N.G.A., A/C 4/SR 885-A/C 4/SR 890, November, 1959, passim; U.N.G.A., A/C 4/414, September, 1959, pp. 1-2; U.N.G.A., A/4354, 1960, p. 26; U.N.G.A., Year Book of the United Nations 1959, 1959, pp. 363-368. The analysis in this paragraph regarding the role of the United Nations is based on the speeches which the members of that organization made, to be found in these documents, and the voting pattern at the United Nations.

125. Chem-Langhee, pp. 119-215.

126. Interview with Dr. E. M. L. Endeley held on April 10, 1978 at Buea.

127. "Yaounde," West Africa, July 16, 1960, p. 795; Victor T. LeVine, "Calm Before the Storm in Cameroun," Africa Report, Vol. 6, N°5, May, 1961, p. 4.

128. Southern Cameroons Information Service, "London November Talks," Press Release N°1048, Buea Archives, October 29, 1960, p. 2.

129. Interview with Dr. E. M. L. Endeley held on April 10, 1978 at Buea.

130. Kale, p. 70.

131. U.N.,T.C., T/1556, April 3, 1961, pp. 111-112.

132. U.N.,T.C., T/1556, April 3, 1961, all sections on Southern Cameroons; U.N.G.A., A/C 4/SR 1142-A/C 4/SR 1144, July-August, 1961, passim. For a detail analysis, see Chem-Langhee, pp. 257-277, 204-333.

133. U.N.,T.C., T/1491, November 25, 1959, passim; U.N.,T.C., T/1556, April 3, 1961, all sections on Northern Cameroons; U.N.,T.C., T/PET 4/L 71, December, 1959, p. 1; U.N.,T.C., T/PET 4/L 162, April 21, 1961, p. 1; U.N.,T.C., T/PET 4/L 150, April 17, 1961, p. 1; U.N.G.A., A/C 4/SR 1142-A/C 4/SR 1144, July-August, 1961, passim. For detail analyses, see Chem-Langhee, pp. 220-257, 287-303, and Vanghan in American Anthropologist, Vol. 66, Menasha, Wisconsin, 1966, passim.

3
The Political Culture of Anglophone Cameroon: Contrasts in Rural-Urban Orientations Toward the Nation

Ndiva Kofele-Kale

INTRODUCTION

The problems associated with the creation of a sense of national identity are shared by most of the nation-states of the world. However, it is in the emergent nations of Africa and Asia that these problems confront nation-builders with particular urgency. There, the need to create a sense of common citizenship on the basis of shared political values has become the principal challenge, compli-cated by other equally important challenges having to do with economic development and modernization. Put simply, the demands to create a single psycho-logical focus shared by all segments of the popula-tion must contend with demands for bread and butter--the basic issues of survival.

Students of political culture agree that every political system engages in the process of manufac-turing symbols which can be manipulated and trans-lated into values which individuals hold, and operationalize through some form of loose ideology structure. It is widely recognized that, short of coercion, no political system can maintain itself over time without enlisting the unsolicited support of its members. To build a reservoir of support for its institutions, personnel, and policies, the nation's leadership must strive to create among its citizens some positive feelings of identification with the nation. Verba has forcefully argued that, "unless the individuals who are physically and legally members of a political system (that is, who live within its boundaries and subject to its laws) are also psychologically members of that system (that is, feel themselves to be members) orderly patterns of change are unlikely." (Verba, 1965: 529) In this essay the concept of "we are all Cameroonians;" i.e., the feeling that Cameroonians all belong to the same political community by long inheritance and choice is examined. Cameroon is used here because it shares with the emergent African nations their full array of problems. It is also significantly different in a number of respects including its unique colonial experience. The country has been scarred by political, regional, and ethnic cleavages in addition to its checkered colonial history which left behind a dual linguistic and a Euro-cultural legacy (Le Vine 1964, 1971; Johnson 1970). Thus, Cameroon provides a useful laboratory for the comparative study of political culture.

This study of Cameroon's political culture is comparative inasmuch as it analyzes the political attitudes of rural folk as well as those of urban people. Of particular importance in the analysis of rural-urban differences is the fact that the population of Cameroon, like that of most African nations, is still overwhelmingly rural. A 1970 estimate places fewer than 500,000 Cameroonians or 7 percent of the population in communities of over 20,000 people. Thus, a staggering 93 percent of Cameroon's population is rural-based. (Roser 1970: 15).[1]

Until we are reasonably well-informed about the contents of the political "baggage" carried by all Cameroonians no meaningful statements can be made about the way a people's sense of national identity is shaped.

THEORETICAL FRAMEWORK

The purpose of this study was to explore empirically the relationship between environment and political orientations toward the nation. The view taken here is that political orientation is as much the result of responses to environmental stimuli as it is of political socialization. In short, the specific geographic location (village, town, or city) of an individual or of groups of people influences their values and behavioral patterns. The conventional viewpoint held by students of political socialization interprets the antecedents of political orientations in pedagogic terms. Most studies assume that political behavior develops largely through a learning process.

66

(Langton 1969: 8-16). Thus, the focus has usually
been directed toward an examination of certain
major institutions in society (family, school, peer
group, etc.) deemed central in the transmission of
political values and attitudes to members (Easton
and Hess; Hess and Torney 1970; Jennings and
Langton 1968, 1969; Langton 1969).

Valid as this assumption is, it fails, however,
to underscore the importance of non-pedagogical
factors in the acquisition of political orientation.
More to the point, it leaves unanswered the
question: how much does environment influence
political behavior? Therefore, this study tested
the hypothesis that individual and group conformity
to patterned political values and behavior varies
with exposure to environmental influences. That is,
variations in geographic location are accompanied
by parallel contrasts in political orientation, resulting in different patterns of political attitudes
toward the nation by urban and rural residents.

This analysis will present some of the observations that have been made respecting the putative
difference between rural and urban communities and
their populations. The distinction between rural
and urban culture and behavior and the debate over
its validity is an old one indeed. Its roots reach
back to Maine, Tonnies, and Durkheim, all of whom
contributed important dichotomies of societal
characteristics. Others have since carried on with
this tradition (Redfield 1930; Wirth 1938; Simmel
1955). Venerated as this dichotomy came to be for
some social scientists (Redfield 1930, 1947) it has
however generated much adverse criticism from the
academic community (Murdock 1943; Herskovits 1948;
Lewis 1951; Miner 1952; Qadeer 1974).

In attempting to draw "causal" links between
locality and manifest political attitudes one ventures into territory that has only been partly explored. The problem has been noted and commented
upon by several scholars (Banfield 1962; LePalombara
1965; Rustow 1965; Frey 1968). The evidence, still
fragmentary and not quite representative of the
universe of political systems, indicates that significant differences exist between rural and urban
people with respect to their national political
sentiments.

In a study of Italian political culture,
LaPalombara notes the strong impact that traditional
structures and values have on the political orientations of rural Italians. In a similar vein Banfield's investigation of the behavior of villagers

in a southern Italian village uncovered a strong attachment to the family and the kin group. So extreme was this "amoral familism" among Montenegrians that it severely undermined any sense of community or national identity. Both studies conclude that the majority of rural southern Italians still remain firmly tied to the family, adhereing to affective, diffuse, and particularistic standards in contrast to the more affectively neutral, specific, and universalistic standards found among urban northerners.[2]

Frey's study of the political orientations of Turkish peasants confirms the findings of LaPalombara and Banfield. Frey also found that rural village Turks had a lower incidence of nationalistic sentiments than their urban compatriots, and even village youths seemed to be notably less oriented toward the nation than their urban peers attending public Lycee-level schools.

STUDY DESIGN

The data for this report were gathered during a larger survey of political attitudes of English-speaking Cameroonians undertaken between October 1972 and July 1973.[3] Interviews were held with and questionnaires distributed to about 900 adult Cameroonians drawn from three types of localities: villages, plantation camps, and towns. The non-probability sample was selected in order to facilitate subgroup comparisons in line with the major thrust of the larger study which was to investigate the impact of environment on ethnic group values and political orientations. Accordingly, respondents were drawn equally from three major ethnic groups in Cameroon, the Banyang, Grassfields, and Kpe.

Interviews were conducted in the towns, camps, and villages, all of which were geographically located in the coastal south. Care was taken in selection of the villages to insure that they were far removed from any major town. All the villages were relatively underdeveloped and economically deprived. None had electricity (although all save one of the towns and camps enjoyed this facility), pipe-borne water or a good road system. All were served by primary schools but only one had a health clinic with a resident mid-wife. The nearest hospital for any of the villages was 15 or more miles away, a journey usually made on foot, since there was no public transportation system nor any commercial taxis serving these areas. In terms of access to very basic goods and services provided by the national government, all the towns and camps were better endowed than any of the villages.

The response rate was about fifty percent. Four hundred and fifty-seven schedules and question- naires were retrived, of which 56 were discarded for incomplete information. The sampled n is 391 about 35 percent of which were self-administered questionnaires.

Independent Variables

Locality was the independent variable for this study. Locality was operationally defined as (1) rural ethnically homogeneous villages, (2) multi- ethnic plantation camps, and (3) towns. Camps and towns were treated as polar opposites of rural villages. However, plantation camps and towns were considered different in the one sense that the towns have developed through a form of laissez-faire urbanization as opposed to the "forced" urbaniza- tion of the camp. [4]

Dependent Variables

The dependent variables examined in this study were two broad dimensions outlined in Devine's identity system (1972) and Easton and Hess's political community (1961): (1) national identity meaning the vertical relationship between members and their political system; and (2) community identity which refers to the horizontal identifica- tion among members of the same nation.

These two were selected for emphasis in this study because they constitute critical dimensions within the nation-building process. The psycholo- gical proximity between members and their political system and among subjects themselves is a strong measure of how well integrated such a polity is. [5]

FINDINGS

Sense of National Identity

Three levels of national identity were meas- ured: (1) Political Awareness; this term refers to the degree of involvement with the political process by members of a political system. This dimension of political culture has been bifurcated by Almond and Verba (1963) into input cognition, the frequency with which people follow or pay attention to political and governmental affairs; and output cognition, the extent to which people perceive the political process as having an effect on themselves. (2) Political Knowledge; i.e., the ability of people to identify their national and local leaders. (3) System Affect; i.e., the emotional attachment an individual has for his/her country.

Political Awareness/Input Cognition. In trying to assess the extent to which citizens are involved in governmental affairs and with what degree of infrequency, as expected the data show that more camp (80 percent) and town (78 percent) respondents stayed close to governmental and political affairs than did villagers, only 53 percent of whom shared this position (as shown in Table 3.1).

However, when respondents were asked whether they thought politics was beyond the comprehension of the average citizen, a noticeable shift occurs with 69 percent of the village and 68 percent for the town respondents compared to only 40 percent of the camp subsample subscribing to the view that the

TABLE 3.1
Relation Between Community and Political Awareness: Input Cognition Aspect

	Community		
Exposure to Political Affairs	Rural Village	Plantation Camp	Town
Regulargy	27.6%	28.4%	30.6%
From time to time	25.0	52.9	48.1
Never	47.4	13.5	17.5
N.A.	0.0	5.2	3.7
Total	100.0%	100.0%	100.0%
N	(76)	(155)	(160)

$$x^2 = 42.22 \ p = <.001$$

average citizen is incapable of comprehending
governmental and political affairs.

Since the item did not ask how the respondent
himself felt about politics but called upon him to
give an opinion about the average citizen's reaction, the responses cannot be interpreted as indicative of the actual level of political comprehension among respondents. To bring this out, i.e.,
the citizen's own opinion of his level of political
comprehension and awareness, the following item was
put to the respondents: "Do you think you can
understand some of the policies and programs that
the national government has been undertaking? For
example, the construction of the Tiko-Victoria
highway?" The results indicate that the majority
of respondents in all three communities understood
(or thought they did) the significance of this
particular governmental program. However, more
town and camp respondents (68 percent and 67 percent respectively) than village respondents (52
percent) report a higher level of political awareness with respect to the input process.

This finding is of interest since it is consistent with findings drawn from the data on media
exposure. That is, village folk lag somewhat behind
camp and town residents with respect to their exposure to the news media and the level of involvement with day-to-day happenings in the political
arena. Since camp and town folk, as the data reveal, tend to listen more to political broadcasts
than village residents, they are also more aware of
important policy announcements and programs than
people from the village.

Political Awareness/Output Cognition. Does
the citizen perceive that the government has an
impact on his day-to-day life? How does he assess
this impact? Is it favorable or not and why? Large
majorities of village, camp, and town respondents
see their national government as having some impact
on their daily lives. On one extreme are the camp
respondents, 92 percent of whom attribute some impact (either great or some) to their national
government. The other extreme is occupied by 86
percent of town respondents and the middle with 83
percent respondents attributing some or great impact
to their national government is the village subsample. Less than 4 percent of the camp respondents
and under 15 percent of the village and town respondents attribute no effect to their national
government. When the results of the question to

71

determine whether citizens considered the impact
favorable or not, the pattern that emerged is
similar to the one just discussed (though of course
there were some substantial drops in the frequency
score). A higher proportion of respondents in all
three communities considered the impact of government as beneficial to their lives.

The broad picture presented so far seems to
suggest that Cameroonians no matter where they live
feel the impact of governmental activities and
policies. Although the majority of the respondents
evaluate this impact as favorable, camp (77 percent)
and town (65 percent) folk subscribe more highly to
the view than village residents (47 percent). This
may reflect the fact that camps and towns are
closer to the centers of national decision-making
and so receive more amenities from them. As
Table 3.2 shows, of those village respondents who
found the impact of government far from beneficial,
an overwhelming majority gave as their reason the
unequal distribution of goods and services in the
country which not only expanded an already wide
developmental chasm between the towns and rural
areas but also reinforced the stratification between
"haves" and "have-nots." Although the picture is
slightly blurred in Table 3.3, we still find that
many town respondents who found government impact
to be beneficial mentioned the rapid pace of social
and economic development; while a higher proportion
of camp respondents cited the stable political
situation. Clearly political stability and steady
economic growth seem to be positive factors of
governmental policies, although the responses of
the camp community emphasize one while those of the
town emphasize the other. Table 3.3 also indicates
that village respondents who found government to be
favorable saw this in the light of the stable
political climate and the strides in the area of
socio-economic development.

In summary, village, camp, and town respondents
are agreed on the general impact of government on
the lives of its citizens though they differ on the
direction (whether positive or negative) of this
impact. Majorities in camp and town tend to see
its effects as salutary. In contrast, village
respondents assess the impact of government on their
lives in a very negative way.

Political Knowledge. The pattern of responses
illustrated in Table 3.4 which deals with the ability to identify government Ministers indicates that

TABLE 3.2
Reasons Given by Respondents Who Found Government Impact
Unfavorable

		Village	Camp	Town
1.	Poor Economic Policies Widened Gap Between Haves and Have-Nots	59.46	14.28	30.95
2.	Unemployment	8.11	8.57	9.52
3.	Civil and Political Liberties Denied	8.11	8.57	28.57
4.	Other	0.0	5.71	2.38
5.	No Reason	0.0	2.86	19.05
6.	MD/MA	24.32	65.71	7.14
	Total	100.00%	100.00%	100.00%
	N	(37)	(35)	(42)

$$x^2 = 52.2922 \ p = < .001$$

TABLE 3.3
Reasons Given by Respondents Who Considered the Impact of
Government to be Favorable

		Village	Camp	Town
1.	Peace and Political Stability in the Country	26.31%	43.33%	16.34%
2.	Big strides in economic development	34.21	26.67	40.38
3.	No Reason	39.47	30.00	43.26
	Total	100.00%	100.00%	100.00%
	N	(38)	(120)	(104)

sharp differences exist between camp/town, on the
one hand, and village on the other. The table reveals that only 32 percent of the village respondents can correctly identify three cabinet Ministers
compared to 60 percent for the camp and 62 percent
for the town. This low frequency of uninformed
village respondents is consistent with the low

percentage of the village subsample not exposed to the news media and whose level of political awareness is relatively low. The village group comes out to be the least exposed to the communications media and the most poorly informed and politically knowledgeable of all three communities.

TABLE 3.4
Ability to Identify Cabinet Ministers

| | | Community | |
Can Identify	Rural Village	Plantation Camp	Town
3 Ministers	32.9%	60.0%	61.9%
2 Ministers	15.8	9.0	9.4
1 Minister	21.1	3.9	5.6
0 Minister	30.0	26.5	22.5
N.A.	0.0	0.0	0.6
Total	100.0%	100.0%	100.0%
N	(76)	(155)	(160)

$$x^2 = 34.9699 \quad p = <.001$$

TABLE 3.5
Ability to Identify National Party Leaders

| | | Community | |
Can Identify	Rural Village	Plantation Camp	Town
4 Bureau Members	14.5%	7.7%	18.1%
3 Bureau Members	2.6	8.4	8.1
2 Bureau Members	5.3	6.5	8.7
1 Bureau Member	21.1	11.6	7.5
0 Bureau Members	56.6	65.8	56.9
N.A.	0.0	0.0	0.6
Total	100.0%	100.0%	100.0%
N	(76)	(155)	(160)

$$x^2 = 10.8553 \quad p = <.01$$

74

TABLE 3.6
Ability to Identify Local Party Leaders

	Rural Village	Plantation Camp	Town
Identify Section President	17.1%	18.7%	32.5%
Not Identify	81.6	80.6	66.2
N.A.	1.3	0.6	1.2
Total	100.0%	100.0%	100.0%
N	(76)	(155)	(160)

$$x^2 = 10.8553 \ p = <.01$$

Tables 3.5 and 3.6 which report respondents knowledge of the National and Local Party leaders reveal no variation in levels of information along community lines. These tables strongly suggest that large majorities of respondents in the three communities cannot identify their local party leaders or even name one national party official. This phenomenon is evenly spread through all three communities. However, the town does enjoy a slight edge over the other two communities with a fairly high, relatively speaking, proportion of well-informed residents.

The data also indicate that locality is significantly related to respondent's knowledge of national and local political party leaders, on the one hand, but not related to knowledge of national Cabinet Ministers, on the other hand. (The latter when cross-tabulated with location where respondent lives yielded a Chi square of 33.848 with 8 degrees of freedom which was not significant at the .01 level; failing to confirm the null hypothesis that locality affects respondents' civic knowledge.) Cross-tabulations of community with respondents' knowledge of party leaders at both the local and national levels resulted in Chi squares that were significant at the .01 level of significance, thus confirming the first relationship between the two sets of variables.

Certainly, after reviewing the whole body of data for this section, the most evident conclusion

that can be drawn is that Cameroonians have very
low knowledge of who holds public office, and this
is more so for their party leaders than cabinet
Ministers. Two questions logically arise. How
does one explain the apparent imbalance in the
pattern of political knowledge revealed by the
data? Why is it that respondents have less difficulty identifying cabinet Ministers (given their
high turn-over rate in Cameroon) than they have the
relatively stable party leaders? This discrepancy
becomes even more significant when we take into
consideration the fact that in practice, the
Cameroon political system allows for an overlap between Cabinet position and national party office.
Thus, many cabinet Ministers also combine active
duties and functions within the ruling and only
party in the country--the Cameroon National Union.
This is consistent with official doctrine where
party and government collaborate greatly and
operate as a unity. Most surprising is the
apparent inability of a large majority of the respondents to even identify local party leaders--
those with whom presumably they are most likely to
come into contact.

Several explanations can be advanced for this
low level of political knowledge in general and the
coincidental high information level on cabinet
Ministers. The high success in recognizing
Ministers, as demonstrated by respondents, is in my
view, idiosyncratic; in the sense that it is a by-
product of sampling biases of either a reactive or
interactive nature occurring in the course of the
testing (Campbell and Stanley 1966). These biases,
were probably occasioned by the fact that interviewing took place during a period of intense
political activity in the wake of a momentous constitutional change in the country's political set-
up. The shift from a federal system to a unitary
state took place in May, 1972. This move resulted
in the appointment of a new cabinet and the reorganization of provincial administrative services.

The reorganization of the reconstituted provincial administrative services necessarily involved new appointments and movement of personnel.
The investiture ceremonies for these new appointees,
especially in the upper echelons, were well attended
by the public and usually presided over by the
Minister in whose ministry the officer was a functionary. It may well be that the presence of
Ministers during these ceremonies afforded the
public unparalleled opportunities to get acquainted

with their national leaders. For the Ministers too, these occasions also heightened their visibility to the masses. As a result, when in the course of interviewing, respondents were asked to identify their cabinet Ministers, only relatively few had difficulty recalling the names of some of these Ministers whom they had seen only a few months back. Thus the high visibility of Ministers occasioned by their frequent (even if brief) exposure to the populace during this period of constitutional change increased the recall capacity of respondents.

For this intervening factor (timing of the testing), respondents' ability to recognize cabinet Ministers would have been just as low as their ability to name their party leaders. This, of course, leads one to wonder whether there is a high level of mass alienation from the Cameroon political system, especially the national leadership.[6] To test if this was the case and whether it was not limited to only the party hierarchy, an item was included in the instrument which sought to tap people's affective images of their cabinet officials. Respondents were asked, "If you had to choose a career for your child, what would you not want him/her to become? A lawyer, businessman, government Minister or nurse?" On the whole, more people rejected a cabinet post for their children. Discounting the 38 percent who elected not to express an opinion, only 4 percent of the respondents did not want their children to become nurses; 11 percent were against them becoming business entrepreneurs; 14 percent were opposed to a career in law; while the plurality of respondents--32 percent--were dead set against their children becoming government Ministers. The most frequent reason given for this diffident attitude toward cabinet ministers is the public's belief that ministers are very corrupt and generally more involved in the pursuit of self-interest than the public good. The evidence leads me to conclude that the Cameroon public, regardless of geographical locality domiciled is highly critical, very cynical, and generally distrustful of its national leaders. This undifferentiated public also experiences great difficulty in correctly identifying its national leaders. The one apparent difference-- a greater ability to recognize cabinet Ministers-- appears to be a clear example of coincidental reaction to external stimulus (i.e., the setting and timing of the research act).

The inability of Cameroonians to recognize their party leaders can be attributed to either or both of the following reasons: the fact that (1) party leaders are not well exposed to their constituents; and (2) the imperfect integration between the only party in the country (Cameroon National Union) and the mass public. The evidence reviewed so far suggests that Ministers were easily recognized because of this high visibility. The fact of exposure does not go far in explaining respondents' failure in correctly identifying other leaders for, as I indicated earlier, many Ministers also double-up as party officials (either in the national bureau or section executive). Nor does it help to explain why the overwhelming majority of respondents failed to even identify by name any of their local party leaders--those with whom presumably the public has greater access to and enjoy some degree of familiarity. The low information level uncovered by the data strongly suggests the existence of a gap between the C.N.U. and the Cameroonian masses.[7]

To begin to understand this gap between party and people, a brief word must be said about the organizational structure and general orientation of the Cameroon National Party.[8] The Cameroon National Union is what Johnson (1970) and Rubin (1971) have described as an elitist/patron party as opposed to a mass political party of the Leninist type. It began as (and has remained) a party which united the leadership of the nation rather than the membership of the various constituents (Rubin: 153). Although the party's original intentions were to transform itself into a mass movement to mobilize the Cameroon people toward the goals of national unity and socio-economic development, the CNU has not succeeded in casting off its elite/patron image. Nor is this problem of passing off an elite party for a mass movement uniquely Cameroonian. It is a problem shared by some of the more prominent one-party states in Africa (Zolberg 1966; Bienan 1970).

It is this writer's impression--and it must remain nothing more than an impression--that the orientation of the Party is directed at rewarding those political leaders and their clients who had given up leadership positions in their respective parties in order to join Ahidjo's Union Camerounaise. The composition of the 1973-78 Parliament is a case in point. The elections of May, 1973, far from slating a completely new cast of political leaders merely returned to power

carry-overs from the dissolved assemblies of the
former federated states (i.e. former C.U.C.,
C.P.N.C., K.N.D.P., and U.C. politicians.)[9] Although the continuity at the leadership level is
remarkable since it has succeeded in giving Cameroon
one of the more stable African governments.[10] Yet
the fact that it represents an unbroken chain of
command of patron/leaders who have dominated the
Cameroon political stage for two decades further
suggests that the elitist profile of the CNU has
not changed. A party organized as an elite/patron
club runs into serious credibility problems when
it seeks to pass itself off as a mass movement.

Another dimension of this imperfect integration between party and masses may well be a function of the historical recency of the CNU and less
of its organizational edifice. The CNU did not
come into existence until late 1966. (It existed
prior to this date as the Union Camerounaise and
confined all its activities to the francophone
sector of the country.) Consequently, the party
(1) still in its definitive stages is still going
through its birth pangs (so to speak) to be in any
strong position to evoke widespread grass-roots
partisan attachments; and (2) the C.N.U.'s historical recency especially in English-speaking Cameroon
only serves to demonstrate that this sector of the
country, quite literally never had a single party
political culture until the arrival of the CNU
(West Cameroon enjoyed a measure of parliamentary
democracy between 1954-1969). This factor in itself
is capable of generating sufficient and powerful
centrifugal forces to seriously challenge, if not
repeal, efforts at the national center to popularize
the party at the mass level.

In summary, the data on political information
suggest that a gap exists between the Cameroonian
people and their national party. A gap which, in
this writer's opinion, reflects in part the structural and orientational deficiencies inherent in
the CNU, and in part historical factors to which
the party may have become an unwitting victim.
Without reading too much into the data, it would
appear that the impact of the CNU on the population
has been limited, leaving open for debate the
party's claims of having mobilized mass support
for its goals and programs.

System Affect. In examining the first two
dimensions of the identity subsystem of political
culture, we were able to discern gaps between

town/camp, on the one hand and village, on the
other with respect to exposure to the communications media, level of political awareness, and
content of political information on their national
leaders. The system affect dimension is concerned
with the feelings people have for their nation, its
institutions, leaders, etc.
One of the items respondents were confronted
with required them to select between a movie on how
Cameroonians celebrated their tenth anniversary of
independence from colonial rule and another depict-
ing America's space explorations.[11] Although large
majorities in the three communities chose to watch
the movie on Cameroon, the distinction between town
and countryside revealed in earlier analyses still
lingers. Comparatively more town and camp respondents (81 percent and 73 percent respectively) than
village respondents (65 percent) opted for the
movie of their country's independence celebration.
Respondents were then asked an item aimed at
discovering those attributes of the nation in which
they took pride. The responses are displayed in
Table 3.7. Two attributes--enlightened Presidential

TABLE 3.7
Pride in Country: As a Cameroonian, What Things
About This Country are you Most Proud of?*

	Village	Camp	Town
Political institutions & policies	3.9%	12.2%	16.8%
Political leadership	36.8	49.7	43.1
Economic development	13.2	29.7	18.8
People, heritage, culture	16.0	1.9	4.9
Nothing in particular	29.0	1.3	8.7
MD	1.3	5.2	7.5
Total	100.0%	100.0%	100.0%
N	(76)	(155)	(160)

$$x^2 = 77.5989 \quad p = < .001$$

*This was an open-ended item

80

leadership and the rapid pace of socio-economic development--need mention here since they received the highest proportion of frequency scores for the entire sample. We find that all three communities rate their President very highly. Two points are germane here. The first is that the distribution of responses is somewhat influenced by community difference. When we examine the proportion of respondents who attribute their pride in the Cameroon nation as influenced by the enlightened leadership of President Ahidjo, faint lines of cleavage appear separating communities. There are more camp respondents (50 percent) than town (44 percent) and village (36 percent) who mentioned presidential leadership as a source of national pride. Secondly, the high regard respondents have of their President contrasts sharply to the low regard they have for his lieutenants (cabinet Ministers especially). Apparently, Cameroonians do make a distinction between their President and the Ministers that serve under him. They not only have little difficulty identifying him (as sharply expressed in the high proportion of respondents who mentioned his leadership as a factor generating high system pride) but are warmly and affectively oriented toward the person of Ahidjo.

The second response category that received relatively high frequency scores was socio-economic development. What is interesting here is that the proportion of respondents who selected this attribute fairly corresponds to that which mentioned national accomplishments in the areas of socio-economic development as one of the salutary effects of governmental policies and programs.

It should be noted that Cameroonians seem to express little pride in the characteristics of the Cameroonian people. Only 12 percent of the village compared to less than 5 percent camp and town respondents even bothered to mention the characteristics of Cameroonians as source for system price. (See Table 3.7).

Finally, respondents were asked whether they would like to swap their Cameroonian nationality for that of another country. On the whole, large proportions of respondents in all three community groups indicate a willingness physically to desert the fatherland (46 percent Village, 47.1 percent Camp, and 55 percent Town). Lest the overall results be hastily interpreted as a sign of low system effect, let it be emphasized that responses to a follow-up item which asked why respondents

81

wanted to change nationalities seem to indicate an urge for adventurism and not an expression of dissatisfaction with the Cameroon polity. A fairly high proportion of respondents who expressed the desire to switch nationalities, indicated a preference for those countries that were considered: "as peaceful as Cameroon;" "politically stable as Cameroon;" "Religious and God-fearing as Cameroon;" etc. In short, the desire to change nationalities was only entertained as long as it was believed that the country for which refuge was being sought was in many ways similar to Cameroon. Cameroonians it would seem would change their nationality so long as the "pain" of desertion was soothed by the belief that the new country was just like the old one.

The evidence indicates that geographical location does not produce significant variations in this one aspect of citizens' behavioral attachment to the nation. (A cross-tabulation yielded a Chi-square of 36.715 with 14 degrees of freedom which was not significant at the .01 level of significance.) As such the null hypothesis was not borne out. Cameroonians, regardless of community domiciled in, generally have a high level of national pride.

SENSE OF COMMUNITY IDENTITY

Attention now will be directed to finding out how widespread the diffusion of this identity value is among respondents. On the strength of the factor analysis results (Table 3.8), sense of community identity will be examined along three dimensions: (1) degree of neighborliness; (2) degree of friendliness; and (3) attitudes toward cross-ethnic marriage.
i. Degree of neighborliness--Did respondents have many friends in the neighborhood in which they resided? Were visits ever exchanged between persons living in the same neighborhood and with what degree of frequency? The responses to these questions provided the material for measuring the "neighborliness" dimension of community identity. It was found to be very high in the total sample. Close to 90 percent of the sampled population had many friends in the neighborhood they were domiciled. Of this proportion, only 11 percent later said they never exchanged social visits. Thus, the overwhelming majority of respondents visited each others homes with varying degrees of frequency.

TABLE 3.8
R Factor Analysis: Rotated Factor[a] Matrix Showing Factor Loadings on Dimensions of Inter-Group Contact

Items	Factor I[b]	Factor II[c]	Factor III[d]	Factor IV[e]
Speak any indigenous language	.00388	.00140	.04970	.51630
Recognize anybody from neighborhood	.13491	.00233	.13749	.00570
Have friends in neighborhood	.59627	.09845	.14228	.06493
Ever visit with them	.61604	.00564	.01072	.01552
How often are these visits	.56104	.04203	.18069	.06498
Have difficulty making friends with non-ethnics	.14220	.04798	.55885	.14121
Close friends come from which ethnic group	.28036	.00583	.51746	.07996
Language spoken with fellow ethnic	.03664	.02798	.29605	.45278
Reaction to cross-ethnic marriage	.01405	.12040	.18246	.09063
Any preference for ethnic group	.04304	.71066	.01899	.11195
Any particular reason	.06732	.66599	.03921	.12332

[a]Factor I accounts for 43 percent of the total variance, Factors II and III for 46 percent and Factor IV 10.3 percent.
[b]Children in Family Decision-making Factor.
[c]Images of Parental Authority Factor.
[d]Typology of Family Decision-making Factor.
[e]Typology of Ethnic Group Decision-making Factor.

When geographic location was controlled, it was found that degree of neighborliness was comparatively higher among plantation camp and town respondents than for village respondents.

ii. Degree of friendliness--This dimension of the identity subsystem sought to examine the ease or difficulty which respondents experienced in trying to establish friendship networks with non-ethnics. Secondly, to discover the composition of respondents' friendship networks; whether recruitment and participation are solely determined on the basis of cultural similarity or other non-particularistic criteria. The data show that over two-thirds of the sampled population experienced no problems establishing friendly ties with non-ethnic people. About the same proportion of respondents also indicated that their close friends were drawn from persons who belonged to different ethnic groups.

Although the majority of respondents could be classified as friendly, this attribute varies to some extent with geographic location. As expected, more presons from ethnically heterogeneous communities (camps and towns) than from ethnically homogeneous rural villages, have no apparent difficulty establishing friendship contacts across ethnic boundaries. The same is true for composition of friendship network; more people from the village subsample than from the camp and town subsamples appear to have developed airtight friendship bonds which exclude persons from other ethnic groups. Sixty-four percent of the village respondents admit to having their close friends from among co-ethnics while only 31 percent of the camp respondents and 34 percent for the town subsample share this trait-- a spread of almost 30 percentage points separates town from countryside. The division parallels that which was evinced in the analysis of data on neighborliness.

It is easy to see why camp and town residents appear to be more neighborly and participate in a varied and heterogeneous friendship network than village folk. One of the definitive characteristics of camps and towns is their heterogeneous population as opposed to rural villages that are essentially ethnically homogeneous. Plantation camps and towns within the Cameroon context have served as magnets attracting all kinds of peoples from all over the country. These people flock into these areas for a variety of reasons--greater educational and employment opportunities, adventure, escape from the constraints of traditional life, etc. From a purely statistical standpoint, a person living in a multiethnic urban context has a greater probability of coming into frequent contact with individuals from other ethnic groups than an isolated villager; and are, therefore, most likely to participate in a wider variety of overlapping activities. Such opportunities do not exist in rural villages, and even when they do on a much lower scale. The data confirm the hypothesis that persons from ethnically homogeneous rural villages will have relatively more difficulty establishing friendship ties with non-ethics than those persons from camps and towns. (A cross-tabulation of location by ability to make friends with non-ethnics produced a raw chi-square of 13.389 with 8 degrees of freedom at .0991 significant level. It sustains the theoretical hypothesis that location affects cross-ethnic social relationships.)

The data also confirm the hypothesis that the actual composition of respondents' friendship group would be significantly affected by community differences, such that comparatively more camp and town respondents than village ones will have a singularly heterogeneous friendship network. So it was found, for instance, that in the village sub-sample 64 percent of the respondents draw their close friends from co-ethnics. About the same proportion which had difficulty making friends with persons from other ethnic groups. As expected, majorities in camp (65 percent) and town (63 percent) had most of their close friends from different ethnic groups.

On the whole this writer's observations draw strong support from previous studies of camp attitudes which found a high sense of community identity among workers that transcended narrow, local ethnic particularisms (Ardener 1961; DeLancey 1973). The most recent study by DeLancey found on the basis of quantitative analyses that the more heterogeneous the labor camp and labor force the more diversified the sociometric patterns; i.e., a pattern of friendship network that cuts across ethnic differences. He cites as reasons for this high level of community consciousness among plantation camp workers: (1) the fact that there are no totally exclusive neighborhoods, professions, or work places which would reinforce ethnic differences; (2) a marked preference by workers themselves for ethnically mixed living and work arrangements; (3) both (1) and (2) are supported by a deliberate policy of the

employer to ignore ethnic background in job,
housing, and other assignments; and (4) the fact
that institutions provided by the employer--schools,
clubs, sports teams, community hall activities--
were generally multi-ethnic as were other facilities
not provided by the employer but serving the entire
camp like the churches. Thus, the structural and
institutional set-up of camp society reinforced by
a willing predisposition on the workers' part to
ignore ethnic differences have led to the cementing
of interethnic bonds and high level of community
identity among camp workers.

iii. <u>Propensity for cross-ethnic marriage</u>--
In ethnically plural societies, a good test for
feelings of community identity is examining the
extent to which members will tolerate cultural
differences. One practical way to do this is to
examine marriage patterns in order to find out
whether they are strictly endogamous or exogamous.
Thus, the intensity of inter-ethnic antagonism can
be expressed very sharply in the willingness or
reluctance of members to participate in exogamous
marital relations. Thus, where there is a willingness then a sense of shared community identity can
be inferred; but where there is a general preference
for endogamy then one can conclude that feelings of
community identification are absent or weak at best.

The data reveal that a substantial majority of
respondents are neutral on the question of marriage
across ethnic lines. On one extreme, only 12 percent of the respondents clearly and unequivocally
stated a preference for a non-ethnic marriage
partner; while on the other end of the pole, 33
percent--a fairly high proportion--of the respondents were inclined toward endogamy. Nestled in
between were a plurality of respondents, 41 percent
of whom expressed no particular preference as to
which ethnic group a marriage partner should come
from.

When respondents' place of residence was taken
into consideration, the data confirmed the broad
patterns that have already been sketched. Within
each of the three communities, the majority of
respondents have no fixed and rigid preference for
any ethnic group as the likely pool from which potential in-laws can be drawn. On the one hand are
the camp respondents, 50 percent of whom said any
ethnic group was good enough while on the other,
are the village and town each with 35 percent of
their respondents falling in the neutral zone (i.e.,
did not care one way or the other). Across

localities more town and village respondents (37 percent and 34 percent respectively) than camp respondents (27 percent) favor endogamy. Interestingly enough, of the three localities, comparatively more of the village respondents (20 percent) than camp (12 percent) and town (9 percent) respondents come out clearly in favor of cross-ethnic marriages.

The data fail to confirm the null hypothesis (raw chi-square of 16.453 with 6 degrees of freedom at .0115 significance level) of no significant relationship between place of residence and attitudes toward inter-ethnic marriages.

The data show that the sense of community identity is widespread among the anglophone Cameroon population, though it varies in intensity and geographic location. Cameroonians, it would appear, are generally friendly and outgoing. Although the majority participate in broad-based friendship networks that cut across ethnic group boundaries, there is still some reluctance or hesitance to expand these networks to embrace cross-ethnic marriages.

This finding sustains the conjecture that inter-group behavior is conditioned in a well-defined field of communication which is circumscribed by what one may call "permissible sectors of interaction" among ethnic groups. Such interactions are characterized by, "an approach-avoidance complex." Although members in the broad political community do establish contact based on common functional interests and associational ties, such contracts only result in interactions that operate along narrowly defined limits, (e.g., friendship networks.) This is so, I believe, because of powerful internal ethnocentric forces within the respective ethnic populations that constitute the political community which prevent friendship contacts to spill-over into another realm; for example, cross-ethnic marriages. The absence of cross-ethnic marriages does not _prima facie_ indicate intense inter-group antagonism. If anything it probably reflects people's fear that such relations may seriously compromise ethnic individuality. Thus, a strong advocacy for exogamy is tantamount to a call for cultural suicide. Therefore, a low indidence of exogamy could be interpreted as a positive sign of ethnic pride and not ethnocentrism as such.

Finally, the data also demonstrate that broadly speaking, people from ethnically heterogenous

communities (camps and towns) have a higher level
of community identity than their counterpart in the
ethnically homogeneous rural villages. This distinction holds only on two dimensions--degree of
neighborliness and friendship. That is to say,
camp and town residents tend to have a high degree
of neighborliness and experience no difficulty
making friends from among non-ethnics. The opposite holds for rural village folk. They, interestingly enough, come out more in favor of exogamy
than those persons resident in the two multiethnic
communities.

CONCLUDING STATEMENTS: ENVIRONMENT AND POLITICAL
    ORIENTATIONS

     Tests of independence have shown that on cer-
tain political culture dimensions community differences are associated with contrasts in national
political orientations. This was very much in
evidence in the examination of the identity system
which among other things was reflected in measuring
how informed and critical Cameroonians are of their
political system. Although all three community
groups reported very low scores on the political
knowledge dimension, nonetheless, camp and town
residents were found to be generally better informed, more interested and critical spectators of
their political system than village respondents.
Secondly, all three community groups manifested a
high sense of system pride. Respondents' sense of
their "Cameroonianness" was not found to be latent
or marginal but overt and long internalized. Many
attributed their pride for the Cameroon nation to
the President, El Hadj Ahmadou Ahidjo, as the
symbol of national identity and unity. However,
this close and intimate identification with the
Cameroon President contrasts sharply with the low
degree of familiarity the population has of his
Cabinet Ministers. On the whole citizens' behavioral attachment to the Cameroon nation was not strongly affected by community contrasts. The data show
that a sense of community identity varies with geographic location. Residents from the three
communities had a tendency to participate in broadly
based friendship networks that cut across ethnic
group boundaries through many were reluctant to
expand these networks to embrace cross ethnic
marriages. Using extra-ethnic patterns of interactions as indicators of feeling of identification

88

among members of a political community, the data strongly support the position that camp and town groups have a proportionately higher level of community identification than rural village people.

This is a very significant finding in that it points us to the fact that urbanization is not altogether a bad thing, as many critics have argued over the years. It has been usual to view urbanization as a phenomenon that has had a profound dislocative impact on traditional African values and institutions. Sifting through some of the literature one is left with the impression that although these writers are in agreement that urbanization is clearly one very important dimension of that complex of irreversible transformations African societies are undergoing, they are not prepared to look beyond those problems that are, by definition, built into the urbanization process (i.e., urban unemployment, congestion, crimes, inadequate sanitation, anomic violence, etc.), in order to see some of its beneficial aspects. The data in revealing the other side of urbanization underscores its inherent functional role in nation-building. What the evidence suggests is that urbanism can actually help in minimizing or defusing inter-ethnic conflict (a major problem in the majority of plural societies.)[12]

Whether it is the controlled urbanization of plantation camps or the laissez-faire type characteristic of towns, the process has resulted in the bringing together of people from diverse cultural backgrounds under a common umbrella. People so pushed together by force of circumstance tend to relate to each other more on the basis of functional needs and shared interests and less on ascriptive considerations. It is through such cross-cultural interactions that people begin to develop a sense of respect for each other and become more sensitive to, and understanding about, cultural differences. Within such situations of culture contact stereotypes are steadily replaced by knowledge. In this regard, urbanization serves the important function of broadening the scope and framework for inter-ethnic contact and interaction. It provides the seminal material from which a genuine sense of national community identity can be erected. From this standpoint, it is desirable and functional in the nation-building process.

That rural residents expressed such low feelings of community identity seems to suggest that people cannot remain captive in their

homogeneous ethnic capsules, isolated from the
other members of the national society and still be
expected to develop strong bonds of community
attachments. Thus, the more isolated people are
the lower their chances for interacting with other
people not from their immediate vicinity and ultimately the lower their sense of national community
identity.

But the weak sense of community identity ex-
hibited by rural people also alerts us to the fact
that if change in the underlying political cultural
configuration of the Cameroon nation is to take
place then rural attitudes must be radically transformed. This would mean extending to the countryside those facilities that have proved helpful in
raising the level of community identification
among urban residents.

While many planners may deplore the large
scale migration of people from rural communities
(since this inevitably leads to an overload of demands on the limited facilities in the urban
centers) caution must be exercised in advocating a
reversal of this trend. Coercive measures aimed at
arresting the flow of rural migration to cities may
ease urban congestion but will not solve the underlying problem; namely, what is it that attracts
people to labor camps and large towns? After all,
it is in these communities that government has
historically concentrated all its best efforts.
When you say town or city, you immediately conjure
up images of medical and public health facilities,
schools, pipe-borne water, electricity, paved roads,
etc., and of course greater opportunities for entry
into the working force. Caught in the so called
"revolution of rising expectations," everybody,
rural and urban alike, wants a share of the national
cake. This gives rise to a tendency for evaluating
the government in very instrumental terms, what it
does, or can do, for me? It is, therefore, to be
expected that town residents should manifest a more
favorable disposition toward the nation than their
deprived rural compatriots. The data strongly bear
out this conclusion.

NOTES

A shorter version of this paper was originally published as "Patterns of Political Orientations Toward the Nations: A Comparison of Rural-Urban Residents in Anglophone Cameroon," African Social Research, No. 26 (December, 1978). It is being included here with the permission of the Institute of African Studies, University of Zambia. Field research for this study was made possible by a fellowship from the Woodrow Wilson National Foundation and a grant from the Program of African Studies, Northwestern University. The author wishes to express his gratitude to these organizations. He is also indebted to Professors Victor T. LeVine, Paula Wolff and the several anonymous readers who read and offered constructive suggestions to an earlier draft of this paper. However, none of these individuals is responsible for the views expressed here.

1. This statistic is slightly misleading in view of Rosser's observation that "national definitions of the urban population vary widely from country to country--and sometimes from one government department to another inside country." For some countries "urban" is defined as localities of 1000 or more persons while others use 5000 inhabitants as the cut-off point. Colin Rosser, Urbanization in Tropical Africa: A Demographic Introduction. New York: Ford Foundation, 1972, p. 13. There are about 22 urban centers in Cameroon with populations of 3000 and above. Combined they account for close to 600,000 people. See Victor T. LeVine, The Cameroon Federal Republic. Ithaca: Cornell University Press, 1971, p. 51.

2. Although rural people tend to be more parochial in political culture terms, this is not to imply that urban residents are wholly participant citizens. The emphasis here is on the higher order of parochialism typical of rural people when contrasted to urban residents. LaPalombara did find that Italian political culture was generally fragmented, isolative, and alienative and although these profiles were fairly widespread they were certainly more pronounced in the rural south than the urban, industrialized north. J. LaPalombara "Italy: Fragmentation, Isolation, Alienation," in Lucian W. Pye and Sidney Verba (eds.), Political Culture and Political Development. Princeton, N.J.: Princeton University Press, 1965, pp. 282-329.

3. N. Kofele-Kale, "The Impact of Environment on Ethnic Group Values in Cameroon," in John N.

Paden (ed.), Political Culture and National Integration in Africa: Research Reports. Evanston,
Ill: Northwestern University Press, 1979. Also
chapter on "The Impact of Environment on National
Political Culture," in Paden (ed.), ibid.
    4. The terms "forced" and "laissez-faire"
urbanization were first suggested to me by Professor Remi Clignet of Northwestern University's
Department of Sociology in a personal communication.
A detailed account of rural migration to plantation
camps in Cameroon can be found in Edwin Ardener et,
al. Plantation and Village in the Cameroons. London: Oxford University Press, 1962.
    5. Eleven items were included in the survey
instrument for measuring sense of national community. These were later submitted to a factor analysis
from which three clusters of factors with loadings
of .50 and above were extracted. On the basis of
the factor analysis, three levels of community were
discerned: (1) degree of neighborliness--the
willingness on members' part to maintain good
neighborly relations with persons who live in the
same neighborhood irrespective of their ethnic or
regional origin; (2) propensity for inter-ethnic
marriage; and (3) degree of friendliness--represents
members willingness to establish friendship networks
across ethnic lines. See Table 3.8.
    6. The phenomenon described here may not
necessarily be alienation but what Nelson Kasfir
calls "departicipation"--the end product of a process by which popular input is minimized. I am
indebted to Professor Victor T. LeVine for bringing
this point to my attention. The reader should however consult Kasfir's The Shrinking Political Arena:
Participation and Ethnicity in African Politics with
a Case Study of Uganda. Berkeley, California: University of California Press, 1976.
    7. The low information level, as Professor
LeVine suggests, could also be attributed to several
other possible reasons, many of which touch on the
weaknesses inherent in survey research methodology.
The instrument, for instance, may have been suffering from the problem of validity in the sense that:
(a) the questions asked were not the right ones;
(b) respondents preferred not to answer, or when
they did respond, to respond truthfully; and/or
(c) respondents just did not give a damn. I am
willing to dismiss the question of low validity on
the grounds that the errors generated could at the
very best be considered random with built-in

allowances for self-cancellation. At the worst, if respondents failed to reply truthfully on this item, then it is equally possible that they did the same on the other items. However, this study remains an empirical question to be resolved through replication of this study.

A more substantive rival explanation for the low information level may have to do with the possibility that respondents had other ideas about what (or who) was politically relevant. That is, my choice of politically relevant actors in Cameroon was not consistent with the public's. Had I asked them to identify, for example, the local préfet or sous-préfet, the local traditional chief, or former high officials (like Jua, Foncha, Kemcha, etc.) they would have done much better. Although this may well have been the case, I am still unpersuaded for two reasons. First, many of these former officials are still playing an active role in the CNU both at the local and national levels. Second, the close ties between government and party usually means that in all party functions, rallies, etc., the government is represented by its préfets or sous-préfets. Thus, Cameroonians who conscientiously participate in these rallies should not only be able to recognize important government officials but also party commissars. That they were unable to identify the latter indicates not so much differences in perception on who are the relevant political actors rather the indifference of the Cameroonians masses toward the C.N.U.

8. What follows ignores a certain amount of official party line. It is my view, not always that of the CNU leadership, of the reality.

9. Seventy-five percent of the members of the 1973-78 Cameroon National Assembly were former deputies in either the now defunct state legislative assemblies or the Federal House of Yaounde. Fifteen of the deputies (out of a total of 24) representing the two English-speaking provinces owe their parliamentary seats to their long period of association with the KNDP, CPNC, and CUC--the three political parties from former West Cameroon that joined Ahidjo's ruling Union Camerounaise in East Cameroon to form the Cameroon National Union in 1966. Three English-speaking members of President Ahidjo's cabinet (as of May, 1975) also owe their positions to their former ties with the dissolved political parties from West Cameroon. It would be difficult to escape the conclusion that the CNU is

93

a patron/elite party which has, to some extent, united and continues to reward that faction of the country's leadership that was favorably disposed toward the idea of unification.

10. It is so easy to conclude that because nothing ever seems to happen in a country everything must be in order. In acknowledging that Cameroonians have maintained one government in office for two decades is not to suggest that all is fine, the people are happy and satisfied and therefore see no need nor have any desire for change. This blanket of deceptive calmness that appears to shroud the authoritarian countries of the Third World was only recently lifted in Iran; and in the process, exploding once again the political folklore that machine guns, torture chambers and secret police remain the best antidotes for combatting the revolution of rising expectations being waged by the masses. Only time will tell whether or not the price Cameroonians have paid for the country's remarkable degree of stability and leadership continuity far outweighs the benefits.

11. The purpose of the question was to pose respondents a difficult choice in order to test their attachment to the Cameroon nation. The widespread interest in America's space explorations evidenced by the large number of Cameroonians who went to exhibitions of Apollo 13 at various U.S. consular centers demonstrates that the American documentary offered an attractive alternative to the movie on the 10th anniversary of Cameroon's independence.

12. There is some evidence to contradict this position. Some scholars take the view that ethnic ties and identities do get reinforced in towns (rather than disappearing). Hanna and Hanna are of the opinion that "most residents (in towns) are to some extent 'encapsulated' within their own network which serves as a barrier between them and the wider urban social system. Striking cultural differences among many groups further hamper the development of an interethnic sense of community." Hanna and Hanna, op. cit., p. 106. For the same argument, see also Jean Rouch, "Second Generation Migrants in Ghana and Ivory Coast," in A. Southall, (ed.), Social Change in Modern Africa, London: Oxford University Press, 1961, pp. 300-304; Paul Mercier, "Remarques sur la signification du 'tribalisme' actuel en Afrique noire," Cahiers Internationaux de Sociologie, 31 (1961), pp. 61-80; and Hilda Kuper

(ed.), <u>Urbanization and Migration in West Africa</u>.
Berkeley, California: University of California
Press, 1965, pp. 1-22.

REFERENCES

Almond, Gabriel and Sidney Verba. The Civic
    Culture. Boston: Little, Brown & Co., 1963.
Almond, Gabriel and Sidney Verba and Bingham
    Powell, Jr. Comparative Politics: A Develop-
    mental Approach. Boston: Little, Brown &
    Co., 1966.
Ardener, E. W. "Social and Demographic Problems of
    the Southern Cameroons Plantation Area," in
    Aidan Southall (ed.). Social Change in Africa.
    London: Oxford University Press, 1961.
Banfield, Edward C. The Moral Basis of a Backward
    Society. Glencoe: The Free Press, 1962.
Barth, Frederick (ed.). Ethnic Groups and Bounda-
    ries. Boston: Little, Brown & Co., 1969.
Beals, R. C. "Urbanism, Urbanization, and
    Acculturation," American Anthropologist. Vol.
    3, No. 1 (January-March, 1951), 1-10.
Bienen, Henry. Tanzania: Party Transformation and
    Economic Development. Princeton, N. J.:
    Princeton University Press, 1970.
Campbell, D. T. and J. C. Stanley. Experimental
    and Quasi-Experimental Designs for Research.
    Chicago: Rand McNally & Co., 1966.
Delancey, Mark W. "Changes in Social Attitudes and
    Political Knowledge Among Migrants to Planta-
    tions in West Cameroon." Unpublished Ph.D.
    Dissertation, Indiana University, 1973.
Devine, Donald J. The Political Culture of the
    United States: The Influence of Member Values
    on Regime Maintenance. Boston: Little,
    Brown & Co., 1972.
Durkheim, Emile. The Division of Labor in Society.
    Trans. George Simpson. New York: Macmillan
    Co., 1933.
Easton, Dennis. A Systems Analysis of Political
    Life. New York: Wiley, 1955.
_____. A Framework for Political Analysis.
    Englewood Cliffs, N.J.: Prentice-Hall, 1965.
_____, and R. D. Hess. "Youth and the Politi-
    cal System," in S. M. Lipset and Leo Lowenthal,
    (eds.). Culture and Social Character. New
    York: The Free Press of Glencoe, Inc., 1961,
    pp. 226-251.
Frey, Frederick W. "Socialization to National
    Identification among Turkish Peasants,"
    Journal of Politics. #4 (November, 1968).
Foster, George M. Traditional Cultures and the
    Impact of Technological Change. New York:
    Harper & Row, 1962.

96

Gluckman, Max. "Anthropological Problems Arising
     from the African Industrial Revolution," in A.
     Southall, (ed.). Social Change in Africa,
     1961, pp. 67-82.
_____. "Tribalism in Modern British Central
     Africa," in Markovitz, Irving L. (ed.),
     African Politics and Society. New York: The
     Free Press, 1970, pp. 81-95.
Hanna, William John and Judith Lynne Hanna. Urban
     Dynamics in Black Africa: An Interdiscipli-
     nary Approach. Chicago: Aldine-Atherton,
     1971.
Herskovits, Melville. Man and His Works. New York:
     Alfred A. Knopf, 1948, especially pp. 604-07.
Hess, R. D. and Judith V. Torney. The Development
     of Political Attitudes in a Fragmentary
     Society. Princeton: Princeton University
     Press, 1970.
Johnson, Willard. The Cameroon Federation: Politi-
     cal Integration in a Fragmentary Society.
     Princeton: Princeton University Press, 1970.
Kale, Paul Monyongo mo'. Political Evolution in
     the Cameroons. Buea: Government Press, 1969.
Kasfir, Nelson. The Shrinking Political Arena:
     Participation and Ethnicity in African
     Politics, with a Case Study of Uganda.
     Berkeley, California: University of Califor-
     nia Press, 1976.
Kofele-Kale, Ndiva. The Political Culture of Anglo-
     phone Cameroon: A Study of the Impact of
     Environment on Ethnic Group Values and Member
     Political Orientations. Ann Arbor: Univer-
     sity Microfilms, 1974.
Jennings, Kent M. and Kenneth P. Langton. "Politi-
     cal Socialization and the High School Civics
     Curriculum," The American Political Science
     Review. September, 1968.
_____. "Mother versus Fathers: The Formation
     of Political Orientations among Young Ameri-
     cans," Journal of Politics, May, 1969.
LaPalombara, Joseph. "Italy: Fragmentation, Isola-
     tion, Alienation," Lucien W. Pye & Sidney
     Verba (eds.). Political Culture and Political
     Development. Princeton, N.J.: Princeton
     University Press, 1965, pp. 282-329.
Langton, Kenneth P. Political Socialization. New
     York: Oxford University Press, 1969.
Le Vine, Victor T. The Cameroons From Mandate to
     Independence. Berkeley and Los Angeles:
     University of California Press, 1964.

_____. The Cameroon Federal Republic. Ithaca,
    N.Y.: Cornell University Press, 1971.
Lewis, Oscar. Life in a Mexican Village: Te-
    poztlan Restudied. Urbana: University of
    Illinois Press, 1951.
Maine, Henry. Ancient Law. London: J. Murray,
    1961.
Mayer, Lawrence. Comparative Political Inquiry.
    Homewood, Illinois: The Dorsey Press, 1972.
Miner, Horace. "The Folk-Urban Continuum,"
    American Sociological Review, Vol. 17,
    October, 1952.
Murdock, George. "Review of the Folk Culture of
    Yucatan," American Anthropologist, Vol. 45
    (January-March, 1943), pp. 133-136.
Pye, Lucian and Sidney Verba, (eds.) Political
    Culture and Political Development. Princeton:
    Princeton University Press, 1965.
Redfield, Robert . Tepoztlan: A Mexican Village.
    Chicago: University of Chicago Press, 1930.
_____. "The Folk Society," American Journal
    of Sociology. Vol. LII, 1947.
Rosser, Colin. Urbanization in Tropical Africa: A
    Demographic Introduction. New York: Ford
    Foundation, 1972.
Rustow, Dankwart A. "Turkey: The Modernity of
    Tradition," in Pye and Verba, op. cit., pp.
    171-198.
Rubin, Neville. Cameroon: An African Federation.
    London: Pall Mall Publications, 1970.
Stein, Larry N.; L. Douglas Dobson and Frank Scioli.
    "On the Dimensions of Political Culture: A
    New Perspective," Comparative Political
    Studies. Vol. 5, No. 4 (January, 1973),
    pp. 493-511.
Tonnies, Ferdinand. "Gemeinschaft and Gessell-
    schaft," (1st ed., 1887), trans. and ed.
    Charles P. Loomis, Fundamental Concepts of
    Sociology. New York: American Book Co.,
    1940.
Verba, Sidney. "Conclusion" in Lucian W. Pye &
    Sidney Verba (eds.), op. cit.
Wirth, Louis. "Urbanism as a Way of Life,"
    American Journal of Sociology. Vol. 44,
    (1938), pp. 1-24.
Zolberg, Aristide. Creating Political Order.
    Chicago: University of Chicago Press, 1966.

Part 2
The Distribution
of Political Power

4
Federalism in Cameroon: The Shadow and the Reality

Frank M. Stark

INTRODUCTION

When the Federal Republic of Cameroon official-
ly became the United Republic of Cameroon on
June 2, 1972, it marked the end of a highly
centralized federalism. In October 1961 the former
British Trusteeship Territory of the Southern
Cameroons, and the newly independent Republic of
Cameroun formerly the French Trusteeship Territory
of Cameroun joined together to form the Federal
Republic made up of two states, West Cameroon and
East Cameroon. Eleven years later, the federation
ended by a referendum announced May 8, 1972, and
voted on May 20. Henceforth this event was
officially known as "The Glorious Revolution of
May Twentieth." However, although the name and
the outward structure of government changed, little
revolutionary change took place. The Anglophone
leaders of West Cameroon long before had given up
hope of any political or economic power for their
state. There was little opposition to the event
among these minority leaders and even relief among
many. Why was this change conceded so easily by
West Cameroonians? Why was it trumpeted officially
as a "revolution"? To answer these questions
demands an examination of the kind of political
relationship that federalism in Cameroon actually
was. This paper is divided into three sections
reflecting the birth, life, and death of a federation which was more shadow than reality.

I. THE BIRTH OF FEDERALISM: THE END BEFORE THE
   BEGINNING

The old German colony of Kamerun had been
divided between the British and French after World
War One by the League of Nations. They brought to
their Trusteeship territories of the British
Southern and Northern Cameroons, and the French
Cameroon, administrative styles which contrasted
with the stereotypes most often associated with
them. The French might have followed the centralized tradition which was rooted in the French
Revolution but the fact that its share of Kamerun
was a Trusteeship Territory prevented it from
integrating the new territory with the rest of its
colonial possessions. The British, on the other
hand, felt free to incorporate their share into
the colonial Federation of Nigeria, but as part of
the Eastern Region and not as a separate entity.
Thus a certain paradox exists. The French, noted
centralizers, were obliged to decentralize their
relationship with Cameroon, while the British,
noted for their decentralizing tendencies,
integrated their part of Cameroon into a region of
Nigeria. These differing treatments resulted in
different economic and social development patterns
in the two trusteeship territories. French aid was
relatively greater than British aid to its trusteeship territory which received less than its fair
share of British grants to Nigeria. Further, the
economy of the "British Cameroons" was based on
the old German plantations centralized into a
single corporation which dominated the economy,
leaving other aspects of economic development to
fall behind both Nigeria and the "French Cameroons"
where African entrepreneurship was already taking
root.[1] The Southern Cameroons was caught between
two groups of aggressive traders, the Ibo who
dominated the economy of the Souther Cameroons on
the one border, and the Bamilike in the French
territory who were interested in expanding their
trade and escaping some of the hardships of French
colonial rule on the other border.
      The idea of the reunification of the two
trusteeship territories seems to have originated in
early 1948 in the Kumba and Tiko areas of the
Southern Cameroons among the Bamilike who had
resettled there and wished to improve trade by
making border crossing easier. They were still
relative outsiders in the Southern Cameroons. They
wanted unification or at least a customs union.

From the Bamilike appeal, it was adopted as a major part of the political programme of the Union des Populations du Cameroon, the first nationalist party on the French side. From the U.P.C. platform it was adopted by Dr. E. M. L. Endeley on the one hand, and the Bamilike who were seeking to enhance their own trade on the other.

In the Southern Cameroons, Dr. E. M. L. Endeley used reunification as a wedge to pry the Southern Cameroons away from tight Nigerian control. Both he and the U.P.C. made representation to the U.N. Visiting Mission in May, 1949, but neither said anything about federalism; Endeley because he was really preoccupied with Nigeria, and the U.P.C. because they saw "unification" as a means to gain the United Nation's attention for Cameroon and the U.P.C.'s fight for independence.

It was not under the guidance of either Dr. Endeley or the U.P.C. that reunification and independence were to be finally achieved. By 1955-56 with the granting of regional status for the Southern Cameroons within Nigeria, Endeley had cooled to the idea. The U.P.C. continued to advocate it strongly, and Um Nyobe's speeches at the United Nations in 1952 greatly aided the movement, but the U.P.C. was banned in May 1955.[2]

Many of the U.P.C. leaders fled to Kumba, in the Southern Cameroons, a town close to the border, where they tried to make contact with pro-reunificationists in the Southern Cameroons. John Foncha had split from Endeley's party in 1955 on the reunification issue and had formed his own party, but although he was wary of co-operating with the U.P.C. Foncha did feel the strength of the issue among the "mass" of the Southern Cameroonians, especially in the northern grasslands area where the Ibo economic domination was partially resented. He gradually built a following based upon it; while personally hoping that independence and reunification would be a long way off. In this way it is likely that he saved the issue from extinction, needing it as a popular, partly anti-Ibo movement to help his political fortunes and ultimately defeat both Dr. Endeley and a U.P.C. political challenge in the Cameroons.

Although Endeley was one of the two university graduates in the Southern Cameroons, Foncha defeated him decisively in the 1957 elections fought on the issue of reunification. Foncha was a good "grass roots" politician who travelled to the villages by bicycle and on foot. A primary school teacher with

a secondary school education, he placed more
emphasis on personal contact than his more intellectual rival. Endeley, a Bakweri from Buea was
aware of his coastal sophistication, and consequently was not as well liked in the grasslands in
the northern part of the territory where Foncha's
personality and ethnic connections stood him in
good stead.

Pressured by the election campaign and the
exiled U.P.C.'s continued efforts at the U.N.,
Foncha seems to have originated the idea of
federalism during the 1959 election campaign as a
way of bridging the gap between the ideas of
independence and reunification.[3] In a speech at
Douala in November 1958 he suggested a Cameroonian
federation with three regions; North, South, and
"French" Cameroons.[4] Federalism thus seems to
have been Foncha's idea and Foncha's perception of
the potential relationship between his territory
and the French one. But as yet he had not met his
younger counterpart Amadou Ahidjo who had become
Prime Minister of the French "Cameroon" only in
February 1958. Amahou Ahidjo was from Garoua in
the Northern Cameroons. Like Foncha he had only
secondary school education, a fact attributable to
the relative backwardness of the north. A progressive Moslem, Ahidjo was only one of a small group
of Northerners at the time with "modernizing" ideas
and legislative experience: he had been a member
of the Cameroonian territorial assemblies from 1947,
and had been a member of the Assembly of the French
Union from 1953-1957. In May, 1957 he was appointed
Vice-Prime Minister in the government of Andre
Mbida and succeeded to Mbida's position upon
Mbida's resignation in February 1958. His style of
leadership was and is conservative, and is seen to
reflect the values of the Fulani north.[5] When he
took office as Prime Minister he was only thirty-
four years of age.

During 1958 he was lukewarm to the idea of
reunification.[6] He had adapted the main planks of
the U.P.C. programme, "independence" and "reunification," under the pressure of proving that his
government represented the population to the
international community in spite of the agitation
of the U.P.C. But he was still undoubtedly more
aware of the problems of cementing the unity of
Northern Cameroon and controlling the southern
part of the country during the first year of his
government than he was of the Southern Cameroons.
The idea of federalism was not a particularly

welcome one to him at the end of 1958. Mbida, after resigning, appealed to France to divide the French Cameroons up into a Federation "like British Nigeria or Switzerland."[7] The outspoken Catholic newspaper L'Effort Camerounais opposed the idea on the grounds that it might create ethnic divisions, would be costly, and besides was "totally against French political tradition by which we have been brought up for forty years," in contrast to the "English empiricists who would have created Northern, Eastern, and Western Regions."[8] The idea of federalism was also associated among the more radical nationalist groups with neocolonialism and France's efforts to maintain its French Union.[9] Therefore it is not surprizing that Ahidjo would be hesitant about federalism, a political relationship thrust upon him by Foncha to solidify reunification, which in itself was a symbol forced upon him by the U.P.C.

But the Cameroons, English and French, were still United Nations Trusteeship Territories. Foncha and Ahidjo finally met during the important United Nations sessions in March of 1959 shortly after the South Cameroons election. Foncha later recalled that no real discussion took place since Ahidjo wanted to discuss the issue as "brothers" on Cameroonian soil.[10] Foncha and other Southern Cameroons cabinet ministers met with the Vice-Prime Minister of the French territory, Michael Njine, and Paul Monthe, an economic counsellor at Nkongsamba, in April 1959.[11] Foncha reiterated that reunification would take place on a federal place on a federal basis after the Southern Cameroon's secession from Nigeria.[12] Arrangements were made to meet with Ahidjo himself the next month in Yaounde, French Cameroons. The May trip to Yaounde was made to represent the arrival of a potential political partner. He was received by Ahidjo at the airport, met the cabinet and spoke to the Legislative Assembly. The final day of his three-day visit he participated in celebrations for the May 10 national holiday.[13]

The official communique noted that Foncha spoke of a federal union which would pave the way to a complete reunification and assure a harmonious transition. Ahidjo denied any desire to "annex" the Southern Cameroons.[14] These positions show that Ahidjo had accepted the idea of a federal union, and that Foncha was already speaking of a more complete union than he himself realized.

105

Four months later, Ahidjo and Foncha were both invited to the first Pan-Cameroonian Students' Congress held August 22, 1959. Foncha was extremely reluctant to go. A bilingual student envoy sent to Buea found him hesitant about unification as well, and during three days of informal discussion. Foncha was apparently thinking of a four-state federation with both British North and South Cameroons, and a French Cameroon divided on north-south lines. In any case, as late as two days before the conference, he claimed that no official invitation had been made and announced that he had no intention of going.[15]

He may have been aware of the opposition of the French High Commissioner to Cameroon, M. Torre, to the radical aspects of the conference which included U.P.C. supporters. The Minister of Education, Michael Njine, was to lose his cabinet post, apparently for allowing it to take place. In any case, minutes of the conference reveal that Foncha sent a message which showed his "secession from Nigeria first" stand. "Everybody who makes reunification a condition for secession is an enemy working in favour of integration in the Nigerian Federation."[16] Here, the question of Southern Cameroons independence was most important. Foncha seemed to be following Endeley's path.

No other Anglophone-Francophone contact was made until after the next fateful U.N. Trusteeship Council meeting. The story of how Foncha and Endeley were pressured by the four committee members to hold a plebiscite not later than March 1, 1961, with alternatives to join Nigeria or Cameroon has been told in detail.[17] The result was that the conditions for reunification were determined: the Southern Cameroons would have to join a country--Nigeria or Cameroon--that was already independent. Not only would its small size and population stand against equality in such a relationship, but the two parts of the federation--if federation was to be the link--would be unequal in terms of sovereignty at the beginning of the relationship. The U.N. had taken away Foncha's bargaining position. He was forced to join the country which the voters favoured without being able to use future withdrawal as a lever.

It was perhaps partially because of this strategic loss that in the next discussions on November 25, 1959, between a member of Foncha's cabinet and members of Ahidjo's the Anglophones would request a relatively loose federation.

106

S. T. Muna did the negotiating for the Southern
Cameroons side. The press release after the meeting announced that

> Without entering into any comment, the Hon.
> Muna expressed a view that unification between
> the Southern Cameroons might take the form of
> a loose federation with the aim of preserving
> the individuality of the Southern Cameroons
> state which at the same time would enjoy the
> advantages of federation with the Republic of
> the Cameroons. He expressed a view that a
> committee might be established to examine the
> possibilities of such a federation. His views
> found favour with the French ministers who it
> appears had been thinking along similar
> lines . . . it was agreed that the union
> should be a union of brothers from which both
> sides would draw strength.[18]

This press release also said that it was agreed
that the individual nature of the respective territories should be preserved as far as possible
because of the differences in cultural tradition.
But Ahidjo was involved with the independence of
the new Republic of Cameroon on January 1, 1961,
and made no new statement about a federation or
even about reunification after a brief mention of
reunification a week after independence. There is
no evidence that any meeting took place between the
two leaders.

Foncha was anxious for Ahidjo to come to the
Southern Cameroons and lend his presence to the
plebiscite campaign that Foncha's party, the
Kamerun National Democratic Party, was waging in
favour of reunification. He announced several times
that Ahidjo's arrival was imminent. Ahidjo for his
part seems to have been in no hurry to visit Buea.
He may have still had ambivalent feelings about
adding to the population of the southern part of the
Cameroons and certainly he had more natural interest
in the referendum for reunification which was also
to be held in the Northern Cameroons. The Northern
Cameroons bordered Ahidjo's own area and the
addition of this territory would have helped to make
the north a smaller minority vis-à-vis the south.
In any case, he finally came to Buea in July 1960
for an official visit. Foncha was ecstatic. He
declared that "given the time and the opportunity a
united Cameroon can be transformed into a paradise
in Africa." But even paradises must take concrete

forms. Still, Foncha anticipated no unsettling
intrusion from this direction.

> Our people are eagerly listening to what we
> have to say about their future. . . . All
> that we shall pronounce after our meeting will
> be an outline of what the setup of a United
> Cameroon government will look like. We know
> our place in the Federation of Nigeria. The
> place which we hope to get in the unified
> Cameroon will not be the same. It will be
> like that of divided brothers who have
> regained their liberty and returned home to
> their fatherland.[19]

The joint communique of the July meeting
announced the following fair resolutions: firstly,
"we affirm the people's strong desire for reunification"; secondly, "we agreed to unify on a federal
basis adaptable to conditions peculiar to all
sections of Cameroon"; thirdly, "we decided to set
up a joint committee to study the various constitutional problems that may result from reunification";
fourthly, "we resolve that a conference to
represent all sections of the Cameroons be held at
a later date to examine the proposals of the joint
committee."[20]
This was regarded by Foncha as the "first
public communication of the way reunification will
be achieved."[21] In a speech to the Union of Pan-
Cameroon students in Buea on August 25, Foncha
revealed that he and Ahidjo were in agreement on
most points in their July meetings and that
meetings had been continued in Yaounde by cabinet
ministers from August 9 to 14 and "a large measure
of agreement" was reached. It was agreed to set up
a committee of experts to study the economic
arrangements and the external trade of a unified
Cameroon not tied to the sterling or the franc zone.
The third formal reunion between Foncha and
Ahidjo took place from October 11-13, 1960.[22]
Foncha was anxious to have an agreement to show the
Southern Cameroons population in his plebiscite
campaign against Dr. Endeley. Evidently he was
ready to agree with Ahidjo, and the communique after
this meeting showed that the important aspects of a
potential constitution had already been negotiated.
There are two slightly different versions of
the constitutional proposals which emerged from this
meeting. The first version was published by the
West Cameroon Press Service. The second version was

the one transmitted by the Foreign Office of the
Republic of Cameroon. It was published officially
in the document The Two Alternatives[23] which
emphasized the differences in the two stages of
federal power. It noted that

> /̄a̱/ list of powers which would fall within
> the competence of the Federal Government in
> the second stage will be set out in the
> constitution

and also specified, that "Federal services will be
established to carry out Federal Administration,"
a sentence of vital importance for the future of
the federation. It seems clear that Ahidjo with
the help of French advisors had already prepared
their plans for a reunification, and that these
October meetings were really crucial to the federal
relationship. The major points of the federation
were established: provision that additional
unspecified powers would be taken over by the
federal government in a second stage without an
accompanying entrenchment of strong and specific
state responsibilities; the dominant place of the
President in the federal system; and the provision
of "federal services." These federal services may
have appeared vague and innocuous to Foncha and
his colleagues but it seems clear that to Ahidjo
they meant the reaffirmation of the system of the
Federal Inspectorate, an administrative system the
French colonial parallel to that of federal government. One of the main hypothesis of this paper is
that in October of 1960, Foncha had already agreed
to the shape of things to come. This communique
was the real stuff of reunification. These
agreements rather than any later conference
represent the agreement between elites which shaped
the future of Cameroonian federalism.

Foncha's party won the plebiscite in the
Southern Cameroons but Ahidjo had already enough
control of the situation to be able to shape the
coming reunification. Whereas Foncha had wanted a
period of independence, he was forced by the U.N.
to join either Nigeria or Cameroon. Now he had
won the plebiscite but in the effort to have a
constitutional proposal to put before the people
during the campaign he had made agreements with
Ahidjo which removed any small room for manoeuvering
which might have remained to him. But how great
was this room to manoeuver? The dominance of Ahidjo
in the political relationship was set. In fact

legally Ahidjo did not have to accept a federation
at all since the Southern Cameroons was obliged to
form the Republic in any event. This situation was
not clear in the Southern Cameroons. The debate on
the form the constitution would take was just
beginning when in fact the preliminaries had
already ended. Foncha himself, with only the
Nigerian federal experience behind him and operating virtually along without advisors, was no doubt
also confused. He was still publicly committed to
a relatively loose and decentralized federation in
spite of the implications of the October agreement.
He was to lead the Southern Cameroons delegation to
the Foumban Conference like "lambs to the slaugh-
ter."

Meanwhile in the Republic there was more
reaction to the decision of the Northern Cameroons
to stay in Nigeria than there was to the victory of
Foncha. Ahidjo's government had hoped for an
increased northern population to bolster his
support, and it was extremely disappointed by this
loss. The National Assembly of the republic
unanimously rejected the results of the plebiscite--
even U.P.C. supporters could agree to this--and
Britain came in for the most criticism.[24]

But there was some popular acceptance for the
idea of a temporary federation with the Southern
Cameroons. Immediately afterwards a conference
titled "Reunification of Federation" was held by
the Cercle Culturel Camerounais, a group founded
by Cameroonian students in France. The conference
concluded that federalism was not the best form of
reunification, but appropriate for the immediate
situation since it would take time to "harmonize"
the different cultures and habits of two
territories.[25]

> Donc, a moins d'être démagogue, tout le monde
> doit convenir que c'est une fédération qu'il
> nous faut aujourd'hui. Mais une fédération
> fondamentalement provisoire, transitoire et
> dont le dynamisme puisse nous acheminer, le
> plus tôt possible, vers un Etat unitaire,
> seul idéal de tous les heros du nationalisme
> camerounais et que plusieurs ont déja payé
> de leur sang. . . . Il faut pour cela un
> délai, mais un délai n'est qu'un délai.

Thus, their preferred model was clearly a
unitary state. Their suggestions for federation
in Cameroon included:

(1) One legislative chamber--because of the lack of divisions they saw in the "nation" and the cost of a second chamber.

(2) A strong executive.

(3) The President elected by universal suffrage should also be the head of the federation and "gardien de la constitution."

(4) The states should not have prime ministers, for the sake of economy.

(5) All foreign relations should be in the hands of the federal government.

These young members of the Francophone elite, some of whom were to become cabinet ministers in Ahidjo's government, suggested as centralized a federation as possible. It will be interesting to note how closely the Federation resembled their recommendations. However, they represent only one organization which put pressure on Ahidjo for a more centralized position. U.P.C. supporters including Abel Kingue put themselves on record at the time of the plebiscite as being for unitary government.

> Nous soutenons que seul un gouvernement unitaire peut garantir la securité et l'unité d'une Cameroun reunifie . . . font preuve que, de deux Etats a caractere national soumis au même regime economico-social l'Etat unitaire assume infiniment mieux que l'Etat federal sa securité, son unité et la consolidation de son independance nationale.[26]

Ahidjo then, while committed to a federal union, had pressures upon him to make it as unitary as possible. Foncha on the other hand had stressed a loose federation from the beginning.

Some of these differences in the interpretation of the concept of federalism might have come to light at the Foumban constitutional conference in August 1961. However, partly because Ahidjo was aware there was no need to hammer out a bargain, this interaction did not take place.

According to the original schedule of the conference, the President was to talk privately with Foncha and then receive the delegates of Southern Cameroons one at a time. The startled West Cameroonians thinking that they were there to argue out the constitution insisted on a meeting of the whole conference. This meeting of the two groups lasted only one hour and thirty-five

minutes.[27] All the previous time had been taken up
by the meetings of the Southern Cameroon delegates
who had not been aware of the detailed proposals of
the Republic until only a few days before the
conference. The Southern Cameroonian negotiators
were no match for the carefully prepared proposals
of Ahidjo and his French advisors the importance
of whom whould not be understated. There was no
suggestion of equality. It was made clear that the
President would accept suggestions but that he and
his delegation would be the final arbiters of what
would be accepted. The "Westerners" gave their
"observations" on Ahidjo's proposals back to
Ahidjo who accepted those that he wished to and
ignored those he did not.[28] Ahidjo agreed to
omit the word "indivisible" from the constitution,
but rejected the notion of a two-level legislature
on the grounds of cost and efficiency. Thus one of
the main means of safeguarding regional interests
in many constitutions was eliminated. He accepted
the idea of the President being elected by
universal suffrage rather than an electoral
college of the legislative assemblies, but he was
also under pressure from his own Republic on this
point, the "Cercle Culturel" had called for it.
Ahidjo's clinching argument for dominance was his
statement that:

> It was incumbent on the Republic of Cameroon
> which was already independent to revise its
> constitution in order to make possible this
> union.[29]

This was why the Republic's proposals were the
basis for discussion, and why Ahidjo became the
arbiter. In legal position, in strategy, and
finally on paper. Ahidjo swept the day.
Foncha had several meetings with Ahidjo before
reunification actually took place but the mask on
the reality of the federal relationship had been
lifted. Ahidjo would not commit himself to a quota
of ministers from West Cameroon. Another line in
the defense of the autonomy of the Southern
Cameroons within the federal system had thus
collapsed.
In summary, although federalism took its
public form in the conference at Foumban, its
reality had been shaped in the discussions between
Foncha and Ahidjo before the drummers of Foumban
had started their welcoming flourishes. Although
federalism's birth was formally celebrated, as a

political system it was doomed to perish in the cradle. This was not immediately apparent to the southerners.

Under Articles Five and Six of the constitution, the responsibilities of the central government were broad enough to include any powers the Federal government might wish. Article Five listed powers which would be adopted by the central government gradually. Perhaps Foncha saw these as state powers and only ultimately as federal ones. In any case by 1965 most of them were assumed by the Federal government. An important point was that revenue allocation between the two states was never finally fixed. West Cameroon was to give up its sources of customs and other revenue and was to be financed by federal subventions until a formula could be fixed. However, such a formula was never found and West Cameroon continued to be dependent on the Federal government from the beginning to the end of the Federation.[30]

One issue which was soon a source of disagreement between Cameroon leaders was the question of territorial administration. There is little indication that the West Cameroon delegation at Foumban gave a thought to the clause dealing with federal administration in the Cameroon Republic's constitution proposals. But Ahidjo was ready with the legislation immediately after Reunification: Decree 61-DF-15 of December 20, 1961, specified that the whole federation should be divided into administrative regions under the authority of Federal Inspectors of Administration who were to be directly responsible to Ahidjo and be responsible for representing the Federal government in "all acts of civil life and in judicial matters," to "supervise the enforcement of federal laws and regulations," to "maintain order according to the laws and regulations in force," having at their disposal the police force and gendarmerie, and federal services. Under this system West Cameroon was designated as only one of the six regions.

Ahidjo thus created an administrative system which basically ignored the "federal" nature of the country. The Federal Inspector in West Cameroon considered himself the equal of the Prime Minister, and there was a constant battle for jurisdiction between the two officials until the late sixties. West Cameroonian politicians (the Southern Cameroons had become "West Cameroon") found that state officials were at the same time exercising federal responsibilities. As federal powers

expanded, these officials, including the District
Officers, spent more and more time on federal
rather than state work and began to resolve conflicts of jurisdiction in favour of federal
authorities.[31] All reports and correspondence--for
either state or federal matters--were to be copied
and sent to the Inspector. Foncha countered by
pressuring the President to issue a directive that
all state officials, whether or not they were also
federal officials were to direct all communication
with federal bureaus through the office of the
Prime Minister.[32] Foncha's own understanding of
the federal agreement was quite different on this
point. He declared in the legislature:

> Administration is a federal matter, but not
> totally federal. It is concurrent in some
> cases. It is unfortunate that the word
> "concurrent" has not been inscribed in the
> Constitution, but the practice can not be
> otherwise. While administration is a con-
> current subject, the District Officers are
> directly responsible in the first instance
> to the Federated State. They do their duties
> to the Federated State. They deal with the
> Head of State, the Government and the people.
> So, in the first instance, they are
> responsible to the Head of the Federated
> State. There has now been created a post
> which is a co-ordination between the Federal
> Government and the Federal State Government.
> This is the post of Inspector of Administra-
> tion. This new post is equal to that of
> Commissioner in the other independent African
> countries, but manned by a civil servant
> instead of a politician. . . . The work of
> the Inspector of Administration is co-ordina-
> tion and direction. . . . His first duty is to
> tell the District Officer the relation between
> the Gendarmes, the soldiers, and the civil
> population.[33]

One postscript might be added. Willard
Johnson reports that Foncha seems to have claimed
privately that the administrative system violated
his agreements with President Ahidjo before reunification. This recalls differing versions of
October 1960 agreements. The Francophone proposals
included a sentence providing for federal administration and the West Cameroonian Press Services

version did not, as we have seen from the above passage.

Another area in which federalism was important in the minds of West Cameroonians was the area of language, culture, and education. Higher education was included in the Article Six list of subjects for immediate takeover. Secondary and technical education were included as subjects to be taken over gradually. Foncha had been concerned about the protection of cultural autonomy at Foumban and he consistently maintained this attitude throughout his period as Prime Minister of West Cameroon.

A federal representative in the educational system of West Cameroon was created in 1962.[34] The "Cultural Delegate" had a position parallel to the Director of Education of West Cameroon, and split his responsibility between the Federal and West Cameroon governments until 1965. The West Cameroon government insisted on paying half his salary to retain "half control" of his services. When it was learned in the summer of 1962 that the Federal government planned to take over the secondary school system, Foncha was displeased, and having received a letter from Ahidjo on the subject, proceeded to ask the Catholic Church to open two new secondary schools in his capacity as Vice President without notifying the Federal Minister of Education or the Cultural Delegate.[35] By using his dual powers of Prime Minister and Vice President, Foncha tried to delay federal takeover in the education area. However, although the secondary school system was federalized, pupils were still prepared for the British General Certificate of Education, and no major departure from the British school system was made.

The issue does not revolve around merely the jurisdiction over the school system, but the cultural implications of federation. As Foncha's opening speech at the Foumban conference shows, he was concerned with a "new Cameroonian culture" less than with the preservation of the English-speaking one, and he clearly feared French domination.

Ahidjo in a national speech saw Cameroon as being a laboratory of African Unity, and a bridge between states speaking English and French, but the differences in languages between regions were never to be stressed in quite this way again; and three years later Ahidjo gave another speech to the nation in Buea in which African unity was to be aided by the development of a new culture.

115

As far as culture is concerned we must in fact refrain from any blind and narrow nationalism and avoid any complex when absorbing the learning of other countries. When we consider the English language and culture and the French language and culture we must regard them not as the property of such and such a race but as an acquirement of the universal civilization to which we belong. This is in fact why we have followed the path of bilingualism since we consider not only that it is in our interests to develop these two world-wide languages in our country but that furthermore it offers us the means to develop this new culture which I have just mentioned and which could transform our country into the catalyst of African Unity.[36]

Ahidjo had a different view from Foncha on bilingualism in the primary school, and on the harmonization of the educational systems. He had inspiration for this policy from a West Cameroonian scholar, Dr. Bernard Fonlon, who had been the secretary of the Foumban Conference and later had joined Ahidjo's staff at the Presidency. Fonlon had studied at the Sorbonne, and at Oxford and the University of Ireland where he obtained a Ph.D., and his very real contribution to the Cameroon Federation was to argue strenuously for bilingualism. Bilingualism for Fonlon was a means of preventing West Cameroonian values and cultures from being overwhelmed, but it also stemmed from a sincere intellectual cosmopolitanism. He was appointed deputy Minister of Foreign Affairs in 1964.

However, Fonlon was also a West Cameroonian, and one of the few educated members of the K.N.D.P. He led a group of K.N.D.P. "Young Turks" into a two-day closed door meeting between the K.N.D.P. and the U.C. in late 1964. Fonlon spoke for the group, which included Nzo Ekah-Ngaky, Egbe Tabi, and Muna. Ahidjo, Moussa Yaya and Njoya Arouna were among the U.C. members present.[37] He argued that real accommodation and discussion should take place between elites from both sectors. He wanted consultation on government policy between the parties, and an equal quota of cabinet ministers in the Federal government.

Despite his official policy Ahidjo and his advisors were astonished that West Cameroon would expect more than the token bilingualism of the

secondary school system and civil service that had
already taken place.[38] Fonlon's writings in West
Cameroon Times and Abbia stirred West Cameroon
nationalism briefly in the mid-sixties, but this
effort was in the fact of the reality of Ahidjo's
power and the divisions of the West Cameroonians
themselves and was easily frustrated.

Part of Ahidjo's dominance of the federation
during the first five years of its existence was
his mastery over the political divisions within
West Cameroon. West Cameroon never held a unanimous
voice vis-a-vis Ahidjo and East Cameroon. The party
splits and political fights of West Cameroonians
would fill a small volume. E. M. L. Endeley was
still in opposition--and out in the political cold
for much of this period. There were also divisions
within the K.N.D.P. between Foncha, Augustine Jua
and S. T. Muna. Sooner or later all the politicians
attempted to better their enemies by coming under
Ahidjo's wing. Ahidjo had called for a grand
national party as early as 1961, and as the splits
and squabbles developed, all of these leaders with
the possible exception of John Foncha scrambled to
be the first in.

Dr. Endeley's party lost more ground in a
West Cameroon election in January 1962, and therefore in March he proposed to Ahidjo that his party,
the C.P.N.C., be joined to Ahidjo's Union
Camerounaise on the grounds that his party would
support Ahidjo's views of national unity and
centralized federalism more readily than the
K.N.D.P.[39] However, Foncha in April came to an
agreement with the U.C. which by implications prevented U.C. ties with other parties in West
Cameroon. In the next election in the Spring of
1964 Endeley's C.P.N.C. won more than a quarter of
the votes in West Cameroon. This was a shock to the
K.N.D.P.-U.C. alliance, and reveals some discontent
with the K.N.D.P. administration which Ahidjo was
well aware of.

In the meantime, the constitution required that
the functions of Prime Minister of West Cameroon
and Vice President be separated at the time of the
April 1965 Presidential elections. Therefore, an
internal contest in the K.N.D.P. for the deputy
leadership of the party took place. Foncha being
Life President had decided to be Vice President of
the Republic. His deputy would become Prime
Minister of West Cameroon. Camps grew up around the
two aspirants, Augustine Jua and Solomon T. Muna.
Jua was a good "grass roots" politician, Minister of

117

Finance in the West Cameroonian government, and
Catholic. He was considered as the "states-rights"
candidate. S. T. Muna on the other hand was
Minister of Transport and Communications in
Ahidjo's government. He was a Protestant, and was
considered to be the "federalist" candidate with
his close ties to the northerners in Ahidjo's
cabinet. Jua won the position easily and his ally
Nzo Ekah-Ngaky won the position of Secretary-
General of the Party. Muna still coveted the
position and emphasized the constitutional right of
the President of his own authority to nominate the
State Prime Minister which had not been noted
before.[40] Foncha wavered. In the end an open vote
of the K.N.D.P. favoured Jua twenty-three to seven.
Ahidjo selected Jua despite Muna's appeal to the
members of the West Cameroon House of Assembly,
members of the House of Chiefs, and the federal
deputies.

Jua suspended Muna from the Party so he quickly
formed a new party, the Cameroon United Congress
(C.U.C.) with policies and initials aimed at
reflecting Ahidjo's ideas and obtaining his favour.

Endeley still wanted to be part of the U.C.
Now that Foncha was in Yaounde, Jua made room for
him and the rest of his party in a coalition
"unity" government. Previously Foncha had insisted
that Endeley disband the C.P.N.C. and join the
K.N.D.P. Endeley became a special Leader of
Government Business. However, Jua's selection as
Prime Minister and the incorporation of the C.P.N.C.
into his government did not bring peace to West
Cameroon, particularly thorny was the problem of
who was to be a member of the K.N.D.P.-U.C. unity
group, specifically whether Muna and Egbe Tabi
could continue to be a member. The U.C. supporters
of Muna were claiming that members of the group had
been selected as individuals. The K.N.D.P. having
suspended them from the party claimed they were
ineligible. It was at that point that it was
suggested that a single party be formed. Ahidjo
who had advocated a grand national party since 1961
suggested that the idea be "slept on," and the next
day it was agreed that the parties be joined.[41]

Foncha at first refused to give his approval to
a united party for the reason that the C.P.N.C.
would be gaining ground at the K.N.D.P.'s expense
and he feared the unfamiliar situation that a
single political party would bring. Certainly it
would mean that he would lose his position of Life
President of the K.N.D.P. if it dissolved. However,

it was finally agreed, on Ahidjo's initiative, that
a party would be formed with a steering committee
of thirty with twenty-two each for the C.P.N.C. and
the C.U.C. giving the U.C. a permanent majority of
fourteen. The working committee was to have eight
U.C. representatives, two K.N.D.P. and one each for
the C.U.C. and the C.P.N.C.[42]

This brief history of party relations in West
Cameroon reveals that Endeley, Foncha, Muna, and
Jua all ultimately wished to join their parties to
Ahidjo's. They had divided and conquered themselves. With the arrival of the single party the
Cameroon National Union, Ahidjo's political as
distinct from constitutional right to appoint the
Prime Minister of West Cameroon could no longer be
doubted. A little more of the shadow of West
Cameroon's "federal" nature had slipped from its
grasp. Despite the fact that Jua had suggested the
joining of their parties to his, when Ahidjo
appointed the next Prime Minister of West Cameroun
in 1968, it was S. T. Muna.

Before leaving Jua's time as Prime Minister,
it is illuminating to examine one incident which is
illustrative of his relationship with Ahidjo, and
Ahidjo's conception of Federalism as a symbol in
Cameroonian political life. The incident revolves
around Jua's relationship to the territorial
administration which was previously outlined.

On the first of October 1966, the Cameroon
Mirror of Kumba published a story captioned "Federal
Regions May be Recarved." The story stated that the
administrative regions would be reconstituted so
that East Cameroon regions would cross the border
and incorporate West Cameroon; for example, Victoria
Division would be merged with the Littoral Region of
East Cameroon. The truth of the report is still in
doubt. However, Jua reacted swiftly against the
newspaper for printing what he considered to be
"false and sensational publications." He also
revealed his concept of the Federal relationship.

> It must be emphasized that the Federal Republic
> of Cameroon is a federation of two states with
> the different backgrounds, cultures and
> traditions; the present arrangement was in fact
> envisaged as the most ideal solution to the
> reunification of two parts of a country which
> had been kept apart for over forty years by
> federal powers. Any exericse, therefore, that
> is designed to alter this arrangement as
> speculated by the Mirror will clearly state

119

the basis on which the entire Federation rests
and will throw our present system of government into complete disarray. . . . It is
equally clear that since ours is a democratic
republic a matter of such far-reaching
significance and consequences cannot be
conceived and executed in secret without the
full knowledge and concurrence of the people
of West Cameroon through their accredited
representatives, to wit, the West Cameroon
Government.[43]

Ahidjo reacted quickly to Jua's remarks. He
said that he did not understand what people meant
when they talked of integration and absorption;
there was a single Cameroon and its citizens had
the same rights and the same duties. He said

. . . after the people of West Cameroon
massively voted in favour of reunification and
not for federation, after reunification itself
we freely estimated that it was necessary to
create a federation between the two states,
and to create federal institutions. But that
does not permit us to say that there are two
Cameroonian nations.[44]

Ahidjo went on to state that although he was
committed to bilingualism himself, still it was
true that some unitary countries enforce the
teaching of French and English. The implication is
clear; Ahidjo reacted with some vigour to Jua's
public statement, pointing out that federalism was
not sacred, nor was it inextricably associated with
bilingualism. The most revealing part of his speech
was his conception of the plebiscite vote: that
the majority called for reunification and not
federation. He may have meant the Federation of
Nigeria. He may have meant federalism as a concept
itself. In any case it is perhaps Ahidjo's clearest
public statement in this period.[45] It was also
clearly a slap at Jua.

II. THE SINGLE PARTY STATE

Muna's administration in West Cameroon faced
the same problems that had plagued Jua--the lack of
financial resources, conflict with the Territorial
Inspector and the problems of retaining the
bilingual identity of Cameroon. However Muna set

120

out in the same spirit of "centralist federalism" that had characterized his rise to power. Preparations to "harmonize" the public service with East Cameroon at higher rates of pay, federalize finances and the police were started almost immediately, with land law, roads, and prisons just behind. He talked of West Cameroon as one of the six economic regions of the Federation, and used all of Ahidjo's political slogans especially the French idea of "patrie" or fatherland. Muna attempted to pacify the central government on the issue of the Territorial Administration.

Until 1968, the competition between the Federal Inspector and the West Cameroon officials had been so intense that the Federal Inspector had refused to let the West Cameroon politicians inspect Guards of Honour in ceremonies over which he was presiding. In fact in January 1968, the inspector insisted that he inspect the Guard of Honour in Kumba for the beginning of the judicial year rather than the court magistrate who customarily did these duties. The ceremony was postponed while the issue was discussed. Ngoh's ordering the local D.O. to read a new administration decree aloud gave more power to the Federal Inspector. Ultimately Ahidjo told Ngoh to restrain his activities.[46] This indicated another triumph for Muna.

On August 5, 2969, Muna held a conference of Secretaries of State, Permanent Secretaries and Heads of Departments in Buea in order to "afford an opportunity to check the administrative machine which we are operating and to lubricate it where this is required."[47] Ahidjo had further strengthened the Territorial Administration as a reaction to Jua's administration. Muna on the other hand used a policy of explicit co-operation which he outlined to the West Cameroon government. He produced two "organigrams" which attempted to define the relationship between State and Federal governments, and placed the Federal Inspector below the Prime Minister but on a par with the Secretaries of State.[48]

In October of 1969, Ahidjo urged certain constitutional changes to be made by the National Assembly. The President requested that a law be passed to enable Parliament to extend or cut short its term of office on the initiative of Ahidjo. He also wanted the power to appoint Prime Ministers of the states, and finally requested that the assembly delegate to him the power of legislation.[49] The change by which he appointed the Prime Minister

121

was merely the legal recognition of what he had done in Muna's case as head of the party.

Both Presidential and Legislative elections were held in the spring of 1970. The Executive Committee of the party surprised the general populace by nominating Muna as Vice-President in Foncha's place. This meant the replacement of the symbolic leader of federalism, John Foncha, its original proponent, who has not only a reminder of the federal stage of Cameroonian unity but also could be interpreted as opposing the new values and symbols in Ahidjo's political universe. Clearly too, Foncha's appeal as a grass roots politician was not matched by any real understanding of the goals of the politicians in Yaounde, aspirations reinforced by the Francophone distaste for decentralization.

It was also time again for the nomination of the Prime Minister of West Cameroon. The political in-fighting in West Cameroon had not ended with a single party. In fact there was so much contention about the position that Ahidjo gave it again to S. T. Muna having had to make a special constitutional provision to do so. It was clear that Ahidjo held the alternate political leaders there in low esteem.

In 1970, S. T. Muna saw unitary government as attractive, but foresaw no immediate changes under his government.[50] Still, the trend was moving further away from federalism towards other symbols. The new rules seem to have broken down the concern the West Cameroon political elite had for Anglophone-Francophone differences since, in a sense, these differences had been depolitized. Whereas at reunification the influential West Cameroon politicians had all remained in Buea rather than take federal positions; by 1969, they all had federal positions or none. There was nothing to be gained by clinging to the old boundaries, old parties, and old views of federalism. The single party with Ahidjo at its head completely changed the situation.

Economically, the cash crop economy was expanded, and although West Cameroonians considered French goods as inferior to English ones their relative income rose. The shift in trade was accompanied by new communications infra-structures, including the "Unity Road" from Douala in East Cameroon to Tiko in West Cameroon, and a branch of the railway to Kumba. Both were built by the Federal government with French assistance and aimed

at exporting West Cameroonian products through
Douala to European markets in the classic pattern
of Europe dominated trade.

Muna's administration in Buea was generally
unpopular with the lower level civil servants there.
They looked forward to the day when they would
leave the favouritism of West Cameroon politics
behind and take refuge in Ahidjo's federal civil
service. Muna was still Ahidjo's man, but feared
less by him than Jua or Foncha, perhaps partly
because Muna's Protestantism may have seemed less
dangerous than their Catholicism. Ahidjo had been
actively opposed by the Catholic Bishop Ndongmo,
who was tried for treason, and the government had
also been persistently criticized by the Catholic
Bishop Zoa and the Catholic Newspaper L'Effort
Camerounais. Muna also specifically professed
allegiance to Ahidjo's ideas. Among the "elder
statesmen" Endeley was still suspected by Ahidjo
because of his former opposition to reunification
and his relative lack of popularity.

Bernard Fonlon was dropped from Ahidjo's
cabinet in late 1971. Bilingualism, the cause he
had fought for within the federation was still
official government policy, but it was symbolic
only. Education in neither East nor West Cameroon
was bilingual. Several bilingual grammar schools
were set up in the West but it was bilingualism for
West Cameroon alone. Anglophones in the Ministry of
Education were losing their strength; the bilingual
journal Revue Cameroonaise de Pédagogie was no
longer published after 1967. Abbia, the symbol of
Dr. Fonlon's fight for bilingualism was itself in
serious financial difficulties and was unable to
raise enough funds to publish in the 1969-1970
period until a gift from outside the country paid
for its operating expenses. Dr. Fonlon faced the
challenge of other intellectuals who were close to
the president, intellectuals who stressed a new
indigenous culture rather than bilingualism. In
President Ahidjo's speech to the Garoua conference
of the U.N.C. in March of 1969, he spoke of
bilingualism and biculturalism in connection with
the university;[51] however the university remained
primarily a Francophone institution and a stumbling
block for West Cameroon students who took two or
three years longer to get degrees than their
Francophone counterparts. In fact, its Vice-
Chancellor saw it as a regional university for
Francophone central Africa. Although increasing
numbers of Anglophone students and staff were

123

planned,[52] this territorial concept, and the financial control of the university by France kept the
university in a French cultural milieu. In the
bureaucracy, government circulars and directives
were not always translated into English, and if
translated were months late appearing.[53]

From time to time during the period 1966-1972,
there were rumours and suggestions of the end of
federation similar to the one that provoked Jua's
reaction in 1966. Ahidjo was asked directly about
federalism's future in 1969 but would not give a
definite answer. He said that the way of unity is
mysterious, and that in reality

> we have a strong centralized federation. . . .
> I repeat national unity does not necessarily
> mean that you must have a unitary state and
> there are examples of very solid unity in
> Federal States or even Confederation.[54]

The end came quickly when it finally arrived.

In April 1972, Ahidjo shuffled the officers of
the territorial administration in both East and
West Cameroon. He made a visit to West Cameroon on
April 17 and 18, and inaugurated the regional centre
of the National Insurance Fund.[55] This speech was a
strong reminder of the progress West Cameroon had
made since reunification and the attempts of the
government to reduce the disparities between the
two states and integrate their economies.[56] On
April 22, the Political Bureau issued a communique
announcing an Extraordinary Congress of the Party
to be held June 2 and 3. A sudden meeting of the
Political Bureau was summoned on May 7, and at that
meeting President Ahidjo announced the end of federation. In a long speech the next day to the
National Assembly and diplomatic guests specially
invited for the occasion, he announced the changes
and outlined the plans for a referendum. On May 9
the draft constitution for the unified state was
announced; the next day the referendum campaign
started. On May 15 members of the territorial
administration met with the chiefs. It had been
made the responsibility of the Divisional Officers
to get out the vote, and they were probably asking
for co-operation. The results were overwhelming in
favour, with 99 per cent turnout and 99 per cent in
favour of the end of the federation.[57] The official
results were announced on May 29. On June 2 and 3
the Extraordinary Congress of the party took place.

124

There is evidence that Ahidjo had considered ending the federation at various times, the most recent having been the Garoua conference of 1969. However there was no inkling of coming events in October of 1971 during the speeches commemorating the tenth anniversary of reunification. It is possible that he changed officers of the Territorial Administration in response to specific local events or conditions. He then may have felt it necessary to visit West Cameroon himself on April 17 and 18 to view the situation for himself. The call for an Extraordinary Congress of the Party then followed. It can be hypothesized that the decision had been made, and the constitution drafted in the next two weeks before the Political Bureau met and the change announced. Certainly, there was no opposition within the party; Federalism in Cameroon was over, only needing ratification in the national referendum. All the action to end the federal drama had taken approximately two months from Ahidjo's initial reaction to the "Glorious Revolution of May 20th."

The question remains what sort of conditions or events precipitated Ahidjo's action at that particular time--the position of the C.N.U. was secure. No political movement had existed in West Cameroon since 1966 which could claim adherents in the forest and grassland parts of the State. It is possible however that in the wake of the trial of Bishop Ndongmo for treason in Spring 1970, rumours of a Catholic political party in the grasslands made the difference. Only a party based on religion could gain allegiance in both the northern and southern parts of the state. Whether or not these rumours were true, it may have been enough for President Ahidjo to end a Federation which he seems to have only tolerated.

The new cabinet, announced July 3, 1972, included nine more members than the previous one. West Cameroonians held nine portfolios and were led by Solomon Muna who was named Minister of State, since there was no Vice President under the new constitution. Muna's role in this new unified government was to emerge as President of the National Assembly, still second to Ahidjo, at least in formal position. Three weeks after the new constitution went into effect, Ahidjo redesigned the regions of the territorial administration. Contrary to earlier rumors that he would combine West Cameroon with East Cameroon regions, Ahidjo divided West Cameroon into two Provinces: the North West

Province with Bamenda as capital comprised the departments of Bui, Donga, Mantung, Momo, Mezam, and Menchum; and the South Western Province centred at Buea and including Fako, Manyu, Meme, and Ndian departments. This division reflects the division between grasslands and forest peoples in West Cameroon previously mentioned, and was a delayed response to the demand for two provinces which had first raised its head in the period of British administration.

A province under the new plan was to be placed under the authority of a governor, a department under the authority of a perfect, a department subdivision under a sub-perfect, and a district under a district head. The first three of these were to be appointed by decree and they represent the final triumph of Ahidjo's directly appointed territorial administration system and the final eclipse of the pretense of political autonomy in West Cameroon.

III.   CONCLUSION

There are many details that this brief historical account must leave of necessity to a longer study. However perhaps enough of the events and circumstances have been outlined to suggest that federalism was a rather empty symbol of reunification from its inception. Other commentators have also suggested that Ahidjo always intended to ultimately end the federation. The evidence brought forward here goes further and casts doubt on whether a federation in the sense of a voluntary relationship between political units ever existed. When we attempt to answer the questions posed at the beginning of the paper, this must be kept in mind.

The West Cameroon elite who arranged "federation" were badly advised, had little experience or education, and were confused by the early arrangements for independence. Ahidjo on the other hand had the legal advantage because of the absolute necessity of the Southern Cameroons to join the republic after the plebiscite in 1961. He had tactical superiority in his argument that a new constitution was not necessary since the Republic of Cameroon was already independent and this gave him the superiority to arbitrate what changes he would accept. He also had the skill and patience to make federalism irrelevant to the West Cameroonian elite through the single party system, and higher salaries for federal civil servants.

He played West Cameroonian political factions off
against each other. He eliminated from positions
of power those West Cameroonians who might hold
views different from his own, such as Jua, but did
not martyr them: most have important positions in
the C.N.U. if not in the government. He created
physical communication links between East and West
Cameroon; from Douala, the main sea port in East
Cameroon to Kumba in the West Cameroon; and the
"Unity Road" from Douala to Tiko in the west. In
the end, he used the rumour of a Catholic political
party and dissatisfaction with Muna's West Cameroon
administration to end quickly what was from the
beginning not a real federalism but a shadow of one.
As one politician put it, it was better to have a
unitary state than a phoney federation.

An analogy which suggests that West Cameroon
is the "Quebec of Cameroon" has limited value.
Quebec had a degree of sovereignty and financial
security that West Cameroon never had. The fundamental difference is that the federal divisions in
Cameroon were based on colonial cultures and values
which had to be broken down into a new indigenous
culture; a breakdown that all Cameroonians could
agree with. The allegation that in reality French
models of culture and administration were used more
than English ones is a source of some discontent,
but no overt opposition has surfaced.

Federalism was primarily an "elite" symbol and
concept. Ahidjo attempted to suppress its popular
appeal as we noted in his speech in Buea in 1966.
His success in eliminating its appeal to the West
Cameroon "elite" was an important reason Federalism
died a quiet death.

APPENDIX A

The Federal Constitution

The federal constitution which came into force
October 1, 1961, listed a number of subjects to come
under federal jurisdiction immediately upon independence under Article Five, and another list in
Article Six which would temporarily be placed under
the jurisdiction of the respective states.[58]
Under Article Five were included:
nationality, the status of aliens, regulations concerning conflicts of laws, national defence,
foreign affairs, the internal and external security
of the federal state, emigration and immigration,
development and planning, the monetary system,
taxes and revenue of all kinds, higher education
and scientific research, information services and
radio, foreign assistance, postal services and
telecommunications, aviation and meterology, regulations governing the civil service and judiciary,
the federal court of justice, the territorial
boundaries of the federated states, organization of
services pertaining to these matters.
Under Article Six--the items to be assumed by
the federal government include:
public liberties, law of persons and property, the
law of obligations and contracts in civil and
commercial matters, judicial organization, criminal
law, transport and ports, prison administration,
legislation relating to state lands, labour legislation, public health, secondary and technical
education, administrative organization, weights
and measures.
Most of these powers were assumed by 1965.
As far as the states were concerned, the powers
are dealt with as follows:

Any subject not listed in Articles Five and
Six, whose regulation is not specifically
entrusted by this constitution to a Federal
law shall be of the exclusive jurisdiction of
the Federated States, which within those
limits may adapt their own Constitutions:
(Article 38 (1)).

No specific powers are listed although by implication customary courts and primary education "have
some constitutional warrant for being taken as state
subjects."[59]

Articles Five and Six are so broad that they might include virtually any powers beside these. Therefore in terms of powers shared, it is a centralized federation without doubt.

NOTES

This paper is based on research in Cameroon during 1969, 1970, and 1971. I gratefully acknowledge assistance of the Canada Council.

1. Other authors who have written on the subject of reunification include: Edwin Ardener, "The Nature of the Reunification of Cameroon," in Arthur Hazlewood (ed.), African Integration and Disintegration (Toronto: Oxford, 1967), pp. 285-338; David Gardinier, "Cameroon," United Nations Challenge to French Policy (London: Oxford, 1963); Willard R. Johnson, "The Cameroon Federation: Political Union between English and French Speaking Africa," in William H. Lewis (ed.), French Speaking Africa (New York: Walker, 1965), and The Cameroon Federation (Princeton: Princeton University Press, 1970); Victor Levine, The Cameroons, from Mandate to Independence (Berkeley: University of California Press, 1964), and Claude Welch, Dream of Unity (Ithaca: Cornell University Press, 1966).

2. There is a debate on this point. Victor Levine favours a theory that the idea originated with the U.P.C. itself, Claude Welch suggests that it existed before the U.P.C. was formed in April 1948. Interviews with Dr. E. M. L. Endeley and N. N. Mbile in Buea in March 1970 on which I base my interpretations tend to support Dr. Welch's interpretation. See also U.N. Document T/Pet. 4/61. Trusteeship Council Official Records, Annex, Volume 11. Sixth Session 1950, p. 115.

3. This point is made by Edwin Ardener in "The Kamerum Idea," West Africa (1958), p. 559.

4. L'Effort Camerounais, 30 novembre, 1958, p. 4. Electoral speech of J. N. Foncha, President-General of the K.N.D.P. 1/9/59 (mimeo), p. 6.

5. Whether or not Ahidjo has accepted it deliberately, his personal style seems to conform to the "Pulaku code" which governed the behavior Moslem Fulani leaders in traditional Fulani society. This style earns him respect in the North and in the rest of the country as well. The code itself is described in Sa'ad Abubakar, The Emirate of Fombina, 1809-1903, unpublished Ph.D. Thesis, Ahmadu Bello University, 1970, p. 154-155. See also Pierre-Francois Lacroix, Poesie peula de l'Adamawa (Paris, Julliard, 1965), p. 35.

6. According to reports reveived by British security in the Southern Cameroons.

7. L'Effort Camerounais, 29 juin 1958, p. 4.

8.   "Le Cameroun, peut-il devenir un Etat federatif?" ibid., p. 1.

9.   Ibid.

10. See also L'Effort Camerounais, 8 mars, 1959.

11. Ibid., 19 and 26 April, 1959.

12. Ibid.

13. Ibid., 31 mai.

14. Ibid.

15. West Cameroon Press Release, No. 434, Buea, August 20, 1959.

16. Pan Kamerun Student Conference, Yaounde, August, 1959, published by the International Union of Students, Prague. Notes kindly lent by Dr. Claude Welch, State University of New York, Buffalo.

17. Levine, op. cit., p. 210.

18. Southern Cameroon Press Release No. 618, 25 November 1959.

19. Southern Cameroon Press Release No. 909, 18 July 1960.

20. Ibid.

21. Ibid., No. 965, 25 August 1960.

22. Ibid., October 1960.

23. U. N. Document A. 4727. Report of the United Nations Plebiscite Commissioner for the Cameroons under United Kingdom Administration. General Assembly, fifteen session. Official Records, Annexes, p. 17.

24. Welch, op. cit., p. 242.

25. L'Effort Camerounais, 19 mars, 1961.

26. Abel Kingue, speech (mimeo) 16 December, 1960.

27. See Johnson, op. cit., p. 182.

28. Record of the Conference of the Constitutional Future of the Southern Cameroons, held at Fumban 17th July 1961. West Cameroon (mimeo).

29. Ibid.

30. This was a constant source of friction. One West Cameroon official estimated that had West Cameroons retained income from import and export duties, it could have remained independent. Interview, Buea, February 1970.

31. See also Johnson, op. cit., p. 209.

32. Johnson, ibid.

33. West Cameroon, House of Assembly Debates, volume II, section 13, July 1962, p. 118.

34. A "Cultural Delegate" Decree 62-Df-84 of March 1962.

35. Interview, Government Official, Buea, April 1970.

36. A. Ahidjo speech, Buea, October 1, 1964 (mimeo).

37. Interview, Government Official, December 1969.

38. There was no truth to the threat and the divisions between the West Cameroonian participants was real: Muna and Egbe Tabi on one side and Fonlon and Ekah-Ngaky on the other.

39. Interview, E. M. L. Endeley, Buea, February 1969.

40. See the debates in the Cameroon Champion and West Cameroon Times during 1964.

41. Interview, Foncha, April 1974.

42. Johnson, op. cit., p. 284.

43. West Cameroon Times, October 29, 1966.

44. Union et Verité, Bulletin de liaison de l'Union nationale camerounaise No. 3, November 1966, p. 2.

45. It also clearly revealed his dislike of the concept of federalism and lends weight to the argument that he foresaw its end.

46. J. Benjamin, op. cit., p. 300.

47. S. T. Muna, Speech, August 5, 1969 (mimeo).

48. Ibid.

49. West Cameroon Information Services Press Bulletin, October 31, 1969.

50. Interview with S. T. Muna, Buea, February, 1970.

51. Speech, President Ahidjo, Garoua Conference of the Cameroon National Union (mimeo) 1969.

52. Interview, Vice Chancellor, Federal University of Cameroon, January, 1970.

53. Cameroon Tribune, October 10, 1974.

54. Press Conference given by President Ahidjo at the Garoua Congress of the Cameroon National Union (mimeo), March, 1969.

55. This visit was announced the previous week.

56. SW/NW Provinces Regional Press Bulletin, 21 April, 1972.

57. West Cameroon Times, May 30, 1972.

58. E. Ardener, op. cit., p. 309. This is an excellent article on the period under discussion. The constitution is found in the Annuaire National, Yaounde, 1969.

59. Ibid.

132

5
An Imperial Presidency: A Study of Presidential Power in Cameroon

Mbu Etonga

THE PROBLEM

This paper examines the problem of Presidential
power in the Constitutional jurisprudence of the
Republic of Cameroon in the light of the American
practice. A remarkable feature of Presidential
government in Cameroon is the extent to which it
incorporates elements of the American presidential
system. Indeed, it may justifiably be said that
the vital elements of the latter system are the
superstructures upon which presidentialism in
Cameroon is built. However, our analysis will focus on the underlying constitutional and policy
considerations which have led to an almost authoritarian presidency in Cameroon. As the Cameroon
Supreme Court has yet evolved no doctrine in this
matter, this paper will attempt to discover those
grounds which, in various combinations and degrees
of intensity seem persuasive to the Jurist.
Though the analysis will be primarily directed
toward the development of a Cameroonian theory, I
will also consider the extent to which the policy
considerations are similar to those which underlie
the American doctrine.
Politics, in Cameroon as elsewhere, have tended
increasingly to be preoccupied with how to win and
retain power, overriding the need for a due sense
of balance and restraint. Along with economic
development, national integration and stability,
there is a need for ideology, for principles of
government, in short, for constitutionalism--a quest
for appropriate restraints upon the powers of
government in the interest of the protection of
individual liberties. This paper makes suggestions
to this end in the light of the American practice.

PART ONE--THE PRESIDENTIAL EXECUTIVE IN CAMEROON

In this section the nature of the Presidential executive in Cameroon will be examined always bearing in mind that our study is conducted in the light of American practice.

Two main features characterise the executive in a presidential system. It consists of a single individual and it is independent of the legislature and judiciary.

Single Unified Executive

The framers of the American Constitution were much exercised by the issue of whether the executive branch of the new government should consist of one or several individuals. For a people just emerging from a bloody armed confrontation with a monarchical government, monarchy or any other form of government by a single individual was apt to stir up sentiments of fear and hate. Yet, after lengthy discussions at the Constitutional Convention at Philadelphia, the framers, unable to devise a more satisfactory alternative, settled for an executive of one person. Enacting this decision, the Constitution declares in Article II that "the executive power shall be vested in a President of the United States of America."

The first question to address our minds to is whether the vesting of executive power in a single person, named President, requires that the President be the sole repository of the entire executive authority of the State, and that no other executive function exist independently of him or be exercised otherwise than under his direction and control. Alternatively, does the provision admit of other independent executive functions, with the President's being the pre-eminent one, i.e., that of the Chief Executive?

It may be argued against the idea of chief executive that the Constitution does not say that the President is chief executive. That would imply that there are other executives of lesser power associated with him. This position can easily be maintained in the face of the Constitution itself, which, while lodging the executive power in the President, also grants to other authorities functions which, under governmental practice, are commonly treated as partaking of execution. Thus, the creation of office, the declaration of war, and the raising of armies are functions lodged in

Congress, not in the Executive branch. Furthermore, the President's power of appointment and of treaty-making are shared with the Senate.[1]

A Constitution may, of course, so distribute executive power among the President and other executive agencies that it is not easy to say who has the preponderant share of it. The Constitution of the French Fifth Republic is a case in point.[2] It establishes a President with certain significant executive powers--and insures the integrity and continuance of the state.[3] Significantly, however, the power to execute the law is vested not in him, but in a Premier. The Premier, the Constitution declares, is to direct the operation of the government and ensure the execution of the laws. Where the proponderance of executive functions lie under the Constitution is thus inconclusive.

But it is to be noted that the Premier is appointed by the President. He can also remove the Premier from office. The removal power effectively subordinates the person subject to the will of its possessor. Hence, between the President and the Premier, there can be no doubt as to who is boss or chief, even as regards the power to execute.[4]

In Cameroon, no such difficulty arises, since the constitution establishes the paramountcy of the President in the executive field. The Prime Minister is completely under the President, with no independent executive power of his own. The Constitutional amendment creating the post of Prime Minister reads:

Art. 5 (new)

The President of the Republic, Head of State and Head of Government shall ensure the respect of the Constitution and the unity of the State and shall be responsible for the conduct of the affairs of the Republic. He shall define the policy of the Nation. He may charge the Prime Minister to apply his policy in given spheres.

The Prime Minister shall for this purpose receive a delegation of powers to direct, co-ordinate and control the activities of the government in such spheres.[5]

The implication of the principle of a single executive here is that, as regards functions properly within the executive power vested in the President (Head of State and Head of Government) all other executive officers, ministers, etc. have no independent authority. Their authority is merely delegated. The Prime Minister, for instance, is there only in the role of subordinate to assist the President in the exercise of his executive power. He is not a co-beneficiary with the President and his appointment in charge of any departments does not imply an abdication by the President of his power over those departments.

A very important question that arises, however, is whether it can be said that the principle of a single executive is incompatible with the concept of a cabinet.

In the case of Cameroon, no obligation is imposed on the President to accept or act on the advice of the "cabinet." The establishment of a cabinet, provided in Art. 8 of the Constitution, has been made completely pointless as the President is free to convene it and use it as he wishes. Surely, the intention of providing for a cabinet among other things should be to minimise as much as possible the possibilities of a personal government, such as occurred in America during the Civil War.[6] In Cameroon, Presidential consultations are for the most part with individual ministers, and with occasional cabinet meetings. Without question, the failure of the constitution to subject the President to cabinet advice and influence is an open invitation to despotism, caprice, and intrigues. There is no doubt that in any regime, an obligation to consult a cabinet operates to fetter any advance to assume dictatorial powers.

Executive Independence

The makers of the U.S. constitution were conditioned as much by the tyranny of monarchy as by the excesses of an omnipotent legislature. The revolution against monarchy had led to the enthronement of the omnipotence of the legislature. But this omnipotent legislature became despotic and fell out of favour. Americans began to look up to an independent executive as the guardian of the people, even of the lower classes against legislative tyranny and against the great and wealthy who in the course of things will necessarily compose the legislative body.[7] Thus did executive independence come to be enshrined as a principle of the governmental system established by the Constitution.[8]

Executive independence requires freedom from control by the legislature as regards appointments

and tenure. The American President is not chosen
by Congress but independently of it--by the people
at large. If he were to be elected by Congress, he
would be subordinated to it through a desire to
curry its favour in order to obtain re-election.

The real significance, however, of having the
President elected by the people rather than by the
legislature lies in the fact that it gives him an
independent right to govern. The right flows
directly from the people who elect him, and, argua-
bly, is greater than the legislature's because it
is more nationally based.

A further point arises concerning the system of
checks and balances and its relationship to the
principle of independence. How do we reconcile independence and check? Checks and balances, a conspicuous feature of the American constitution seeks
to reconcile the need for a strong executive with
democracy. Thus, under the Constitution, the President's power in regard to appointments and making
of the treaties is checked by the necessity for the
Senate's approval. Again, he, the Vice President
and other civil officials are liable to impeachment
before Congress for treason, bribery, or other high
crimes and misdemeanors, and, upon conviction, to
automatic dismissal from office.[9]

It may be thought that the checks made the
President dependent upon Congress and thus contradict the principle of the separation of powers.
This would mistake the nature of the system of
checks and balances. Its effect is not to subordinate the person checked to the authority exercising
the check. For, writes Nwabueze,

> It neither divests him of discretion in the ex-
> ercise of functions vested in him nor makes
> such functions a joint responsibility. And
> far from being contradictory to the doctrine of
> separation of powers, its purpose is to make
> the separation a more effective instrument of
> constitutionalism.[10]

Take, for instance, the position of the Senate in
the matter of appointments under the American constitution. The fact that some appointments can only
be validly made with the advice and consent of the
Senate does not make appointments the joint responsibility of the Senate and the President. In
Myers v. United States, the Supreme Court held the
consent of the Senate does not make an appointment;
this still remains the act of the President, and is

137

also a voluntary act.[11] Alexander Hamilton put the matter quite lucidly, almost as if it admitted no controversy.

> It will be the office of the President to
> nominate and with the advice and consent of
> the senate to appoint. There will, of course,
> be no exertion of choice on the part of the
> senate. They may defeat one choice of the
> executive, and oblige him to make another, but
> they cannot themselves choose.[12]

However, for executive autonomy and independence to be fully effective, the President must have a discretion in the discharge of his functions not only in the political agencies but in the courts as well.

In Cameroon, on the other hand, Presidential independence and autonomy means that: (i) the legislature is subordinated to the executive, (ii) the judiciary is subordinated to the executive, and (iii) the whole concept of checks and balances is largely abandoned.

We shall attempt an explanation of the situation by looking at the Office of the President for an understanding of the rejection of these constitutional guarantees.

PART TWO--THE OFFICE OF THE PRESIDENT

Formal Source of Presidential Power

In the political development of a country just recently emancipated from colonialism, national sentiment has important significance, even in matters of pure form. A sentiment of national consciousness and identity has to be inculcated in the people in order to arouse them to a feeling of loyalty to the new state. Thus their constitution is seen as an instrument of cultural revival of national restatement reflecting the peoples choice of a frame of government, as well as their traditional political concepts, if not specific institutions and procedures.

A titular or even moderate Head of State is said to be un-African. The late Tom Mboya, Kenya's Minister for Constitutional Affairs, said:

The historical process by which, in other
lands, Heads of States, whether Kings or
Presidents, have become figureheads, are no
part of our African tradition.[13]

Thus, while a weak Head of State is denounced
as meaningless in the light of African political experience and history, a strong or even extremely
powerful executive presidency is extolled as being
in accord with it.

Thus, the most striking feature of the presidency in Cameroon is its tremendous powers. Its
formal powers exceed those of its American proto-
type--not in nature but in extent. This presidentialism, in the context of the restraints which the
constitution imposes upon power, differs quite
markedly from its American counterpart; so markedly
indeed that the somewhat pejorative qualification
"African" has been applied to it and others. Some
term it Presidentialist. Professor Carl Friedrich
has observed almost accurately that:

It is part of the major perversion which ac-
companies the adaptation of American constitutional ideas in foreign lands that where one of
the major institutions of American constitutionalism such as the presidency has been re-
produced, federalism and judicial protection of
human rights have not been.[14]

The "Africanness" of the presidency in Cameroon
refers to the fact that it is largely free from
limiting constitutional devices, particularly those
of the rigid separation of powers and federalism
which was abolished in 1972.

Every kind of separation or division in governmental authority is rejected. The legislature is
subordinated to the executive; bicameralism, which
existed before, has been replaced by unicameralism,
and federalism by unitarism. The judiciary is subordinated to the executive as regards appointments
and dismissals. All this was but a foundation for
the emergence of that political monolith, the one-
party state, which itself finally consummated the
personalisation of rule, i.e., the centralisation,
within the single party, of all power in the hands
of the leader. The whole concept of checks and
balances is largely abandoned. President Julius
Nyerere made this point for the rest of them in
terms, intellectual and trenchant:

Our constitution differs from the American
system in that it avoids any blurring of the
lines of responsibility and enables the executive to function without being checked at every
turn. For we recognize that the system of
checks and balances is an admirable way of
applying the brakes of social change. Our need
is not for brakes--our lack of trained man-
power and capital resources and even our climate, act too effectively already. We need
accelerators powerful enough to overcome the
inertia bred of poverty, and the resistances
which are inherent in all societies.[15]

Thus, for example, the power of the President
to appoint ministers, judges, and other public
servants and to enter into treaties with foreign
countries is not limited, as in America, by the
necessity of obtaining the approval of the legislature.[16]

Informal Sources of Presidential Power

Myth, charisma, and tradition. The constitution is only one of the sources of presidential
power though no doubt a supremely important one.
The reality of power depends on other factors besides its formal structure.
It may be said that the circumstances of
Cameroonian society favour an authoritarian presidency. To begin with, the presidency is clothed
with a considerable amount of mystique which bestows
upon it an authority transcending that of any ordinary Head of State. The mystical quality derives
partly from the achievement of the present leadership generally, as heroes of the nationalists
movements, which overthrew colonialism. The leader
incarnates the spirit of that struggle and the aspirations of those engaged in it. The apparent re-
alisations of those aspirations have elevated him to
the status of a deliverer, a messiah. As the per-
petuation of the inferiority of the African and
particularly of the illiterate Northerners was central to the philosophy and technique of colonialism,
a Northerner who was able to challenge the myth of
white and Southern superiority was considered a man
of extraordinary qualities and all the awe and
mystique associated with the white man is now trans-
ferred to him. In the words of Professor Nwabueze:

140

The reality is brought home to the people by
the spectacle of the leader occupying the
former colonial governor's official residence,
that symbol of the glory and glamour of
empire. There he sits, perhaps in the very
chair used by the embodiment of white power,
directing affairs of state, and giving instructions to all functionaries of the state, both
white and black.[17]

A fantastic myth has been built up around the
leader to arouse a charismatic appeal among the
people. The charisma and mystique have engendered
the belief that the leader is a kind of demi-god
specially commissioned by Providence to deliver the
people from neo-colonialism, poverty, ignorance,
and disease. An authority based on this kind of
charisma needs constant nurture; since the myth on
which it is based is liable to evaporate if exposed
to public contact. The cult of personality is
resorted to for the necessary nurture. A cult of
incorruptibility and infallibility is accordingly
built up around the leader. His name and his activities are kept tirelessly in the public view.
His image is glorified in songs praising his
achievements, in posters showing his photographs,
in institutions and streets named after him, and in
statues of him erected in the most conspicuous
centres of the city.[18]

Also, tradition has inculcated in the people a
certain amount of deference towards authority. The
chief's authority is sanctioned in religion, and it
is a sacrilege to flout it. Though customary sanc-
tions of abuse of power may exist, there is considerable toleration of arbitrariness by the Chief.
This attitude towards authority tends to be trans-
ferred to the modern political leader. The vast
majority of the population, which of course is still
illiterate and custom-bound, is not disposed to
question the leader's authority, and indeed disap-
proves of those who are inclined to do so. The
president, in effect, is the <u>chief</u> of the new nation, and as such entitled to the authority and
respect due by tradition to a chief.

<u>Conditions of underdevelopment</u>. There is yet
another respect in which conditions in Cameroon are
a source of power for the President. In a situation
where the state is the principal employer of labour
and almost the sole provider of social amenities,
and where a personal ambition for power and wealth

and influence rather than principle determines political affiliations and alliances, power to dispense patronage is a very potent weapon in the hands of the President, enabling him to gain and maintain the loyalty of the people at various levels of society. Loyalty of this type secured by patronage produces an attitude of dependence, a willingness to accept without question the wishes and dictates of the person dispensing the patronage. Patronage has therefore been one of the crucial means by which the Cameroon president has secured the subordination of the legislation, the bureaucracy, the police, and even the army.

Tribalism. Cameroon embraces a large variety of peoples of differing origin, culture, language, and character. This heterogeneous collection needs to be integrated into a unity, infused with a sense of common destiny and common national aspirations. It is the role of the President as leader to serve as a focal point of unity. This integrating role of the President involves the exercise of power-- power to prevent the inevitable cleavages of tribalism from destroying the state. The tribal conflicts create a condition of instability. In the view of some authorities, the state of affairs is comparable to a state of emergency, and a state of emergency, even in the most advanced democracies, demands actions of an authoritarian type to preserve the peace and integrity of the state. The experience of the United States illustrates the great potency of a situation of emergency as a source of presidential power, for it is during such periods that the presidency has attained its zenith of power, as is illustrated by Lincoln's "dictatorial" regime during the civil war; by Wilson's highly centralised World War I administration, and by Franklin Roosevelt's executive dominated government during the emergencies of domestic depression and global conflict.[19] Tribalism has also operated in another way to put greater power in the hands of the Cameroon President. For in the clash of interests between various tribes and their leaders, an "atribal," northern and Moslem politician often becomes a kind of counterpoise holding the balance of power in the state.

Personal ambition. However, the authoritarian style of the President cannot be explained solely in terms of the pressure of circumstances. For as Hirschfield has pointed out, while circumstances and

142

particularly crisis conditions can make vast
authority available to the President, yet they cannot by themselves guarantee an appropriate presidential response; only he can make the decision to
use it.[20] Personal ambition for power, and the
wealth and prestige that go with it, are also decisively important. Of course a personal love of
power has always been a prime motive in politics
everywhere, but in Cameroon power carries very high
stakes indeed, and the stakes have an especial significance because of the general poverty of the
society. Fortunately, Cameroon's President, Ahmadou
Ahidjo, tries to live a life of Moslem simplicity
and morality, without the kind of ostentatious display of wealth which characterises Presidents and
ministers elsewhere in Africa. Yet, while this may
mitigate, it cannot remove the stark reality of the
economic and social gap between him and the huge
peasant and labouring masses.

Again, one would like to know how many terms of
office the President is permitted to have. The two
alternatives have been a life presidency or indefinite eligibility for election with or without a
break. A life presidency has not had many advocates
in Cameroon but indefinite eligibility without a
break is the constitutional principle. Art. 7(1) of
the Constitution of the Republic provides:

> The President of the Republic shall be elected
> for five years and may be re-elected.

This unequivocally reflects a desire to perpetuate the rule of the president indefinitely. It
is worth noting that the current President has ruled
for twenty years. The explanation for perpetuity
involves a complex of factors, but a desire for
power and its prerequisites is at the root of it
all. Once a President, a person feels it incon-
ceivable that he can thereafter be anything else
but a president. The power is so intoxicating, the
adulation so flattering, and the prestige and
grandeur of the office so dazzling as to be almost
irreconcilable with a new life as an ordinary citizen. Hence the temptation to cling to the office
for life--in fact the constitution has provided for
a de facto life president!
We will proceed in the next sections to discuss
the features of Cameroon presidentialism mentioned
in the closing paragraph of Part Two and in the
opening paragraphs of this paper, namely, centralism
in the organisation of governmental powers, and the

subordination of the legislature and the question of human rights.

PART THREE--CENTRALISM AND POWERS OF THE PRESIDENT

From Federalism to Unitarism

In an address to Parliament on May 6, 1972, President Ahidjo announced his intention to change the nature of the Cameroon republic. Two weeks later (May 20), the Cameroonian people by a vote of 3,177,846 to 176 adopted a new constitution, which the President of the Republic promulgated by decree 72-270 of June 2, 1972. Under its provisions, the Federal Republic of Cameroon became a unitary state and changed its name to the United Republic of Cameroon. The legislative houses of the two former federated states were abolished and the state authority was henceforth to be exercised by the President of the Republic and the National Assembly.[21]

Was the desire for unitarism part of the aim to achieve concentrated power under a presidential system? The federal arrangement under the 1961 constitution[22] unquestionably operated to limit presidential power and that is why federalism proved an effective cornerstone, although of a relatively short interval, of Cameroon constitutionalism. Its limitations were quite severe, going beyond that of the separation of legislative, executive, and judicial powers. It involved a division of powers that was both functional and territorial.

It is to be expected thus, that a leader with ambition for centralized power might be impatient with such a scheme of division and the restraints which it imposes. While, however, personal ambitions for power might have been relevant and important factors, the argument for moving Cameroon from federalism (1961) to unitarism (1972) was based on other grounds. It was argued that federalism or regionalism impeded development. Also, it was thought that federalism undermined national unity by providing an institutional base for tribal politics and that it fostered all the cleavages and conflicts between Anglophones and Francophones who belonged to separate states. Then there was the fear that the Anglophones were harnessing power and influence for eventual secession; an argument I personally consider far-fetched.

As with unitarism, the question is also
prompted as to the reason for the institution of
the one-party system in Cameroon.[23] Was it attributable to the centralising propensity of an executive presidency or was it dictated by the genuine
needs of the country?

Many reasons have been advanced to justify
this shift from multipartism to the one-party state.
Of the most forceful is the oft-cited argument
based on national unity, stability, and economic
development, admittedly the most imperative needs
of the country. It is argued that in a new nation,
riven by tribal or racial divisions and conflicts,
the unity of a single political party is necessary
for stability and economic development. The masses
were led to expect that independence would bring
about an immediate improvement in their conditions,
and the non-realization of these expectations had
been blamed on multipartism and had in turn bred a
mood of impatience. Unless, therefore, improvement
could be effected as speedily as possible, this
mood of impatience might explode into violent hos-
tility--to endanger, if not destroy, the state itself. The urgency of the task, it is argued,
admits of no diffusion of energies in an unbridled
competition for power.

Secondly, political unity is necessary to fight
neo-colonialist forces trying to subvert the newly-
won independence. Having taken a forced exit, the
imperial powers are suspected of wanting to exploit
the inexperience and poverty of the new nation in
order to perpetuate their economic stronghold or to
discredit it as incapable of self-government. Neo-
colonialism is represented as insidious, working
through paid agents among the disgruntled elements
in the state, and as such is perhaps even more
sinister than colonialism. Only by imposing unity
through the medium of a single party can the government check or neutralise those prone to fall prey to
the mechanizations of neo-colonialism, so the argument goes.

The plain truth as experience in Cameroon has
shown, however, is that the one party is far from
erasing tribal loyalties. Unity can only be
achieved through the evolutionary process of education, social intercourse in trade, intermarriage,
and other social and cultural interactions, professional and business life, a functional re-align-
ment of people cutting across tribal or racial
divisions, and a shared community life generally.[24]

145

Personally, I will not quarrel with the system
if in fact it maximized the opportunity for popular
participation in government in a meaningful way.
However, experience of the actual working of the
Cameroon National Union Party (CNU) shows, that
participation is far from being maximized. (See
Bayart's chapter in this volume.) And, in any case,
can participation be really meaningful where there
is only a minimal scope for dissent and where
organized dissent is not permitted at all? Can debate conducted on the basis of only one set of
programmes lead to a really meaningful consent?
And, as Professor Busia has remarked, even where
there is agreement on objectives, the differences
on methods and priorities by which to achieve the
objectives can be very important and fundamental.[25]

Subordination of the Legislature

The importance of an independent legislature
needs no special emphasis. Unless parliament is in
fact independent of the executive, then the sovereignty of parliament to which Cameroonians are fond
of referring, means simply the sovereignty of the
executive. An executive possessed of the legal
sovereignty of the state (i.e., power to legislate)
is unquestionably a danger to liberty and democracy.
However, it may be conceded that, in the interests
of governmental efficiency and effectiveness, the
executive should have control of policy and therefore of the legislative initiative. But the final
process by which policy is legislated into law
binding on the community must not only be separated
from, but needs also to be independent of, the executive. For it is in this that the real essence of
liberty lies. Liberty is not secured by a constitutional guarantee of rights alone. No Constitution,
however strongly entrenched, can be guaranteed
against the temptations of power on the part of the
executive, unless there is an independent legislature to act as a counterpoise against such temptations. In Cameroon, a young and largely illiterate
country where public opinion is underdeveloped and
slow to form and to articulate, an independent legislature can be the rallying force of the people
against incipient tyranny.
In Cameroon, the parliament can rightly be
characterised in the words of Dr. Lee, as "a passive
and decorative organ."[26] The National Assembly
serves almost entirely to rubber-stamp decisions
taken by the executive. The nature of this

subordination may perhaps be best perceived by considering how the powers and functions involved in
legislation are shared between the legislature and
the executive. Our examination will comprise two
main heads: (i) legislative power, and (ii) legislative initiative. All along, we shall draw on the
American experience and practice.

(i) Legislative power. The general rule of
law is that a legislature cannot be said to be completely sovereign if it does not possess the en-
tirety of the legislative power of the state. The
sovereignty of parliament demand that it alone shall
have the power of legislation, and that no other
body can legislate except by its authority and with
its consent. This is not true in Cameroon where the
President is as much a constituent part of parliament as the assembly, their title to the legislative
power being joint and equal in the sense that, in
the absence of a contrary provision in the constitution, the concurrence of both is indispensable to
its exercise.

Subject to the Constitution, neither the one
nor the other alone can exercise the power. Art.
2(1) of the 1972 Constitution provides:

Art. 2(1) National Sovereignty shall be vested
in the people of Cameroon who shall exercise
it either through the President of the Republic
and the members returned by it to the National
Assembly or by way of referendum; nor can any
section of the people or any individual
arrogate to itself or to himself the exercise
thereof.

This must be accounted a serious qualification
upon the autonomy of the legislature, a qualification which it is difficult to justify in a republican constitution. It is a relic of monarchy, and is
explicable only in that context. It is an attempt
to reconcile monarchy with popular sovereignty. The
monarch is the sovereign, and the cardinal essence
of sovereignty in the legal sense is the power to
make laws. Such a devise should have no place in a
republic. It has none indeed in the first modern
republic, the United States. The American constitution vests legislative power in Congress alone.

The point here should not be confused with the
question of authentication or the President's legislative role. It was the fear that the executive
might be reduced by the legislature to the mere

147

pageant and shadow of magistracy that led the
framers to provide for the participation by the
President in the legislative process. The power
thus to participate, it was hoped, would serve as a
shield to the executive, ensuring that it would not
be left at the mercy of the legislative department.[27] Again, legislation being a solemn and
authoritative act of state, it would need to be
authenticated by the state functionary who personi-
fies the authority and majesty of the state. The
President's signature is necessary to bestow the
seal of authority of state upon a law passed by the
assembly. But this fact alone does not by itself
make him a co-beneficiary of the legislative power--
although some commentators, notably Benard Schwartz,
has argued that it does.[28]

In Cameroon, the executive does possess inherent lawmaking power. Article 9(g) of the Constitution provides:

> The President of the Republic shall have the
> power to issue statutory rules and orders.

In Cameroon, the administration is vested with the
inherent authority to promulgate rules and regulations which have the force of law (force de
droit).[29] This inherent authority based on the
generally accepted principles of administrative law
is merely reinforced by the constitutional provision
that the President has the power to issue statutory
rules and orders.

The situation is foreign to American concep-
tions of executive power. In the American theory,
the executive possesses only the lawmaking power
which has been delegated to it by Congress. It is
true that such power of delegated legislation has
increased tremendously in recent times. Without
doubt, the President may issue proclamations, termed
social acts of the highest official[30] and in the
field of foreign affairs. Yet, though such proclamations and the like may have an impact on the
community, it is inaccurate to characterize them as
exercises of inherent executive lawmaking power.
They are lacking in the chief characteristic of true
acts of legislation, for their violation is not
attended by recognized legal consequences, of the
kind which ensur when laws are violated. They are
lacking in the sanction against person or property
which gives to the lawmaking power its efficacy.
Again, they may not be backed by the force of

society, unless such consequence has been provided for by the Congress.[31]

That the U.S. President may act as lawmaker only in virtue of a Congressional delegation is clear from the Steel Seizure case. The opinion of the court there declares:

> The founders of this Nation entrusted the lawmaking power to the Congress alone in good and bad times.[32]

The organic document refutes the notion that the President is to be a lawmaker: "The Constitution," declares Justice Black, "limits his functions in the lawmaking process to the recommending of laws he thinks bad. And the constitution is neither silent nor equivocal, about who shall make laws which the President is to execute."[33]

Another exception in Cameroon, to the statement that parliament is the sole repository of the legislative power is in the question of transitional legislation after adoption of a new constitution. A change of constitution creates a necessity for adapting existing laws to the new constitution. Such adaptation is an exercise of legislative power by way of amendment of existing laws in order to bring them in conformity with the new order. In Cameroon, it is considered both expedient and desirable to give this power to the president. The nature of the necessary adaptations are often extensive, involving the whole body of existing legislation.

Perhaps the most potent qualification upon the exclusiveness of parliament's legislative authority is emergency legislation by the President. The principle of executive legislation during an emergency is almost universal throughout the world. Its normal scope and purpose is to enable the executive to make such regulations as appear to him necessary or expedient during an emergency to secure the public safety, and defence of the state. There is perhaps nothing objectionable in giving this power to the executive subject, however, to strict parliamentary control. The difference in Cameroon is the wider scope and overriding force of emergency powers, the absence of parliamentary control and the fact that the declaration is absolutely in the sole discretion of the president (Article II, paragraphs 1-3, 1972 Constitution).

It is ironical that it is at such times as this, i.e., states of emergency or siege, when the possibility of abuse is greatest, that parliamentary control is <u>absent</u>. This in itself is tragic, especially when it is remembered that, apart from war, an emergency is whatever else the leader regards as such.

(ii) <u>Legislative initiative</u>. Theoretically, every member of Parliament has the right to initiate bills, motions, and questions in parliament quite independently of the government and without its prior approval. This right is limited in matters involving the raising and expenditure of public funds. Usually such matters are initiated only by government through the President or his ministers. The reason for this is said to be that good and orderly government requires that only those who administer the government and therefore have an intimate connection with it, should propose national expenditures, and how the money needed can be raised, and to avoid financial chaos since members may compete among themselves to secure as much of public funds as possible for the constituencies or interests which they represent.

The second limitation comes from limited opportunities available for the exercise of initiative. It is the President who summons a session of parliament and brings it to an end by prorogation, though he is constitutionally bound to call a session once every year at intervals of less than twelve months.[34] In Cameroon, meetings of the Assembly are too few and short to provide members ample opportunity to discharge their functions adequately and effectively. No doubt therefore that government business should have priority over that of private members, since without the approval of the assembly, in the form of legislation, the government cannot implement its policies and programme. So complete has this monopoly of government business become that most M.P.s are not even aware that they have a right to initiate legislation.

There is another reason advanced why legislative initiative must be a function of the government. Much of it is of an extremely complex and technical nature with wide-ranging ramifications, which at once put it beyond the capacity of an individual M.P. to manage or even to comprehend. The dimensions of the issues with which it deals are usually beyond their vision given their generally <u>low</u> academic standing. Also, many issues arise in the administration of the departments and other

150

institutions of state about which only someone inside the government or a technocrat can have
knowledge. Such are questions of fiscal policy,
economic development, and social reform, etc.
Their complexity and technical nature require special expertise which M.P.s lack.

What seems of greater importance is not that
the assembly should control the initiation of legislation, but rather that legislation introduced by
the government, or the organ better able to do so,
should be thoroughly scrutinized and discussed in
the Assembly. It is this scrutinizing that should
form the chief concern of the parliament. In dis-
charging this function, the Cameroon National
Assembly has failed to demonstrate any sense of
independence or effectiveness.

PART FOUR--HUMAN RIGHTS AND NATIONAL SECURITY

Human Rights and National Security

The question here is whether a strong, centralised government, such as characterises the presidential regime in Cameroon, permits of adequate en-
joyment of human rights. The record would seem to
indicate a negative answer. Concentrated power as
we know it, is very sensitive to criticism and very
jealous and suspicious of rivals or competitors;
hence the institution of the one-party system in an
already tight atmosphere.

The point of controversy is, however, in what
circumstances and subject to what safeguards should
individual rights yield to the claim of extraordinary powers by the government to preserve the
nation? Should every threat to peace and security
of the state, justify encroachment upon the rights
of the individual?

(i) The American Legacy. The American approach
to the conflict of state security versus individual
liberty is particularly relevant both because
America had undergone a similar experience of colonial rule and independence and also because it is
governed under a written constitution. The keynote
in the American approach is contained in the
following words of the U.S. Supreme Court in the
great civil war case of Ex parte Milligan in 1866.[35]

The constitution of the United States is a law
for rulers and people, equally in war and

peace, and covers with the shield of its protection all classes of men, at all times, and under any circumstances. No doctrine involving more pernicious consequences was ever invented by the wit of man that any of its provisions can be suspended during any of the great exigencies of government. Such a doctrine lends directly to anarchy or despotism, but the theory of necessity on which it is based is false; for the government, within the constitution, has all the powers granted to it which are necessary to preserve its existence.[36]

These words were echoed by the same Court in another great constitutional case arising from World War II.[37] We may here also recall the similar words of Lord Atkin in his famous dissenting judgment in another World War II case, Liversige v. Anderson.[38] "In England," amidst the clash of arms, he said, "The laws are not silent. They may be changed, but they speak the same language in war as in peace." In the view of the U.S. Supreme Court in the Milligan case, it is just at such times of grave exigency that liberty requires to be protected against the pretentions and abuses of unlimited power; the Court observed that a nation preserved at the sacrifice of the cardinal principles of liberty is not worth the cost of preservation.

The Court was not denying any form of extraordinary power for the government to deal with an emergency endangering the peace and security of the nation. But an exigency, such as will justify interference with individual liberty, must not only be real but also grave and immediate. The most obvious situation is war, or other civil strife.

A war creates an extreme situation calling for sterner measures, such as a general suspension of the writ of habeas corpus, that greatest of all muniments of Anglo-American Liberty.[39] The U.S. Constitution itself authorises its suspension in an invasion or rebellion if the public safety requires.[40] The Supreme Court in Ex parte Milligan laid it down, however, that the suspension of the writ does not authorize the arrest of anyone, but simply denies to one arrested the privilege of this writ in order to obtain his liberty[41] though a minority of the court, dissenting from this view, took the contrary position that where the writ of habeas corpus is suspended, the Executive is authorised to arrest as well as detain.[42]

Even in the face of the American Civil War,
the Court refused to sacrifice to the exigency of
public safety the individual's right not to be
deprived of his liberty or life in pursuance of the
judgment of military court. It rejected the argument that in time of war, state necessity justifies
the assumption by a military commander of absolute
power to suspend all civil rights and their
remedies, and to subject civilians as well as
soldiers to the rule of his will. In the Milligan
case, the majority rested its decision on the
ground that trial of civilians by a military court
cannot be authorized, whether by the President or
Congress, except when, as a result of military
operations, the ordinary courts have ceased to
function. Those who founded this nation, said
Justice Murphy, knew full well that the artibrary
power of conviction and punishment for pretended
offences is the hallmark of despotism.[43]

(ii) The position in Cameroon. Security
powers in Cameroon have a frightful reality. They
are formally very wide and drastic both in and out
of an emergency. As noted before, the constitution leaves undefined what constitutes an emergency,
war apart. There is also no check on the power to
declare it. It is the President's power and he
uses it the way he desires; "thereafter, he shall
inform the nation by message of his decision."[44]
It is perhaps on personal liberty that security
powers have impinged most. The power of detention
and restriction is extensive. The ordinary legal
limitations on arrest are usually dispensed with.
It is a precondition of a lawful detention that the
arrest must have been effected in accordance with
the requirements of law. The preventive detention
laws of Cameroon authorise arbitrary arrest for this
purpose. In anticipation of the sort of question
that has arisen in the U.S. Supreme Court, they
provide that a detention order shall constitute an
authority to any police officer to arrest the person
in respect of whom it is made and for any police or
prison officer to detail such person as a civil
prisoner.[45] The regulations under all the emergency
and security statutes made a similar provision. The
effect of this is thus to dispense with the ordinary
requirements for a lawful arrest.
Perhaps the most critical feature of the power
of detention and restriction is that it permits no
scope for challenge in the Court. The authority to
issue a detention order is in all cases, both under

the emergency legislation and under the preventive
detention laws, an absolutely discretionary one,
requiring only that the President or other detain-
ing authority be satisfied in a subjective sense
about the necessity for the order. Neither the
reasonableness of the President's satisfaction nor
the truth of the facts providing the grounds for
the order can therefore be enquired into by the
court, for otherwise the court might be substituting
its own subjective satisfaction for that of the
president.[46]
The reality of power lies more in the manner
and extent of its use rather than in its formal
existence. A repressive law is in itself objectionable even if it may not be used at all, but when it
is used extensively and oppressively, then tyranny
is created. The record in the use of security
powers is perhaps no better than that of our colonial predecessors; in some respects it is certainly
worse. Under such circumstances the constitutional
guarantees set out in preambulary form are a
nullity.
It is tempting to condemn out of hand the
republic for its extensive and oppressive use of
security powers. But it might be that the situation
with which it has to deal is peculiar. No one, of
course, not even the leaders themselves question
that these measures, particularly that of detention
without trial, are extremely dangerous to freedom
and the rule of law. It means /in the rather
telling words of President Nyerere/ that you are
restricting someone's liberty and making him suffer
materially and spiritually for what you think he
intends to do, or is trying to do, or for what you
believe he has done. Few things are more dangerous
to the freedom of a society than that. For freedom
is indivisible, and with such an opportunity open to
the Government of the day, the freedom of every
citizen is reduced. To suspend the rule of law
under any circumstances is to leave open the possibility of the grossest injustices being perpetrat-
ed.[47] In somewhat oratorical style, an editorial
in the Kenya Daily Nation had said:

> A Preventive Detention Act, by its very nature,
> degenerates into a sordid instrument of
> tyranny. It destroys the judiciary. It
> destroys the freedom of the press and academic
> freedom. It turns citizens into spies for the
> administration--it destroys their morals; and
> it might be used by some citizens to blackmail

others. It corrupts the morals of the whole
nation.[48]

This without more summarizes the reality of
security powers in Cameroon.

CONCLUSION

Doubtless an executive President who holds and
exercises executive power in his discretion and who
also controls the process of legislation arouses
fear of dictatorship. While instituting such
leadership, the constitution might also have established a cabinet and by this cast upon the
President an obligation to consult it. The influence of the cabinet, to which this consultation ex-
poses the President, might perhaps have created
conditions favourable to the minimisation of the
danger of personal rule, without however disabling
the President from acting unilaterally when speedy
action is needed or when disagreement among cabinet
members makes it necessary for him to impose his
will. Presidentialism in Cameroon has tended
towards dictatorship and tyranny not so much because of its great power as because of insufficient
constitutional political and social restraint upon
that power, and because conditions in Cameroon are
particularly favourable to the growth of dictatorship.

NOTES

1. U.S. Constitution.
2. French Republic Constitution, 1958.
3. Ibid., Art. 15.
4. B. O. Nwabueze, Presidentialism in Commonwealth Africa, p. 21.
5. Constitution of the United Republic of
Cameroon, 2 June 1972, Amendement of Law No. 40--
PJL--AN of June 5, 1975.
6. Louis W. Koenig, The Chief Executive
(1969), p. 20. See also Nwabueze, p. 26.
7. E. S. Corwin, The President, Office to
Powers, p. 12.
8. Madison, Federalist No. 48.
9. U.S. Constitution--Impeachment.
10. Nwabueze, p. 30.
11. Marbury v. Madison, 1 Cranch 137, 155
(1803).
12. Federalist No. 66.
13. House of Rep. Debate, Vol. III, Part III,
Oct. 1964, cols. 3881-3.
14. Carl J. Friedrich, The Impact of American
Constitutionalism Abroad (1966), p. 8.
15. Julius Nyerere, "How Much Power for a
Leader?" Africa Report, Vol. 7, No. 7, July 1962,
p. 7.
16. Cameroon Constitution (1972), Arts. 8-10.
17. Nwabueze, p. 108.
18. Ibid., p. 109.
19. Hirschfield, "The Reality of Presidential
Power," pp. 382.
20. Ibid., p. 381.
21. Constitution of Oct. 1, 1961, creating the
Federal Republic of Cameroon. See Constitutions of
the World, ed. by Albert P. Blaustein, p. 12.
22. Ibid., pp. 9-10.
23. In Sept. 1966, Cameroon adopted a one-party
system with the formation of the Cameroon National
Union which amalgamated all of the local and legal
parties. Note, however, that the Constitution
(1972) places no ban on the formation of political
parties as is generally believed. Rather, it
provides:

> Article 3(1) Political parties and groups may
> take part in elections. They shall be formed
> and shall exercise their activities in
> accordance with the Law.

24. Nwabueze, p. 231.

25. *Africa in Search of Democracy*, p. 40.

26. J. M. Lee Paul in *Ghana*. *Parl. Affairs 1962/63*, V. 16, p. 376.

27. The Federalist No. 73.

28. Bernard Schwartz, *A Commentary on the Constitution of the USA*, Part I, p. 26.

29. See Schwartz, *French Administrative Law and the Common Law World*, 89-92 (1954).

30. Corwin, *op. cit.*, *supra* n., p. 392.

31. Leading case in U.S. v. Eaton, 144 U.S. 677 (1892).

32. 343 U.S. at 589.

33. Id. at 587.

34. *Ibid.*

35. 4 Wall 2 (1866).

36. *Ibid.*, p. 120-21.

37. Duncan v. Kahanamokn, 327 U.S. 304 (1945), concurring judgment of Justice Murphy, pp. 325-35.

38. (1942) A. C. 206.

39. Corwin, p. 144.

40. Art. 1, § 9.

41. 4 Wall 2, p. 115. *See* *also* Luther v. Border, 7 How. at p. 62 (1849).

42. At p. 139.

43. Duncan, 327 U.S. 304.

44. C. Const. Art. 11(3).

45. Ex parte Milligan, *ibid*.

46. R v. Home Secretary, Ex parte Greene (1941), 3 AER 104 Ca., Liversideg v. Anderson (1941) 3 AER 338 (HL).

47. "Development and State Power," Speech inaugurating the University College, Dar Es Salaam, reprinted in Thomas Franck, *Comparative Constitutional Process* (1968), p. 231.

48. *Daily Nation* editorial, May 26, 1966.

6
One-Party Government and Political Development in Cameroon

J. F. Bayart

The political development of East Cameroun, formerly a trust territory under French rule, has followed an unusual course. Its national movement, the Union des Populations du Cameroun (UPC), in contrast to those in most English-speaking and some French-speaking African countries, failed to reap the fruits of its struggle for independence and was forced into illegality by the clumsiness and intransigence of the colonial administration. Through the latter's manoeuvring, the moderates were able to seize power: following M. Mbida in 1957, M. Ahidjo became Prime Minister in February 1958. The UPC, driven underground from 1955 onwards, carried on guerrilla opposition against what it regarded as puppet regimes; nor did its attitude change when in January 1960 Paris handed over power to M. Ahidjo at independence. Yet the part played by the UPC was substantial: its pressure forced the moderates to take over and progressively put into effect the nationalist programme: independence, the reunification of French and British Cameroon, and subsequently the establishment of a unitary state. Meanwhile the British trust territory of West Cameroon, following the lead of Mr. John Foncha, in 1961 rejected incorporation in Nigeria and opted for union with East Cameroun within the framework of a federal republic. From that time to 1972, Cameroon political life has resolved itself into two main and closely linked themes: the maximization of the power of M. Ahidjo, the president of the republic, and the growing centralization of government. From 1961 to 1966 M. Ahidjo's Union Camerounaise (UC) in East Cameroun (where multipartyism ceased to exist after 1962), and Mr. Foncha's Kamerun National Democratic Party (KNDP) in Western Cameroon worked in collaboration at the

federal level. After much political manoeuvring
and bargaining, the two leading parties decided to
merge in the Union Nationale Camerounaise (UNC),
sweeping away in the process such opposition as
remained. The single party--or in official parlance
the 'united' party--was born. It should be
appreciated that in East Cameroun the UNC is
essentially simply the continuation of the old UC
party; the analyses that follow of the UNC's
machinery and functions hold generally true for
both. In fact it is only in West Cameroon that
there has been a real break. Between 1968 and 1970
the extension of federal legislation, and the
discarding of Mr. Foncha and his colleagues as too
'particularist' in favour of the 'federalist' Mr.
Tandeng Muna; in 1971 the formation of a single
central trade union organization, L'Union Nationale
des Travailleurs Camerounais (UNTC)--these were the
chief stages leading up to the establishment in
1972 of a unitary state by way of a referendum. Is
this indeed the apotheosis of M. Ahidjo's regime,
with its much-vaunted outstanding degree of
stability? It is perhaps worth looking beneath the
surface appearance of overwhelming political support
for the regime to examine its roots, to take a look
at the hidden mass of the iceberg.

In the hope of avoiding the ethnocentricity
which too often vitiates the concept of political
development, I shall make use here of the definition proposed in a recent article by Rajni Kothari.
He distinguishes, following S. Huntington, between
'development' on the one hand and 'modernization'--
socio-economic growth taken as such--on the other.

> Development . . . consists of building these
> processes into well-defined and predictable
> structures and institutional systems and--we
> may add--into traditions of national and
> cultural life.[1]

Kothari's originality, as against Huntington
and Pye, lies in the importance he attaches to the
cultural tradition of societies affected by socio-
economic change: he speaks of political development when 'traditions of modernity' emerge; when
the established society and culture prove themselves capable of traditionalizing and assimilating
changes.[2]

In Cameroon the ideology of M. Ahidjo's regime,
based on the theme of nation-building, and which I
have accordingly labelled 'ethic of unity,'[3] sees a

contradiction between modernity on the one hand and
the political tradition inherited from the societies
of the pre-colonial and colonial periods on the
other: the UNC is contrasted with multi-partyism
and the old UPC, national unity with 'tribalism.'
But students of African politics have shown that
ethnic factors do play an important role and do
express present-day socio-economic realities; this
is surely just the kind of traditionalizing of
change that Kothari has in mind. The case of
tribalism would seem to give a priori validation to
my research hypothesis: that the 'ethic of unity'
and the political monolithism which it seeks to
justify are dysfunctional from the point of view of
genuine political development.

To test this formulation, it will be convenient to translate Kothari's theoretical proposi-
tions into an operational problem. I propose to
select arbitrarily four functional requirements
characterizing all categories and/or individuals
(viewed as sociological units): (1) integration
with a group; (2) the sense of identity; (3) expression of interests; and (4) the management (or
participation in the management) of the affairs
that most closely concern them. The satisfaction of
these four fundamental requirements results in an
'integrated' cultural/political personality
(according to Kothari's development model); their
non-satisfaction leads to the disorders which may
be designated by the broad and ambiguous concept
of 'alienation.' The content of these terms will
be defined more closely below.

Cameroon has experienced rapid and far-reaching
social change. Between 1965 and 1970, the urban
population grew from 16.4 per cent to 20.3 per cent
of the total; and while the numbers in the traditional sector of the economy dropped from 82 per
cent to 74 per cent of the active population, those
in the modern private sector and in administration
rose from 3 to 10 per cent and from 2 to 8 per cent
respectively. As E. W. Ardener has emphasized for
West Cameroon,[4] these changes do not affect the
urban sector alone; the expansion of export crops,
the building of main roads and railways, the
arbitrary re-grouping of villages, the transfer and
compulsory settlement of scattered groups (such as
the Pygmies in the east and the Kirdi mountain
peoples of the north)--all these things are
revolutionizing the whole fabric of rural society.
And, to a greater degree than in most African
states, the country's recent political experience

has been one of fear and tension, with civil war
from 1955 to 1964, and the UPC still able to create
incidents as late as 1970. All this economic,
social, and political change affected--indeed
completely broke down--the established modes of
meeting the four requirements referred to above. I
shall endeavour to show that the Ahidjo regime has
not succeeded in supplying anything to take their
place.

PARTICULARIST LOYALTIES AND JACOBINISM

    The model of development implied by the 'ethic
of unity' is of the Jacobin type: particularist
loyalties (identifications) are systematically
suppressed in the interest of national consciousness. Conscientious 'nation-building,' as enjoyed
by the regime's propaganda and prescribed by its
legislation, is posited as excluding attachment to
any other community--notably ethnic, regional or
social ones--and is naturally equated with support
for the government. The equation is none the less
real for being latent rather than explicit. On the
one hand 'there is established . . . a phenomenon
of identification between individual, party, people,
and nation:' on the other are ranged 'the forces
of evil,' the 'maquisards.'[5]
    In the first place, the authorities condemn
'tribalism' in all its forms. Officially, it is a
question only of 'transcending the tribe without
ceasing to acknowledge it.'[6] In East Cameroun
multi-partyism (which was often an expression of
ethnic pluralism) was suppressed in the interests
of the Union Camerounaise. In 1962 the great flood
of more or less spontaneous adhesions had nevertheless given to the dominant--and subsequently single--
party a submerged structure: within it were
discernible groups that had been dissolved; above
all, the basic local units remained ethnically
homogeneous.[7] On the basis of Article 6 of the
Party Rules the leaders of the UC required their
supporters to operate within the areas where they
lived, and seem to have been largely successful in
this. The measure however was limited in its
effects: the homogeneity of the cells is often no
more than the reflection of the composition of
quartiers and of villages. But the party deliberately declined to make systematic use of traditional structures and so to reconcile political with
ethnic identifications. Moreover, the authorities

162

tried to extinguish other manifestations of
"tribalism." The Law of June 12, 1967, banned "any
associations exhibiting an exclusively tribal or
clan character"--the definition of this (in Article
4) being singularly vague: (a) "any association
which claims to admit as members only those coming
from a named clan or tribe; (b) any association
which, without altogether excluding those from
other clans or tribes, in fact pursues an object
contrary to national unity." Here too, the legislation is only very imperfectly applied; nevertheless it runs counter to the political consciousness
of the Cameroonians. In 1970 M. Njiensi, Minister
of Youth and Sport, tried to detribalize football
in the name of "the national interest,"[8] arbitrarily reducing the number of teams; M. Ahidjo,
however, concerned over the resentment aroused by
this decision, disavowed him and postponed the
implementation of the reform. The campaign against
"tribalism" extended beyond the organizational level
to the suppression of particularist cultures--al-
though it is true that the regime claimed not to be
in contradiction to these.[9] But, on the one hand,
its effective achievements in this sphere affected
only a limited circle--that of the intellectuals.
And, on the other hand, they rested upon erroneous
ideological premises: those of Negritude, of "the
acknowledged unity of traditional civilizations,"[10]
of the possibility of synthesizing these in a
national culture: diversity was stubbornly denied.
The culture thus conceived is dead and reified--
culture in its museum and university sense. As its
secretary-general acknowledged,

> The mission /of Ngondo--the traditional
> assembly of the Duala/ is no longer limited
> exclusively to the protection of tradition
> . . . we are striving to act in such a way
> that 'Ngondo' shall be a veritable library of
> our culture.[11]

At the popular level the exigencies of practical politics are setting Cameroonians in conflict
with their customary values and artistic expressions,
or at least are de-vitalizing these traditions. The
state schools systematically discredit the vernacular languages--which do nevertheless transmit a
global cultural vision; thus the child is torn
between his own milieu and the political system.
The UNC is less intransigent than the schools, in
that it appears to have tolerated the use of these

vernaculars at lower levels, but it has given up
the publication of its bulletin in Ewondo,
Esamndzigi.[12]

The ambiguities of government cultural policy
are well illustrated by the occasion of the celebration of the annual festival of Ngondo, in July 1972.
The Duala took the opportunity of a recent controversy between the historian M. Dika Akwa, an old
UPC member, and Din Same, Secretary-General of the
Ngondo, to re-examine their historical and political
role. In a resolution addressed to the President,
they expressed rather more explicitly than in
previous years their desire for regeneration and
the reawakening of their consciousness as (coastal)
Sawa. But they knew that the local administrative
authorities suspected them of wanting to set up an
alternative political structure in collaboration
with a number of West Cameroonians, and were
advising Yaounde to abolish the Ngondo. So the
authors of the resolution made a point of stressing
their respect for national unity and for the regime;
it would even seem that the Duala, hitherto very
reticent towards the ruling single party, had
decided at this point to join the UNC en masse and
to protect their interests from within it. The
reply from the Presidency was cautious and somewhat
self-contradictory: while rejoicing in "any
initiative directed towards the development and
strengthening of militancy within the UNC," it also
recalled the 1967 law on ethnic associations in
order to ensure that traditional forms of expression
which "contributed to the building up of a genuine
national culture and which could offer incentives
that would facilitate the mobilization of the masses
in favour of national objectives" should be contained within the framework of the party, "so that
they should effectively serve the cause of unity
and national construction." Here too, particularism
was reified; it was acceptable only insofar as it
contributed to national unity, not in itself. The
Catholic weekly, L'Effort Camerounais, was in no
doubt as to the meaning of the President's reply:
it was an "exhortation for the whole of the
Cameroonian peoples to die to their clans in order
to be born as a nation."[13]

The contradiction is no less acute as between
the present regime and the colonial tradition. In
Eastern Cameroun, we have seen multi-partyism condemned; the past role of the UPC is denied or
forgotten: yet the phase of the movement for
liberation from colonial rule has in fact left deep

marks on popular political culture and remains vivid in people's memories. Above all, the integration of Western Cameroon in a predominantly French-speaking Federation has plunged that territory into a serious crisis of identity: the 'harmonization' between the two federated states has in large part turned out to mean simply the erosion of Western particularism.[14] The establishment in 1972 of a unitary republic heralds its eventual disappearance, and the economic justifications invoked are in reality secondary:

> It is, undoubtedly, a matter of providing the nation with institutional structures capable of giving the greatest possible effectiveness to its will for progress. In the final analysis, it is also a matter of completing a cycle of national history: that which, starting from independence and passing through reunification, must lead to the apotheosis of total national unity.[15]

Western Cameroon has already ceased to exist as a single entity and has been divided into two provinces, that of the South West around Buea and that of the North West around Bamenda. It is true that the President has undertaken to respect bilingualism: but such an undertaking, coming from his lips, elicits from the West Cameroonians the wry rejoinder "bilingual in French . . ."[16] The predominance of English in the western state is generally respected: but a number of national institutions are openly unilingual (such as the army) or are only very imperfectly bilingual (such as the university and the territorial administration).

Thus the regime makes no attempt to reconcile tradition and modernity. Moreover, the latent crisis of identity which it is provoking is the more serious in that it has not been able--or willing--to supply substitute identities of a "modern" type. The "ethic of unity" denies the existence of social classes in Africa and rejects all consciousness of class, whether of worker or peasant. The idea of building up the UNC, as at one time envisaged, on socio-professional foundations seems to have been abandoned for this reason.[17] The disappearance of overt opposition has inhibited the political loyalties/identifications which were in evidence on the eve of and immediately following independence: the "UN-ist" (like the "UPC-ist") was often a

genuine militant: it is significant that no such
familiar term is applied to the UNC supporter of
today. A national consciousness is however emerging. M. Ahidjo is anxious that it shall give birth
to a Cameroonian cultural personality.[18] But is
not any such national cultural synthesis an
illusion when it is achieved by the suppression of
particularisms and an acculturation forcibly
imposed from above?[19]

THE EXPRESSION OF INTERESTS

It should be made clear that I am not discussing here the expression of interests in a socio-
economic perspective--in terms of social stratification, of the lowering or raising of living stand-
ards--but from a political standpoint; that is, in
terms of the mechanisms of communication, and of
the political-cultural forms which such communication takes.
As the authorities argue for loyalty to the
national cause over against "tribalism," so also
they invoke the general interest to withstand local
and sectional interests; "Does not History teach us
that national unity is always incompatible with
private interests?"[20] This Jacobin myth clearly
does not dispose of economic exploitation and social
stratification; in working to the advantage of the
most favoured groups, it in fact strengthens their
position. The foreign--particularly the French--
industrial circles of Douala maintain a more or
less continuous dialogue with the secretariat-
general of the Presidency through the medium of
Minister M. Sengat Kuo. After a long period of
disillusionment with the economic policy of the
regime, they have since 1971 been able to secure a
renewal of interest on the part of the President,
and the setting up of official co-ordinating
bodies.[21] The civil service, omnipresent, dominat-
ing everything, and held together by an esprit de
corps that openly exalts the regime, is in a position of evident material and political privilege.
The army, though less conspicuous, has nevertheless
for several years occupied a similar position. On
the other hand, the situation of the national
bourgeoisie is ambiguous: the "planned liberalism"
which is the economic doctrine of the regime leaves
it in theory a part to play; in practice it is held
in check by the power of the administration and by
the apprehension in which the Fang and the Muslims

hold that most enterprising of ethnic groups, the Bamileke.[22]

The white-collar workers, manual workers, and peasants for their part no longer have available specific channels through which to express their demands. The main trade union organizations have never managed to establish roots in the rural sector. It is true that, immediately after independence, there were a number of professional organizations functioning locally, of which the best-organized was L'Action Paysanne of Gaston Medoux. This was attacked by M. Assale when he was prime minister (it was in competition with his own political and economic "machine" in the cocoa zone); and it was from 1962 absorbed by the Union Camerounaise, which was unable however effectively to take its place. Today, the farmers can put forward their interests only when administrative tours take place; prefects and sub-prefects have become their sole representatives, particularly within the framework of the regional planning commissions.[23] Manual and white-collar workers do have their own organizations, but the autonomy of these is purely nominal. Their internal divisions, the fear of being labelled as belonging to the subversive camp, the political eclipse of M. Assale in 1965, have steadily weakened the trade unions. The unification of the three main organizations, which M. Ahidjo had called for at the Congress of Garoua in 1969, was effected in 1971. The elections of trade union officials have in effect been suspended since 1967; single candidacies, controlled by the departmental offices of the UNC, will for the future rob them of any significance. The new main union organization, the Union Nationale des Travailleurs Camerounais (UNTC) will be tightly bound to the party: unification has taken place under the auspices of a joint committee of the unions and the Political Bureau of the UNC. The regional organizing committees of the local unions also include a representative of the BPN of the UNC (along with the Regional Inspecteur du Travail and trade union representatives). It is the same with the Assessment Committee, which controls the management of the central body's finances. In private those responsible for the government's social policy do not conceal that trade union unification will make it easier to discipline the world of labour. However, collaborationist trade unionism has for a long time prevailed over more challenging attitudes; no professional organization has launched a strike

167

since 1960--if one excepts the National Federation
of Private Instructors working in the denominational
schools who went on strike in 1968 and 1970. In
these circumstances the unions are in no position
to carry out their role of communication: they do
not put forward the expectations of the workers in
relation to the public authorities, and they do not
explain government decisions to the workers. Thus
in 1971 for example, the coming into force of a
new system of wage classification provoked serious
discontent among the manual and white-collar workers
of Douala, who had not been properly informed: the
reduction in the number of categories of wage
earners convinced them that they were being down-
graded; there were frequent misunderstandings over
questions of seniority of service and qualifications. There were also a number of the genuine
consequences of this reform measure which caused
dissatisfaction among the workers. Generally
speaking, they were expecting a more substantial
rise in wages. More specifically, in the textile
industry, the abolition of piece-work led to an
actual decrease in workers' earnings, despite the
establishment of a compromise system of payment.
Moreover the social climate was bad for reasons
specific to particular enterprises; in the Régie de
Chemins de Fer Camerounais (Regifercam), for
instance, the unions failed to express in the form
of demands a discontent which was of long standing
and of which they were well aware.[24] The last
resort of the workers thus continued to be strike
action. Yet the 1967 Code du Travail prescribed
compulsory procedures of conciliation and then of
arbitration before such action could be taken, and
this implied the participation of professional
bodies. Accordingly in 1971 manual and white-collar
workers of Douala, in order to voice their griev-
ances and their aspirations, were obliged to in-
fringe the law: these "wild-cat" strikes were
regarded as subversive, and were all the more
vigorously repressed in that the authorities were
able to invoke the state of emergency maintained on
the coast since the days of "UPC-ist" terrorism.
The instigators of the strikes were interrogated by
the police and their homes were searched; despite
official denials, it seems that some of them were
given prison sentences--although these did not
exceed one month. (In the Regifercam, the solidarity of the workers and the manifest justice of their
demands made any repression impossible.) The position of the students at the Federal University of

Yaounde is much the same as that of the wage-
earners; in 1969 they boycotted mid-course examinations in order to register a number of demands;
some of these demands were in fact met in the
following year, but in the meantime the most
dynamic of the leaders of the student organizations
had been expelled from the Faculty, and the
Association of Christian Students had been dissolved. At the end of 1969, the Fédération
Nationale des Etudiants Camerounais (FENEC), linked
to the UNC, was openly given the monopoly of student
representation. As it proved unable to contain the
student discontent and agitation at the beginning
of the 1972 academic year, it is not impossible
that the party will take direct action to establish
local cells within the university.

The same means, the ethic of unity and organizational monolithism, are employed to hold ethnic
and/or regional interests in check. Although the
distribution of posts--in particular of ministerial
posts--does to a very small extent reflect these
interests, the regime in theory rejects the principle of ethnic/regional representation.[25] At the
local level, tribal or clan rivalries project themselves naturally on to the political scene; multi-
partyism has been succeeded by electoral competition
within the party, on the occasion of re-elections
within its local units. The ethic of unity regards
these as simply struggles for influence and ignores
their socio-economic content ("tribalism" and
"personal animosities," are often no more than a
form of words).[26] Thus in Mungo, for example, the
departmental office at the UNC section--as also the
Catholic bishopric--has been the object of a bitter
rivalry between the local people and Bamileke
settlers and traders. At the national level, it is
the West Cameroonians who seem to have suffered
most from government Jacobinism: in 1963, the
decision in London to discontinue the preferential
tariffs given to bananas from English-speaking
Cameroon was particularly bitterly resented at Buea,
where the political leaders hotly criticized federal
diplomacy, in the belief that they would have
obtained a better deal if the constitution had
allowed them to negotiate directly with the British
government; subsequently they complained of the
fact that British and American aid was being cut
back--on the grounds of the growing centralization
of the federation.[27] English-speaking Cameroonians
held generally that the federal institutions and
political processes did not allow them to give

effect to their regional interests. A key instance
of this was the 1972 referencum on the unitary
state; the issue was one which primarily concerned
them, but the results of the referendum were determined by the demographic disparity between the two
regions. The unitary structure which has since
been set up will be no more effective in assuring
their representation. As J. Benjamin has implicitly shown, the English-speaking region is to
Cameroon as Quebec is to Canada. The case of West
Cameroun shows, even more clearly than that of the
trade unions--self-determination (autogestion) is a
distant ideal--the correlation between the expression of interests and the distribution of power.[28]

THE DISTRIBUTION OF POWER

The effects of the stranglehold which we have
seen at the level of the expression of local and
sectional interests are aggravated in Cameroon by
the growing--and now almost absolute--concentration
of power in the hands of the state.[29] It is not so
much the UNC that is strengthened by this process
of centralization as the territorial administration
and in a lesser degree the police.
Local democracy has been steadily emptied of
its content. The Cameroun chiefs are still, as in
the colonial period, closely subjected to the
administration; they are no more than its auxiliaries. Only the notables of the North, Foulbes or
Muslims of pagan origin, have managed to regain some
part of the autonomy granted to them by the colonial
power within the framework of 'indirect rule'--which
M. Ahidjo's government for a time took away from
them: but their own political practice is auto-
cratic or authoritarian rather than democratic.
Again, the Law of July 7, 1966, and the two
Laws of March 1, 1967, put an end to municipal
liberties by handing over to the government the
task of nominating mayors for the three types of
municipality (sometimes from outside the municipal
council in the case of mixed rural communes); the
executive power over the towns of Yaounde, Douala,
and Nkongsamba has thus been put in the hands of
government nominees.

In deciding, admits one observer (who is in
favour of the new measures), that the chief of
the municipal executive shall for the future
be nominated in all the communes de plein

exercise, the law is directed in fact at the suppression of this type of commune, even though the name is retained.[30]

At the same time, the representative character of the municipal deliberative bodies was reduced; proportional gave way to majority voting; candidates had to be members of a party (in other words the UNC); in the small groupements and the commercial quartiers of the rural communes sections carrying only a single seat were suppressed as being conducive to "clan-ism." For the elections of May 28, 1967, it was the departmental offices of the UNC which maintained control of the candidacies, in collaboration with the prefectural authorities and under the formal control of the Provisional Comité Directeur; and it was they that subsequently nominated the presidents and vice-presidents of the municipal councils. It is significant that the local cells had no say in the choice of candidates, since the government was unwilling that those elected should represent particular quartiers. The role of the municipal councils, confronted by this supervisory authority (basically that of the Ministry of the Interior up to 1972, and now that of the Ministry of Territorial Administration) and by the presence of the government delegates, is very much circumscribed. "Of communal democracy," we may conclude with Ph. Lippens, "there remains no more than the existence of a decentralized administrative organ with financial administrative autonomy."[31] In West Cameroon Tandeng Muna's government, which since 1968 has been anxious to weaken the natural allies of KNDP sympathies within the UNC, has undermined the "local councils" freedom of action by interfering with appointments to them.[32]

The situation is not substantially different at the regional level. Regional division (formerly into six federal "inspections," today into seven provinces) is no more than administrative "de-concentration." West Cameroon was alone in enjoying for a time--thanks to the federal structure--some degree of autonomy. Yet that region quickly came to regard this measure of autonomy as inadequate, and in particular complained that it was largely bypassed in the working out of federal policy. In September 1964, on the occasion of a meeting between the UC and the West Cameroon KNDP, the Anglophone delegation requested that the constitution should be revised before the end of the transition period, and more specifically demanded that the role of the Council of Ministers should be enlarged: but to no purpose.[33] The victory of Muna's "federalists" over Jua's "particularists," followed by the formation of a unitary republic, set the seal on the process of centralization and dispossession; English-speaking Cameroonians are still represented in the ruling circles of the regime, but West Cameroon no longer conducts its own affairs as a distinct entity.

The concentration of power is in some measure a response to obvious dysfunctions--the administrative and financial cumbrousness of the federal institutions, the deplorable mismanagement and fantastic corruption of the municipalities and co-operatives; but it is also a reflection of the regime's aspiration towards absolute unity and the civil service's ambition for power.[34] Potentially this evolution is itself dysfunctional from the point of view of political development. The impact of the ordinary Cameroonian on his most pressing problems and interests is severely limited; he is losing (or has already lost) control over his daily life; the socio-economic changes which are taking place seem all the more incomprehensible to him. These changes, planned and carried out entirely without reference to him, do violence to him in an almost physical sense; the evictions in the urban areas, the regrouping of villages, arbitrarily determined and applied, are only the most striking examples. It is true that the institutions which the state has taken over were in any case probably ill-adapted to their cultural environment; local democracy should have expressed itself on the basis of the village and not of the commune,[35] the co-operative should have been discarded in favour of some other less western-based structure. But it should be a matter of urgency to restore--or to give--to Cameroonians some rights that will make them feel less helpless in the face of modernity. As an answer to this need, the solution of one-party government has up to the present proved a sham. "A militant is an agent and, as such, he must not indulge in personal initiatives."[36] In the event, this exhortation by M. Arouna Njoya, sometime vice-president of the Union Camerounaise, carried the day over the appeals in favour of popular participation in economic development put forward by other leaders, M. Ahidjo among them. The local units are not centres of decision-making--no rights are

recognized in them--nor are they in general effective auxiliaries of the civil service; at all
levels the substance of power is in the hands of
the administrative machine.[37]

INTEGRATION AND SECURITY

Socio-economic change is a disturbing experience. In Cameroon there have also been political
changes: the adventure of independence, the phase
of terrorism and, in West Cameroon, the anxieties
aroused by reunification. The regime did succeed
in bringing about security through the establishment of civil order: but at the same time, the
establishment of monolithism brought back afresh
the atmosphere of fear.[38] Laws have been passed
giving the public authorities the power to define
absolutely and arbitrarily what is legal and what
is legal and what is subversive. Thus, according
to the Ordinance of March 12, 1962, (the basic text
of the regime):

> Whosoever shall give utterance to or propagate
> false reports, news or rumours, or tendentious
> commentaries on accurate news when such news,
> rumour or commentary may tend to the damaging
> of the public authorities, shall be
> punished . . .

In 1963 Emah Ottu, one of the ex-UPC leaders
who has subsequently joined the UC, was placed
under house arrest for having been "convicted of
subversive action," in that he had

> brought serious accusations against other
> Camerounians--accusations which, if not a
> threat to public order, were at least of
> substantial moral and material prejudice to
> those Camerounians.

As Ahidjo acknowledged at the time, "the word
'subversion' covers a great many activities."[39]
Who is subversive? Who is not subversive? Ahidjo
alone knows, in that he is the source of all power.
Party membership confers no physical or psychologi-
call security. The leaders of the UC and, after
them though to a lesser degree those of the UNC, in
exhorting their militants to vigilance against
"internal opposition," "dubious attachments," and
"double-crossers," have maintained this atmosphere

of distrust and insecurity within the very heart of
the organization. In this light, the rites of the
'anti-terrorist cadi' that were organized on a
large scale in the west of the country take on all
the character of exorcisms. In a regime which has
suppressed all competition in the field of
political life, everything has become political:
the Ngondo celebration, the schism within the
Presbyterian church, funeral processions, even
family gatherings.

     In consequence of these feelings of general
guilt there comes about a need for integration with
a community that can offer security--an aspiration
nurtured by physical, social, and cultural
déracinement. In its own way the ethic of unity,
being single-minded and therefore integrationist,
does provide a response to this, but it cannot be a
real substitute for integration within a limited
group. In the latter sense ethnic associations are
admirable communities: they are at once economic
(mutual aid, investment), social (high entrance
subscription linked to an initiation rite), and
existential (common origin, festivals, age sets).
The religious denominations, thanks to their
missionary spirit and to the militancy they inspire,
and in spite of the internal crisis dividing them,
also instill into their members a strong group
consciousness. It is otherwise with the local units
of the party organization--something that was bound
to happen from the moment when the UNC became a
community without limits, a "party/people." Since
there is no "out-group" there is no longer an "in-
group." The annual party subscription seems often
to be regarded as a supplementary tax; it is the
same with trade union subscriptions, now auto-
matically deducted at source by the employer.
Ultimately party membership cards and official
identity papers merge into a single category in the
popular mind. The leaders maintain that the local
cell is "the basic unit where the members should
live in a quasi-family relationship, on a permanent
footing."[40] In practice, although the party rules
provide for the holding of meetings at least every
fortnight, many local cells do not meet more than
two or three times a year--when they do so to
organize the processions which mark every festival
occasion of the regime. Moreover, the effectiveness
of political involvement and the group consciousness
of the militants are diluted by the weight of
numbers.[41] And the meetings of these local committees are taken up with interminable personal

quarrels. The Garoua Conference found itself
obliged to appoint arbitrators for the disputes at
section, sub-section, and local unit level. In
future, "the Political Bureau will not take cog-
nizance of quarrels and disputes between militants
or local units except on appeal."[42] In the
machinery of the UNC as in the plays of Sartre,
"L'Enfer c'est les autres." In short, the party--
save for a few of its cadres--is of little use in
fulfilling this function of social integration.[43]

POLITICAL ALIENATION IN CAMEROON

The regime seeks to control the whole of social
life. But, as we have seen, the structures which
it builds are only very poor working substitutes
from the point of view of the four requirements
under discussion. New social fabric is not being
legislated into being; it is weaving itself gradually from the depths of the crisis. As Durkheim
once observed, "This kind of operation cannot be
devised from the seclusion of an office desk; it
can only emerge step by step from within itself."[44]
Mr. Ahidjo's political regime does not combine the
conditions needed for such a social re-structuring--
or rather perhaps re-invention. The widespread
sense of fear and guilt inhibits all initiative.[45]
Nothing can be done outside the party, but the
party does nothing. American political scientists,
notably Pye and Huntington, have made pluralism
into a dimension of political development: their
work however is marked by a strong Anglo-Saxon
"democentrism"--to use A. L. Madian's expression.[46]
This adaptation to socio-economic change can take
place through many kinds of institution, processes,
and patterns of behaviour. It would be better,
rather than talking of associations or of intermediate groups--specifically western concepts--to
use the term "small political communities" (petits
collectifs politiques), a concept which embraces
equally social structures that are of imported
origin (parties, syndicates, elections), indigenous
(associations or originaires, palavers, bands), and
even informal social relations (gatherings,
expeditions).[47] In Cameroon there are formidable
obstacles to the formation of any similar social
units: in police surveillance, and in the extension of the practice of requiring preliminary
authorization to the press, to meetings and in
particular to associations of any kind. The Law of

June 12, 1967, is effectively designed to bring
about in the long term the steady extinction of
freedom of association, by providing--subtly but
inexorably--for the assimilation of autonomous
groups into the structures of the regime. In a more
general sense, political monolithism is intolerant
of anomic and deviant groups; yet the important
contribution of these to social change has often
been stressed by perceptive sociologists.[48] The
regime established by Mr. Ahidjo is a poor response
to the need for integration and identification, for
the expression and meeting of interests. It frus-
trates the adaptation of the Cameroonians to
modernization; it is dysfunctional from the point
of view of political development.

The present tendency of political science is
perhaps to fight shy of the concept of alienation.[49]
Yet such an attitude makes impossible the use of
the only research techniques whereby the serious
study of the Cameroon political culture can be
undertaken--the application of a detailed question-
naire to a limited sample and/or interviews in
depth. By the ambitious term "political alienation," I will therefore limit myself to pointing
out certain features indicating the gap that has
grown up between the Cameroonians and economic/
political modernity. And I shall confine myself to
an impressionistic description of these features.

The Cameroonians do seem broadly to accept,
and to interiorize, the ethic of unity.[50] The
provisional necessity of one-party government is
admitted, a negative view of politics is widespread,
a national consciousness is expressed, the
authorities and the regime are in general validated,
the western-based modernization is not on the whole
rejected. These undoubted facts may seem to contradict my conclusions. Yet there are a number of
tensions, consciously experienced, which characterize this political culture: the frustration of
the West Cameroonians at the growing centralization;
of the intellectuals and social cadres, robbed of
all initiative; of the Bamileke, constantly suspect
for their economic dynamism; and of others.

The spirit of opposition is not wholly dead.
While the students outside the country and the
Duala have appeared over the past year to rally en
masse to the regime, it must not be forgotten that
in some quarters there is talk of Mr. Foncha
quitting the UNC and forming a rival party of a
Christian Democrat complexion; and that the brusque
and unforeseen suppression of federalism was just

the thing to give it fresh impetus. In a more
general way, there are substitutes for political
pluralism making their appearance: the religious
organizations; the personal popularity of Mgr.
Ndongmo, leader of the Catholic liberals; and football (which under pressure of popular opinion
refused to be 'unified' by the authorities in 1970).
Movements of rejection have asserted themselves:
thus the Jehovah's Witnesses, 50,000 strong and
increasing fast since they were proscribed for boycotting the 1970 elections, are probably to be
regarded as an expression of protest both against
imported civilization and against the regime. This
would explain why they have taken particular hold
in the west and on the coast, notably among the
Bamileke--a group often guarded in its relations
with the UNC and one particularly affected by social
change. The persistence or aggravation of the
socio-economic disequilibrium prevalent in Africa
today--such as delinquency and prostitution--also
demonstrate the inability of the regime to take up
the challenge of modernization. The ordinances of
September 28, 1970, threaten these deviant movements
with heavy penalties--even death; but they fail to
go to the roots of the trouble.

In any case, from a theoretical point of view,
the non-consciousness of alienation (or in Marxist
terms, false consciousness) cannot dispose of the
fact of alienation. An attempt at analysis--or
rather an outline analysis--in depth is therefore
needed, to delineate this concealed state of
alienation. The inability of the regime to nurture
an integrated cultural/political personality will
then become clear. It is in fact developing vertical relationships (of a family type) at the cost of
horizontal ones (with groups of similar social and/
or biological structure):[51] we have seen how the
petits collectifs politiques (in particular age-
groups, trade unions, autonomous youth movements)
have degenerated to the advantage of political
authority and particularly of administrative power.
I use the term 'degeneration' less in a develop-
mentalist perspective--which is dangerously ethno-
centric--than in its psycho-analytical sense; in
place of egalitarian relations between the
Cameroonian and his tribe, his age-set, his
association, there is substituted a relationship of
dependence on power, liable to acquire the projec-
tion of parental images.[52] In fact, power is in
considerable measure personalized in the popular
mind: not only Mr. Ahidjo but also, in the rural

context, the prefect and sub-prefect assume the
character of father-figure.[53] The contradiction
between rallying to the President and attachment to
tradition is experienced and is a source of guilt
feeling:

> The voice of the child-people echoes with pleas
> for your help and your pardon.
> With beating heart, in shame and in confusion,
> we come to bear true witness to our demagogy,
> Only you do we hear, for sky and earth no
> longer remain unaware of your vocation.
> Give counsel to us, as a father to his erring
> children
> And above all do not deal with us according to
> the measure of our errors and our trans-
> gressions.[54]

In another aspect, and related to the father-
figure in a way that requires clearer definition,
there are mother-figures--in the concepts of
national independence, reunification, national
unity, and the UNC. This relationship of dependence
means an infinite extension of the role of the
public authorities: the Cameroonians look to them
for everything.[55] Thus for example the rural
people, when the administrative tours come round,
recount their "doleances"--a term which admirably
expresses the role of dependence--and confine
themselves to a strictly passive attitude; making
no effort to address themselves to their own needs
by the application of their own human resources.
The vertical links might appear to be solid
ones, for in theory parents do not betray their
children.[56] In practice, however, the authority
cannot live up to this absolute expectation, and
this provokes in the Cameroonian the sense of
desertion:

> The militant often has faith in the Party and
> believes with conviction that through its agen-
> by everything will go well. But instead the
> militant finds himself in fact neglected by
> the upper levels of the Party; the /procès
> verbaux/ and the reports appear not to be
> studied, and doleances are not given considera-
> tion.[57]

Such feelings of abandonment are of course disturbing and set up reactions of resentment or guilt.[58]

The political alienation revealed by these
symptoms is not wholly to be attributed to the
regime. Other factors are involved: external
economic conditions (which subject the farmer to
the harsh and distant dictates of world market
forces), the influence in the past of the colonial
power (which helped to instill this passive subject-
mentality), the cultural heritage (in which the
entrenchment of chiefly authority seems to have its
roots). The present regime does however perpetuate
this alienation in a context of rapid socio-
economic change and on a national scale. It is true
that the alienation is not equally felt in every
sector of the socio-political system; it is worse
for the West than for the East Camerounians; for the
peasants, manual workers and white-collar workers
than for the officials; for the masses and for the
grass-root militants than for the notables and the
cadres of the UNC. Nevertheless, there emerges
overall the model of a frustrating political
culture, which could be labelled as Jacobin--by
analogy of course with the case of France: a
strong national consciousness, the suppression of
local and sectional loyalties and interests, a
relationship of dependence between those administered and a highly centralized power.[59] Contrary
to the view often postulated by American political
scientists, national integration is not necessarily
an indication of political development.

BY WAY OF CONCLUSION

It remains to determine what is really to
blame for this alienation. Is it one-party government and monolithism as such, or is it the form
which they take in Cameroon? All criticisms of
one-party government tend to irritate African
ideologists, who regard them simply as ethnocentric:
but the thesis of a specifically "African" kind of
democracy which they cherish is generally greeted
with scepticism. Rightly or wrongly? In Cameroon,
the quickening of urban life in the Nylon quartier
of Douala, a number of ethnic associations, and in
the rural sector the Zones d'Action Prioritaires
Integries (ZAPI), seem to provide examples, as yet
partial and incomplete, of political development
within the framework of one-party government, that
are highly original by comparison with imported
European solutions. Their most interesting feature
would seem to be the displacing of the vertical

relationships between those administered and the
central authority by the formation of autonomous
decision-making centres which nevertheless continue
to respect the legality of the regime; thus for
example the inhabitants of Nylon have taken over the
management of their quartier, making use of the
local units of the UNC as a structural framework.
If the success of such experiments is confirmed,
the definition of the degree of pluralism necessary
to political development could be made clear. In
short, the number of competing social structures
should be regarded as less significant than the
diffusion of power.

The Cameroon case-history suggests a second
research hypothesis. There would seem to be a contradiction between what appear to be the overwhelming support and resources of the ruling
African one-party governments, and the real depth
of popular following that they enjoy. Subconscious-
ly at least, people can hardly remain attached to
regimes which cannot satisfy their underlying
desire for integration, for a sense of identity,
for self-expression and for the care of their
interests. They will accordingly regard their disappearance with indifference, or more probably, in
their gnawing sense of abandonment, with positive
pleasure. In the end they may even take the
initiative in overthrowing them: as in Upper Volta
and Dahomey in 1966, in Madagascar in 1972. But,
as prisoners to their own role of dependence, they
will succeed only in establishing new vertical
relationships, and will make no attempt to bring
about a qualitative political change.[60] This
explains how it is that apparently solidly-estab-
lished regimes such as those of Ghana, Mali and
Madagascar have suddenly crumbled or been over-
thrown--only to be succeeded by similar authoritarian models and by the continued suppression of
any genuinely radical political innovation.

NOTES

1. R. Kothari, "Tradition and Modernity Revisited," Government and Opposition, 3 (Summer 1968), p. 287. Author's italics.

2. By "traditional" I understand the social, political, and cultural system prior to the establishment of the one-party state (1962 in East Cameroun, 1966 in West Cameroon). African research has conclusively demolished the primitivist and static view of "traditional" societies. On the one hand pre-colonial societies certainly experienced profound changes: on the other, the idea of tradition equally encompasses the colonial period-- the contribution of the colonizers, the nationalist era. See S. Amin, "Sous-developpement et dependance en Afrique noire contemporaire," Partisans, 64, March-April 1972, p. 19; and A. Zolberg, Creating Political Order: the party-states of West Africa (Chicago, 1966), pp. 143-5.

3. The central theme of unity in the ideology of the regime is sufficiently explicit to warrant my preference for the concept of ethic rather than that of ethos--as denoting the whole body of both rules and non-formulated beliefs that regulate the conduct of members of a society. Cf. E. Banfield, The Moral Basis of a Backward Society (Glencoe, 1958).

4. E. W. Ardener, "Social and Demographic Problems of the Southern Cameroons Plantation Area," in A Southall, ed., Social Change in Modern Africa (London, 1961), p. 95. These figures are quoted from Direction de la Statistique et de la Comptabilite Nationale, Evaluations et projections demographiques en République federale du Cameroun (Yaounde, 1970).

5. "Le Secret de la réussite," L'Unité, 230, week October 1-8, 1971, p. 4. L'Unité is the official organ of the UNC (and was formerly that of the UC). A. Ahidjo, Contribution a la construction nationale (Paris, 1964), p. 28. My italics.

6. M. Ahidjo, "Discours de Quebec," Bulletin quotidien d'information de l'agence camerounaise de presse (ACAP), September 13-14, 1970.

7. Cf. Sadou Daodou, "Tribalisme au niveau des militants comme au niveau des responsables," Premier Conseil Nationale de l'Union Camerounaise, tenu a Yaounde du 14 au 20 avril 1963 (J. Colombet, 1964), p. 13 sqq.

8. Discours de Douala, ACAP, September 12, 1970.

9. See esp. Mr. Ahidjo's speeches to the Ebolowa Congress of the UC (July 1962), and to the Garoua Congress of UNC (March 1969).

10. Proposition No. 5 of the UNC Charter (adopted in 1969), week September 1-10, 1971, p. 1.

11. Interview with M. Din Same, Douala, July 8, 1971, 1 p. mimeograph. My italics.

12. The use of vernacular languages in black Africa has met with considerable obstacles. See e.g. P. Alexandre, Langues et langage en Afrique noire (Paris, 1967), Ch. 4; and R. Santerre, "Linguistique et politique au Cameroun," Journal of African Languages, 8, 3 (1969), pp. 153-9.
In Douala, however, the (Catholic) College Libermann-though with no official encouragement--offers its pupils the choice of one or even two vernacular languages as an additional subject, with the idea of giving the children a genuine African cultural foundation.

13. "Du clan a la nation," L'Effort Camerounais, 827, August 13, 1972, p. 1 (my italics). For the texts of the Ngondo resolution and the reply from the Presidency see ACAP, August 2, 1972.

14. See W. R. Johnson, The Cameroon Federation (Princeton, 1970), p. 426; and J. Benjamin, "Le Sort des Camerounais occidentaux, 1961-1969" (Paris, doctoral thesis, Foundation Nationale des Sciences Politiques, 1970), p. 442.

15. Speech by Mr. Ahidjo to the National Federal Assembly, La Presse du Cameroun, May 9, 1972, p. 5. My italics.

16. Quoted by Benjamin, Camerounais occidentaus, p. 325.

17. From personal interviews. It seems however that there do exist some cells of officials. And socio-economic criteria do seem to have been a factor in the effectiveness with which the UNC was built up: it was less effective amongst civil servants, intellectuals, and probably manual workers than among the mass of the people. Source: sectional reports of the Congress of Garoua, 1969.

18. A. Ahidjo, Nation et développement dans l'unité et la justice (Paris, 1969), pp. 14 sqq.

19. In France, the Jacobin concept of development flowed into a Parisian-aristocratic-bourgeois culture labelled "national culture," and killed the popular (regional, peasant, worker) cultures. See R. Lafont, Decoloniser en France: les régions face a l'Europe (Paris, 1971), p. 197.

20. Ahidjo, Contribution a la construction nationale, p. 28.

21. Note de Service No. 24/PRF, of December 3, 1971, threw open to representatives of the private sector the Comité Technique Interministeriel pour les Affaires Economiques et Financieres, set up in June 1970. For the difficulties of the private sector and its contacts with the Presidency, see esp. "Rapport moral du President," in Procès-verbal de la 43 session de l'Assemblée generale ordinaire du G.I. CAM, 13 december 1971, pp. 9-11.

22. For Mongo Beti (a nationalized Frenchman, and fierce opponent of the regime) M. Ahidjo's government, in the pay of western or Lebanese/ Syrian economic interests, is actually bound to oppose itself to the formation of a genuine national bourgeoisie. In this perspective the author analyses the arrest and conviction in 1970 or Mgr. Ndongo, bishop of Nkongsamba and himself a Bamileke. See Main basse sur le Cameroun: autopsie d'une decolonisation (Paris, 1972). His argument seems to me to be carried too far.

23. See Ph. Lippens, "La démocratie economique et la democratie sociale au Cameroun," (Paris, doctoral thesis in public law, 1967), p. 181.

24. See "Les Impressions d'un manoeuvre," L'Effort Camerounais, 687, May 4, 1969, p. 2. The author, Luc Mebenga, was a militant of the USSC-- the Christian trade union--and personnel delegate.

25. Ahidjo, Nation et développement, pp. 20, 21.

26. Besides the well-known studies of P. Mercier, I. Wallerstein, and G. Balandier, see S. Bonzon, "Modernisation et conflits tribaux en Afrique noire," Revue Française de Science Politique, 17, 5 (October 1967), pp. 862-88; and T. Yannopoulos, "Luttes de classes et guerre nationale au Nigeria," Ibid., 18, 3 (June 1968), pp. 508-23.

27. Benjamin, Camerounais occidentaux, pp. 95- 100. This sense of frustration is particularly interesting from a political point of view in that West Cameroun seems to have benefited economically from the reunification, and that its development is heavily subsidized from the federal budget.

28. G. Lavau's concept of fonction tribunitienne (see "Le P.C.F. dans le systeme politique francais" in Le Communisme en France, Paris, 1969) comes close to that of the expression of interests. In Cameroun the party may take on this function at local administrative levels--e.g. by intervening with the police at the request of families in cases of what are regarded as arbitrary

arrest; the cadres are free to accept or decline
this role. Besides this, the UNC quite often acts
on behalf of purely personal interests: local
cadres may intervene with private enterprise or the
central administration; or members of the Bureau
Politique may recommend their "proteges" to the
departmental presidents, in the hope of getting
them jobs.

29. In discussing the distribution of power in
the following section I shall deal only with the
ability of social groups to determine their immediate interests and to provide for them. For a
brief account of the participation--or more accurately the non-participation--of the Cameroonians
in national power, see J. F. Bayart, "L'Union
nationale camerounaise," Revue Française de Science
Politique, 20, 4 (August 1970), pp. 706 sqq.

30. Mintya, "Les Communes du Cameroun oriental," Revue Juridique et Politique, 22, 2 (April-
June 1968), p. 359. The institution of government
delegates has generally been quite well received as
being a guarantee against corruption. Moreover the
government cannot afford in its choice to displease
the local people; thus M. Fonda, who enjoyed some
prestige as mayor of Yaounde, only quitted that
office in order to become government delegate.

31. Cf. Ph. Lippens, "L'institution communal
permet'elle a la population des s'administrer elle-
même?" (Douala, 22 pp. manuscript).

32. Benjamin, Camerounais occidentaux, Ch. 6.

33. For this episode, see ibid., pp. 294 sqq.;
and Johnson, Cameroon Federation, pp. 312 sqq.

34. M. Mannoni, Enfance aliene (Paris, 1972),
p. 17. See also M. Crozier, La phenomene
bureaucratique (Paris, 1964).

35. See J. C. Pauvert, J. L. Laucrey-Javal, Le
Groupement d'Evodoula (Cameroun): étude socio-
economique (Paris, 1957), p. 35; and Mintya,
"Communes du Cameroun oriental," loc. cit.

36. Arouna Njoya, "Le Militant et les elections," Deuxieme seminaire de l'Union camerounaise
tenu a Yaounde du 15 au 28 juin 1964, p. 73.

37. See J. F. Bayart, "Cameroun: l'illusion du
parti unique," Le Mois en Afrique, 65 (May 1971),
pp. 44 sqq.

38. The term is not too strong. See the remarkable texts published in the religious denominational press, and especially "Muets comme des
carpes, ou psychose de la peur," L'Effort
Camerounais, 351, August 19, 1963, p. 6; and

"Cessons d'avoir peur," ibid., 576, January 20, 1967, p. 3.

39. Press conference by M. Ahidjo, A.C.A.P., July 2, 1963.

40. Circular No. 1/UNC/BPN/SO, dated June 1, 1969, and signed by M. Kame.

41. A cell may number more then 100 members, even though theoretically the maximum is 30. In 1969 there was a demand from the local level for the breaking up of various committees, and indeed of sections, on the grounds of population-growth and of the great distances militants were obliged to travel to meetings. It was only in September 1971 that the Bureau Politique accordingly decided to appoint a commission to restructure the local units. It is difficult at present to estimate the scale of this movement.

42. Circular No. I/UNC/BPN/SO, quoted above. A vivid picture of these local disputes may be gleaned from the records of the sub-section meetings, unfortunately too long to be quoted here.

43. This decline in the integrative function of African government parties was early discerned by Ruth Schachter; see "Single-party Systems in West Africa," American Political Science Review, 55, 2 (June 1961), p. 304. For Cameroon my conclusions are supported by the observations of C. Dikoume and J. Luetke-Entrup, Mouanko: étude socio-economique generale en vue du développement (Douala, Institut panafricain pour le developpement, October 1971), pp. 63-4.

44. E. Durkheim, De la division du travail social (8th edn. Paris, 1967), p. 406.

45. L'Effort Camerounais has given a vivid description of how this happens. "I can't undertake such a step," one hears on all sides. An official, for instance, is working at Yaounde and has a certain amount of weight with the youth of his village, and would like to get work parties going there. But he can't. He is afraid. He has been active at some time or other in such and such a political party. It wouldn't be well regarded if he put himself at the head of some association, even just a work-party. And in any case, he has joined the new party. But he knows that people are afraid of him, and he in turn is frightened of them" ("Cessons d'avoir peur," loc. cit.)

46. A. L. Madian, "The Anatomy of a Failure," Government and Opposition, 4, 2 (Spring 1969), p. 288.

47. Cp. the petits collectifs de travail (co-

185

operatives, small waterworks etc.) which according
to R. Dumont disseminate social and economic change
more smoothly and more effectively than the giant
economic enterprises. See esp. his Cuba,
socialisme et développement (Paris, 1964). The
petit collectif politique implies the autonomous
and localized power of a group as contrasted with
national-scale structures (the main press organs,
unitary movements of all kinds).

48. See esp. J. Duvignaud, "Anomie et mutation
sociale," pp. 63-81, and Ed. Morin, "Remarques sur
la 'commutation' des traits sociaux," pp. 145-56,
in Sociologie des mutations, ed. G. Balandier
(Paris, 1970).

49. Cp. J. Israel, L'Alienation de Marx a la
sociologie contemporaine (Paris, 1972), and the
seminar of G. Lavau at the Foundation Nationale des
Sciences Politiques devoted to political integration and alienation (Paris, 1971/2).

50. It should not necessarily be regarded as
an ideology of foreign origin, artificially imposed
upon the country. The ethic of unity is to be
found in the colonial period, and characterizes for
instance the clan movement of the Banyang. See M.
Ruel, Leopards and Leaders: constitutional politics
among a Gross River people (London, 1969). It is
possible that l'unanimisme really has its roots in
pre-colonial political philosophy, as African
political leaders commonly maintain. The dysfunc-
tions of the ethic of unity would then account for
the transition from (local) unanimisme to
(national) Jacobinism, as is suggested by the case
of Operation Nylon, see below.

51. See O. Mannoni, Psychologie de la
colonisation (Paris, 1950), pp. 68, sqq.

52. Ibid.; and G. Mendel, Pour decoloniser
l'enfant: sociopsychanalise de l'autorite
(Paris, 1971).

53. "Ahidjo is our father"--old man in Edea
(La Presse du Cameroun, April 6-7, 1963); "Papa
Ahidjo, Papa Ahidjo"--chant the under-twelves in
Douala (A.C.A.P., October 16, 1971). At the extreme,
M. Ahidjo is deified--which is more remarkable in
that divinity is not systematically sought; the
President has never attempted to acquire a charis-
matic legitimacy.

54. G. N. Anyon Mbida, "Long life to our
beloved President El Hadj Ahmadou Ahidjo, on this
tenth anniversary of our independence," La Presse
du Cameroun, December 31, 1969, January 1, 1970,
p. 3. The beginning of the poem compares

M. Ahdijo to Moses leading the Jews out of Egypt.

55. See e.g. the interview with M. Djambon, Commissaire Central de Police at Douala, by Ph. Lippens (June 16, 1970): "The people have substantially extended the role of the police. These folk seek from the police material and moral security." We are very close to the culture of subjection" described by G. Almond and S. Verba, The Civic Culture: political attitudes and democracy in Five nations (Princeton, 1963).

56. Cp. Mannoni, Psychologie de la colonisation, p. 70.

57. Report on the political situation of the New-Bell III sub-section (Wouri section) March 26, 1971.

58. Cp. Mannoni, Psychologie de la colonisation, Ch. 4; and E. H. Erikson, Enfance et societé (Neuchatel, 1966). This analysis requires modification or even substantial revision. On the one hand, M. Ahidjo is also seen as (a) big brother, "grand camarade," usually by the party militants; (b) son, by the old matrons: "Come, take me, Death, for now I have seen my son Ahidjo," exclaims one of these. A.C.A.P. January 19-20, 1969. On the other, there is the lack of definition of the relation between father-images and mother-images.

59. Cameroon more or less explicitly takes France as its model for successful national integration. But there the politics of unification, in denying diversity and particularisms as such, impinged simultaneously on a strong national consciousness and a growing ethnic discontent: some minority groups experience national unity as alienation. See Lafont, Decoloniser en France; P. Serant, La France des minorities (Paris, 1965); and especially Morvan Lebesque, Comment peut-on être Breton? essai sur la democratie francaise (Paris, 1970).

60. In Madagascar, the formation of the KIM (committees for co-ordinating resistance) and the ZOAM (Madagascar young unemployed), as the result of the movement of May 1972, would seem to open up new perspectives in this field: confronted by the more classic power of General Ramananisua, which one can safely predict as moving towards greater authoritarianism.

Part 3
The Shaping
of an Economic Order

7
The Impact of Federal Institutions on West Cameroon's Economic Activity

Jacques Benjamin

CENTRIFUGAL FACTORS IN CAMEROON'S ECONOMIC ACTIVITY

Welch points out in his comparative work that economic structures represent the basic criterion which enables one to distinguish the two different entities in Cameroon as well as in Senegambia.[1] West Cameroon's autonomy is inherent not only in its economic structures but also in the actual economic situation (wages and prices) and in its own institutions.

Economic Structure

In East Cameroon, priority is accorded to industrialization; from 1967-1971, 20 billion CFA francs were invested in this field: 4 billion for food industries, 3.5 for chemical industries, 3 for textile and 2.8 for aluminum industries. Now these industries have a business turnover of 29 billion CFA francs (60 billion if one includes water and electric power production). The number of wage earners is 142,500 in the industrial sector.[2] These wage earners work in more than 700 industrial firms, the most important component of which is the ALUCAM complex. The other is made up of the Pechiney group of aluminium processing factories. For the past five years, 50,000 tons have been, on the average, produced at EDEA annually. Ever since, Cameroon's industry has stood third in francophone black Africa.

In West Cameroon by contrast, the industrial sector records very low figures: a 4.5 billion business turnover; 40,000 wage earners; and 27 industrial firms (most of them are processing plants for agricultural products).

191

The agricultural structures of the two former federated States also differ in nature. In the West, most of the production is ensured by the Cameroons Development Corporation, which employs more than 11,500 wage earners.[3] In the East, family-type plantations are the general rule.

Once again, West Cameroon forms an autonomous unit with its own agricultural production: rough timber, palm oil, bananas, and rubber are on its priority list. The East accords preference to cocoa, robusta coffee, cotton, bananas, and tobacco.[4]

We are told in Yaounde that Cameroon is a coffee-producing country. In francophone Africa, it stands second after the Ivory Coast. Ninety percent of this commodity is produced in the East, where robusta coffee, which grows in the lowlands or in lands of average altitude, accounts for 70% of the total production. In the West, on the contrary, it is the arabica type, especially suitable for the highlands, that accounts for 70% of the production.

Likewise, in West Cameroon, the banana zones of the industrial plantations are planted entirely with Poyo and Cavendish types, while in the East, the latter represents only 40% of the total, the rest being of the Gros-Michel type.

Experts explain that the cultivation of the Gros-Michel type is quite suitable for mixed planting while a profitable farming of the Poyo and Cavendish varieties are not. Furthermore, banana trees are attacked by many parasites but the banana-tree weevils cause greater damage to the Poyo and Cavendish types. These types are sensitive to threadworms.

West Cameroonians pointed out that their brothers in the East err in wanting to grow only the Gros-Michel type. They explained that in well-managed plantations, the Poyo variety produces 74.10 tons per acre while the Gros-Michel type only yields 19.76 tons.[5] West Cameroonians seemed to have made their point to some extent since the Yaounde government called for a conversion of production. According to all those involved, however, the process will be a long and slow one.

And lastly, these different crops are marketed under two independent systems. West Cameroon inherited from the trusteeship period the single Marketing Board system for all commodities; its agents buy at guaranteed prices in official buying depots and export the commodity themselves. These

192

agents are cooperative groups (Bakweri, Nso, Bamenda, Kumba), commercial firms and individuals (Atabong Enterprises, Cameroon Trading, Transporting and Crop Company, S. Latani and Sons, S. Roger, N. Stephanon, etc.).[6]

In the East by contrast, there are several Price Stabilization Boards--one for each major product. None of them dealt with exports.

From all viewpoints therefore, the economic structures differ in both states.

Economic Situation

The above difference in economic structure is coupled with a difference in the actual economic situation. On both sides of the Mungo River, everyone is concerned about wages and prices. The standard of living is very different from one federated State to the other: the income of some 150,000 wage earners in the East is about twice as high as that of 45,000 workers in the West.[7]

The disparity in the cost of living is also striking. But the difference in prices is smaller depending on whether the products are local or imported. It fluctuates between 20 and 50%.[8] Some years ago in West Cameroon, this variation was complicated by the absence of purchase price control for the producers; in fact, all the moves made to this effect early in the federation affected only East Cameroon. The Journal officiel stated each time that the presidential decrees referred to East Cameroon only.[9]

This disparity in incomes and prices induced the federal government to maintain the internal border until 1966, especially since it was accompanied by as wide a gap in both infrastructure investments and production. In 1966, the per capita gross domestic product was 46,000 CFA francs along the East Coast and 19,000 in the West. In the Douala region in 1968-1969, investments reached 12.6 billion CFA francs, that is, 8 francs per capita. They only amounted to 2 billion in the Victoria region, i.e. 2.5 francs per capita.[10]

Faced with this economic imbalance, the federal government consented to keep the internal border. When the latter was non-existent, the rise in prices had been disastrous for West Cameroon since the purchasing power (wages) was half that of prices. Thanks to this border, West Cameroonians do not have to pay prices which were increased as a result of the external tariff levied by the federal

State on all goods coming from countries other than those of the European Common Market, i.e. from Great Britain and Nigeria in particular.

However, this decision sheds light on two elements which seem contrary to concepts usually associated with federalism. In their theory, K. W. Deutsch and his colleagues stress that for a federation to be successful,[11] there is a need for smooth and frequent contacts between men and an easy flow of foodstuffs between the federated States. The maintanance of the border goes against this principle. However, both West Cameroonians and federal leaders desired it. They looked upon the border as a means of preventing the entry into East Cameroon of rebels who, according to them, were taking refuge in West Cameroon.

One also associates federalism with the concept of equalization. The latter is a mechanism by which the federal government attempts to normalize the standard of living of the federated States.[12] Now while the per capita gross domestic earnings were 2.5 times higher in Douala than in Victoria, public investments were still three times higher eight years after unification.[13]

The decision to keep the internal border seemed to have had two contradictory effects. On the one hand, it of course benefits West Cameroonians since goods imported from Commonwealth countries actually enter Tiko and Victoria ports at prices well below those from the same origin arriving at the Douala-Bonaberi port. On the other hand, these foodstuffs are subsequently smuggled into the East in quantities that cause firms established there to lose an average of 20% of their transactions. While these firms would have paid the State a sale's tax on these transactions, the smugglers make the State lose significant amounts of revenue because they do not keep any accounts of their dealings. The West Cameroon government became aware of the "social costs" of smuggling; it noted that smuggling forced the firms involved to reduce their distribution networks in East Cameroon and the Victoria-Tiko area. This caused loss of work and food shortages at localities in West Cameroon which were suddendly excluded from the networks. On November 24, 1965, West Cameroon's government officially asked the federal authority to impose a tighter control over the internal border in order to curb smuggling.[14]

The federal government itself wanted to encourage the importation of certain West Cameroon goods into the East duty-free. This would earn even larger profits for West Cameroon cooperatives. In May 1966, the Federal Minister of Planning and Economic Affairs disclosed, however, that facilities granted for interstate trade "were being flagrantly abused at the moment."[15]

Nevertheless, we must not modify our first hypothesis: agreements signed in 1965-1966 indicated that the federated government had been attempting for the past six years, out of a genuine concern for equalization, to facilitate the movement of goods. Furthermore, these aspects of the economic situation seemed to disclose not only what is termed "sociological federalism" but also a federalism sanctioned by agreements and encouraged by the government. This is clearly demonstrated in the external customs system: comprehending its principles is a matter of reading the Journal officiel.

External Customs System

At the time of unification, the import and export duties on goods were lower in the West than in the East. This situation was justified by its lower standard of living. Because this domain was passing over to federal jurisdiction (article 5) the government wished to harmonize Cameroon's customs systems. However, it proceeded in stages in order not to wholly upset West Cameroon's economic structures.

Because the non-repayment of West Cameroon's public debt was caused by loss of customs revenues, the federal government agreed to discharge it. The amount then was 288,000, i.e. about 200 million CFA francs.

With a view to avoiding a disruption in the importers' supplies, a decree promulgated on March 31, 1962[16] fixed a temporary system of exchanges and foreign trade. The latter was regulated by another decree in ten clauses[17] which were "made necessary by West Cameroon's special situation."[18] Despite its claim of controlling external trade in a "definitive"[19] manner, the latter decree took West Cameroon's particular situation into consideration since it came into effect on July 1, 1962, for export transactions only. The March 1962 temporary decree mentioned above remained in effect for import transactions until an order from the Federal Ministry of National Economy declared it had lapsed."[20]

The same day, another presidential decree reorganized the "technical import distribution

committee." The first article of this decree
stated that "/. . ./ In order to facilitate the
supply and equipping of the West, importers established in this part of the Republic had at their
disposal a special quota on credits and imports
from foreign countries into the franc zone. /. . ./
Goods imported on a quota basis had to be cleared
at a center in West Cameroon."21

The same decree stipulated that the five new
members of the committee be West Cameroonians;
under the decree, they formed a special section
which could hold meetings "to discuss the distribution of special quotas." But it also stipulated
that they be appointed by the federal president.22
Would the president consult the West Cameroon
government before making these appointments?
Federalism's theory requires that West Cameroon
have its say. The presence in Yaounde of West
Cameroon's prime minister (the federal vice-president) facilitated matters considerably.

In July 1962, a clause of the decree which
dealt with the establishment in the Federal Republic
of a common external customs tariff for Cameroon
and the United States of the Equatorial Customs
Union (UDE) stated that "the provisions of this
text are suspended on matters relating to West
Cameroon until such time as decrees which make the
customs system of both states uniform are
published."23

Likewise in 1963, two decrees took West
Cameroon's particular position into specific consideration. The first one brought about a 50% reduction in customs duties on its banana exports for
the period running from October 1, 1963, to June 30,
1964,24 when the Commonwealth's preferential
tariffs ceased to apply. The other one had more
positive aspects. It fixed the customs tariffs on
certain West Cameroon imported and exported goods
while taking into consideration its particular
position.25

The slow economic integration of West Cameroon
had to take place within the framework of an economic and customs union which included more than just
the Cameroon federation since on January 1, 1966,
Chad, Gabon, Congo-Brazzaville, the Central Africa
Republic and Cameroon decided to integrate their
economies. Furthermore, the Central African
Customs and Economic Union (UDEAC) was more than an
ordinary customs union since its duty was to enable
member states to harmonize their industrial establishment projects and to compensate, with the

help of financial mechanism, for "the unequal
development which the coastal regions benefited
from to the detriment of the mainland areas."[26]
West Cameroon's geographical position did not help
her in this case. However, the federal government
took into consideration West Cameroon's lower
standard of living when it decided that tariffs on
goods imported by the latter from Commonwealth
countries would be applied only gradually.

The economic activity of the past ten years
was set forth in detail to avoid making hasty
generalizations. During this period, this activity
was not uniform, but varied, a fact which is at the
very heart of federalism. To be more precise, one
could add that the form of relations between Buea
and Yaounde be described as "asymetric federalism"
because the type of structures and economic situations were very different from the pattern existing
in these domains in the East.[27] The future of this
form of federalism in the economic field seems to
depend on the vitality of West Cameroon's economy.
One West Africa correspondent had probably already
answered the question when he wrote in 1962 that
West Cameroon's economy suffered from "chronic in-
solvency."[28] Until then, the territory has been
nothing but a small province of Nigeria, relatively
remote from the country's large centers and therefore very much neglected from the viewpoint of infrastructure.

West Cameroon's Economic Institutions

By any standard, the 1961 federal Constitution
does not facilitate West Cameroon's task as a
government. It does not stipulate the mechanism
of income distribution between the two levels of
government. Under article 5 of the Constitution
customs taxes--the most important source of government revenues--go directly and entirely into the
federal government's coffers. The constitutional
text is silent about the means of recourses of the
federated States; it does not prevent them from
levying taxes, but it deprives them of their main
source of revenue.[29]

"Regional" taxes (i.e. those of the federated
State) reached 418 million CFA francs in 1966-1967
and 677 million (rough estimate) in 1968-1969;
licenses amounted to 125 to 130 million respectively.[30]

The establishment of commercial firms and
factories had limited success. Private investments

197

which were worth 215 million CFA francs in 1958
fell to 113 in 1962.[31] With the hope of cushioning
the shock caused by the reduction in commercial
firms after unification, the Cameroon Commercial
Corporation (CCC) was founded at the beginning of
1964; five years later, except for the two warehouses in Victoria and Kumba, all its retail shops
were forced to close down. The corporation has
been founded with the financial help of the West
Cameroon Development Agency.[32]

It seems that this financial help to the CCC
enabled certain people to increase their salaries
by misappropriating funds.[33] But the closure of
the retail shops in February 1969 was poorly welcomed by the population which considered their
services indispensable. In certain remote areas,
in fact, only they dispensed these services. One
edition of the Cameroon Express headed that "the
launching of the CCC was politically motivated."
But in light of the protests from the people, "the
prime minister asked the State Secretariat to study
the possibility of reopening them."

The establishment of factories encountered
little more success and for the same reasons. One
pot-casting factory was opened at Tiko in 1963. It
was short-lived. An inquiry revealed that the
project was submitted directly to the prime minister
by three businessmen with foreign names (Messrs.
I. Shivdasani, De Cavallo, and K. Masters) who in
order to obtain his assent reminded him of their
financial support of the KNDP. And yet steel pots
had not been in use in West Cameroon for a long
time.[34]

In fact, the value added of West Cameroon firms
was evaluated at 2 billion CFA francs (88% of which
was for the agricultural establishments) compared
to 152 billion for East Cameroon firms.[35] And the
total water and electric power production was 110
times less in the West.[36]

Lastly, the government had contributed its
financial support for the establishment of the
Cameroon Bank Ltd. whose duty was to ensure a
certain autonomy for West Cameroon. Because of an
excessively liberal policy on credit, and an un-
approved non-repayment of loans granted,[37] the
salaries of state officials could not be paid in
1966. President Ahidjo agreed to intervene personally and the federal government invested sums in
the bank. He created a National Credit Council
which was responsible for ensuring the supervision
of banks through a six-member commission comprised

entirely of francophones.[38] Then the governing body of the Cameroon Bank was dissolved while the credit committee was conducting an inquiry.[39] Furthermore, the change in government facilitated the matter. The new Prime Minister, Mr. Muna, did not share the same "independentist views" (term rejected by Mr. Muna) as Mr. Jua.[40]

As early as 1961, the federal government had, according to the equalization principle, paid out grant-in-aids which represented two-thirds of West Cameroon's budget. This grant has remained the same since the beginning (1,600,000,000 out of a total of 2,818,935,000 CFA francs in 1968-1969). But the aid left the West Cameroon government at the mercy of the federal government. The State Secretary of Finance, Mr. Kemcha asserted in 1966 that these ad hoc grants were "thoroughly unsatisfactory."[41]

Mr. Jua wondered how a state could develop according to its own priorities if it could not be sure of how much it possessed. According to him, it was necessary to create a mixed committee on revenue sharing which would set a permanent distribution of government revenue between the two component Governments of the Federation.[42] He added that if not, West Cameroon would not be able to act much longer as a true government which makes decisions in domains where it "has sovereignty."

The federal government reacted by federalizing certain areas which were under the jurisdiction of the federated States (the West Cameroon police force in 1969). It thereby reduced the expenses of these states!

The analysis of economic structures and circumstances, of West Cameroon's special status in Cameroon's external customs system, and of West Cameroon's own economic institutions has given a clear picture of the scope and limitations of what some anthropologists have called West Cameroon's "economic space."[43]

A CENTRIPETAL INSTITUTIONAL FACTOR: INTRODUCTION OF THE CFA FRANC INTO WEST CAMEROON

Currency is both an essential characteristic of a state's sovereignty, an instrument of commercial life, and an essential factor in development planning. Viewed from these three angles, the introduction of a single currency into Cameroon seemed to have caused, in its western part, what

Mr. Jua, the former Prime Minister, called "considerable anguish."[44]

Consequences for West Cameroon of Adherence to the Franc Zone

Until July 1, 1959, the currency used in British Cameroons had been that of the West African Currency Board. On that date, the new Central Bank of Nigeria issued a special currency for the new State and it was this currency which was put in circulation in British Cameroons. The government of the Republic of French Cameroon asked a Norwegian expert, Mr. M. K. Andersen, to undertake a study of the economic aspects of a possible merger with British Cameroons. Drafted between December 1960 and February 1961, the purpose of the study consisted in weighing the following alternatives: should the Federal Republic retain the pound sterling in West Cameroon and the CFA franc in East Cameroon; should it allow the use of both currencies concurrently in both federated States (it was believed that this type of precedent existed in Morocco), or should it introduce the CFA franc into West Cameroon while abolishing the use of the pound sterling? Andersen chose the third alternative.[45]

From the early days of federation (January 17, 1962), a presidential decree imposed the CFA franc in West Cameroon.[46] Traders and buyers were particularly affected.[47] The federal government claimed that it had never concealed its belief that federalism required integration into a single monetary zone and the establishment of different commercial channels.[48] The franc zone was protected by a system of exchange controls and import-export licences. The extension of these controls to West Cameroon in 1962 created serious misgivings since the federated State continued more than ever to trade in the sterling zone and had no valid reason to change its policies: as a result of forty years of colonization, West Cameroonians had been accustomed to Nigerian and British food supplies.[49]

West Cameroon's authorities protested vehemently on many occasions. Any time he was questioned in the Assembly on this matter, the finance minister was openly pessimistic.[50] Even if the decree which controls foreign trade included a clause which indicated that "the application of /this/ regulation could be changed later when West Cameroon's[51] special conditions were taken into consideration /. . ./," the federal government

200

believed that national unity required the lack of
any such compromise. In 1965-1966 there was a
shortage of salt and rice; the new minister of
finance repeated the same promise as his predecessors: "We are making efforts to convince the
authorities of the need to change this system."[52]
    The "system" included the federated State's
imports and exports. The "narrow economic symbio-
sis" alluded to by the president of the Republic[53]
seemed to be accomplished in this domain at the expense of the West Cameroonians once again.

West Cameroon's Foreign Trade: Problems

    The federalization of both states brought this
commercial agents of these territories into competition. Prior to this, each group had exported its
goods into a particular monetary zone. Great
Britain was West Cameroon's major client. It received 60% of the latter's exports. In numerical
value, bananas represented 50% of West Cameroon's
exports in 1958. Coffee accounted for 15%.[54] Now
that West Cameroon belonged to the franc zone, the
question arose as to whether it could continue exporting its products. As Burdeau showed in his
Traite,[55] federalism in fact does not attain its
true objective unless it standardizes all the
different economic data involved.

    West Cameroon bananas. Since it no longer
belonged to the sterling zone, West Cameroon could
not benefit from the imperial preferential tariffs
for its bananas (a price which was 15% higher than
the world price). Great Britain agreed to continue
applying these tariffs until the end of 1962.
Problems of commercial outlets after that date were
feared.[56] In fact, French Cameroon also exported
bananas. And France, Cameroon's main client, found
it difficult to increase the purchase of this commodity which had already glutted the French market.
    Under the 1961 Constitution, foreign trade was
under the federal republic's jurisdiction. During
a visit to London, the Minister of External Affairs,
Mr. Jean Betayene was promised that these bananas
would benefit from preferential tariffs until
September 30, 1963. Faced with criticism from West
Cameroon,[57] the federal government stoutly maintained that it had done everything to obtain the extension of these privileges and that London's decision to abolish them was unilateral.[58]

201

But in light of repeated protests from West Cameroon, the federal government decided in January 1964 to deal with this particular commercial problem on the other side of the Mungo River by creating a Coordination Committee on the Banana Industry.[59] The creation some months later of the Federal Banana Organisation induced the Federal Minister at the time, Mr. Tchongi, to declare that "thus Cameroon has acquired the legislative and administrative tools necessary to restore /West Cameroon's/ bananas to a prime place in the economy."[60] In November 1968, in a brief official comminique, the CDC announced, however, that it would be compelled to completely discontinue the growing of bananas in 1972 because of ("the limited and protected French quota allocation of this crop to the CDC."[61]).

For their part, West Cameroon's top officials openly accused France of granting Ecuador a higher quota than West Cameroon.[62] They asserted that France must lead the struggle to create "free" markets since access restrictions to present organized markets were the major obstacle to the growth of West Cameroon's banana exports. To guarantee equitable incomes to the planters, the policy of the Federal Board of primary commodities in Yaounde had, however, always been to adapt the demand as closely as possible to the market needs. Now according to federal officials, these markets are glutted since "a banana consumer unfortunately has but one stomach."[63]

Decisions relating to the quota are taken each month in Paris by the Interprofessional Banana Committee, an international but officially non-governmental body. However, it was the French minister of finance who appointed the members: Cameroon's representative was a Frenchman who controlled one of the largest plantations in East Cameroon. Now "despite the fact that West Cameroon belongs to the Federal Republic of Cameroon, it succeeded in obtaining part of this country's banana quota at the end of 1966 only. Very attached to their privileges, East Cameroon's producers were able, until then, to prevent the West Cameroonians from taking away any of those privileges."[64]

And since 1966, two different aspects of this new situation has particularly irritated West Cameroonians. The quota allocated by France to Cameroon has not been honoured,[65] while West Cameroon's bananas could contribute to this quota. Furthermore, part of West Cameroon's low tonnage bound for France was refused on arrival in port.

202

The inspectors maintained that certain bunches were
spoiled but as the planters pointed out "it is impossible for all the eight or nine bunches in a
package to be unacceptable."[66] The inspectors for
their part affirmed that they accepted all healthy
bananas. One probably should not forget that this
controversy increased the anxiety and frustration
of West Cameroonians. In the East, no one knew
whether to blame France, the federal government in
Yaounde, or the port inspectors. But as the CDC
communique indicated, what was clear was that ten
years after federalization and after having accounted for 50% of the State's exports, bananas were no
longer exported. (As Hapi pointed out, in 1962,
West Cameroon supplied more than 50% of Cameroon's
banana exports).[67]
     Coffee is another West Cameroon export
commodity. In this case, there is an international
coffee agreement. As one West Cameroonian pointed
out, this accord should allow West Cameroonians to
know very well who to blame if matters go wrong!
What is perhaps important for our study is that
West Cameroonians hoped that by increasing their
coffee exports they would compensate for part of
the foreign exchange losses caused by the reduction
in their banana exports..

     West Cameroon's coffee. It is the federal
Board of primary commodities and it alone that sets
West Cameroon's part of the coffee quota that can
be sold each year: this part is only 12.20% of the
total.[68]
     Despite the West Cameroonians' claims, it is
uncertain whether they are basically poorer than the
East Cameroonians. It is obvious in fact that more
coffee would be produced in both states if no quota
existed. In light of this, criticism of the federal
government is perhaps not very fair. It is always
possible for the West Cameroonians to obtain more
by direct negotiations but the OAMCFC would refuse
to accept West Cameroon as a full-fledged member of
its organization. However, West Cameroon can obtain
a share higher than 12.20% whenever European plantations in the East encounter harvest difficulties
as has been the case since 1968-1969. This was
what the Cameroon Express of that time suggested
for instance.[69] Furthermore, federalization perhaps
implies West Cameroon's representation on the administrative and management committee of primary
commodities. It probably involves not only West
Cameroonians, which would perhaps already be a way

of indicating a better comprehension of the federalist spirit, but even the federated States' representatives who are members of the
commission in charge of establishing quotas and of
representing Cameroon at the OAMCFC. At the present time, the Marketing Board is apparently kept
informed and that's about all. But under the
residual clause of the 1961 Constitution, it is the
West Cameroon government which is responsible for
coffee-growing. Logically then, the federal government has not been empowered to enforce article 48
of the International Coffee Agreement which urges
it to adjust its production to consumer needs.[70]
Federalism encourages this lack of planning since
each level of government is sovereign in its own
areas of jurisdiction.

Currency as a Factor in Development

Other than being a symbol of sovereignty,
currency is primarily a highly important factor in
development. As a State, West Cameroon does not
exercise any control as such over this factor
(article 5 of the 1961 Constitution). When setting
the expenses for the 1968-1969 fiscal year, the
president of the Republic stressed the strictness
with which provisions had to be applied "in order to
deal with the ups and downs of economic and financial situations."[71] Contemporary examples of the
federalist type of government seems to prove that
the multiplicity of governments, each one of which
is sovereign in its own areas of jurisdiction, and
the heterogeneity and dispersion of economic factors
cause a certain number of economic difficulties.
In fact, it seems very clear that the effects of
several economic policies counter-balance one another if these policies do not belong to an integrated process. A federal budget which shows a
surplus can for instance have a significant influence on the country's inflationary tendencies if
a federated State's budget indicates a deficit
which is equal to the federal surplus. This was why
a presidential decree of May 8, 1965, abolished the
"interim period allowed for the functioning of West
Cameroon's Treasury."[72] From then on, the treasury
was to belong to an administrative region and it
was placed under the authority of a treasurer
appointed by presidential decree.[73]
The president of the Republic considers the
implementation of this federal planning as an essential factor in the economic stability of the

country: to leave the autonomous West Cameroon budget completely free would be disastrous for a developing economy such as Cameroon's. As someone freely asserted in Yaounde, federalism is probably suited to a laissez-faire economy. But it is contrary to the idea of development planning. This control must be exercised over all the instruments of economic development, including the CDC.

An important producer, the CDC was, since its inception in 1946, charged with the economic development of British Cameroons. From 1946-1960, the corporation invested five billion CFA francs in its plantations and three billion in road and construction projects. Likewise, it contributed to sustaining the economy of the country by paying more than three billion CFA francs in taxes.

Would the corporation remain a firm of the West Cameroon State or would it become federal public property? Representatives of both governments and of the Commonwealth Development Corporation met in London during the summer of 1963 and discussed the projects which this corporation undertook: medical services, ports, roads, schools, domains which under article 6 were all to fall later under federal jurisdiction. The CDC itself seemed to be completely willing to hand over these domains to whoever would assume the responsibility--the medical costs alone had reached 82 million CFA francs in 1962. By contrast, the numerous CDC workers believed, for their part, that these projects would be better administered under the continued responsibility of the CDC. The West Cameroon government defended this viewpoint in London; and the federal government yielded (medical care cost the CDC 100 million francs in 1969). The latter even agreed in 1965-1966 to assist the corporation in its efforts to borrow on the international market. It was this government which negotiated with IBRD and IDA and obtained, in 1966-1967, a loan from the former (2,700 million CFA francs) and credit advances from the latter (1,700 million).[74] But it applied pressure to obtain certain controls over these amounts which now form part of the corporation's shares as though invested by the federal government itself.[75] The latter is now represented by one of the eight members on the board of directors of the company by virtue of what a Financial Times commentator called "a discreet right of inspection."[76]

Certain people maintained[77] that since the division of economic leverages of development

between the two levels of government is contrary to
the spirit of planning, the introduction of the CFA
franc into West Cameroon would have remained a
purely formal decision if it had resulted only in
substituting control over the issuing of one
currency for another. In order that it have some
influence on the economic situation, it had to lead
to a reorganization of former economic channels.

Reorganization of Economic Channels

The reorganization of economic channels implied
that West Cameroon's trade with the outside world
should pass through Douala, the only important port
of the franc zone in central Africa rather than
through Nigerian ports as has been the case for
several years. Furthermore, given the apparent
inelasticity of demand of its agricultural products
on the world market, West Cameroon is compelled
under penalty of suffocation to increase its trading
with East Cameroon. Both ways, it is at the mercy
of its fellow State for its exports.

Thus any federal government's decision in this
realm, which on the surface is economic only, was to
have political consequences. To centralize the new
communications thoroughfares with Douala, as had
been done in the past, was to put West Cameroon's
economy at the mercy of East Cameroon. To open them
to the sea, on the other hand, was to grant West
Cameroon a greater political and economic autonomy.
The centripetal pressures or the willingness to
compromise would thus become apparent from Yaounde
since the 1961 Constitution reserved this domain of
jurisdiction for the federal level of government.
Therefore the railway and highway networks deserve
to be studied from this viewpoint in particular.

Railway system improvement. Before the railway
was built (its dimensions made it national and it
was consequently baptised Trans-Cameroonian), what
existed in this sector did not amount to much:
some 150 miles of narrow track installed between
East Cameroon's plantations near the coast and which
served to transport the palm-cabbage and the banana
harvest.

One of the avowed goals of the Trans-
Cameroonian line is to develop the rich but isolated
Kumba region in West Cameroon.[78] However, this
construction was frowned upon in Buea. What created
the belief that the federal government wished to
dampen West Cameroon's independentist spirits by

206

economically developing this region was, on the one hand, the huge cost of the construction (13% of the federal budget estimates for 1964-1965 when the decision was made)[79] and on the other hand the lay-out itself. If, with such amounts the federal government intends to develop our State, why did the line stop at Douala and not go on to the ports of Victoria and Tiko which are located at barely a few kilometers from there?

Perhaps in this regard one should stress the reply of Belgium's Prime Minister, Mr. Eyskens, to the Walloons' protests following the decision to build a "super-port"[80] at Flanders when this part of the country had a better developed infrastructure. It was pointed out that the Walloon infrastructure would mean the building of the Walloon highway which was to be "a true link between the neighbouring countries, France and Germany." Certain Walloons asserted that "the billions we squander on a so-called national port would likely have provided us with an excellent highway network." Mr. Eyskens replied that "for compensations to be accorded to the Walloons, each one must define what he considers /as/ national if indeed one wishes to maintain the /Belgian/ State alive. /Of course/, the efforts on behalf of the regions must be balanced. That does not necessarily mean a generalized parallelism."[81]

Highway improvement. Early in the federation, the federal government devoted a portion of its budget to highways by providing sums only for the building of East Cameroon's inter-state routes and completely neglecting West Cameroon's. A presidential decree of November 1962[82] allocated a sum of 600 million CFA francs for equipping and improving the highway; article 2 of this decree excluded West Cameroon since it mentioned that "the details of this program's operations will be the subject of an order-in-council from East Cameroon's prime minister." Actually, West Cameroon would also be in need of funds to improve its highways. "Lacking roads, part of the production is dispatched by water and half of the value of certain agricultural produce is spent just to pay for the transport. The fact that there was too frequently an overloading of trucks, the premature wear and tear of the trucks and the high rate of traffic accidents involve considerable depreciation and insurance spending."[83]

But while the West Cameroon government requested some amounts from the federal government for the

improvement of its own network,[84] the federal
government decided in October 1965 to undertake the
building of a road to link Douala in East Cameroon
to Tiko in West Cameroon. (Furthermore, Mr. Ahidjo
ammounced in March 1970 that the building and maintenance of interstate roads would from then on fall
under the jurisdiction of the federal government).
Constituting the first direct and permanent link
between both federated States, "Reunification Road"
was opened in April 1969. Certain independentists
maintained that no one doubted that it would
facilitate the assimilation of West Cameroon. The
attraction of Douala "the big city" on the one hand,
the need to learn French because the French demanded
that they be spoken to in French at petrol stations
and hotels on the other hand, had already made
themselves felt a year after the opening of the
road. But federalism also implies the development,
at the federal level, of a "sense of community"
which the opening of this road was to facilitate.
We are already familiar with the theories of North
American researchers: the degree of development of
a political community is measured not only by studying the development of federal, political, and
economic institutions but also by analyzing the
development of a political consensus (political
culture) at the federation level.[85] The relationships between persons which the opening of this
road facilitates certainly count in support of
federalism. Furthermore, the economic activity of
the federated State would gain enormously from it.
The first people to benefit from it were the inhabitants of the rich and populated villages along
the road. Unable to dispose of their production,
they had reduced it to the level of self-consump-
tion. Now they could ship their produce not only to
Douala but to Tiko, Victoria, and Buea as well.[86]

Lastly, this road would enable as yet un-
imaginable quantities of foodstuffs to be transported from East Cameroon to the West.

On the other hand, the Prime Minister himself,
Mr. Muna, had predicted that Victoria would have its
deep-water port.[87] It was certain that it could not
be developed before 1975 but the Douala port which
was already over-crowded could not be enlarged without destroying the Wouri bridge.

It was pointed out in Buea that after the
introduction of the CFA franc into West Cameroon
and the "considerable suffering," such as lack of
rice and salt, the departure of John Holt Ltd.,
the closure of outlets, etc. that it had caused, the

building of this port was to be the first institutional "adjustment" of East Cameroon's economy to the federal economic situation as a whole.

CONCLUSION

The administrative, political, economic, and legal institutions seem to exercise a certain number of constraints on the minority in a bi-communal federation. To use a Marxist term, the "superstructures," for the same reason as the infrastructure, exert tremendous pressures on the minority.

But it is interesting to note that Ardener stressed two unexpected effects of centralizing influences. In two oral statements, he in fact emphasized that 1) the relative physical isolation of West Cameroon, with no railway nor direct road link with Douala, contributed at the beginning to the prevention of total control over the federated State by the federal inspector and the police, and that 2) the non-bilingualism of the francophones enabled the officials of the federated State to retain a larger autonomy of action than the organigram in the second chapter indicates.[88]

Ardener however does not deny that the federal presence in West Cameroon, through its police, its language, and its goods has such weight that the centralizing aspect of the 1961 Constitution (articles 5 and 6) was even accentuated.

These aspects of the matter throw some light on constraints of a completely different nature: those which political culture exercises over the minority. In certain cases, these contraints are added to institutional ones and in other cases they markedly reduce their scope as evidenced by the incidents touching on the ignorance of the English language.

As Alfred Grosser emphasized with respect to traditional comparisons,[89] institutions and their true functioning were juxtaposed. Most recently, national political systems had been compared on the basis of criteria such as their stability or their ability to transform requests into decisions. Would it not also be necessary to study the latitude of choice which external constraints** on the national political system leave for the leaders? And what about the lack of latitude which might be a consequence of their ethnic origin** or of the country where they had studied?**

These are the three criteria which will be retained for further discussion. Did the exogenous forces tend to protect the minority or to strengthen the political weight of the majority community? Are intercommunal relations cordial and were they so before the merger? And does the political philosophy of the leaders of both communities lend itself to the protection of the minority or to their assimilation?

NOTES

*The paper is based on a Chapter in Benjamin's
West Cameroonians: A Minority In a Bicommunal Republic. Montreal: Montreal University Press 1972.
Chapter 3.
*Translator's Note: In italics in the original
text.
1. Welch, Dream of Unity, p. 250.
2. Europe-France-Outre-mer, no. 474-475,
July-August, 1969, p. 40.
3. The balance sheet of the Cameroons Development Corporation (CDC) is impressive: 19 large
modern industrial plantations which are fully
equipped and divided into four zones; an annual
budget of 4 billion CFA francs. At the moment, the
corporation produces 77% of West Cameroon's rubber,
48% of its palm products, 45% of its bananas, 38%
of its tea and 80% of its pepper for sums of 706,
490, 245, 167, and 6 million CFA francs respectively.
4. West Cameroon -- rough timber: 29,500
tons; palm oil: 22,500t; bananas: 16,500t; rubber:
8,500t; cabbage-palm: 8,500t; cocoa: 6,500t;
arabica coffee: 6,500t; roubusta coffee: 3,000t;
tea: 1,000t. East Cameroon -- cocoa: 105,000t;
wood: 625,000t; cotton: 65,000t; bananas, 57,000t;
robusta coffee: 5,000t; arabica coffee: 15,000t;
cabbage-palm: 18,000t; rubber: 5,000t; tobacco:
2,000t (cf. Federal Republic of Cameroon, Budget de
l'exercise 1969-1970, Yaounde, Imprimerie nationale,
1970, p. VIII).
5. Interview: Mr. Epale, Buea, September 19,
1969; Marches tropicaux et mediterraneens, no. 1154,
December 23, 1967, p. 3291; Europe-France-Outre-mer,
no. 474-475, July-August, 1969, p. 23.
6. The Marketing Board's choice of "Greek and
foreign firms" as commercial agents continues to
generate protests in West Cameroon; in 1969, it
chose six cooperatives, 12 firms and individuals
most of whom were actually Greeks and foreigners.
The Bamenda Cooperative Marketing Association
Limited made the following comment: "Greeks are
rich enough and could limit themselves to the sale
of our products abroad. Rather than make foreign
firms realize profits, we would prefer to sell to
East Cameroon's UCCAO."
In certain parts of West Cameroon (the Mamfe
and Gwofon regions), they are the only cooperatives
chosen as the Marketing Board's agents: where there
are firms, the Board considers them more capable
"of selling the products more quickly. Consequent-

ly, it is advantageous to the peasants themselves."
It is uncertain whether this argument is satisfactory to the Bamenda Cooperative.

7. While the average is of minor significance,
"the available income" is obtained by adding the
value of the self-consumed products to the salaries,
the family allowances and the value of gross trading returns. The salaries and social benefits are
the amounts distributed among workers either by the
administrations or by the companies or by the individuals who rented services. An equitable distribution of this money would ensure an income of
9,600 CFA francs per capita in East Cameroon and of
4,600 in West Cameroon." (Cf. interview: Mr.
Simon Epale, Buea, September 19, 1969; cf. also
Pierre Chauleur, "Cameroon and Cameroonians,"
Marches tropicaux et mediterraneens, no. 1093,
October 22, 1966, p. 2688-2689).

8. The purchase prices of arabica coffee for
instance varied in East Cameroon from 197.5 CFA
francs/kg in 1960-1961 to 270.9 now, and in West
Cameroon from 139.2 in 1962-1963 to 183 now.

9. For instance the decree of December 24,
1963, concerning coffee, the decrees of September
25, 1962, and of September 15, 1964, concerning
cocoa, and the decree of November 4, 1964, concerning groundnuts.

10. Interview: Mr. Epale, Buea, September 19,
1969.

11. K. W. Deutsch et al., Political Community
and the North Atlantic Area, Princeton, Princeton
University Press, 1957, p. 88.

12. Jean-Luc Pepin, "Cooperative federalism,"
le Devoir, September 30, 1964, p. 4 and the portion
of the talk given by Mr. Robert Bourassa, Quebec
Prime Minister at the Victoria Conference on this
matter, cf. le Devoir, June 15, 1971, p. 5.

13. The 2nd Five-Year Plan (1966-1970) provided, however, for some per capita total investments
(i.e. both public and private) which were higher
in West Cameroon's coastal region (2.5 times per
capita higher than in West Cameroon's coastal
region). Because private capital was lacking, it
does not seem that these estimates were met in
1970. In all fairness, however, the intention of
the federal government deserves to be mentioned.

14. Africa Report, January 1966, p. 32.

15. While allowing free passage, without payment of limited quantities of bananas from Kumba
cooperatives, the federal government understood
that these operations were carried out only within

212

the framework of agreements signed to this effect
between West Cameroon's Banana Cooperatives. It
was its hope that the financial benefits resulting from this trade would have pervasive repre-
cussions on the activities of West Cameroon's cooperatives. The abuses which the minister alluded
to derived from the conditions under which these
bananas were transported; the Kumba cooperatives
did not have the required trucks, and according
to the minister, the East Cameroon truck drivers
who were to collect the banans refused to pay the
price agreed upon. They resold the bananas themselves once they arrived in East Cameroon. Thus,
the middlemen intervened "in such conditions that
West Cameroon planters benefited only slightly
from the profit which they would have realized".
The minister therefore insisted that the police
should let trucks belonging to the General Union
cross the border at the rate stipulated in the
agreements. (Cf. "The interest of banana producers
should be safeguarded on both sides of the Mungo
River", l'Unite, no. 278, June 1-8, 1966, p. 1).

16. Decree no. 62-DF-98.
17. Decree no. 62-DF-204 promulgated on June
16, 1962.
18. Cf. article 11 of this decree, Journal
officiel, July 1, 1962, p. 627.
19. Cf. article 1, Journal officiel, July 1,
1962, p. 626.
20. Cf. article 12, Journal officiel, July 1,
1962.
21. Cf. Journal officiel, July 1, 1962, p. 628.
22. Cf. article 2 of this decree, Journal
officiel, July 1, 1962.
23. Article 16 of decree no. 62-DF-223 of June
27, 1962, Journal officiel, July 1, 1962, p. 672.
24. Decree no. 63-DF-343.
25. Decree no. 63-DF-244 of September 30, 1963.
26. Interview: Mr. A. Foalem, Head of Economic Affairs at the OCAM, Yaounde, September 10,
1969.
27. Tarlton, The Journal of Politics, vol. 27,
no. 4, p. 871.
28. West Africa, July 7, 1962, p. 745.

29.   TABLE

West Cameroon's autonomous
financial resources
(estimates for 1968-1969)

Direct Taxes	CFA francs
a) on personal income	52,000,000
b) on companies	75,000,000
c) pay-as-you-earn	70,000,000
d) self-employed persons (business and liberal professionals)	300,000,000

Sales Taxes	
cocoa	20,000,000
cabbage-palms	10,000,000
palm oil	30,000,000
coffee	85,000,000
licences	129,000,000
court costs	13,800,000
ministerial depart- ments' incomes	59,726,000
rental and interests	61,249,000
repayments and others	254,936,000
Total autonomous resources	1,160,711,000

Source: Federal Republic of Cameroon--West
           Cameroon, Estimates of West Cameroon,
           1968-1969, Buea, West Cameroon
           Government Press, 1968, p. 13.

30. Already in 1959-1960, an enquiry had been
conducted to determine the "fiscal viability" of
the territory if it were to separate from Nigeria:
the report had concluded that the survival would
amount to a hand to mouth existence. There were
too few factories, plants, and trading firms in the
State. (cf. Sir Sydney Phillipson, Financial,
Economic, and Administrative Consequences to the
Cameroons of Separation from the Federation of
Nigeria, Lagos, 1959, mimeo.)
     31. Interview: Mr. S. Epale, Buea, September
19, 1969.
     32. The (Dervish) Commission of Inquiry which
was responsible for studying the activities of the
West Cameroon Development Agency heard witnesses

214

disclose that the latter had not withdrawn its funds from the CCC at the express request of the then Secretary of State for Internal trade, Mr. Tamfu (cf. Cameroon Times, vol. 8, no. 78, May 29, 1968, p. 1).

33. Cameroon Express, no. 14, July 11, 1968, p. 3.

34. "CCC Launching Had Political Motive", Cameroon Express, no. 13, July 9, 1968, p. 3 and 7.

35. Interview: Mr. S. Epale, Buea, September 19, 1969; cf. N. Etienne, les Donnees essentielles de l'economie de la Republique federale du Cameroun, Yaounde, 1965, pp. 27 and 127, mimeo.

36. Federal Republic of Cameroon (Statistics Department), Note trimestrielle de statistique, 3^e trimestre, 1968, pp. 9-10:

Total production of electric power
(unit: 1,000 kw/h)

	1966	1967	1er Semestre 1968
East Cameroon	1,003,451r.	988,046	505,453
West Cameroon	8,992	9,537	5,080

37. Cameroon Express, no. 78, December 17, 1968, pp. 1 and 4.

38. Article 26 (which is new) of the decree no. 67-DF-238 promulgated on May 29, 1967, Journal officiel, June 1, 1967, p. 951 which modifies the decree no. 62-DF-90 of March 24, 1962.

39. "Cameroon Bank Board Dissolved--Commission Named to Probe Money Matters", Cameroon Express, no. 67, November 15, 1968, p. 1 and no. 78, December 17, 1968, pp. 1 and 4.

40. Mr. Jua, at first as Secretary of State for Finance and later as prime minister had tried to set up these self-financing methods after the federal government had refused to give him fixed and regular revenues every year. In fact, Mr. Jua stated that: "the present system through which the federal government grants an annual subsidy to the federated State to balance the deficit caused by the projected surplus in expenditure in relation to revenue, makes the estimate of the federated State's expenditures a risky job since the federated State cannot know beforehand the amount it will receive in a particular year from the federal government." (quoted in Claude E. Welch, "Cameroon since Reunification--3: The Finances of Federation", West Africa, November 2, 1963, p. 1241 [the translation is ours]).

41. The federal government demonstrated this
fact when it stated in 1968 that: "The financial
difficulties which the federal budget encountered
in its task of finding a fair balance between its
resources and the means required by its services
fixed from the beginning a limit on the contribution the federal government could make to the federated States. [...] West Cameroon was to receive
a 1,600 million grant which was [then] lower than
the amount granted in 1967-1968 by 200 million."
(cf. Federal Republic of Cameroon, Budget de
l'exercise 1968-1969, p. XXXVIII).
42. Estimates of West Cameroon, 1966-1967, p.
94.
43. The term belongs to Mr. Ardener, in Hazlewood, African Integration and Disintegration, p.
328.
44. Quoted in Claude E. Welch, "Cameroon since
Reunification--3: The Finances of Federation",
West Africa, November 2, 1963, p. 1241.
45. Since British aid had been very limited for
the past forty years, the entry into the franc zone
of the Federated State of West Cameroon enabled the
latter to receive "generous" aid from the French
Republic; and because the Federated State separated
from Nigeria in a rather abrupt manner, the latter
would insist that another currency replace "its"
pound sterling in any case. (When, in 1969-1970,
West Cameroonians pointed to the Moroccan case,
they perhaps forgot that the use of both currencies
concurrently only lasted for a short period of time
and that the peseta was then the stronger currency.)
Cf. Kjell Andersen, Report on the Economic Aspects
of a Possible Reunification of the British Cameroons with the Republic of Cameroon, Yaounde,
February 18, 1961, mimeo.
46. Presidential ordinance no. 62-DF-3 of
January 17, 1962; decree no. 62-DF-66 of February
24 fixed its terms and conditions.
47. Nigerian traders in West Cameroon were
accustomed to the exchange rate of 800 CFA francs
to the pound sterling: they accepted rather poorly
the new official rate of 692 francs to the pound
which the London Times (of September 8, 1961)
readily described moreover as "over-valued". Considering this rate to be artificially raised themselves, they envisaged only one solution: to raise
the selling price on their products since otherwise,
they would receive, in sterling currency, less than
they would have received before for the same sale.

It was, however, the illiterate women who encountered more difficulties in using this new currency
to make purchases at the public markets. Furthermore, the traders took advantage of this confusion.
As a result, West Cameroonians lacked confidence
in the CFA franc and they tended to hoard the pound
sterling to buy smuggled Nigerian products. (This
currency was exchanged on the black market for much
more than 692 francs per pound). The 1 shilling
coins inspired more confidence than the notes (of
25 or 50 CFA francs). The government therefore
decided to replace the notes with coins. These
aluminium coins, called "white francs" had not yet
been fully accepted in 1972. In 1963, the KNDP
Congress suggested forcing the traders to accept
them. In 1964, the Cameroon Times published letters
to the editor reaffirming the distrust of West
Cameroonians in this matter. The devaluation of
the pound sterling and later that of the franc
caused a rather painful imbroglio and a rapid look
at the Kumba, Mamfe and Bamenda markets in the
autumn of 1969 revealed that eight years after unification, no one was using the CFA franc; not only
did they refuse the coins but they seemed to be surprised to even see them. The three most common
reactions were expressed thus: Weti be dis? "Wuse
cana moni dis? I no di take dis cana moni".
    48. Those West Cameroon top officials question-
ed by this author in 1969 did not conceal the frustration they felt in such a situation. Here are
some questions and answers: "Certain French Cana-
dians speak of English Canadian imperialism in
Canada. If one admits as a hypothesis that an East
Cameroon imperialism exists in Cameroon, what field
of public activity will first come to your mind?"
"The introduction of the CFA franc in West Cameroon
without consulting us. They should have asked for
our opinion." "And what would you have suggested?"
"That we keep two currencies. The second will no
longer be the Nigerian pound but the currency in
circulation before 1959, the West African one."
The new control of import licences (decree no. 62-
DF-204 of June 16, 1962) forced the West Cameroon
wholesale traders to order their goods outside the
franc zone a year in advance. Several firms from
this federated State then decided to trade in the
franc zone since it was much easier to purchase
goods without having pound sterlings or special
licences. The John Holt Co., which had been operating in West Africa for eighty years, decided to

close its business firms in Cameroon.

In 1962-1963, Great Britain's important share in West Cameroon's market recorded a rapid and substantial drop due to a massive entry of French goods into the East. These were sold by East Cameroon's wholesale firms: during these two years, East Cameroon's export to its fellow state multiplied quantitatively by 40. In monetary value, it multiplied by 28 and with predictable consequences: those goods which were imported in large quantities remained on the counters of the traders and in the warehouses. Thus the statistics of the commercial exchanges between the federated States recorded what was far from the whole truth!

50. "Exchange control and import licensing are still the vexing question they have been since their introduction in West Cameroon. [...] Not much success has been achieved in convincing the authorities concerned to modify them or to fit them to the particular circumstances of West Cameroon. [...] [But] the initial irritation they caused to businessmen when they were newly introduced has lost much of its sting as people are learning to accommodate, or maybe to resign themselves to the new situation." (Estimates of West Cameroon 1964-1965, p. 126).

51. Cf. article 11 of the decree no. 62-DF-204 of June 16, 1962, Journal officiel, July 1, 1962, p. 627.

52. "The difficulties inherent in Exchange control and import licensing system are still plaguing the trade of West Cameroon. Recent short-age of salt and rice are thought to be attributable to the rigidity of the system. Efforts are still being made with a view of convincing the authori-ties as to the necessity of modifying the system." (Estimates of West Cameroon 1965-1966, p. 122).

53. Press conference, in ACAP, no. 259, November 12-13, 1961.

54. Cf. Bederman, The Cameroons Development Corporation, p. 31.

55. Georges Burdeau, Traité de Science politique, vol. II: L'Etat, 2nd ed., Paris, Librairie generale de droit et de jurisprudence, 1967, p. 470.

56. Even if the 1963 West Cameroon banana harvest was in fact sold--and at prices which were until then unattainable--because of a hurricane in the West Indies, the traditional suppliers for several countries, the fear of harvest losses re-

duced production substantially.

57. Can one blame the federal government for the loss in preferential tariffs? West Cameroon's top officials were convinced that they would have been able to retain this tariff if the Constitution had allowed them to put the necessary pressure on the British government, and that in this sense, federalism had been very harmful. The Federal Minister of Commerce pointed out that West Cameroon's prime minister and secretaries of state went several times to London during this period and that they had the opportunity to present their viewpoint themselves, even if it was privately.

58. "As regards the elimination of imperial preferences, I should say that since reunification, we have been in a fair-play position vis-a-vis the British government. [...] One cannot say that even if the principle of preference was abnormal, the unilateral elimination of this preference was fair-play. [...] As for the preferences themselves, they benefit [...] bananas in particular. [...] Thus West Cameroon's producers, particularly [those] connected with the CDC earned between 200 and 300 millions; this is what they should lose after the elimination of preferences." (cf. Mr. Ahidjo's press conference, in ACAP, July 2, 1963).

In a statement to the House of Commons, a British minister seemed to have agreed completely with the Cameroon government: the latter was in no way responsible: Jamaican planters had exerted pressure in order that their bananas have preference. Cf. House of Commons Debates, July 22, 1963, col. 1204: "Jamaica and the Windward Islands [are] both concerned to increase their export earnings and worried about the tendency, especially in the winter months, for the British market to be oversupplied with bananas. These countries have made it clear that they are strongly opposed to sharing their preferential advantages in our market with West Cameroon given that the territory is the only area in the world which enjoys preference both in Britain and in the EEC." (Minister of State at the Board of Trade.)

59. Decree no. 64-DF-3 of January 2, 1964 creating a Coordination Committee on the Banana Industry and on Banana Growing Areas; decree no. 64-DF-180 of June 1, 1964 creating the Cameroon Banana Organization; and decree no. 64-DF-480 of December 12, 1964 appointing a technical director for this organization.

60. Cf. SP. P. Tchoungi, "The gradual economic integration of both federated States", Europe-France-Outre-mer, no. 416, September 1964, p. 49.

61. Cameroon Express, no. 70, November 28, 1968, p. 3.

62. The State Secretariat for Aid, located on Rue Monsieur in Paris, refuses to let itself be involved in a controversy which it believes involves only the Cameroonians themselves. There is no international agreement on bananas as there is on coffee. What exists is a special agreement with France. Under this, preferential prices are accorded to the West Indies, the Ivory Coast, Cameroon and the Malagasy Republic. Each year, France establishes its needs in this field after taking into consideration the Treaty of Rome and the needs of the market. The so-called "German" protocol which is annexed to the Treaty of Rome is no help at all to West Cameroon. When France in 1957 in Rome applied for the overseas colonies and territories maintaining special relations with it to be associated with the EEC, West Germany obtained, through a special protocol, the right to import a certain quantity of bananas without paying the duties included in List F of the common customs tariff. The latter protects the European Community against imports from other countries. This tariff, which applies to all the member states, has been about 20% since July 1, 1968. Calculated on a scale which takes into consideration a national consumption growing at a constant rate, along with quotas which complete it, this tariff quota in fact authorizes West Germany to import almost all its needs without paying any customs duty. Thus Germany preserves for its industry its traditional commercial links with Latin American customers while realizing substantial profits from the bananas it buys from them. In its article 2, the Yaounde Convention formally repeats the German protocol. West Cameroonians believe, however, that it tends to make it more flexible. By contrast, Annex IX of the Convention however, seems to reinforce it. This Annex in fact stipulates that the associated States (including Cameroon) will be consulted on the possibility of supplying Germany "under suitable conditions" with the quantities of bananas it would request in addition to the ordinary quota that the Protocol grants it. The expression "under suitable conditions" seems to damage any good that Annex IX could have as an advantage for the associa-

ted States; in fact, West Germany never stopped imagining conditions which the Africans and Malagasians could not fulfill at the moment when it formulated them: demand for specific banana varieties, refusal to send them in plastic-covered bunches, unacceptable prices, etc. Thus West Germany continues to take advantage of its privilege; 93% of its bananas in fact come from Latin America. Furthermore, banana-exporting associated countries include not only Cameroon, the Ivory Coast, and Madagascar but also Somalia, the two Congos and Surinam. Thus Cameroon only supplies 300 tons of banana to Germany in prosperous years (out of the 615,000 tons which Bonn imports)...One cannot exactly describe this as a market for West Cameroon's bananas. Furthermore, the average price for South American bananas arriving at the European ports is 0.70 CFA franc/kilo and if one deducts 0.70 CFA franc from the common customs tariff, one has 0.84 franc, a price which is still lower than the Cameroon price. Why then should France's partners within the EEC have to increase their purchase of Cameroon's bananas to please West Cameroonians!

63. Because the normal ceiling was fixed at 10kg/person annually, it is actually attained in West Germany (10.4), but not in France (9.2) nor in Belgium (9.6). According to CDC leaders, it is not obvious that "Bulgarians do not even know that one has to remove the peel of a banana before eating it!" as federal officials maintain in order to explain their decisions not to make an effort to open the market to Bulgaria.

Cameroon can even export to France 53,420 of the bananas consumed there following a quota specified by a bilateral agreement. This rate is fixed, but the tonnage varies according to the estimated French consumption. It reached 65,6000 tons in 1965, 52,000 tons in 1966, 46,000 in 1967 and 44,000 in 1968. Furthermore, since the beginning of 1968, there has been, in France, a standardization decree specifying the number of acceptable and unspoiled bananas that would be accepted. Ecuador which is particularly disliked by West Cameroonians exported 16,000 tons of bananas to France in 1965, 8,000 tons in 1967 and 6,000 in 1968. Why bananas from Ecuador? General de Gaulle's visit to Latin America had something to do with this decision. Furthermore, while labour cost/kilo of bananas in Cameroon or the Ivory Coast is 0.12 franc, it is 0.03 franc in Ecuador. But it seems that France

takes advantage of this fact essentially to stabil-
ize prices: the quota exists because to glut the
French market would amount to lowering the prices
of bananas; but when France considers it appropriate to lower prices, it is bananas from Ecuador
that it imports!

64.   "Despite the fact that West Cameroon is
part of the Federal Republic of Cameroon, it did
not manage to obtain a share of the country's
banana quota until the end of 1966 as the producers in East Cameroon, jealous of their situation, successfully kept West Cameroon producers
from infringing upon their share." (Bederman,
The Cameroons Development Corporation, p. 31).

65.   Cameroons Development Corporation. Annual
Reports and Accounts for the Year Ended 31st
December 1966, Victoria, CSC, 1967, p. 11; and
Europe-France-Outre-mer, no. 474-475, July-August
1969, pp. 30-31.

66.   "During the last two years, the percentage of wharf rejects for boxed Poyo bananas has
increased. Bananas shipped these days are con-
signed in hands and put into cartons. One wonders
how a whole carton of any eight to nine hands will
completely be unfit for export.

"These bananas are graded and boxed at the
various boxing stations by supervisors skilled for
this job, yet a staff of the Marketing and Inspection unit rejects these bananas. [...] The only
place to grade and inspect boxed bananas [should]
be the boxing station, and not the wharf." (cf.
"What's Wrong with These Bananas?", Cameroon Express, no. 76, December 12, 1968, p. 2).

67.   Hapi, "The marketing of tropical products....", p. 57.

68.   The International Agreement on Coffee,
signed in 1962 and renewed in 1968 between producing and consumer countries creates mechanisms
of control and quotas on world coffee production.
The five-year basic quota was established for each
country according to the annual statistical account for coffee production in that country during
the previous ten years. The purpose was to
identify "the trend of production". Thus Brazil
obtained an export quota of 20 million 60 kg bags
for the five years, Colombia received 7 million,
the Ivory Coast 3 million, Cameroon 1 million, etc.
For Cameroon in particular, what these statistical
data reveal harms its interests because the troubles
in the coffee-producing areas prevented a normal

production of coffee to take place during the period they took into consideration. Furthermore, this is why the 1 million bag quota is slightly higher than the statistical extrapolation. And yet, Cameroon had asked for a 1.5 million bag quota.

It was from this five-year quota that the annual one was fixed for the African countries. This time, this was established as a unit. One simply established the import estimate (consumer nations) and one distributes the goods in proportion to the basic quotas. This was the technical explanation which officials of the Federal Board of Raw Materials gave to West Cameroonians who complained of not being able to sell their production. And they added that there was a structural over-production of coffee at that moment (production exceeded consumption); consequently, article 48 of the International Coffee Agreement obliges us "to adjust our production."

The eight coffee producing African countries form the OAMCAF (African and Malagasy Organization of Coffee Producing Nations) which was created in 1960. Since 1963, the latter has been responsible for ensuring the coordination of the coffee policies of its member states. Since 1969, which was when the renewed statutes of the OAMCAF were signed, the eight members, however, have preferred to limit the role of the organization to that of "a shield": the countries present a united front only at the International Coffee Organization.

As it is described by the Raw Materials Board itself, its work method is the following: each year, at the end of the coffee campaign, the International Coffee Organization offers a quota to the OAMCAF under article 30 of the International Agreement; at the end of September, this organization gives Cameroon a quota for the following three months basing its judgment both on Cameroon's reserves (article 49 of the International Agreement) and on the production prospects during the current year. Thus the quota is a percentage of the total reserve and estimates. But it is the Federal Raw Materials Board and it alone which fixes West Cameroon's portion of this quota.

69. Cameroon Express, no. 99, February 19, 1969, pp. 1 and 8.

70. "Each producing State promises to adjust its production such that it does not exceed the quantities required for domestic production, for

the exports allowed and for the building up of
reserves...." article 48, paragraph 1, Accord
international sur le café 1968, Paris, OAMCAF, p.
27). Interview: Mr. Joseph Ndi, general secretary of the OAMCAF, Paris, November 15, 1969.
    71. "Before the Federal National Assembly,
the Head of State invokes the need to balance the
public finance and currenty", l'Unité, no. 85, May
15-55, 1968, p. 1.
    72. Cf. Decree no. 65-DF-163, Journal officiel,
May 15, 1965, pp. 515-516.
    73. Even if this treasury is also in charge of
certain services as the Federated State of West
Cameroon, its status as Federal Treasury prevents
its financial account to show a deficit at any time.
"Since revenues ony come in late to the government,
this presidential decree reduces the activities of
the federated governments to their simplest expression." In fact, the federated State was no
longer even allowed to disburse the sums authorized
by its own legislative Assembly, a fact which seems
contrary to the essence of federalism itself. This
measure was poorly received, for it seemed to constitute at the time the official government's reply to Mr. Jua's. The latter requested that fixed
sources of revenue be provided for in the Constitution; he asserted that revenues authorized annually
by the federal Assembly did not enable its government to plan ahead in terms of the economic development of the federated State. Cf. "[...]
Connected with this was the [...] federalization of
the former West Cameroon Treasury. This move which
is very important has had interesting consequences
in the operation of the West Cameroon budget and
will have a modifying effect on the philosophy on
which the West Cameroon financial operations have
so far been based. In the first place, the Treasury
now serves merely as a bank. By Decree No. 66-DF-
155 two accounts were opened in the Treasury one
each for the Federated States of East and West
Cameroon. Article 5 of the Decree stipulates that
those accounts must always be in credit. Whenever
they are in debt, the Federated State concerned
must apply to the Central Treasury for some accommodation, with agreed terms of repayment. Until this
is done by Presidential Decree, the Federated
State whose account is in debit cannot make any payments arising out of its budgetary operations even
though provision for such payments may exist in the

Budget.

"As is only well known, revenue does not come in as fast as expenditure proceeds. The Treasury motivation, therefore, would mean that unless State expenditure is not only carefully controlled but also judiciously phased and programmed the possibility that even the salaries of Government officials will not be paid at a particular time would not be remote." (Secr. of State, Mr. Kemcha, Estimates of West Cameroon 1966-1967, p. 92).

74. Cameroons Development Corporation, Report and Accounts 1966, p. 8; West Cameroon Estimates 1967-1968, p. 82.

75. In 1969-1970, CDC's capital thus included the following: 685 million CFA francs invested by the West Cameroon government, 519 million by the West Cameroon Marketing Board, and 278 million by the federal government.

76. Paul Lewis, The Financial Times, February, 19, 1969.

77. Cf. A. H. Birch, "Opportunities and Problems of Federation", in Leys and Robson, ed., Federation in East Africa, Oxford University Press, 1965, pp. 6-7.

78. This forest zone annually sends about 65,000 tons of timber to the coast while about 90,000 tons are felled and 145,000 could be felled if the region had the facilities required to transport the timber to the coast.

79. "Both federated States are now linked by rail and will soon be by road", Europe-France-Outre-mer, May 1966, pp. 25 and 27.

80. Cf. "Problems at the ports", le Soir, January 16, 1970, p. 2.

81. Le Soir, January 28, 1970, p. 2.

82. Decree no. 62-DF-409 of November 23, 1962, Journal officiel, December 1, 1962, pp. 1333-1334.

83. Interviews at the West Cameroon prime minister's office in September and October 1969.

84. Cameroon Times, July 9, 1965, p. 3.

85. "To what extent is a "sense of community" developing? The development of a political community is considered as a parallel process of developing political institutions at one level and increasing consensus for their acceptance at the other level." (John H. Sloane, "Political Integration in the European Community", Revue canadienne de science politique, vol. I, no. 4, December 1968, p. 459).

86. Adolf Dipoko, "Reunification Road is New Link for Commerce, Leisure", Cameroon Express, no.

49, October 5, 1968, p. 5.

87. "Muna--Victoria to Become Cameroon's Largest Port", Cameroon Times, vol. 8, no. 37, March 13, 1968, p. 3.

88. Cf. also Edwin Ardener, in Arthur Hazlewood, African Integration and Disintegration, pp. 335-336 for an outline of this organigram.

89. Cf. meeting paper "Governments and politics: criteria of analysis and comparison", 3rd cycle seminar, Institut d'études politiques de Paris, année universitaire 1969-1970.

8
The Political Economy
of Regional Economic Development
in Cameroon

Wilfred A. Ndongko

INTRODUCTION

It has been argued that "the questions of
social and economic justice in the distribution of
the fruits of economic progress are as important
and as difficult in terms of regions as in terms of
social classes."[1] It is, indeed, in recognition of
this vital problem, that Cameroon with its diverse
culture, ethnic, economic, and linguistic background,
has since independence adopted a regional approach
to planning with a view to attaining a balanced distribution of investment resources and the fruits of
economic progress. Specifically, Cameroonian experience in regional planning began with the Second
Five Year Economic and Social Development Plan
(July 1966--June 1971), and has continued with the
Third Five Year Plan (July 1971--June 1976) and
Fourth Five Year Plan (1976--1980).

Economic planning in Cameroon has been region-
alized in the sense that it has all along taken into
account the specific problems of the regions. However, regionalization of development planning has
not meant regionalism but rather integrated development with a view to achieving optimal growth of the
national economy. This is because prior to independence Cameroonian economic and social development
policy reflected the influence of the colonial pact
which never took the local structures and conditions
into consideration.

Indeed, the differential impacts of the
British and French economic policies laid the foundation for the economic disparities which existed
between the different regions of Cameroon before
independence and have continued to persist till
today.[2]

Because of the increasing concern for this trend of development by Cameroonian authorities, the purpose of this paper is to examine the dimensions of regional development problems and the development objectives with a view to proposing a theoretical framework which will be used to analyse the functioning of the national investment legislation which was intended to encourage both private domestic and foreign investments in Cameroon. Specifically, an attempt will be made to find out whether or not the approval and location of investment activities have been carried out within the framework of balanced regional development objective of the Cameroon Government.

To this end, the paper is divided into eight sections. The present section is the introduction. The dimensions of regional development problems are discussed in section II. The objectives and process of regional planning are the subject matter of section III. The analytical framework for examining the performance of the investment incentives takes up section IV. The nature of investment incentives and the results of their application are examined in Sections V and VI, respectively. The analysis of the policy implications and the recommendations are taken up in section VII. Finally, section VIII is devoted to the concluding remarks.

THE DIMENSIONS OF REGIONAL DEVELOPMENT PROBLEMS

The regional problems of Cameroon like those of many other developing countries do overlap in many respects. To this extent, therefore, the development policies and programmes initiated since 1960 under the Five Year Development Plans to combat regional disparities have been to a large extent complementary. A glance at the regional problems in Cameroon will indicate that they range from low per capita incomes, poor and inadequate social and physical infrastructure, unequal distribution of industrial activities, to low growth rates. In general, the regional disparities in Cameroon have existed mainly between the northern and southern parts of the nation.[3] Table 8.1 and Table 8.2 provide some economic data on the former six regions of the Republic.

It will be observed from Table 8.1 that three regions--North, South-Central, and former West Cameroon--all have had populations of over 1 million inhabitants. However, former West Cameroon, has had

a higher population density than any of the three
regions. Further, former West Cameroon, North, and
East are the three areas which have had about 90%
of their total population living in backward rural
areas. This reflects the "relative underdevelopment
of these regions," especially when they are compared
with the Littoral and Centre South.

In terms of the percentage of the school-age
population (6-13 years) attending primary school,
the North, East, and former West Cameroon have been
among the regions with less than 60% of the school-
age population receiving some primary education. In
particular, the Northern region (with only 27%) is
far below the level attained by any region. On the
other hand, by 1970, the Littoral, South-Central,
and Western Regions had over 80% of the children
with primary school age attending school. (See
Table 8.1).

As regards the major crops produced for domestic consumption and export, it can be observed from
Table 8.1 that all the regions, except former West
Cameroon, produce almost all the main products. In
addition, they also produce a wider variety of goods
than that region. For example, the South-Central
region produces all crops except cotton, which is
produced only in the North.

In general, the problems of the Eastern region
include inefficient organization of agricultural,
livestock, and industrial production; depletion of
forestry resources; insufficient infrastructure, and
sparse population distribution which hinders large
scale industrial development in that region. All
these problems prevail in the other five remaining
regions except that of sparse population, which is
a unique feature of the Northern region.

For the Western region, the problem of rapid
urban population growth (8.0% per year) has been
very acute whilst the Northern region has had some
300,000 people living below subsistence level.
Further, it has inadequate medical facilities and
medical education, and the rapid movement of population Southward coupled with widely dispersed rural
population has created difficulties in the development of transportation network essential for the
industrial transformation of the region.

The Littoral region, where most of the industrial activities concentrate, has inadequate capacity in both public and private secondary schools to
absorb primary school leavers. Furthermore, the
urban-rural economic and social disparities in this
region, have given rise to a rapid movement of

229

TABLE 8.1
The Regional Structure of Cameroon – 1970

	East	West	North	Littoral	Centre—South	Former West Cameroon
A. AREA (Sq. Kilometres)	109,000	14,100	153,589	21,000	118,000	42,400
B. POPULATION (1969)	288,000	800,000	1,400,000	680,000	1,170,000	1,250,000
Rural Population (%)	90%	80%	92%	32%	70%	90%
Population Growth Rate	2.0%	1.5%	1.3%	4.5%	2.0%	2.3%
Population Density	2.6 Km²	56 Km²	9.7 Km²	30 Km²	23 Km²	28 Km²
C. EDUCATION—Primary Sch. Attend.	63%	80%	27%	81.2%	88.8%	57%
% of Population in School	n.a.	45%	20%	n.a.	n.a.	14%
The Labour Force	n.a.	310,000	n.a.	300,000	632,000	600,000
No. of Wage Earners	n.a.	16,000	n.a.	60,000	73,000	33,000
D. HEALTH—No. of Persons per Dr.	28,000	29,000	83,000	n.a.	14,500	40,000
E. MAIN PRODUCT						
Coffee (tons)	6,297	32,600	260	27,380	5,406	11,430
Cocoa (tons)	7,500	n.a.	n.a.	3,368	94,200	8,000
Cotton (tons)	—	—	68,000	—	—	—
Bananas (tons)	—	—	—	28,000	350	61,036
Groundnuts (tons)	7,200	16,000	53,000	—	19,988	—
Maize (tons)	18,000	112,000	26,000	—	28,000	—
Plantain (tons)	153,000	73,000	—	200,000	273,000	n.a.
Manioc (tons)	111,700	—	119,000	92,000	180,390	—
Yams (tons)	—	18,000	—	26,000	12,000	n.a.
Sweet Potatoes (tons)	560	47,000	35,000	—	5,000	20,000
Palm Oil (tons)	—	n.a.	—	9,700	10,000	17,215

Source: Data compiled from Cameroon, Ministry of Information and Tourism, Yaounde, 1970 and Elaboration de IIIe Plan Quinquennal 1971–76, Regional Synthesis, November, 1960. Third Five Year Economics & Social Development Plan: 1971/72 – 1975/76 – The Regions, Yaounde, June, 1972.

TABLE 8.2

Cameroon: Regional Economic Indicators 1966 and 1971

Region	Population Size		Growth Rate of Population	% Share	Regional Per Capita Products (Francs CFA)		Total Increase 1966-71	Annual Growth Rates of Regional
	1966	1971			1966	1971		
Centre-South	1000000	1220000	2.5%	20	40000	610000	21000	2.5%
Littoral	60000	709000	3.9%	12	70000	92250	25250	10.0%
West	70000	881000	3.0%	14	40000	45400	5400	7.0%
East	25000	26000	2.0%	5	20800	33700	12700	5.0%
North	1400000	1648000	2.6%	28	15000	18200	3200	4.0%
Former West Cameroon	1100000	1304000	2.5%	21	25000	25700	700	5.0%
Cameroon	5505000	5988000	2.8%	100	35000	38050	3050	6.8%

Source: The Second Five Year Plan 1966 - 71 Yaounde, June 1966.
"Elaboration of 3rd Plan 1971 - 76: Regional Analysis," Yaounde 1969.

population from the depressed rural to urban centres. Finally, for the former West Cameroon region, the major problems facing it include insufficient energy production which limits industrial development, deficient transport and communication system; inadequate medical personnel and equipment, and poor methods of producing foodstuffs in the villages and rural areas. The rapid increase in population (2.3%) per annum calls for an increase in the production of foodstuffs and the adaptation of education and manpower training to the development needs of that region.[4]

The consequences for former West Cameroon (now South-West and North-West Provinces) of the creation of a unitary state have been far-reaching. Having a weaker economy, former West Cameroon has not been able to absorb the shock caused by its sudden integration with the more virile economy of the former East Cameroon for example, the transfer of virtually all civil servants and politicians from Buea and Victoria--the major administrative and commercial centres of West Cameroon before reunification--has greatly reduced an important source of purchasing power and the closing down of many shops. To this extent, the departure of high income earners has affected the expansion of retail trade and large businesses.

There are strong apriori reasons for expecting a high and growing degree of regional inequality in the Cameroon. This trend may continue because the frequently observed negative correlation between the degrees of economic development and inequality,[5] is particularly due to the process of "cumulative causation" and the general weakness of the spread effects relative to backward effects in underdeveloped countries.[6] These factors have been instrumental in aggravating these disparities, but the government policy of maintaining equilibrium between the sectors and regions may certainly help in alleviating the differences.[7]

THE OBJECTIVES AND PROGRESS OF REGIONAL PLANNING

In any country, the objectives of policy at the regional level are bound to conflict in any development plan which runs the entire gamut of the social and economic life of the regions. Their reconciliation is always a difficult and delicate task. These objectives, some of which can only be defined in quantitative terms, are not necessarily comparable.

232

For example, the requirements for rapid economic growth are to a large extent in conflict with national, social, and political objectives.

Although, it can be argued that it is to rapid economic growth that countries like Cameroon, must look to in order to free themselves from the grips of poverty, disease, ignorance, and economic and social inequalities, it must be noted that such a policy may not necessarily be progressive. In the circumstances, therefore, it would appear that economic growth can be carefully and continuously traded off with other social goals to meet the requirements of social and economic justice.

To this extent, a fundamental preoccupation of the Cameroon authorities since reunification in 1961, has been the problem of economic development. To a large extent the complex and challenging problems of independence have taken on a new dimension within the framework of the larger demands and aspirations of national economic growth. For this reason, therefore, the prevailing official meed in the nation has been one of optimism that Cameroon could achieve self-sustained growth and balanced regional development.

To be sure, it does appear that the designation of economic regions in Cameroon has been carried within the context or framework of most of the requirements for rational delineations of the regions. Because of the unique cultural, ethnic, economic, and social characteristics of Cameroon, economic regions fall under the Provincial Governors who are in charge of regional plans. It would, therefore, appear that the over-riding consideration in the division of the nation into six administrative and economic regions since the inception of the second Five Year Plan for Economic and Social Development (1966-71) and later to seven provinces following the creation of the United Republic in 1972 was to hasten the removal of the economic disparities which have existed between the different regions of Cameroon since independence.

The process of preparing regional development plans consists of two stages. Firstly, an exercise which consists of the identification of the potentials for economic and social development and problems impeding growth in each region, including specific public private investment programmes which can help develop those potential, is carried out. Further, areas which in each region's judgement are most likely to have the potential for future growth and centres from which the population can be served

233

in order to promote the overall development of the region, are also identified. Following this exercise, a determination of investment priorities is undertaken with a view to ensuring maximum gains from public and private capital invested.

These benefits are in the form of improved opportunities for permanent employment and increased levels of income on a continuing rather than on a temporary basis. A further exercise involving a scheduling and programming of feasible projects for implementation is undertaken. On the basis of this work, the Head of State issues directives to all Ministries and Provincial authorities reiterating the basic guidelines and fixing the objectives of the plan and the strategic operations to be adopted.

The second stage consists of the meeting of the national and provincial planning boards. During these meetings the regional/provincial boards are responsible for:

(i) defining the conditions under which strategic investments concerning their respective areas would have to be put into operation so as to have maximum effectiveness, coherence, and induced effects, and

(ii) taking into account the strategic operations and their effects, defining regional objectives and the methods they propose to achieve them.

Finally, the provincial and divisional programmes are established by the national planning boards in collaboration with the provincial and national administrative structures. It should be noted that the total cost of the projects approved for all the regions does not usually exceed the total projected investment for Cameroon as a whole for each five year plan.

Apart from the fact that sectoral projects in each region/province are weighed and ranked according to their productivity, Cameroonian regional development policy aims at maintaining:

(i) "equilibrium between ethnic groups and regions, none of which can be treated with special favour or disfavour but which must certainly improve their knowledge of each to promote friendship;

(ii) equilibrium between town and country, agriculture and industry, manual workers, and civil servants; so that economic development can be realised in a climate of national solidarity; and

234

(iii) equilibrium between culture, which must give birth to authentic Cameroonian civilization."[8]

It should be pointed out that the sole political party--the Cameroon National Union--plays a dual role in ensuring that the foregoing regional development objectives are achieved. Firstly, by remaining in permanent contact with the population, it is supposed to observe and make known the aspirations, desires, and reactions of the masses of the people with a view to guiding national decision-making. Secondly, it is supposed to mobilize and organize the masses with a view to ensuring their effective participation in the implementation of the regional development policy.

THE ANALYTICAL FRAMEWORK

Because of the importance placed by the Cameroon Government on the objective of balanced regional development, it is essential that the policy instruments at the disposal of the institution and legislations created to implement the objective are capable of making an effective and lasting contribution to the realization of the objective. To this extent, the purpose of this section of the paper is to set up an analytical framework which will aid in the examination of the nature of the provisions and application of the national investment incentives with a view to determining whether or not they have so far reflected the Cameroon Government policy of maintaining equilibrium between ethnic groups and regions.

The basic hypothesis which will guide the analysis of the problem posed in this paper is that investment incentives which place greater emphasis on the spatial dimension of economic activities in any country could redress the adverse effects of the economic and social disparities and the uneven development of the economic and administrative provinces, particularly as the pattern of industrial location is too great a political and social consequence to be subjected entirely to economic calculus.

On the basis of this postulate, the problem presented in this paper is tackled in two stages: Firstly, an economic analysis of the provisions of the Cameroon Investment Code is undertaken with a view to determining whether or not they originally reflected the Cameroon development objective of balanced regional development. Secondly, an

235

examination of the actual application of the provisions of the Code since its creation, is also
undertaken. This analysis is made with respect to
the location of the industries which have benefited
from the incentives provided by the Code, the size
of the investments undertaken by each investor, the
income, and the employment generated.
  The results of the above exercise will reveal
whether or not the application of the investment
legislation has led to the decentralization of
economic activities (which will be in keeping with
the Cameroon policy of balanced regional development) or has instead encouraged the concentration
of industrial activities (in which case that will be
inconsistent with the stated development objective).
  Assuming for the moment that an analysis of the
application of the provisions of the investment
legislation reveals that it has so far widened the
economic and social disparities between the different regions and provinces of the United Republic,
then the question arises as to whether they did not
originally take into consideration the balanced
development objective of the nation or they have
deliberately deviated from their original mission
of ensuring that their application encourage the decentralization of economic activities with a view to
correcting the fundamental structural disequilibrium
between the economies of the provinces. If both are
true, then some corrective measures will have to be
introduced so as to redefine its functions and to
revise the present incentives in order to enable the
attainment of the development objective.
  Alternatively, if the analysis reveals that its
application has reflected the national objective of
balanced regional development, then the question
arises as to why there are still wide economic and
social disparities between the different regions
and provinces of the United Republic. Whatever is
the outcome of the analysis of the provisions of the
investment Code and their application, the stubborn
persistence of the economic and social differences
in the Cameroon economy at various levels of
development, may be identified as a peculiar facet
of the process of economic and social change.
  To be sure, this frame of reference could be
utilized in examining the activity of such public
financial institutions like the Cameroon Development
Bank and the National Investment Corporation with a
view to determining whether or not they have so far
reflected Cameroon's development policy of reducing
economic and social disparities between the

different regions and the provinces through the re-
tional planning process and institutions.*

THE NATURE OF THE INCENTIVES

The need for industrial incentives arose from
the fact that since the initiation of the First
Five Year Development Plan (1960-65), the total
projected investments have far exceeded the expected public savings. For example, under the
1966-71 plan, foreign private investment was expected to account for 36% of the total planned investment whilst domestic private investment was to
account for 4%. Thus, private investment was to
account for 40% of the total planned capital expenditure.
Considering the fact that virtually all private
investments were to be directed to productive economic sectors, which have traditionally been employment and income-generating, it became necessary to
create investment incentives which would attract the
required domestic and foreign private investments
within the framework of the major objective of the
Five Year Development Plans--namely, the maintenance of equilibrium or balance between the various
sectors and regions of the national economy.
As concerns the investment incentives which
are administered by the National Investment Commission, it should be noted that they were first
approved by the Cameroon National Assembly on
June 27, 1960. Although, they were introduced prior
to the reunification of former French Cameroon with
Southern Cameroon, they were later extended to the
entire Republic.[9] In view of the importance of the
incentives, as part of the Government's programme to
foster the expansion of domestic and foreign private
business, within the general policy of balanced
development, it is necessary to give a summary of
each of the four categories into which they are
divided.
i. Preferential Treatment A, permits duty-free
entry of the required raw materials and capital
goods for a period of up to ten years and allows

_____

*Such institutions include the Regional Devel-
opment Councils, Divisional Development Committee
and Rural Action Committees.

237

reduced rates of, or exemption from, indirect taxes (for example, the single Tax on production) on finished products for a period of up to three years, including exemption from new taxes and changes in the rates of existing ones.

ii. Under Preferential Treatment B, enterprises may be eligible to obtain, in addition to the benefits under Preferential Treatment A, exemption for a period of up to five years from taxes on profits and, in the case of mining and timber companies, from the payment of royalties. They are also eligible for many benefits from new tax laws that might be introduced during the first ten years of their operations.

iii. Under Preferential Treatment C, large corporations may conclude an agreement with the government under which they may receive all or part of the privileges of Preferential Treatment B. The agreement in each case will also define other government guarantees in the legal, economic, and financial fields, including the undertaking to assure stable conditions for financial transfers and the marketing of the enterprise's goods for a period of up to 25 years. The enterprise in its turn, must guarantee a minimum volume of production and grant to its employees certain minimum social benefits, including housing.

iv. Preferential Treatment D, which applies to enterprises making investments of particular importance to the long-term economic development of the country, gives to the enterprises all the benefits of Preferential Treatment C as well as a guarantee that new taxes and tax rates will not apply to such enterprises for up to 25 years.

Although it would appear from the above incentives that they were intended to have reaching and lasting effects on national development, it should be pointed out that in general, the Investment Code does not define the areas of the economy in which foreign and domestic private capital can be channelled, in view of the broad national development objective of balanced development and the prevalent regional income disparities which have continued between the provinces till today.

It should also be pointed out here that two other public financial institutions were created--

namely, the Cameroon Development Bank* and the
National Investment Corporation--to mobilize and
oriented national savings towards the promotion
of investment operations of economic and social interest in the fields of industry, agriculture and
Commerce. Like the Investment Code, the provisions
of these financial institutions have not reflected
the regional dimension of development in Cameroon.

THE GRANTING OF THE INCENTIVES

An examination of private investments, approved
under the Investment Code by the Investment Commission during the 1962-63 financial year, reveals
that eleven firms were granted benefits.[10] The investment activities of these firms involved some
2,445 million francs CFA and the creation of 1,000
jobs.[11] Further, during the same period, about
twenty applications were received from other firms
which wanted to undertake investments to the volume
of 5,700 million francs CFA. However, the number of
applications that were approved is not known.
During the 1963-64 fiscal year, private investment approved under the Code, amounted to 158
million francs CFA. These investments went into
hosiery, pin, building material, and manufacturing
industries. By June 30, 1965, a total of 38 companies with capital investments to value of 10,393
million francs CFA had been approved under the Code.
These companies also generated 8,000 new jobs.[12]
The distribution of the companies approved, by
sectors of economic activity, is presented in
Table 8.3.
During the 1965-66 fiscal year, 15 new firms
which provided investments to the amount of 4,180
million francs CFA were approved under the Code.
These firms also generated 2,500 new jobs. Amongst
the companies approved were a flour mill, a plywood
factory, a wooden-box factory, and several saw
mills--most of which were located in the littoral
province. In the former West Cameroon, four firms
were granted relief under the Code--the Brittind
Industries Ltd., and Emen Textiles--both of which

---

*c.f. Wilfred A. Ndongko, "Development Bank
Lending: The Cameroon Experience," World Development, Oxford, Vol. 3, June 1975.

TABLE 8.3
Companies Approved Under the Investment Code as of June 30, 1965

	Location	No. of Firms	Amount of Investment proposed Mill. CFA	No. of new jobs created
Power-based industries				
Mineral Products industries	(L)	9	1,735	346
Timber industries	(C-S, W-C, E)	8	1,061	1,648
Textile and Clothing industries	(N, L)	2	192	385
Food industries	(W, L)	5	3,440	1,875
Miscellaneous industries	(x)	14	3,965	3,795
		38	10,393	8,049

Source: Second Annual Report of the National Credit Council, 1964-66 (Yaounde, June 1967), p. 101.

L = Littoral, E = East, W-C - West Cameroon
N = North, X = Location not Known
W = Western Region, C-S = Centre-South

were engaged in assembly of umbrellas and plastic shoe manufacturing. It should be noted.

Between July 1966 and June 1968, 12 firms were approved under the Code. These included one oil prospecting firm, six food processing firms, two in textile and clothing manufacturing, and one in cement production. Additional companies approved were one flour and one glass industry. The total investments undertaken by the 12 firms amounted to 1,089 million francs CFA. In addition, these firms also created 5,000 new jobs.[13]

Between 1961 and 1969, a total of 133 firms were approved under the Investment Code. These firms created 37,927 million francs CFA worth of investments, in addition to generating 32,757 new jobs. The sectoral distribution of the new investments created is presented in Table 8.4. Again, it

240

TABLE 8.4
Industries Approved Under the Investment Code: 1961-1969
  (Millions francs CFA)

	Location	Volume of Investment
Energy Industries	(L)	10,854 million francs
Primary Products Processing industries	(W.L.)	10,847 million francs
Aluminium Production	(L)	9,827 million francs
Forestry Industry	(C-S, W.C., E)	3,200 million francs
Textile and shoe Production	(W.L.N.)	2,710 million francs
Chemical Industry	(W.L.)	489 million francs
TOTAL INVESTMENTS		37,927 million francs

Source: "Investments and Economic Development: Cameroon,"
        Bulletin de l'Afrique, (Paris, July 1970), pp. 12,
        251-254.

will be observed from Table 8.4 that over 90% of the
investments approved were in Littoral.

Scholars and practitioners are deeply divided
on whether the Investment Code has so far facilitated the promotion of economic projects and regional
programmes. To what extent has the Code encouraged
the movement of business undertakings to the less
endowed regions of the country? The answer to this
question may be discovered if one examines the information available in Table 8.5 on the various
economic sectors and industries which have benefited
from the provisions of the National Investment Code
as of June 30, 1975.

To this extent, it should be noted that the
agricultural industries approved under one of the
schedules of the Code can be classified into two
groups: forestry industries and agro-industries.
It will be observed from Table 8.5 that there were
some thirty-four wood and forestry undertakings in
the Centre-South Province as of June 30, 1975.
Their investments amounted to some six milliard nine
hundred and sixty-two million CFA francs. Their

TABLE 8.5
Forestry Industries

Province	No.	Investments	%	Turnover	%	Employ-ment
Centre-South	34	6,962 mm frs	55	9,000 mm frs	54	6,044
East	15	3,549 mm frs	28	5,430 mm frs	32	3,641
Littoral	8	1,437 mm frs	11	1,299 mm frs	8	937
South-West	4	540 mm frs	5	614 mm frs	4	683
West	3	115 mm frs	1	195 mm frs	2	266
Cameroon	64	12,603 mm frs	100	16,527 mm frs	100	11,571

annual turnover was in the neighborhood of nine milliard (eight milliard eight hundred and fifty-two million) francs CFA. In addition, they generated some six thousand and forty-four jobs.

For the East Province, fifteen undertakings realized investments worth three milliard five hundred and forty-nine million CFA francs with a turnover of five milliard four hundred and thirty-nine million. The labour employed was in the neighborhood of three thousand six hundred and forty-one. As for the Littoral Province, eight undertakings made a turnover of one milliard two hundred and eighty-nine million CFA francs from investments worth one milliard four hundred and thirty-seven million CFA francs. They employed some nine hundred and thirty-seven people.

In the South-West, there were four undertakings. Their turnover was six hundred and fourteen million for investments totaling six hundred and forty million. They employed some six hundred and eighty-three people. In the West Province three undertakings invested one hundred and fifteen million and had a turnover of one hundred and ninety-five million with two hundred and sixty-six people working for them. In the other provinces there were no undertakings of this nature classified under special schedules of the Investment Code.

242

With respect to agro-industrial undertakings, it will be observed from Table 8.6 that the Littoral had investments amounting to twelve milliard two hundred and thirty-eight million francs and a turnover of fifteen milliard seven hundred and eighty-seven million francs CFA. This made up three quarters of the national total. These investments created some three thousand and one jobs. There were four milliard seven hundred and two million francs worth of investment undertaken the Centre-South Province. These resulted to an overall turnover of three milliard four hundred and sixteen million and generated five hundred and forty-three jobs. The other Provinces were hardly considered even though they sometimes hosted undertakings of obvious national importance. This is the case of the North-West with the Wum Area Development Authority and the South-West with PAMOL and Cameroon Development Corporation.

TABLE 8.6
Agro-Industries

Province	No.	Investments	%	Turnover	%	Employ- ment
Littoral	18	12,238 mm frs	63	15,787 mm frs	77	3,000
Centre- South	5	4,702 mm frs	25	3,416 mm frs	16	553
North- West	2	398 mm frs	3	100 mm frs	1	924
North	4	719 mm frs	4	534 mm frs	3	325
South- West	3	1,081 mm frs	5	418 mm frs	3	3,295
Cameroon	32	19,132 mm frs	100	20,255 mm frs	100	8,097

In the industrial sector, one can distinguish undertakings that make products for day to day consumption (beverages, kitchen utensils, wrapping paper, etc.) from those which can be described as basic industries (aluminium, for example). As concerns the basic products, it can be observed from Tabke 8.7 that fifty-five undertakings out of the

243

seventy that were approved for these activities
were in the Littoral Province (and Douala for the
most part). They realized twenty-seven milliard
one hundred and seventy-seven million francs CFA
worth of investment and a turnover of thirty-seven
milliard nine hundred and thirty-four million.
They also generated eleven thousand five hundred
and forty two jobs. The Centre-South Province with
nine undertakings and the South-West Province with
four, were the only other provinces which benefited
somehow from the incentives available for this
economic sector. The other provinces had practically no activities in this sector. This was perhaps
because of their remoteness from accessible markets,
or because of the absence on the spot of primary
products of intermediate inputs.

TABLE 8.7
Manufacturing Industries

Province	No.	Investments	%	Turnover	%	Employ-ment
Littoral	52	26,479 mm frs	91	36,297 mm frs	90	11,374
West	1	266 mm frs	1	na.n	--	82
North	1	3 mm frs	0,05	16 mm frs	0,03	150
Centre-South	9	1,587 mm frs	6	3,823 mm frs	8	631
South-West	4	575 mm frs	1,95	609 mm frs	1	733
Cameroon	67	28,910 mm frs	100	40,205 mm frs	100	12,970

With respect to the basic industries, it can be
observed from Table 8.8 that once again the Littoral
Province and more particularly Douala, had the
lion's share. As a matter of fact, thirty-nine
undertakings had their registered offices there.
They invested twenty milliard four hundred and
forty-five million CFA francs and had a turnover of
twenty milliard one hundred and eighty-two million.
There were also three thousand nine hundred and
seventy-eight workers on their pay roll. The
Centre-South had nine companies which undertook one

TABLE 8.8
Basic Industries

Province	No.	Investments	%		%	Employ-ment
Littoral	38	20,445 mm frs	85	20,182 mm frs	80	3,978
West	3	229 mm frs	1	159 mm frs	1	50
Centre-South	9	1,188 mm frs	4	1,764 mm frs	6	626
North	2	1,049 mm frs	4	2,216 mm frs	8	82
South-West	3	1,299 mm frs	6	1,083 mm frs	5	150
Cameroon	55	24,210 mm frs	100	25,404 mm frs	100	4,886

Source: Compiled from files of Ministry of Economic Affairs
and Planning, Yaounde.

milliard one hundred and eighty-eight million francs
CFA worth of investments with a turnover of one
milliard seven hundred and sixty-four million and
six hundred and twenty-six employees. The West had
a few units of little importance. In the North
Province, there was the annex of an important unit,
CIMENCAM. But this was indeed, marginal.

Thus, on the basis of the available data, it
can be argued that the Littoral and to a less extent the Centre South stood out clearly as the
largest beneficiaries of the incentives given the
substantial number of companies approved under the
Investment Code as of June 30, 1975.

THE POLICY IMPLICATIONS AND RECOMMENDATIONS

In view of the available evidence, it is clear
that the application of the industrial incentives
have not taken into consideration the regional
dimension of Cameroonian development problem. There
is clear indication that most of private investment
and the income generated have concentrated in the
Littoral and Centre-South Provinces dispite the
fact they were the most developed areas. This undesirable outcome has been as a consequence to the
nature of incentives which did not reflect the fact

245

that some backward provinces such as South-West, North-West, North, and East deserve special investment incentives with a view to attracting private capital with a view to closing the gap between the other provinces and the Littoral and Centre-South. This has inevitably led to a lop-sided distribution of investment and the resulting income between the various economic and administrative regions of Cameroon. Consequently, there is an urgent need for a new regional investment incentive policy which should incorporate the existence of wide economic and social disparities between the different provinces.

An investment location policy which lays greater emphasis on the spatial dimension of economic activities in Cameroon in the 1980's, could redress the adverse effects of regional income disparity and the general uneven development of the economic and administrative provinces. In this respect, it will be recalled that the redistributive effects of the incentives have been negligible in such backward provinces as North-West, South-West, North, and East as compared to the Littoral and Centre South which have absorbed the cream of private capital.

This is because the location of many firms, which have so far benefited from incentives provided under the Investment Code, including capital support from the Cameroon Development Bank and National Investment Corporation, has not been guided by any conscious or deliberate policy of achieving a rationally distributed pattern of economic activities among the provinces. In particular, the industrial location policy, if it exists at all, is nothing but a process of persuasion addressed to foreign and domestic investors.[14]

Such a policy of persuasion has had no regional income distributive dimension because the active competitive inducement for firms in general to invest in any area of the country has been determined in the final analysis by the future potential returns on private capital rather than by the wider context of maintaining regional balances. As a consequence, the only provinces which have attracted the largest proportion of private investments are the Littoral and Centre-South. These two provinces have all or some of such obvious locational advantages as adequate transportation system, power supply, export outlets, (Douala and Kribi ports respectively) skill labour and accessibility to raw materials.

In order for Cameroon to achieve spatial equilibrium and diversification in the distribution of economic activities, a deliberate government policy on the dispersion of investments amongst the various provinces is, indeed, necessary. Important as the influences of geography, labour supply and wages, access to markets and the availability of essential services in determining the location of economic activities are; the pattern of investment location is of too great a political and social consequence to be subjected entirely to economic calculus. In the process of closing inter-regional income gaps, the less developed areas should be regarded as "infant industries" needing special investment incentives and attention, with a view to ensuring that the adverse effects of rapid economic growth of richer regions on the poorer are minimized. To this extent, the economics of the backward areas will be rapidly transformed in the long-run. The offshot of this process is that the gaps will be narrowed.

To achieve this objective, the provisions of the present National Investment Code and the investment policies of public financial institutions should be revised and tailored to achieve this result. Specifically, greater tax incentives-- longer tax holidays, low corporation tax rates, free duties on imports of essential intermediate inputs for production should be offered to firms willing to invest in the backward and neglected provinces. To complement this policy, financial institutions like the Cameroon Development Bank and National Investment Corporation, whose activities have also not reflected the objective of balanced development should set aside sizeable proportion of their resources for financing long-term industrial projects in the backward provinces. These policies will lead to the full exploitation of the developmental potential of those areas and as a consequence raise their industrial location quotient, employment levels and incomes.

A regional approach to the specification of investment incentives could be successful even if for private investment, government policy is tailored to the special needs of particular provinces. To be able to sustain balanced regional economic development in Cameroon, the possibility of less-than-optimum allocation of private resources between the provinces through investment incentives cannot be ruled out.[15] To the extent that spatial considerations, political and social issues enter into

247

regional development process, and particularly as the long-run objective of economic development extends beyond the conventional limits of maximization of national product; a short-run malallocation or inefficient allocation of resources through discriminatory investment incentives will not necessarily be disfunctional. To be sure, the political stability of the collectivity and the contentment of the regional units is imperative and a sine qua non for any rational development policy.

Since the efficiency aim of regional development policy is the fostering of national unity in Cameroon rather than the immediate maximization of aggregate economic growth rate, it can be argued that the justification for sub-optimal allocation of resources is that, after all, one of the essential preconditions of economic growth is political stability--which must be maintained if the economic potential of all the provinces is to be exploited with a view to attaining that objective.

CONCLUDING REMARKS

In this paper I have attempted to examine the dimension of regional development, the objectives, and the investment incentives in the context of the Cameroon regional development policy and the analytical framework which has been developed. I have also attempted to throw light on the need for a revision of the present investment incentives so as to enable private domestic and foreign capital to move to the more neglected provinces and regions of Cameroon. To the extent that the policy of maintaining balance between the regions is a political necessity, the revision of the present incentives to reflect this objective is a must.

There is no doubt that there will be an "opportunity cost" of spreading private investment in order to maintain "equilibrium between ethnic groups and regional units." To be sure, the rate of growth of the conventionally measured national product will be smaller than the of either Y_i or Y_j where Y denotes national product; i a richer province and j the poorer province. The difference between $\Delta Y_i - \Delta Y$ or $\Delta Y_j - \Delta Y$ can be termed the "opportunity cost" of maintaining regional balance or equlibrium.[16] But this "opportunity cost" in the short term cannot be avoided if regional balance or equilibrium has to be achieved in order to maintain national economic and political stability.[17]

NOTES

1.   John Friedmann and W. Alonso (eds.): Regional Development and Planning: Cambridge, 1964,
p. 4.
2.   For additional information see, Wilfred A.
Ndongko "A Comparative Analysis of French and
British Investment Policies in Cameroon," Pan African Journal, New York, Vol. VII, No. 2, 1974.
3.   The U.N.E.S.C.O.'s Report on the Development of Higher Education in Cameroon, Paris, 1964,
notes that, "It is in the South and West of East
Cameroon that the main export crops are grown, and
it is these regions, therefore, which offer most
openings for wage-earners. Economic activity is
much brisker there than elsewhere. In North Cameroon, apart from cotton growing, food production
is about the only activity of a vast area with
poor social infrastructure (in 1960 the school
attendance ration was evaluated at 9%, compared
with 44% for the whole of East Cameroon), and administrative and commercial organization," p. 13.
4.   All these regional problems are summarized
from: Elaboration de IIIe Plan Quinquennal 1971-
76, Regional Synthesis, November, 1969.
5.   United Nations Economic Commission for
Europe, Economic Survey of Europe, 1954, Geneva,
1955, Ch. 6.
6.   These phenomena have been discussed with
special reference to regional inequality in,
Gunnar Myrdal, Economic Theory and Underdeveloped
Regions, Duckworth London, 1957, Chapter 3 in particular.
7.   This required an identification of relevant industries for the backward regions. For the
approach see Wilfred A. Ndongko, "An approach to
Industrial Identification for Backward Regions of
Cameroon," in Annales de la Faculté de Droit,
Yaounde, No. 6, 1973.
8.   Cf. Third Five Year Plan, 1966-71, p. 102.
9.   This extension was done at the Federal
level by the passing of Law No. 64-LF-6 of 6 April
1964 which adopted Law No. 60-64 of 27 June 1960
extending the Investment Code of East Cameroon to
the institution of the Federation.
10. The available data on the various investments and their effects are not broken down in
terms of the volume of investment that was generated
by each category of fiscal incentives.
11. Federal Estimates, 1963-64 (Yaounde 1964)
p. XI.

12.   Second Annual Report of the National Credit Council, 1964-66, (Yaounde, June 1967) p. 101.

13.   Third Report of National Credit Council 1966-68, Yaounde, July 1969.

14.   See Wilfred A. Ndongko, Planning for Economic Development in a Federal State: The Case of Cameroon 1960-71, (Munich: Weltforum Verlag), 1975, Chapter 6.

15.   Cf. Wilfred A. Ndongko, "A Framework of Regional Economic Planning for Development with Reference to Cameroon", Annales de la Faculté de Droit et des Sciences Economiques, Yaounde, No. 7, 1974.

16.   It should be noted, however, that the rate of Y must be greater than that of either Yi or Yj if both were to exist as Balkan States and each minimizing only its own income. Allowing for price differences their total product may be Yz in the long-run. However, under centralized planning which emphasizes regional balance with a view to attaining rapid economic development in the long-run, we will have Y - Yz = 'a' where 'a' is the economic gain to the collectivity.

17.   Wilfred A. Ndongko, "Equal Per Capita Growth Rates as a Regional Development Objectives" Revenue Trimestridle d'Information et d'Etudes Economiques et Francieres", Yaounde, No. 6, 1977.

9
The Cameroon Development Corporation, 1947-1977: Cameroonization and Growth[1]

Sanford H. Bederman
Mark W. DeLancey

The section of the United Republic of Cameroon presently known as the Southwest Province, and especially the Fako and Meme divisions,[2] (Figure 9.1) has experienced both considerable exploitation and development for nearly a century. Since the 1880s an active commercial plantation system has been practiced along the lower slopes of Mt. Cameroon, a physical feature that dominates the whole territory. For the first sixty years, the plantation estates were owned and operated primarily by German entrepreneurs. In December, 1946, the German-owned plantations, which had been expropriated when World War Two began, were subsequently assigned to the newly-formed Cameroons Development Corporation (C.D.C.) to be managed.

This essay is concerned with the events that led to the creation of the C.D.C. and particularly with the experiences of its first thirty years of existence. Between 1947 and 1966, the Corporation was constantly struggling because it never had enough capital to properly conduct any type of major development program. In 1966, however, the C.D.C. negotiated a large loan from the International Bank for Reconstruction and Development (World Bank), the International Development Association, and the Fonds Européen de Développement (F.E.D.). From that time it has had sufficient funds to begin and complete large-scale development schemes without immediate financial liabilities. The Corporation is now in its second development program, with further expansion in hectarage and types of crops underway.

251

FIGURE 9.1

Provinces and Divisions of the English-speaking
Portion of the United Republic of Cameroon. Fako
and Meme divisions until 1972, were known as
Victoria and Kumba divisions, respectively. The
Northwest Province includes the Bamenda Grassfields.

The Cameroon Development Corporation deserves much of the credit for helping to bring about a modicum of positive economic and social change within Western Cameroon, which has ranked as one of the poorest regions of Africa. The story of the Cameroon Development Corporation is an important one to relate for its activities are a unique microcosm of tropical land use and economic development. In many ways, the legacy inherited by the C.D.C. in 1947 can be compared with that experienced in other parts of Africa where plantation agriculture was practiced during colonial rule.

In 1977, the Cameroon Development Corporation was one of the major employers in the country. Throughout its brief existence, its profits have fluctuated as has the size of its labor force. The Corporation's financial success has always depended upon a combination of favorable physical, political, and economic environments. Whenever any of the three has been unfavorable, repercussions have been quickly felt throughout the whole country. Since 1961, the government of Cameroon has consistently depended upon the C.D.C. to be its partner in national development. In the present period, the government is entrusting the Corporation to carry out plantation projects far from its original base in southwestern anglophone Cameroon.

MAJOR PHYSICAL CHARACTERISTICS OF FAKO DIVISION[3]

The Plantations are concentrated in Fako Division, which is the location of Mt. Cameroon (13,353' elevation), one of Africa's most unusual landmarks (Figure 9.2) and the highest peak in West Africa. Its base is at sea level, and it is the only active volcano on the Atlantic side of the continent. Its windward flanks receive the most prodigious amounts of precipitation in Africa, and its deeply weathered volcanic soils by any standards are extremely fertile. Indeed, the natural setting of Mt. Cameroon adjacent to Ambas Bay produces some of the most beautiful scenery on earth.

Almost everyone in Fako Division resides below the 3000' contour. Above that elevation, the terrain is very rugged and because of the porosity of the volcanic material, surface water is not found. Human occupance, therefore, is relegated to the hot and humid lower elevations, which in Latin America would be classified as the tierra caliente. All of the plantations, as well as most of the towns and villages, are located either in the lowland rain forest or in the lower portion of the montane rain forest. This is the least desirable climatic zone of the mountain in terms of health and comfort.

Maximum and minimum temperatures in Fako Division range between 91 F. in March and 70 F. in January. The mean annual temperature at Victoria (at sea level) is 75 F., whereas Buea, situated at the upper limit of settlement at a salubrious 3,000' elevation, registers an annual average temperature of 68 F. Depending upon exposure, precipitation varies considerably from one side of the mountain to another. Debundscha Point, located near sea level on the windward side, averages over 400 inches a year. At nearby Idenau Estate, 320 rainy days and over 430 inches of rain were recorded in 1969. Relatively "dry" conditions prevail in the rain shadow on the northeast side of the mountain. In 1969, Meanja received only ninety-five inches of precipitation. Most of the rainfall in Fako Division occurs between May and October, with a decided dry season experienced between November and April. Although there is more than adequate moisture for crop growth, the availability of drinking water in the region is another matter. Surface water during some months is non-existent.

Severe cyclonic storms that periodically batter the villages and plantations comprise another major element of the region's climate. Line squalls occur with great regularity prior to the onslaught of the heavy monsoonal rains, especially during the month of April. These violent storms locally are called "blow-downs" by banana farmers, and often have been described mistakenly in the literature as being tornadoes. These short-lived hurricane force squalls affect the whole Division, but the most serious damage has been felt in the Tiko Plain where the heaviest agricultural activity is concentrated.

Another major characteristic of the physical geography of the region is that Mt. Cameroon remains an active volcano. The mountain erupted four times in the Twentieth Century--1909, 1922, 1954, and in 1959. No lives were lost during any of the eruptions, and only in the 1922 outbreak was serious property damage incurred, and this was limited to several plantations around Bibundi (near Idenau) on the west coast north of Victoria-Bota (see Figure 9.2).

Regardless of the harsh and unhealthy climate that exists and the natural hazards that plague the area, commercial agriculture has dominated the

FIGURE 9.2

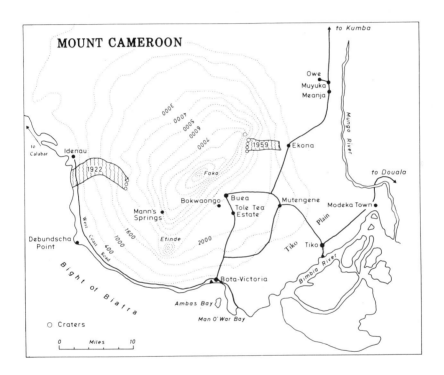

Mount Cameroon in Fako Division.

255

region's economy for decades. For almost ninety
years a variety of Westerners have invested heavily
in the rich agricultural land at the base of Mt.
Cameroon. Although the political history of the
area has been complex, the commercial plantations
have persisted.

THE CAMEROON PLANTATION LANDS BEFORE 1947

Within the past century, the land that is now
managed by the Cameroon Development Corporation has
been controlled in turn by Africans, Germans,
British, and now by the predominantly French-speaking United Republic of Cameroon. As the major
events unfolded, the result was to be a situation
where almost all of the good agricultural land was
initially alienated by a few Europeans with most of
the indigenous population being relegated to the
poorest and least desirable locations. When the
C.D.C. began operations in 1947 this situation was
only partially resolved.

Upon the acquisition of Kamerun in 1884, the
Germans immediately began to exploit the interior.
Among other things, they knew that their interior
territory had to be opened up to trade and also
they had to develop a hinterland for their ports.
The Germans realized rather quickly that the lower
slopes of Mt. Cameroon were suitable for commercial
development.

To facilitate this development, the Germans
had to obtain land.[4] Local tribal chiefs were
forced to cede land after a brief rebellion in 1884.
In 1896, the Germans declared all unoccupied
territory to be crown lands and these in turn were
sold to commercial companies. The Germans also
purchased real estate from the Africans for extremely low prices, taking advantage of the traditional
African concept of land ownership. In the Mt.
Cameroon area alone, the Germans alienated some 400
square miles of the most fertile land. The indigenous Bakweri, who lost over 200,000 acres, were
forced to move either into prescribed restricted
native reserves or to inaccessible territory outside
the alienated lands. Other lands suitable for
plantations were acquired near Kumba and Mbonge in
the present Meme and Ndian divisions.

The current boundary of the plantation lands
essentially was established before 1899.[5] The
greater part of the southwestern, southern, and
southeastern slopes was acquired by private German

256

companies, although only a small portion of the
total concession land was ever placed under cultivation. Alienated land ended at about 3,000 feet
elevation, the primary reason being lack of ground
water and the rugged terrain.

By 1914, the land pattern became more fragmented (Figure 9.3). Additional native reserve lands
were created, and previously undeveloped land on the
Tiko Plain along the Bimbia River was obtained by
the Germans. Throughout the German colonial period,
the most important crops produced on the plantations
were cocoa, oil palm products, and rubber. Minor
crops were kola nuts, tobacco, and coffee. Almost
all were exported to Germany.

In January, 1913, there were 195 non-Africans
engaged in planting in Kamerun. These persons
occupied the managerial and technically-skilled
positions. The African labor force on the plantations numbered 17,827. There were fifty-eight
estates in the colony, and almost all of them were
located around Mt. Cameroon with a few in neighbor-
ing Meme and Ndian divisions.

The plantation economy was not without its
problems. There was a high death rate of workers
because of the crowded living conditions and lack of
medical care at the plantations. The major factor
in the outrageously high morbidity and mortality
rates was the use of forced labor by the Germans, a
process which brought large numbers of Africans
from the elevated, cool, and dry inland regions of
Bamenda and Yaounde to the hot, humid coastal area
with its high incidence of filaria, malaria, and
other diseases.[6] This helped to account for the
rapid turnover of labor and also for a lowering of
the workers' efficiency. The Africans needed
special training in tending each of the large
variety of crops grown on the plantations. A
colonial government edict in 1896, forbidding the
private disciplining of workers, created additional
problems for the estate managers. The Kamerun
government also required the provision of medical
attention for all workers and this proved to be
quite costly to those plantation owners who complied
with the regulation.

Other than in the realm of human relations, the
Germans were among the most progressive of colonial
rulers. Many problems were solved by applying
scientific methods. Planters were taught proper
techniques of tropical agriculture. Technical experts and special commissions were consulted on
forest resources, river navigation, and road

FIGURE 9.3

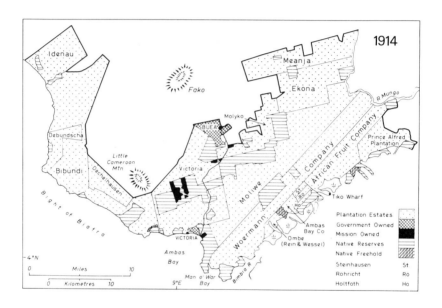

Plantations and Reserves in Fako Division in 1914
(Modified from E. Ardener).   Source: Sanford H.
Bederman, "Plantation Agriculture in Victoria
Division, West Cameroon: An Historical Introduc-
tion," Geography, Vol. LI, No. 4 (November, 1966),
357.

construction. Africans were given training in both missions and government schools. Another aid to planters was provided by the Botanical Garden which was established at Victoria in 1892. [7]

During World War One, British, Belgian, and French troops conquered the Kamerun and eventually the territory was divided into two League of Nations mandates, the smaller, western portion under the control of the United Kingdom and the larger, eastern portion under the control of France. The plantations included in the British mandate were confiscated but were sold, in most instances, to the original German owners in 1924.

In 1938, on the eve of World War Two, Germans constituted the largest group of Europeans in the British mandate, outnumbering British nationals three to one. At that time, the German-owned plantations totalled more than 210,000 acres of which 67,000 acres were under cultivation. When Hitler invaded Austria in March, 1938, there were celebrations throughout the plantation lands, and the Nazi flag was even hoisted in Victoria.

At the beginning of World War Two, the German estates were expropriated again by the Custodian of Enemy Property and German activity ceased in the Cameroons. When the war ended in 1945, the problem of disposing of the expropriated lands arose once more. The Bakweri leaders quickly expressed their feelings. Through a group known as the Bakweri Land Committee, the Crown was petitioned to allow the Bakweri people to reclaim all the territory taken from them by the Germans during the 1880s and 1890s. The initial petition was presented in August, 1946, and as late as 1949 their pleas were still under consideration by both the British Government and the United Nations. The Bakweri Land Committee was unaware in late 1946 that other plans were being made for the future of the Cameroons plantations. In December of that year, it was announced that the Cameroons Development Corporation had been created.

EARLY PROBLEMS OF THE CAMEROONS DEVELOPMENT
   CORPORATION

As the British Cameroons (United Kingdom Trust Territory) was administered along with Nigeria, all of the official documents concerning the land under the jurisdiction of the Custodian of Enemy Property

were prepared in Nigeria. However, the managerial
work for the Cameroons plantations was done in Buea.

The Cameroons Development Corporation came into
being with the passage of two ordinances by a
special meeting of the Nigerian Legislature in
December, 1946. The first was the Ex-Enemy Lands
(Cameroons) Ordinance, 1946, which provided for the
acquisition of the lands formerly owned by German
aliens in the British Mandates of the Cameroons, and
which had been vested in the Custodian of Enemy
Property for the duration of World War Two. Under
the terms of the ordinance, the Governor, upon acquisition of the lands, was to declare them "Native
Lands" and they were to be held for him for the use
and common benefit of all the inhabitants of the
territory. It also provided for the Governor to
grant leases of his newly acquired land to the
Cameroons Development Corporation, which was created
by the second ordinance. The Nigerian Legislature
later amended the Cameroons Development Corporation
Ordinance, 1946,[8] by stating that even though the
Corporation was formed in 1946, it would not legally
begin conducting its business until January 1, 1947.

The Governor of Nigeria, who paid a total of
£850,000 for the German plantation lands, immediately leased them to the C.D.C. In addition to culti-
vating crops and developing and managing the
estates, the C.D.C. was given the responsibility of
constructing and maintaining roads, railways, water-
ways, quays, and wharves; of conducting the export
and import trade; and of constructing and/or acquiring buildings. Another major responsibility was
to provide for the general social welfare (housing,
medical services, and educational and recreational
facilities) of its employees. After all its obligations were fulfilled, it was to pay direct taxes to
the Government of Nigeria and all profits were to
be used for the benefit of the people of the
Cameroons. The C.D.C. was to be managed along
strict business lines, and because it had to pay
taxes, it had the outward appearances of being a
private commercial company, a commercial company
with unusual social welfare responsibilities.

Since the C.D.C. was legally established on the
same day that it assumed possession of the estates
from the Custodian of Enemy Property, very little
preliminary work had been possible in regard to
establishing a proper organization to conduct its
activities. Arrangements were made with that office
to act as Agent for the C.D.C. until the managerial
staff could properly carry out its duties. On

260

June 30, 1947, the Corporation accepted full responsibility for its actions.

On July 1, 1947, the C.D.C. began the difficult task of rehabilitating over 200,000 acres of valuable plantation land. Along with obtaining the estates, the Corporation also gained possession of the Tiko Wharf, which has been owned by the African Fruit Company, Hamburg. Earlier, on January 1, 1947, the Corporation had assumed responsibility for the West Farm in Bota and the Upper and Lower Farms in Buea.

Unfortunately, at the time the Corporation was formed it was not given any working capital. Instead, the second Ordinance provided the authority, with the Governor's approval, to borrow up to a maximum of £1,000,000 at any time. Unwilling to push for a very large loan until all its holdings had been thoroughly surveyed, it decided to obtain a small loan of £100,000 from the Nigerian Government, on which interest was payable at $3\frac{1}{2}$ percent per year. This three-month loan was retired at the end of that period.

Income was needed immediately to pay salaries, wages, and other essential disbursements. Management, therefore, decided to produce bananas and rubber in hopes that they would generate a small profit. At the same time, the Corporation nurtured the production of oil palm, even though it was clear that it would lose money. An acute shortage of oils and fats in Post-war United Kingdom and Europe precipitated this decision.

In the early months of 1947, the C.D.C. was beset with many problems. It was understaffed, but, fortunately, help was again provided by the Custodian of Enemy Property. There was a lack of statistical and other vital information concerning the operations of the estates in the past. Completely absent were detailed survey data relating to both topography and soils. Machinery and equipment were old, and much of what they had was beyond repair. Spare parts were impossible to obtain from war-torn Germany, and the Corporation had to wait its turn for modern machinery since it could not demand high priorities from the British Government.

Without question, the early months and, indeed, the early years of the C.D.C. were difficult. The Corporation slowly acquired the needed trained staff, and eventually it obtained much of the necessary machinery and equipment. Surprisingly, it conducted its business in the early years without

having to borrow huge sums of money.   This situation
was to change radically in the 1950s.

FINANCE AND ORGANIZATION

During its first two decades, the Cameroon
Development Corporation never had enough working
capital available to finance any fullscale crop
development from initial plantings through the first
year of production.   All development had to be on a
year-to-year basis.   Obvious financial and organizational handicaps included the necessity of repaying
short-term loans, taxes, and duties, and turning
over yearly profits, if any, to the Government.   It
is difficult to estimate the cost of fulfilling the
Corporation's responsibility "to provide for social
and other welfare facilities"[9] for its employees.
In 1957 the C.D.C. owned fourteen primary schools,
and managed ten of these.   School buildings, staff,
housing for staff, and etc. were provided by the
Corporation.   Scholarships were provided for higher
education and forty adult literacy centers were
maintained.   Various forms of technical training
were underway.   The Corporation conducted sports
programs and film shows at all estates.   Of greatest
expense, however, was the medical program which included four general hospitals, six auxiliary hospitals, and forty-two aid posts.   These were staffed
and equipped by the Corporation, which in many
instances also paid to train the medical staff.   In
addition to these functions, the C.D.C. was providing quarters for most of its employees, maintaining
road and light railway construction, conducting
stevedoring and maritime shipping activities, and
conducting agricultural research.   Fortunately, the
"Banana Boom" of the 1950s earned considerable
revenue, and much of it was used on estate development.
In the case of the C.D.C., organization and
finance are closely intertwined because the major
contributors of money to the Corporation were given
a voice in its operation.   The ultimate decisions
concerning the Corporation's activities have been
made by the Board of Directors, whose powers
initially were established by the Cameroons Development Corporation Ordinance, 1946.   The regulations
governing appointment to the Board did not change
until 1960, when the Colonial Development Corporation (later the Commonwealth Development Corporation,
or Comdev) loaned C.D.C. £1,000,000 and at the same

time assumed active management of the Corporation, a
relationship which ended in 1974. The composition
of the Board has altered several times in recent
years.

Between 1947 and 1959, the Corporation, through
actions of the Board of Directors, obtained a series
of loans from two sources--the Nigerian Government
and Barclays Bank, Dominion Colonial Overseas
(D.C.O.). Additional loans obtained from the
Nigerian Government are shown in Table 9.1 below.

Between 1950 and 1959, the Corporation received
a total of £600,000 in loans from Barclays Bank,
D.C.O., and that amount was repaid in full in 1959.
As early as the mid-1950s, it became apparent that
the market for bananas was on the decline. The

TABLE 9.1
Loans Obtained from the Nigerian Government, 1950-
    1960

Date	Amount (£)	Repaid (£)	Balance Liquidated (£)
1950	500,000	0	500,000
1953	200,000	200,000	
1954	500,000	24,510	475,490
1955	550,000	0	550,000
1956	258,000	33,490	224,510
			$\overline{1,750,000}$[a]
1960[b]	1,000,000		
1960[b]	750,000	(Southern Cameroons Government)	

Source: Cameroons Development Corporation records.
[a]Liquidated into a new loan shared by the Nigerian
Government and the Southern Cameroons Government in
1960.
[b]The 1960 loans were payable by 18 equal annuities
from 1970.

Corporation realized that it had to diversify its crops, which would entail very costly development programs. In 1958, the Colonial Development Corporation was requested by the C.D.C. to provide a loan of £3,000,000 for development purposes. After considerable discussion, the two corporations finally agreed on terms which were embodied in a Loan Agreement, a Management Agreement, and a Heads of Agreement.

Under the Loan Agreement it was stipulated in principle that Comdev would invest a total of £3,000,000 in the C.D.C. The first £1,000,000 were made available in installments between 1960 and 1962. The remaining £2,000,000 were to follow after the C.D.C. has reconstituted itself from a statutory corporation into a joint stock company. The political events that ensued in the early 1960s precluded this happening.

On January 1, 1960, the former French Cameroon gained complete independence and became known as the Republic of Cameroon. Earlier, in the mid-1950s, sentiment in favor of independence had begun to develop in the British Trust Territory, and in February, 1961, Southern British Cameroons voted in a United Nations-sponsored plebescite to become a part of Cameroon, whereas, Northern British Cameroons and on October 1, 1961, the Federal Republic of Cameroon was born. Southern British Cameroons became West Cameroon, and the former French section became East Cameroon.

Because the former Southern British Cameroons was no longer a member of the Commonwealth, Comdev was placed in a bind as its constitution did not allow for investments outside the Commonwealth. Also, a policy decision to not reconstitute the C.D.C. was subsequently made by the new West Cameroon and Federal governments.

The Management Agreement provided that Comdev would assume the management of the Corporation and would initially be entitled to appoint the General Manager, Personal Assistant to the General Manager, and the Financial Controller. The Management Agreement ran until December, 1974. The change in political status had no effect on this part of the agreement because the first £1,000,000 had already been drawn. In 1964 Comdev agreed that, the initial period being over, the Financial Controller could become a C.D.C. appointment.

The Heads of Agreement between Comdev and C.D.C. provided for the membership of the Board of Directors of the Corporation. Comdev was to have four members (including the General Manager) on the Board representing its interest. The two governments of the Southern Cameroons and the Federation of Nigeria were also to have two members each on the Board. After reunification in 1961, the Government of West Cameroon assumed the rights and obligations formerly held by the Nigerian Government. In the meantime Comdev had voluntarily surrendered one of its seats on the Board to the Government, leaving three Comdev members. The Chairman of the Board and four others, therefore, were appointed by the Prime Minister to represent West Cameroon. The Nigerian Government was still permitted to appoint one member to be an advocate for its investment, although in the 1960s he never attended Board meetings. Presently the Board consists of fourteen members, all Cameroonian, representing various central government ministries and agencies.

In 1963, Banque Camerounaise de Developpement loaned the Corporation £400,000. This debt was retired on December 31, 1968.

The Cameroons Development Corporation in 1966 had debts totalling £3,997,000, but it had assets of about £4,700,000. Profits in 1966 amounted to £83,430 and the Corporation had almost 12,000 tax paying employees. The effective and efficient administration of nineteen estates, including a variety of commercial crops, required constant revisions in the internal organization. The Corporation originally maintained a crop grouping system which involved having a supervisor for each crop grown on the estates. In 1963 the estates were reorganized into four Management Areas, and each Area Manager was made responsible for all the crops grown within his jurisdiction. In 1971 this system was found to be unwieldy; Area Managers were responsible for several different crops and were unable to concentrate their attention on any one set of problems. After 1971, the estates were divided into twelve single-crop plantations, each with a Manager directly responsible to the General Manager through the Chief Production Manager (see Figure 9.4).

LABOR ON C.D.C. PLANTATIONS

One of the major difficulties experienced by growers in all plantation regions is the lack of an adequate labor supply. This has been the case in Cameroon during the German, British, and

FIGURE 9.4

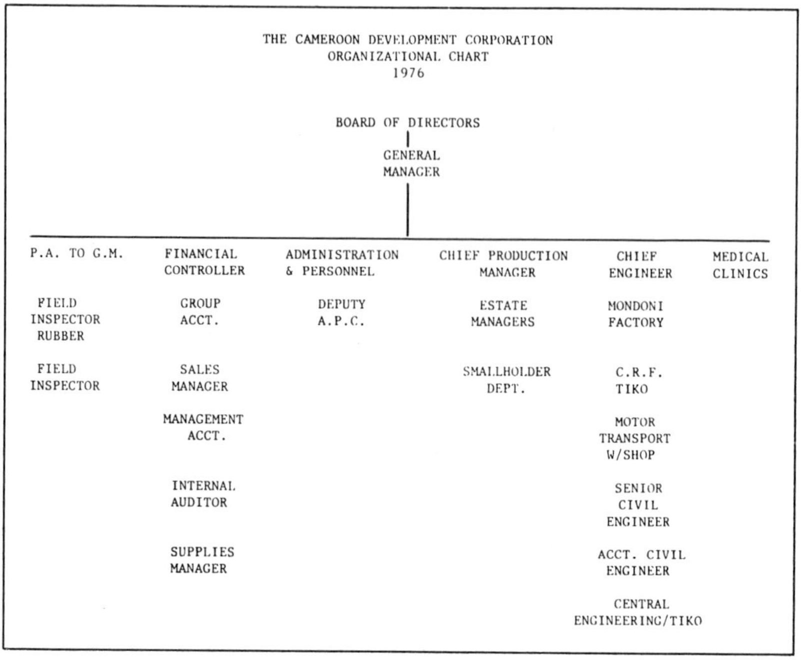

THE CAMEROON DEVELOPMENT CORPORATION
ORGANIZATIONAL CHART
1976

BOARD OF DIRECTORS

GENERAL
MANAGER

P.A. TO G.M.	FINANCIAL CONTROLLER	ADMINISTRATION & PERSONNEL	CHIEF PRODUCTION MANAGER	CHIEF ENGINEER	MEDICAL CLINICS
FIELD INSPECTOR RUBBER	GROUP ACCT.	DEPUTY A.P.C.	ESTATE MANAGERS	MONDONI FACTORY	
FIELD INSPECTOR	SALES MANAGER		SMALLHOLDER DEPT.	C.R.F. TIKO	
	MANAGEMENT ACCT.			MOTOR TRANSPORT W/SHOP	
	INTERNAL AUDITOR			SENIOR CIVIL ENGINEER	
	SUPPLIES MANAGER			ACCT. CIVIL ENGINEER	
				CENTRAL ENGINEERING/TIKO	

SOURCE: Cameroon Development Corporation,
CDC Second Development Programme
(Bota: C.D.C., 1976).

independence periods. The inhabitants of the plantation area were not sufficient in number to provide all of the workers required on the commercial estates and so thousands of persons migrated from French or East Cameroon, Nigeria, and other parts of British or West Cameroon.[10] (See Table 9.2).

The labor force on the plantations has fluctuated greatly in size over the years. World depression in the early 1930s caused a major decline. The "Banana Boom" of the 1950s caused a large increase. The peak year was 1952, with 25,569 persons on the payroll. Between 1955 and 1965, employment decreased as the "Banana Boom" died. The brief increase in the early 1970s occurred as the Corporation undertook a large-scale expansion program (see Table 9.2).

The decrease in the latter part of the 1970s is due to two important factors. First, in order to remain competitive on the international market the C.D.C. has found it necessary to reduce cost of production. This has led to increasing emphasis upon mechanization and the reduction of dependence upon manual labor. Second, again in an effort to reduce costs and rationalize procedures, the Corporation has concentrated on the business of growing and processing agricultural crops with a reduction in social and welfare functions as well as a reduction in ancillary economic functions. This is a continuing process, on-going for several years. For example, in 1964 all primary schools owned by the Corporation were turned over to local government authorities. In recent years large-scale units have been separated from the Corporation. In 1969 the ports at Tiko and Bota, in 1972 the agricultural research station at Ekona, in 1973 the stevedoring operations and facilities, and in 1975 the medical staff and facilities were turned over to the central government.

Two important trends may be observed in the make-up of the labor supply over the years. First, there has been a constant change in the origin of the labor supply. This is in part related to political considerations. In the era of German rule, workers came from all parts of the Kamerun, but especially from the Bamenda and Yaounde areas. After the division of the area into British and French mandates (subsequently trusts), the number of laborers from the French area declined rapidly, but there was in increase from British-controlled areas, including Nigeria. With independence and the reunification of Cameroon, the Nigerian source ended almost

267

TABLE 9.2
Source of Labor on C.D.C. Estates (and Predecessors), 1926-1976

		Percentage of Labor Force			
Year	Total Number	Victoria Kumba Mamfe[e]	Bamenda[f]	East Cameroon	Nigeria
1926[a]	12128	33.3	14.0	52.2	0.5
1930	9040	36.1	22.8	37.6	2.6
1935	15691	33.1	30.8	33.5	2.6
1938[b]	25113	32.0	38.7	19.1	10.0
1947[c]	16262			17.0	19.0
1950	19005	32.2	32.4	12.8	21.4
1955	21664	28.9	35.0	6.3	28.0
1960	17622	27.0	41.5	4.6	26.9
1965	12785	37.9	51.9	5.3	4.9
1970	14670	38.0	55.0	5.0	2.0
1972[d]	13174	37.0	56.0	4.0	3.0
1976	10502	--	--	--	--

Source: Compiled from materials in the Buea Branch
of the Cameroon National archives, the C.D.C.
annual reports, and the annual reports of the
British government to the League of Nations and
United Nations during the mandate and trusteeship
periods.
[a]First year data is available.
[b]Last year of data prior to World War II.
[c]First year data available in C.D.C. era.
[d]Last year data compiled by C.D.C.
[e]Includes present Fako, Meme, Ndian, and Manyu
 Divisions.
[f]Includes present Mezam, Momo, Bui, Menchum, and
 Donga/Mantung Divisions.

completely, especially in 1962 when most Nigerian
workers were declared redundant. In part these
changes are related to economic considerations.
There have been dramatic shifts in supply areas
within English speaking Cameroon; these are not
clearly shown in Table 9.2. Evidence suggests that

migration from any source area declines as economic development occurs within that source area. This provides economically viable alternatives to migration. However, it also provides stimuli to migration from those areas on the fringe of the growth area.

A second important trend has been the Cameroonization of the senior staff of the Corporation. In 1949, there were 114 members of the senior staff and all were classified as "expatriate." A new rank, intermediate service, was opened that year to provide "the means of encouraging younger men with suitable basic education to study for recognised qualifications which, in due course, should fit them for promotion to the Senior Service." A second category was to include those deserving reward but unsuitable for further promotion. Thirty-three African members had been appointed to this rank by 1950.[11] The first promotions of Africans from intermediate to senior staff took place in 1951. In 1966, the 135 members of the senior staff included 88 Cameroonians.[12] By the end of 1969 the twelve highest management positions included six Cameroon citizens (the Assistant General Manager, Development Officer, Chief Medical Officer, Assistant Financial Controller, and two Area Managers).[13] And, in December, 1974, Mr. J. N. Ngu became the first Cameroon General-Manager. His department heads included five Cameroonians and only one expatriate.[14] In 1975, the 133 senior staff included less than six non-Cameroonians.

Similarly, in 1947 the original Board of Directors included one Cameroonian and by 1950 there were only two among its nine members; by 1975 the Board was entirely Cameroonian.

CROP PRODUCTION ON THE ESTATES

The major purpose of any agribusiness enterprise is to produce commercial crops as efficiently and as profitably as possible. In the best of times, the task is not an easy one. To make things even more difficult, the Corporation cultivates five separate crops; a beverage (tea), a spice (pepper), a fruit (bananas), an edible oil (palm oil), and an industrial crop (rubber). In the recent past, cocoa was also grown by the Corporation. Most plantation systems specialize in one crop only. Every one of the crops produced by the C.D.C. is at the mercy of a constantly changing, if not whimsical, world

269

market, although there are large local markets for
palm oil and tea. Additionally, each one presents
local problems for management among which are choosing the best plant material, selecting the best land
on which planting would take place, determining a
proper fertilizer policy, developing a strategy to
combat ever-present pests and diseases, and training
workers to properly harvest each of the crops. To
successfully produce one crop tests any manager's
mettle. That five crops have been cultivated for as
long as they have attests to the unusual ability of
the professional staff that works for the Corporation.

Throughout the 1950s the principal crop grown
on the C.D.C. estates was the banana. In 1958,
roughly 63 percent of all bananas exported from
Southern British Cameroons were produced by the
C.D.C. Banana cultivation started its precipitous
decline in the mid-1950s with the arrival of Panama
Disease in the Cameroons.[15] Between 1958 and 1966,
mature banana acreage fell from 13,450 to fewer than
2,350 acres (for total acreage, see Table 9.3). In
1958, banana production amounted to 58,830 metric
tons, whereas in 1966, the figure dropped to 12,200
metric tons.

By 1966, the Corporation had decided to discontinue any future planting of banana and place
most of its resources in the development of oil
palm products and rubber. Less attention was to be
given cocoa, but tea[16] and pepper were still considered profitable.

TABLE 9.3
Total Planted Acres (by Crop) on C.D.C. Estates

Crop	1951	1956	1961	1966	1971	1976
Bananas	20,524	20,587	10,763	2,790	2,102	1,902
Rubber	14,922	17,109	24,199	29,808	31,873	32,495
Oil Palm	15,968	17,473	20,457	19,998	36,934	41,736
Cocoa	1,480	1,100	1,370	1,156	867	0
Tea		135	738	791	855	815
Pepper	12	44	44	67	124	167

Source: Annual reports of the Cameroon Development Corporation.

The year 1966/1967 marks an important turning point in the history of the Corporation, for at this time an ambitious seven-year development plan was undertaken. For the first time, funds were available for large-scale expansion of land under cultivation and the construction of more advanced and efficient agricultural processing facilities. Funds amounting to $24,482,000 were received from IDA, IBRD, and FED. Total planted acreage increased 40% (from 55,250 to 77,100 acres) during this period. Banana acreage was reduced by almost 50% and cocoa was entirely eliminated. Oil palm and pepper acreages were increased by about 100% and very slight increases were made in tea and rubber. Experiments were undertaken with several new crops, including avocado, coconut, and pineapple. A new mill for expressing palm oil was constructed at Mondoni and older, inefficient mills at Bota and Mpundu were closed. New crumb rubber processing equipment was installed at Tiko and Mukonje. In general, the first development program has been well executed and is considered to have been highly successful.

In 1977 the Corporation embarked upon its second development program (Figure 9.5).[17] This ten-year plan envisions an almost 100% increase in total planted acreage (to 150,000 acres), but in the first five years expansion is limited to 26,250 acres-- 4,000 acres in oil palms and 22,250 in rubber. This will include 5,000 acres in small-holder rubber and palms. The Corporation has conducted minor experiments with small-holders, but this will be the first major attempt to include private growers in rubber and palms. There is general optimism among senior management staff that this aspect of the project will succeed and, indeed, that the planned acreage for small-holders may be increased. Financing for the overall program for the first five years is being provided by the World Bank, Caisse Centrale, and the Commonwealth Development Corporation.

Further expansion in rubber and palms will occur in the second five years, as well as possible expansion of pepper and bananas. It is now planned to undertake large scale production of coconuts at that time. However, planning agricultural expansion this far into the future is a difficult exercise, particularly when sales are dependent upon the rapidly shifting conditions of the world market. The C.D.C. has, quite wisely, not made definite commitments for this second half of the ten-year program.

FIGURE 9.5

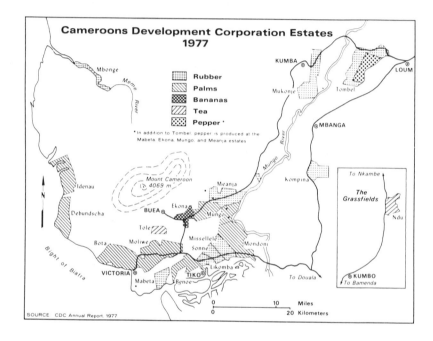

Cameroons Development Corporation Estates 1977

Rubber
Palms
Bananas
Tea
Pepper *

* In addition to Tombel, pepper is produced at the Mabeta, Ekona, Mungo, and Meanja estates

SOURCE CDC Annual Report. 1977

272

In addition to acreage increase, a new oil mill is planned to replace the old facilities at Idenau and new rubber factories will be constructed at Mbonge, Meanja, Tombel, and at the entirely new plantation to be opened at Kompina in francophone Cameroon.

Kompina Rubber Estate is one of three new plantations all located outside of the territory in which the C.D.C. has operated in the past. In 1977 the Corporation acquired the Ndu Tea Estate in the Northwestern Province. This estate, previously privately owned, contains 1,520 acres of tea and 575 acres of firewood. On July 1, 1977, the Corporation took over another tea project, the 4,000 acre estate at Djuttitsa, Dschang in the French-speaking part of the country. No actual planting will begin here until 1980; at present the Corporation is developing nurseries and preparing infrastructure. The Kompina project includes 12,500 acres of rubber and it will become the largest of the Corporation's rubber estates.

The opening of these three new projects is a measure of the government's confidence in the management and development abilities of the Corporation. The movement into two large projects in the French-speaking parts of the country indicates that the C.D.C. has become a national institution, one to which the government can entrust major development projects.

However, there is some reason to fear that the sudden addition of too many new projects could overwhelm the capabilities of the C.D.C. The Kompina project is a part of the Corporation's development plan and provisions for staff needs have been taken. But, the acquisition of Ndu Tea was not planned for, and it was not seen as desirable by all the Corporation's management. The government was faced with the closure of the estate by its foreign owners and the loss of employment by its many workers. An alternative to closure was to turn it over to C.D.C. The estate's fields and equipment were not in good order and the Corporation sustained a $200,000 loss on the first six months of its operation.[18] Discussion of the acquisition of the Djuttitsa tea project does not appear in the development plan or in the 1977 annual report of the Corporation. Again, this suggests that the project has been added to the Corporation's responsibilities without full planning and lead-in time.

THE CDC IN THE CAMEROON ECONOMY

It is difficult to make a full assessment and evaluation of the role of the Cameroon Development Corporation in the economy of the United Republic of Cameroon, for no authoritative study of this question has as yet been published. However, there are some clear indications that the Corporation's contribution has been large and positive. The construction of numerous roads, the building and staffing of schools, the paying of numerous scholarships for training in engineering, business, and medical skills, and the provision of medical care for a large proportion of the inhabitants of Southwestern Province are examples of the indirect contributions the plantations have made for many years. In a more direct manner, the Corporation's exports represent a major contribution to the economy. Production figures and sales values for the year ending June 30, 1976, are shown in Table 9.4. A substantial increase in sales--to $26,940,000--was recorded in 1977.[19]

In 1976 the C.D.C. employed 10,500 persons on a regular basis plus an additional 3,000 seasonal workers. A total annual salary and wages of about $8,700,000 was paid to these employees, all of whom in turn paid taxes to the government. In addition, the Corporation paid $1,270,000 in taxes, duties, and license fees to the central government.

There is no indication of the secondary effects of these wages and taxes. It is clear that employment is provided for many persons in supplying services and goods to the C.D.C. and its employees and there are indications that the employees utilize their savings in economically productive ways.[20] The new small-holder program holds promise for involving a large number of farmers and their families in a profitable exercise.

CONCLUSIONS

Upon reflection, it was a good decision to create the Cameroon Development Corporation to manage the profitable ex-German plantations rather than return the land to the Bakweri. Although heavy resentment was expressed, it is difficult to disagree with the reasoning that lay behind the judgement. The land was very valuable, the Trust Territory was extremely poor, and the indigenous

TABLE 9.4
Production and Sales, 1976, Cameroon Development
  Corporation

CROP	PRODUCTION (TONS)	SALES (US$)
Bananas	11,356	$ 2,574,000
Palm Products	26,520	$ 9,062,000
Rubber	10,421	$ 6,037,000
Tea	975	$ 1,495,000
Pepper	48	$ 62,000
Total	49,320 Tons	$19,230,000

Source: Cameroon Development Corporation, Annual
Report . . . 1976 (Bota: CDC, 1976), 9-10.

population was not at that time competent to obtain
maximum benefit from the estates.

The classic plantation in Africa during
colonial rule stands indicted on three main counts:
(1) the alienation of ownership, (2) the subordination of labor, and (3) the separation from the
surrounding country.[21] By establishing a national
corporate ownership of the former German plantations
for the ultimate benefit of everyone, as was done in
the British Trust Territory in December, 1946, a
successful solution, at least to the first charge,
was found. The new small-holder scheme answers in
some respects to all three charges. And, the contribution of the Corporation to the overall economic
development of the state and its utilization of
profits within Cameroon rather than allowing their
exportation has been a benefit to the entire nation.

NOTES

1. This essay is based upon research conducted by S. Bederman in 1966 and M. DeLancey in 1968-70 and 1976 in Western Cameroon. A large portion of Bederman's work was presented in The Cameroons Development Corporation: Partner in National Growth (Bota: Cameroons Development Corporation, 1968). This monograph is not specifically cited in the essay, although other pertinent works by the authors are footnoted. Bederman's research was supported by the National Science Foundation and DeLancey's by the Foreign Area Fellowship Program (1968-1970) and the Institute of International Studies--University of South Carolina (1975-1976).

2. The most current accepted place names are employed in this study. The Southwest and Northwest Provinces, until 1972, comprised the State of West Cameroon in the Federal Republic. Coastal Fako Division and its neighbor Meme Division were previously called Victoria and Kumba divisions, respectively. After 1972, the Cameroons Development Corporation has been named the Cameroon Development Corporation.

3. For more detailed discussions of the physical geography of Fako Division, see, Sanford H. Bederman, "Mount Cameroon: West Africa's Active Volcano," Nigerian Geographical Journal, Vol. IX, No. 2 (December, 1966), 115-128, and also Geoffrey M. C. Guillaume and Sanford H. Bederman, Subsistence Activity in Five Villages on and Around Mount Cameroon, Victoria Division, West Cameroon (Atlanta: Georgia State College, 1967), 1-5.

4. For a full discussion, see E. Hallden, The Culture Policy of the Basel Mission in the Cameroons, 1886-1905 (Uppsala: Studia Ethnographica Upsaliensia, 1968), passim.

5. Sanford H. Bederman, "Plantation Agriculture in Victoria Division, West Cameroon: An Historical Introduction," Geography, Vol. LI, No. 4 (November, 1966), 354-356.

6. Mark W. DeLancey, "Health and Disease on the Plantations of Cameroon," in Disease and History in Africa, ed. by Gerald Hartwig and K. David Patterson (Durham, N.C.: Duke University Press, forthcoming).

7. The best account of the German experience in this part of tropical Africa is that by Harry Rudin, Germans in the Cameroons, 1884-1914 (New

Haven: Yale University Press, 1938).

8. Most recently altered in United Republic of Cameroon, Decree No. 73-597 of 28th September 1973.

9. Cameroons Development Corporation, Annual Report . . . 1947 (Bota: C.D.C., 1947), p. 1.

10. Migration trends are analyzed in M. W. DeLancey, "Plantation and Migration in the Mt. Cameroon Region," in Kamerun, ed. by Hans Illi (Mainz: Hase and Koehler, 1974), 181-236, E. A. Gwan, Types, Processes and Policy Implications of the Various Migrations in West Cameroon (Ph.D. diss., University of California at Berkeley, 1975), and Y. Marguerat, Analyse numerique des migrations vers les villes du Cameroun (Yaounde: ORSTOM, 1973).

11. Cameroons Development Corporation, Annual Report . . . 1949 (Bota: C.D.C., 1949), p. 19.

12. Cameroons Development Corporation, Report and Accounts, 1966 (Bota: C.D.C., 1966), p. 11.

13. Cameroons Development Corporation, Report and Accounts, 1969 (Bota: C.D.C., 1969), p. 3.

14. Cameroon Development Corporation, Report and Accounts, 1975 (Bota: C.D.C., 1975), p. 5.

15. Sanford H. Bederman, "The Demise of the Commercial Banana Industry in West Cameroon," The Journal of Geography, Vol. LXX, No. 4 (April, 1971), 230-234.

16. The Cameroon tea industry is described in Sanford H. Bederman, "The Tole Tea Estate in West Cameroon," Tijdschrift voor Economishe en Sociale Geografie, Vol. LVIII, No. 6 (November-December, 1967), 316-323.

17. Cameroon Development Corporation, C.D.C. Second Development Programme (Bota: C.D.C., 1976, passim.

18. Cameroon Development Corporation, Annual Report . . . 1977 (Bota: C.D.C., 1977), p. 31.

19. Ibid., 9-10.

20. M. W. DeLancey, "Credit for the Common Man in Cameroon," Journal of Modern African Studies, Vol. XV, No. 2 (1977), 316-322 and "Institutions for the Accumulation and Redistribution of Savings among Migrants," Journal of Developing Areas, forthcoming. Also see the forthcoming issue of Rural Africana devoted to studies of rural savings in Cameroon, particularly, Virginia DeLancey, "Women at the Cameroon Development Corporation: How Their Money Works."

21. D. N. McMaster, "Agricultural Geography," in An Advanced Geography of Africa, ed. by John I.

Clarke (Amersham: Hulton Educational Publications, 1975), 368-370. For a more general indictment of plantations, see George L. Beckford, Persistent Poverty: Underdevelopment in Plantation Economies of the Third World (New York: Oxford University Press, 1962).

Part 4
Aspects of Social Development

10
Language and Language Policy in Cameroon

Beban Sammy Chumbow

INTRODUCTION

There have been, undoubtedly, many successful attempts to build a unified pluricultural and plurilingual nation in developing countries. Most countries of the "third world" are, in fact, pluricultural and plurilingual in varying degrees, for having gone through the colonial experience, they have had to grapple with the problem of grafting a colonial cultural legacy onto a more or less heterogenous traditional cultural heritage. However, the synthesis of cultures in the United Republic of Cameroon is rather unique in that it involves an additional dimension of complexity: the unification of two foreign cultures (British and French) over a background of an extremely complex mould of African cultures and a German cultural substratum.

Cameroon has been called "the centre of gravity of the African continent" because of its geographical position at the juncture of the West, North, and Central regions of Africa. From the linguistic perspective, it may also be considered a miniature continent of Africa because with a population of less than seven million, it is estimated to have over 225 languages (with naturally an even larger number of dialects) distributed among three of the four major language families of Africa established by Greenberg (1966): Niger-Congo to the South and South West represented by the Bantu languages and the West Atlantic subgroup (Fulfude), Nilo-Saharan represented by Kanuri, Afro-Asiatic represented by Arabic-firmly rooted in the Koranic schools of the North. In a word, linguistically, Cameroon does appear to approximate a cross section of the African continent. This already complex linguistic profile was further complexified by the introduction of German before the first world war and then English

281

and French following the split of the country by
the allied nations into a British and French
Cameroons.

On the wake of independence, the will of the
people to reunite into a Federal Republic of
Cameroon after forty years of separation during
which they had each gone separate routes (adopting
English and French cultures), therefore presented an
intergrational problem of considerable magnitude.
It is because of this cultural diversity that
Cameroon was referred to as "the laboratory for
African Unity."[1] Implicit in this characterization
is the somewhat reasonable assertion that the unification of "the Cameroons" with its diversity of
domestic and foreign origin presented approximately
the same problems (on a lesser scale, certainly,
but nevertheless the same divergencies) that the
African continent has to cope with in its search
for unity. The success or failure of "the Cameroon
experiment" would thus serve as a barometer for the
probability of success for African unity.

A fundamental problem in the unification of
divergent cultures is the choice of a language to
serve the machinery of government and other institutions of the nation. To achieve unity in Cameroon,
English and French, the official languages of the
two Cameroons during the colonial era, were both
adopted as the official languages of the Federation.

This paper examines the advent, role, and
significance of the official bilingual policy with
respect to the short and long term needs of the
country. Specifically, it evaluates the present
"language policy" and its implementation, and examines adjustments that would be necessary in order
to evolve a language policy that is more consistent
with the trilingual reality of the Cameroon linguistic situation. However, to understand the dynamics
of the bilingual policy presupposes an understanding
of the background linguistic heritage of which
English - French bilingualism is tributary.

LANGUAGE POLICY IN THE COLONIAL ERA

In terms of its colonial history, Cameroon
passed successively through a period of German
protectorate (1884 - 1919), a League of Nation's
mandate (1919 - 1946) and a United Nation's trusteeship (1946 - 1960). The last two periods saw the
country split into two under the administration of
two of the allied nations (Britain and France).

Thus, between 1919 - 1960 the country underwent only a change of "masters" and consequently no appreciable change in language policy. The two periods would therefore be treated as one.

LANGUAGE IN THE GERMAN MANDATE

The Germans met an already complex multilingual situation in the territory that placed itself under its mandate in 1884. Rudin (1938) reports that there were as many languages as there were ethnic groups and these were so numerous that tribes had ceased to understand one another.[2] Initially, the German government used German as the official language for administration, education, and other public functions. The missionaires (particularly, the protestant missions) used both German and local languages as medium of instruction in their schools. They were quick to realize that the vernacular language was most apt to lodge the word of God right into the hearts of their adherents. To this end, Duala, Bali, Ewondo, Basa (among other languages) were codified by the German Swiss Basler Mission and used as languages of the church in different regions and as the initial language of primary school (with German introduced a little later).[3] The missionary activities were, however, limited to the southern part of the territory.

In the north, another foreign language, Arabic had predated German and was the medium of instruction in the Koranic schools while Hausa and Fulfulde were gaining ground as linguae francae in the area. The Sultan of Fumban, Njoya, had earlier worked out an original orthography for the Bamum language, the first black African script ever invented[4] and wrote an impressive history of his dynasty and empire in the script. Its use was however, restricted to the aristocrats of his Kingdom. English and Pidgin-English had also predated German in Cameroon as a result of British commercial and missionary involvement on the coast (Douala[5], Bimbia, Victoria, Riodel Rey) as far back as 1830.

English and Pidgin-English continued to be spoken in Cameroon under the German mandate. Some missions, (particularly the Baptist mission) persisted in using English in their schools in Douala, Victoria, and elsewhere until 1910. These "clandestine" English schools along with the business influence of British firms (such as John Holt, R & W King, etc. which imported not only British but also Sierra Leonean and Ghanian functionaries) created pockets of English speaking communities in the territory under German mandate.[6]

At first, the German government was indifferent to the status and use of the vernacular languages but was gradually led to modifying its attitudes towards these languages by the need to have the German civil servants know the vernacular languages in order to better cope with their administrative responsibilities as well as curb the opposition and intransigence of the natives - particularly the Duala[7] and other coastal tribes. The Seminar for Oriental Languages founded in Berlin in 1887 did a study of some Cameroon languages and published books or articles on them.

The (German) Colonial Institute was later founded in Hamburg in 1908 to train Germans for administrative duties in the colonies, with local languages of Cameroon on the curriculum. The Germans, therefore, for a time, appeared to have encouraged mother-tongue education in the schools for the first few years of primary education then followed by the introduction of German for the rest of the school period. Faced with the growing influence of the Duala whose language was taught in the schools, the Germans encouraged the use of Bali and Bamum in schools further north to stop the spread of Duala and finally decided to discourage mother-tongue education altogether, apparently, for fear of the political dominance of the people whose languages were used in the schools. Thus, in 1910 (April 24) a decree was issued with the stipulation that grants-in-aid from the government to missions would be restricted only to those who adopted the government's school programme based on German (with no consideration given to the years of mother-tongue education). The government further requested all schools (particularly the American Presbyterian and Baptist schools) to halt the use of English and or Pidgin-English. Moreover, subventions to mission schools would depend on the number of students passing the official government examination in German. These measures had the desired effect of crippling the spread of mother-tongue education in favour of a German language hegemony in the country's institutions until the outbreak of the first world war.

LANGUAGE POLICY DURING THE MANDATE AND TRUSTEESHIP

<u>British Cameroons (Southern Cameroons)</u>--Britain, like every colonial government throughout history, naturally made its language English, the official language in the portion of Cameroon placed under its mandate by the League of Nations. For administrative convenience, she administered it as part of its larger colony, Nigeria, which shares a common frontier with Cameroon. One effect of this was that the famous British policy of <u>indirect rule</u> successfully tried out in Nigeria, was extended to Cameroon and allowed missionaries the option of using the vernacular in all aspects of their work, including education. The Swiss Bosler Mission had two years of mother-tongue education (in Duala and Bali) attached to some of its primary schools and organized adult literacy classes in Duala for the Southern districts (Victoria, Kumba, Mamfe) and in Bali for the Northern districts (Bamenda, Wum, Nkambe). The Roman Catholic Mission preferred the use of Pidgin English (which was already rising to the status of a lingua franca) for church services along with Latin. The Baptist Mission used either English or Pidgin English depending on the locality.

Thus, while establishing English as official language in British Cameroons, the British government allowed the use of local languages in the school system at the lower level of primary education and in local government institutions.

<u>French Cameroons</u>--France introduced French as the official language of its portion of Cameroon. However, whereas the British (consistent with their policy of indirect rule) permitted or at least tolerated the missionary's use of vernacular in schools, the French were categorically opposed to it. Officially, the local language could neither be used as a medium of instruction or figure as a subject on the curriculum. The French intransigence in this respect can be traced to its well-known policy of <u>assimilation</u> as confirmed by a government blue-print to this effect:

. . . the colonial administration is convinced of the impossibility of propagating the achievements of a modern civilization by means of a primitive language . . .[8]

Thus, in accordance with the French colonial policy, it wasn't in the interest of the "frenchification" of Cameroonians to encourage literacy in their own mother tongue--a course of action which would have procured the undesirable effect of strengthening the underlying native culture, making it less easy for the superimposed French culture to penetrate.

The French government's language policy had remarkable success in the government schools as a new class (the "evolue") emerged. In the mission schools, however, the policy was difficult to police as some missionaries, mindful of the importance of the vernacular in the enterprise of evangelization, succeeded in maintaining some degree of mother tongue education in their schools without however, overtly admitting a deviation from the official government policy. Ewondo, Basa, and Bagangte (among other Cameroon languages) were codified and joined Bamum and Duala as vernacular languages of education in the mission schools of the French territory. Here again, not all the missions were eager to use the vernacular and their use was limited to a couple of years. Early transition to French was necessary in order not to arouse government's suspicion and also because of the exigencies of the job market where the school leaver's market value was determined by the degree of "frenchification" attained.

Two types of schools emerged in the French Cameroons as a result of the French colonial administration's educational policy.

(i) the government and government seconded schools, privileged, financed and endowed with recognition

(ii) the "private schools" (a category which in the French administration's categorization includes mission schools and other voluntary agency schools), were often unrecognized and received little or no subventions.

In some mission schools, religious instruction in the vernacular was available and encouraged, not withstanding the government's attitude. Meanwhile, in the Northern part of the country where Islam had taken root, the Koranic schools (more numerous than the French language schools of the government and voluntary agencies combined),[9] continued to use Arabic as in the German era.

In both the French and British Cameroons, there was an important linguistic community, the German-trained Cameroonian civil servants, soldiers, and businessmen who faded out of service either on account of age, or because German had become irrelevant. Though scattered throughout the territory, they remained a significant linguistic community and an important force in the campaign for the reunification of the Cameroons as it was ("in their days") under the Germans.

The picture of the linguistic heritage that emerges on the eve of independence and reunification from the foregoing sketch of language policy in the colonial era is one characterized by complexity, making monolingualism virtually impossible and multilingualism a fact of life in Cameroon. English was the official language of the British sector, superimposed over a background of Pidgin-English, German, and an estimated 70 to 80 indigenous languages, whereas French was the official language of the French sector superimposed over a background of German, Arabic, Pidgin-English (mainly in the West and South-west provinces) and approximately 150 to 170 indigenous languages.[10]

POST INDEPENDENCE LANGUAGE POLICY

The French Cameroons became independent as the Republic of Cameroon in 1960 and the Southern (British) Cameroons (following a United Nation-supervised plebiscite) opted for independence and reunification with the Republic of Cameroon, the two constituting the Federal Republic of Cameroon in October 1961.

THE OFFICIAL BILINGUAL POLICY

The first constitution of the independent Federal Republic of Cameroon stipulated that "the official languages of the Federation shall be English and French." This placed Cameroon in a unique position in Africa in having two exoglossic or foreign languages as official languages in contrast with other African countries where either French or English but not both became the official language at independence.

The factors that gave rise to this choice can easily be surmised from the above background sketch of the colonial legacy. The Federation's official language policy of English-French bilingualism simple involved telescoping the official languages of the two states of the Federation, the State of West Cameroon (formerly British Southern Cameroons) and the State of East Cameroon (formerly French Cameroons). Were there any other alternatives to this choice? What steps were taken to implement

287

English-French bilingualism in the Federal Republic?
What successes (if any) were registered? What adjustments would be necessary to enhance widespread
official bilingualism? These are the issues that
will be taken up in this section.

THE NECESSITY OF ENGLISH FRENCH BILINGUALISM

English-French bilingualism has been dubbed the
official language policy of Cameroon and we shall
continue to refer to it as such. However, it is
important to point out that technically speaking,
it isn't really a language policy and it can be
argued that in this (technical sense) Cameroon is
yet to evolve a language policy; for a language
policy, from the sociolinguistic perspective, is
normally part of a careful and judicious language
planning based on a detailed study of a wide range
of socio-economic-political variables relevant to
the state's developmental needs (both in the short
and long terms). The choice of English and French
as official languages here was not based on any
elaborate linguistic or paralinguistic considerations but rather it was determined essentially by
extralinguistic considerations. It was simply dictated by pragmatism. It would appear to be a necessary choice under the circumstances of the time in
that the atmosphere in both states was charged with
slogans of reunification, and so the leaders were
under political pressure to make reunification work.
The 1960 Foumban Conference that adopted the first
constitution (with delegates from the two states)
felt that reunification should begin with a loose
federation in which each state will maintain considerable autonomy in certain fields during the
first five years. The choice of official languages
of the Federal government was thus made with this in
mind. Besides, the choice could not fall uniquely
on one of the two languages without creating hard-
ship for one of the states, thereby hurting the
enterprise of reunification.
Could an indigenous Cameroon language have been
raised to the status of official language? Not at
that time with the political imperatives before the
government. When it is realized that with a population of only 4 million in 1960, Cameroon had (and
still has) an estimated 200-240 indigenous languages, it can readily be understood that none of
these languages, is extensively spoken in the
territory to constitute a national language (without

the benefit of extensive planning and language engineering).

Despite the merits of a "national" language, particularly with respect to long term needs, reunification, the task at the moment, was so urgent and so immediate that the most expedient solution (i.e., English-French bilingualism) had to be adopted, particularly in the face of demonstrated skepticism regarding the possibility of a successful welding of such divergent cultures as embodied in the French and British political, judicial, and educational institutions inherited by the two states. Such was the skepticism (both from within and without), that an agreement was reached to the effect that the United Nations could intervene and "desolve the marriage" within the first few years of reunification if things did not work out. Given the political imperatives of the time, it would seem that the choice of English and French as official languages was both necessary and justifiable as a temporary measure.

What steps did government take to implement this bilingualism and what has been the response to it?

IMPLEMENTATION OF THE POLICY OF BILINGUALISM

Government's attitude to French-English bilingualism throughout the period of the Federation (1961-1972), (prior to the change to a unitary state) was largely determined by government's political concerns. Just as the policy itself was born out of political speculations so did its fate depend on the government's political concern of consolidation of unification via progressive centralization and elimination of state, or regional autonomy. Several measures were taken primarily in the interest of integration which also had significant repercussions on the implementation of English-French bilingualism.

Bilingual Translators--Recall that the government's primodial task was to make reunification work. This could not be achieved by expecting the use of English and French in all government institutions from the onset since the number of (English-French) bilingual functionaries in the whole Federation was extremely small. The state governments, using only one of the official languages, sailed along more or less smoothly with a pool of translators based in the state's prime minister's office to

translate materials emanating from the other state
or other Federal government. The Federal government was in a hot spot since, in principle, official
documents and correspondences had to be in both
English and French. To this end, a "translation
bureau" was established at the Presidency and some
individual ministries had their own translators.
In practice, however, not all Federal documents were
bilingual since the civil servants who issued them
were often not bilingual themselves. On the other
hand, where attempts were made to have official
documents available in both languages, this often
led to bureaucratic bottlenecks in the administrative process since they had to be sent to the
presidency or some other translation bureau.

Meetings and conferences at the Federal level
were equally difficult to organize since each such
meeting required prior guarantees with respect to
competent automatic interpreters. In a word, the
communication problems of the Federal government in
the first few years of reunification were considerable and it took the will to survive as a nation to
meet with these handicaps and set backs. The
government's immediate reaction was to train or
assemble various degrees of bilingual translators
to cope with the work.

Change in Status of English and French in
School--Most of the secondary schools were monolingual in that the medium of instruction was often
one (not both) of the official languages: English
in schools of West Cameroon and French in schools of
East Cameroon. However, in recognition of the
status of English and French in the Federal
Republic, schools were encouraged to offer or inten-
sify the study of the other official language as a
subject in the curriculum and achieve a respectable
degree of proficiency in it by graduation day.

Bilingual Grammar Schools--The government established bilingual secondary schools ideally conceived as schools for whose products competence in
both English and French would be practically guaranteed by the use of English and French alternately as
media of instruction. In these schools, students
are groomed to receive their lessons in either
English or French by the need of the second year no
matter their linguistic background. The motivation
for an excellent degree of bilingualism is kept
alive by having all students enroll for the French
language examination "Brevet Elementaire du Premier
Cyle" (BEPC) at the end of the fourth year and then
the English language examination "the London

University General Certificate of Education (GCE)
Ordinary level" at the end of the fifth year and
subsequently opt for either the French language
Baccalaureat examination, or the GCE Advanced Level
examination at the end of the seventh and final
year. These are very ambitious goals requiring
qualified bilingual staff and ultra modern learning
facilities. Since 1960, four such schools have been
established: Man O War Bay (now Buea) 1962,
Yaounde 1966, Mamfe 1968, Bonaberi (Douala) recently. Buea and Yaounde grammar schools appear to have
produced good results, approximating a reasonable
extent the goals set for the bilingual schools.
However, whereas it can be said that most of the
graduates of these schools are sufficiently bilingual, less than an estimated 50% consistently
enroll for both the French and English board examinations, although some individual performances in
this respect have been excellent. While the
English-speaking students enrolled in large numbers
for the BEPC, the "francophone" students have tended
to avoid taking the GCE Ordinary level examination.[11] At any rate, these schools constitute a
response to problems of bilingual man-power development: the more successful graduates of these
schools entered the university and other higher institutions while the rest entered the administration and the private sector mainly as translators
and language teachers.

Linguistic Centres--Linguistic centres (which
doubled as cultural centres), are buildings equipped
with a language laboratory and audio-visual facilities among other things.[12] Their main function is
to provide opportunities for workers and the general
citizenry to improve their knowledge of the second
official language with which they are less familiar.
In other words, they are essentially centres for
adult language classes. In the past, civil servants
could be granted a couple of hours off each day to
take language lessons at the Linguistic Centre.
Several courses were run in shifts for a maximum
utilization of the facility and for the convenience
of users. Linguistic Centres are however, too few,
(for obvious financial reasons) and they are located
mainly in the large cities of Yaounde, Buea, and
Douala. The high cost of the specialized equipment
and the rarity of adequately trained personnel have
been determinant factors in restricting the extensive use of linguistic centres all over the country
to aid the cause of the bilingual language policy.
They did, however, play an important role in

stimulating interest in the study of French and English in the early days of the Cameroon Federation.

Radio Language Programmes--Two radio programmes were developed and used in West Cameroon and East Cameroon. In 1967, "Le Francais par la Radio" was aired over radio Buea for English-speaking learners of French over the years, while a similar programme, "L'anglais Chez-vous" was launched for French-speaking learners of English. Tadadjou (1975) has rightly pointed out that the effectiveness of such programmes is hard to determine since enrollment was determined by economic, social, or political motivations, all of which are subject to varying degrees of fluctuation. It is, however, true to say that the motivation for English-French bilingualism was high in the early years of the reunification, making these programmes fairly popular at that time.

Bilingualism in Post Secondary Institutions-- Following the official language policy, English and French are the official languages of the University of Yaounde and its satellite institutions: L'Ecole Normale Superieure, L'Ecole Polytechnique, L'Ecole Nationale d'Agriculture, etc. In practice, what this means, however, is that the lecturer has the choice between English and French as medium of instruction (whichever suits him best) whereas the student has no choice but to do his best to understand lectures, write (and "present" oral) examinations in either language. The pioneer students were essentially monolingual on admission to the University and had to take crash language courses at the university or the language centre in order to make it.

Without ceasing to be problematic, the situation in the university has improved considerably with the improved level of bilingualism in the secondary schools.

For many years, the number of lecturer proficient in French and lecturing in French at the University was superior to staff using the English language; so that despite its constitutional bilingual status, the university was, for over a decade, essentially a French language university (except for the English Department whose programme was patterned after the University of Leeds and remains so patterned). The result of this state of affairs is that during the first decade, more anglophones have become bilingual in going through the university system than francophones. The latter

292

have not had to face the challenge of making
serious linguistic adjustments in the course of
their studies since most of the lectures were in
French.

Responding to the bilingual man-power demands,
a special bilingual degree programme was introduced
in the Faculty of Arts and tailored to meet the
needs of the country with respect to translation
(for the administration) and teaching of the official languages.

The other higher institutions remain highly
monolingual with French alone as the medium of
instruction. French is the sole language of the
army, the National School of Sports and until very
recently, it was the only language used in the
"Ecole Nationale d'Administration et de Magistra-
ture," the highest institution in the country for
training top civil servants for the administration,
as well as for the legal and judiciary departments.

Bilingual Primary Schools--Recently, the
government has introduced official bilingualism in
some selected primary schools. This involved having
one of the official languages taught as a medium of
instruction and the other studied as a subject of
the school curriculum. This measure is coming more
than ten years after Fonlon (1969) had made the
"Case for early bilingualism," by advancing historical, psychological, and educational evidence for
the merits of learning languages early in the
child's maturational growth, preferably in the
nursery and primary school systems. Fonlon's proposal was stiffled, apparently by the more urgent
political problems of the state as well as the
scarcity of bilingual staff. It is the scarcity of
staff along with financial constraints that have
equally limited the present initiative of bilingualism at the primary school level to selected schools.

EVALUATION OF THE OFFICIAL BILINGUAL POLICY

Cameroon's English-French bilingualism is
usually assumed to be a success from within the
country and generally presumed to be a success from
without. What successes have really been registered
and what adjustments would be necessary to enhance
the development of widespread bilingualism?

The success of English-French bilingualism in
Cameroon is largely political in the sense that to
extent that a successful merger of two culturally
different Cameroon states has been achieved (going

from a federal to a unitary government), and to the extent that this was accomplished with English and French as the official languages, this political success has tended to overflow onto the state's official bilingualism issue, crowing and draining it completely. However, a careful look beneath this drain, would reveal that despite some praise-worthy attempts made (see section 2.3), achievements in bilingualism (even for the literate population alone) are considerably limited.

Achievements--Today, almost two decades after reunification, Cameroon has come a long way from the bleak period when communication in human language between average citizen's of the two states was well near impossible, except through interpreters or via a make shift sign language.[12] There is clearly a population of English-French bilinguals in Cameroon today as a result of government as well as individual efforts. The degree of bilingualism, of course, varies and can be represented on a scale from near-zero to near-perfect bilingualism. All Cameroonians can be classified within this scale in a decreasing order of English-French bilingual competence as follows:

(i) The Near-Perfect Bilingual--This is the class with the highest ("excellent or very good") command of both languages in terms of the integrated language skills of reading, writing, oral-comprehension, and oral production. To this class belong the products of tertiary education in Cameroon (i.e.: the products of Yaounde University and allied institutions: L'Ecole Normale Superieure de Yaounde, Ecole Polytechnique, Ecole Superieure d'Agriculture, etc.). More specifically, these are those Cameroonians who through the exigencies of their academic career have mastered their second official language, attaining a near-native speaker's competence in it. To this category may be added those francophone Cameroonians who have studied in the anglophone communities of America, Britain, Canada, or Nigeria, etc., as well as anglophone Cameroonians who have mastered French in francophone countries like France, Belgium, Switzerland, Dakar, etc.

(ii) The Semi-bilingual--This class is characterized by the ability to code switch from English to French and vice versa but with more or less hesitation and a halting but meaningful performance. The hesitation betrays a gap in the grasp of the intricacies of the grammar and language use in terms of lexical categories, lexical functions, etc. Thus

294

for instance, not knowing whether a specific French word is of feminine or masculine gender, can start a hesitation process that is likely to affect not only the rhythm but also the meaning of the utterance. This notwithstanding, individuals in this category succeed in getting themselves understood but with noticeable grammatical errors or performance deficits.

To this category belong a majority of secondary school leavers of the rising generation[13] who have benefitted from the intensified teaching of their second official language (English or French as the case may be), those who have worked in the other "state" for a long time and have made relatively successful efforts to acquire the language (without the benefit of the thorough grounding of a university education) and finally those functionaries who have spent a year in France or Britian specifically to improve their knowledge of the language.

(iii) The Functionally Bilingual--This refers to those whose ability to communicate in the second official language is limited to certain situations or functions. Thus, for example, an anglophone telecommunication technician may be able to converse in French when talking about transmissions, etc. (his job) or about football (his past-time) but gets lost on other topics. Many workers in the government's civil service and some of the private sector have varying degrees of functional bilingualism since they usually have to acquaint themselves with the "jargon" of their profession in both languages.

(iv) The Passive Bilingual--This refers to the individual who can understand the other language but can't speak it at all, or can't speak it well enough. The competence level in this category is best illustrated by an encounter at a check-point between the writer and a "gendarme officer" (a sort of "passe-partout," all-purpose military police):

Officer:	Give me vos pieces, patron.
Answer:	Sorry, my hands are wet. They are all in this envelope (handing it to the officer).
Officer:	Bon, essuyez les mains alors. C'est les pieces que je veux, pas toute cette bagatelle-la!
Answer:	O.K. don't yell at me now! I thought it will be quicker for you to pull them out since my hands are wet and would require drying.

    Officer: (Waving his index menacingly) Vous
                parlex a un chef de brigarde comme
                ca! Comment! attention eh . . . My
                friend, careful.

The Officer, who is French-speaking, demonstrates
passive linguistic competence in English in that he
appears to understand his interlocutor both in
terms of the intrinsic semantics of the discourse
as well as the situational meaning and reacts
appropriately (but perhaps not "correctly") in
French to each response although he cannot verbalize
in English. The speech of such speakers is often
characterized by language interlarding involving an
occasional dose of words from the language which
the speaker does not know well (see the underlined
words in the dialogue above where such language
interlarding results in a sort of "franglais" in
the first sentence). Those who have studied
their second official language without having
opportunities to actualize and verbalize it, often
end up with this type of competence. For many,
however, passive bilingualism is a _transitional
competence_ in that they may, with the appropriate
opportunities, increase their verbal performance
and move out of this category to (iii), (ii), or
even (i).
        (v) _The Near-Zero Bilingual_--Individuals of
this category are either not bilingual at all or
have a bilingual competence that is essentially
lexical. That is, they may know that "garcon" means
"boy" and "pourboire" means "tip" in French without
being able to produce original sentences with these
words in connected speech. To this category, belong
a few of the literate Cameroonians of the _descending
generation_ as well as most of the illiterates.
        Most Cameroonians of the _rising generation_ are
daily code switching from one, two, or three
Cameroonian languages to Pidgin-English (the unofficial lingua franca) and from Pidgin-English to
English or French as the situations arise. We are
in the presence of what Ferguson (1959) calls
bilingualism with diaglossia where each of the languages has some functional autonomy in the sense
that it is associated with aspects of the speaker's
daily life or duties. He speaks Duala, Ngemba
Fe'fe', Basa, etc. at home, Pidgin-English on the
bus or in the market, and then switches on to
English or French at school or in the office. If in
the university, the "bilingual" may discuss History
in English and in the next hour he is discussing

Geography in French. However, the majority of bilinguals of categories (i) and (ii) are to be found
mainly among the rising generation of Cameroonians
who have benefitted most and continue to benefit
from the programmes of bilingualism. Despite these
undeniable achievements, English-French bilinguals
of categories (i) and (ii) are relatively few (in
relation to the potential in this respect). Put
differently, there is still room for wide-spread
English-French bilingualism in Cameroon. Some
factors have been responsible for restricting or at
least slowing down the spread of English-French bilingualism some of which have been identified,
albeit implicitly, in the foregoing discussion.[14]

Factors adverse to Wide-spread Bilingualism[14]

(i) By far the most significant single factor
against the spread of bilingualism is the absence
of clear-cut goals with respect to the implementation of bilingualism. There has never been a
government blue-print with a specific time-table of
expected achievements in bilingualism over the
years, comparable to the various "development plans"
that emphasize economic and political development
projects. There have been no measures to systematically bilingualize and enforce bilingualism in
the school population, for instance. All the
efforts conceded in this respect, (section 2.3),
seem to have been geared towards providing for the
immediate needs in order to make the enterprise of
reunification successfully politically (and perhaps
economically).

Putting it succinctly, there has been no clear
knowledge of the destination of English-French bilingualism in Cameroon and consequently no clear
knowledge of the best way to get there.

It is true that the successive five-year
development plans over the years of reunification
occasionally mention efforts and projects in bilingualism but such efforts and projects are based
on no discernable reasoned language policy. Again,
the recent institution (in 1974) of a language and
linguistic section at the National Institute of
Education, (a branch of the "l'Office National des
Researches Scientifiques et Techniques") may be
regarded as a step forward except that it is not
obvious whether it is a step in the right direction
or not, in the absence of a clear sense of direction
in the form of a meaningful long term language
policy.

(ii) Although constitutionally English and
French have equal status as official languages, the

English speaking part of the country has only a quarter of the country's population; so that from the onset, the scales naturally tilted in favour of French ascendency.

(iii) Furthermore, an analysis of the trend towards bilingualism shows that for over ten years, the trend appeared to be essentially (but by no means completely) unidirectional in that (as has been mentioned before), by far more anglophone conceded efforts and effectively achieved a respectable degree of bilingualism than francophones. This obviously retrogressive ascendency of French over English as a result of the population factor mentioned above and in part to the "frenchification" effect of the French colonial policy which presented the French language to all its colonies as the language of civilization "par excellence." Since French has a de facto popularity and superiority (despite a de jure equality with English), francophones have a less natural urge or stimulus towards acquiring English. This trend was reinforced by the fact that politically, more French-styled governmental institutions, (administration, police, army, etc.) were preferred for the Federal government (and subsequently for the unitary government) over their British-styled equivalents, with the result that francophones had no need to effect major adjustments. These factors are not, however, alone responsible for the unidirectional trend towards bilingualism observed during the first decade of Cameroon reunification. The lack (or in some cases the insufficiency) of English teachers relative to the demands of the francophone schools and federal institutions like the university and the bilingual grammar schools is also a significant determinant of the unidirectional trend towards the ideal of bilingualism in that francophones generally had fewer opportunities for learning and practicing English than anglophones had for learning French.

(iv) For many people, the absence of a powerful motivation and challenging incentives are responsible for the lack of interest in the ideal of English-French bilingualism. Linguistic research on the role of motivation in language acquisition indicates that more people will make the efforts and aspire to be successfully given appropriate motivation (Lambert et al-1968). Afterall, why make sacrifices to learn another language when there is no reason for it?

(v) Language loyalty is, in my judgment, one of the most heart rendering obstacles to be

surmounted in creating an atmosphere conducive to
implementing the government's bilingual policy.
Generally speaking, language loyalty is a phenomenon which corresponds to language as nationalism
corresponds to nationality. More specifically,
"language loyalty" designates the state of mind in
which the language (like nationality) assumes a
high position in a scale of values, a position in
need of being defended (Weinreich 1953: 99).

In this sense, language loyalty need not
always be the object of prejudice and criticism
since there appears to be in each one of us, a
natural inclination, and inescapable emotional involvement with the language we have been speaking
from the cradle or the language used in school as
medium of instruction. However, the extent of
loyalty sentiments attached to individual languages
in a pluralistic society and the consequent display
of resentful loyalty may undermine national interests and thus deserve to come under attack.

Indeed, language loyalty has recently sparked
off integrational problems that have threatened the
foundation of national unity in Canada and Belgium.
In the Cameroon situation the display of language
loyalty is observed less with the diverse mother-
tongue as with the two exoglossic languages:
English and French. There is manifestly a tendency
for some French-educated and English-educated
Cameroonians to cling to the French language and
culture or the English language and culture (as the
case may be) with a naive passion that obscures
national realities and impairs good judgment with
respect to the interests of a pluralistic society
like Cameroon.

Necessary Language - related Adjustments--To
enhance wide-spread English-French bilingualism
within a dynamic national language policy, several
adjustments will have to be made not only by the
government but also by individual citizens:

(i) Individual Adjustments--Individuals,
particularly students, would have to realize the
importance of language to the acquisition of knowledge and to self fulfillment in the society in
which they live. This means recognizing the importance of English, French, and the mother tongue
and making efforts to attain more than a functional
level of competence in all three by exploiting
facilities and opportunities provided for their
acquisition. In short, the reassessment of the
linguistic situation by the individual calls for a

change in individual attitude towards the official languages.

A reapraisal of the linguistic situation and national imperatives also calls on the individual to face up to the divisive effect of language loyalty and to reassign his loyalty by extending it from one official language to include the other official language.

(ii) Government Initiated Adjustments--While the official language policy of English-French bilingualism was necessary on the wake of independence and reunification to ensure the harmonious welding of the Cameroon nation out of two institutionally different factions, there is need, once reunification has been achieved, to make adjustments consistent with the linguistic realities of the country. Government would have to evolve a dynamic policy that considers not only the English-French heritage but also the Cameroon languages heritage without which the Cameroonian is virtually depersonalized.

In an earlier paper, (Chumbow, 1974), I presented the issue in the following terms:

> Due to historical accidents, and factors independent of the intrinsic value of English and French, the two languages have come to acquire a universal status as vehicles of communication and scientific research. Thus, in the short run, if countries of the third world want to participate fully in world affairs and take their place among nations by contributing culturally to the universal fraternity of mankind, these languages (among others) should best serve the purpose. However, this does not imply that our indigenous languages should be neglected or stigmatized; on the contrary, our languages remain the most adequate medium of expression designed to cope with our culture, our world vision, and our cosmogony. An African who cannot speak an African language and speak it well enough to express his innermost-self is like a tree separated from its roots and therefore incapable of contributing something original to universal culture. This, in effect, means that African languages will have to be cultivated, developed, and used to capture, in all their freshness and splendour, the cultural values which constitute our identity, our specificity, and only then will it be relevant to vehicle these values via English and French as a contribution to universal

300

human culture. Thus, English and French as
official (or "national") languages in Africa
must be functionally restricted to specific
aspects of life: education (along with the
indigenous languages), scientific research,
and diplomacy.

In the Cameroon context, citizens who speak
French or English or both, almost invariably also
speak a Cameroon language. So that there is a de
facto trilingual situation for individual citizens.
Consequently, any attempt to construct and enforce
a "bilingual policy" that ignores or precludes the
trilingual reality of the linguistic situation is
bound to lead to a disaster for the Cameroonian
personality (if it leads to anywhere at all). Such
is the importance of a triglossic language policy
that I will return to it in the next and final
section.
Another adjustment that government will have
to make is to provide adequate incentives and
motivations for individual efforts by making its
language policy not only worthwhile but desirable.
At the moment, there is "no appreciable reward" or
gain for achieving a bilingual status, a facotr
responsible for the unidirectional trend towards
bilingualism discussed earlier. Given the demographic imbalance in favour of French (making French
the more dominant of the two official languages),
as long as Francophones are not given a strong
reason for learning English, only an enlightened few
will concede the efforts. For the future of the
government's language policy, it should be obvious
from recruitment, advancement, and promotion requirements that government attaches some premium on
the knowledge of these languages. It is true that
bilinguals of anglophone origin do get top civil
service appointments but since quite often they
share these posts with francophones who are not bilinguals, it would appear that the relevant criterion here is not "bilingualism" but the candidate's
knowledge of French. Indeed, it does appear that
most bilinguals of anglophone origin make the effort
to acquire French mainly because of its dominant
status (which makes it indispensable for job satisfaction and self-fulfillment) and not because of
bilingualism per se.
There is a need to ensure adequate training of
language teachers in sufficient numbers to cope
with the demands. Similarly, language text books
have to take into consideration the heterogenous

301

linguistic background of students. The training of
language teachers will have to include the ability
to adapt standard text books to the needs of the
specific locality where the teaching is carried out.

THE UNOFFICIAL TRILINGUAL POLICY

Mention has been made of the fact that despite
the official bilingual policy, the average English-
French bilingual is in fact trilingual since he
also speaks (at least) one Cameroon language. Considering the cultural value of the Cameroon languages and their significance as medium of education, one is led to the realization that English-
French bilingualism in Cameroon can find its true
expression only in the recognition of the triglossic
linguistic situation by the official adoption and
implementation of the existing unofficial trilingual
policy.

The trilingual policy would involve creating a
favourable climate for the acquisition of English
and French as well as one Cameroon language, preferably the child's mother-tongue or a closely
related vernacular. Since speaking skills are acquired naturally and spontaneously in the family
circles, the problem is reduced essentially to one
of acquiring reading and writing skills.

Recall that throughout the various formal language policies of the colonial era there always was
an informal language policy carried out by missionaries which involved the development and teaching of
vernacular languages for evangelization.

Today a trilingual education operates in some
communities where mother-tongue education is offered
(without any official recognition).

Experts of the UNESCO in a historically important conference on "The Use of Vernacular Languages in Education" (1953) established as axiomatic
that a child will learn to read more rapidly in his
second language if he is first taught to read in his
mother tongue and would achieve a greater mastery
and general knowledge of other subject matter areas
in his second (official language) if he is first
taught these subjects in his native language. Weber
(1970) and Seville and Troike (1971) found that "the
basic skills of reading transfer from language to
another and that teaching reading first in the
child's native language has long term benefits for
the child's learning process. Subsequently, various
experimental mother tongue first education projects

(like the Ife Project in Nigeria-Afolayan 1972)
proved the importance of the use of vernacular languages in education. Tadadjeu (1975) recognizes
three forces in favour of mother tongue education
in Cameroon thereby making the unofficial trilingual
policy a reality inspite of government's non-commit-
tal attitude towards mother tongue education:

(i) The Local Literacy Programmes in vernacular languages which grew out of the missionary
teaching activities into semi-autonomous bodies
without, however, severing their mission connections. One such group and by far the most active,
is the NUFI Programme operating in the Bamileke
region (the grassfield area of Western Cameroon)
since 1961, with organized Bamileke language schools
throughout the country and overseas (wherever there
is a significant population of Bamileke, e.g.
France).[15] The programme is reported to have gradu-
ated over 3,000 people from its schools by 1974.[16]
Other such local, self-financing, non-grant aided
programmes spurred on by a few enlightened citizens
of various communities are believed to function for
Ewondo, Bassa, Duala, Fulfude, and a number of
other Cameroon languages, moved by the same aspirations, geared towards the same goals but achieving
varying degrees of success.

(ii) "Private Schools" (including voluntary
agency schools like the Christian Mission schools
and the Koranic schools of the North) have been
active in encouraging mother tongue education (or
literacy in Arabic for the Koranic schools). In
this category, College Libermann in Douala under the
able leadership of the Jesuit scholar, sociologist
Meinrad Hebga deserves special mention for its
"avant garde" role in introducing vernacular in its
curricula, producing literature materials in these
languages and training teaching personnel with a
view to getting government to officially recognize
the vernacular in the various localities as a replacement of students third language (usually Latin,
German, or Spanish) at the BEPC examination.
College Libermann has been emulated in its mother
tongue education efforts by a number of secondary
schools (mainly mission colleges) in Yaounde,
Douala, and in the grassfield Bamileke region with
the impetus continually flowing from the College
Libermann leadership. Their endeavours in this respect are well supported by the argument that the
vernacular is more relevant to the socio-economic
social needs of the young Cameroonian (along with

English and French) than Spanish and German or even
less, Latin.
   (iii) The opinion of Cameroon scholars expressed in various articles and conferences is an important factor in favour of "mother tongue" education.[17] A number of seminars have been organized
since 1973 initiated either by the College
Libermann or the staff of Yaounde University and the
National Institute of Education to discuss the
linguistic situation. The proceedings of the 1973
seminar were published in a book whose title is
eloquent about its content: "Les Langues Africaines
facteurs de development" (African Languages as
Factors of Development), College Libermann, 1974.
   Another seminar in 1974 was more dynamic and
practical in that workshops for studying selected
Cameroon languages (Duala, Bassa, Bulu, Ewondo
Bamileke) were organized for training secondary and
primary school teachers in the use of phonemic alphabet for the transcription of these languages.
The workshop staff adopted a UNESCO sponsored
phonemic alphabet devised by Professor Bot Ba Njok
in 1970 for reducing Bantu languages of Central
Africa into writing.
   The government's official policy attitude
towards the use of vernacular languages in education
(from all indications) has been rather lukewarm.
In fact, no policy exists in this respect although
government has allowed or in some cases encouraged
the idea to be balloted about in seminars by the
University of Yaounde and the National Institute
for Education.
   The main objectives advanced against the
mother tongue education are:
   (a) the multiplicity of languages in the
country
   (b) the economic implications of providing an
orthography, textbooks and manuals as well as
teachers for each vernacular to be used in education
and
   (c) the possibility of political cleavages
along linguistic lines.[18]
   These problems are not peculiar to Cameroon.
All developing nations that have a pluricultural
background have had to face and surmount these
difficulties. Languages change and linguistic
situations also change (even when "left alone").
The question is, in what direction should the change
(in a given community) go? Can policy makers and
language planners influence the change in a desired
direction? (And in this particular context, does

the haphazard policy of English-French bilingualism
satisfy the needs of the people of an independent
African Nation? If not, shouldn't the nature and
direction of change in language policy be a government priority?) Can any government close its eyes
on the inconvertible linguistic finding that education in the mother tongue, particularly in the first
few years of schooling, has favourable psycholinguistic implications for the overall intellectual
development of the child? These are, of course,
rhetorical questions. The answers are clear.

To surmount the first problem of the multiplicity of languages, the practice has generally
been to isolate a few languages as languages of
<u>wider communication</u> on the basis of significant
sociolinguistic considerations. This involves
spliting the country into a number of Linguistic
zones so that one language in each zone is used for
education. Speakers of other languages thus have to
use the zonal language that is most related to
theirs. Bot Ba Njock (1966) has suggested possible
zonal languages in Cameroon. Although it appears
all the sociolinguistic variables are not taken into
consideration in his paper, this suggestion can constitute the basis for a more refined study and
eventual segmentation into zonal languages. Some
have argued that learning a zonal language for one
who speaks another vernacular language is in fact
learning a foreign language (like English). This is
not entirely true if the zonal language is closely
related to the child's mother tongue. For instance,
because of the "deep" intrinsic relations between
Bantu languages of the same sub-group like Bakweri
and Duala, it would be much easier for a Bakweri to
use Duala as a medium of instruction (and vice
versa) than English or French.

Thus, segmentation into zonal languages limits
considerably, the number of vernaculars for which
textbooks and teachers have to be made available
(without, however, eliminating the economic
problem).

If however, the answers to the series of
rhetorical questions asked above favour the need
for a trilingual language policy with a place for
mother tongue education, then sacrifices have to be
made. The implementation of the policy could be
gradual (as the financial position permits) but the
overall goal and direction should be clear.

The fear that the establishment of zonal languages could create a large entities that can load
to exploiting the linguistic affinity for political

agitation is not a strong argument against zonal languages in that such loyalty sentiments do exist in the form of ethnic identity anyway and can be dealt with by exploiting the socio-economic variables in favour of national unity--which most statesmen (but perhaps, not "politicians") often do.

CONCLUSION

At independence and reunification, the Federal Republic of Cameroon had to cope with a complex linguistic heritage of local and colonial origin. In this study, it was observed that the official policy of English-French bilingualism was dictated by pragmatism and uniquely by considerations of national unity. In the implementation of this policy, such considerations proved too fragile to favour widespread English-French bilingualism inspite of the development of pockets of English-French bilinguals in the country. Implementation also suffers from the lack of a judicious language policy that takes into consideration the linguistic reality of Cameroon, particularly the role of Cameroon languages in the short and long term needs of the people. Finally, it is suggested that English-French bilingualism can find its true expression only in a well-conceived trilingual language policy that takes into account the triglossic situation of the Cameroonian and the various subjective and objective merits of the mother tongue as medium of instruction.[19] The difficulties in this respect are not insurmountable when the policy implementation is envisaged as a more or less long term project. As Bokamba and Tlou (1976) have rightly observed, the problems of dealing with the colonial linguistic legacy are not more insurmountable than those involved in dealing with colonialism itself (in the sixties).

NOTES

1. Among the many references to Cameroon as "the laboratory for African Unity," one of the earliest is by former President Moktar Ould Dadah of Mauritania in his address to the Cameroon people in 1964.

2. Most of these languages had developed a system of talking--drums for inter-village communication whereby two tones of the drum manipulated into intricate rythmic patterns made it possible to transmit any message that could be verbalized. Commenting on this system (which is extensively used in Black Africa), Rudin (1938) acknowledges that "it was an achievement in telecommunication superior to that of the whiteman before the invention of the telegraph."

3. See Rudin (1938).

4. The only other such script is that of the Vai of Liberia (See Eyong Etah and Brain (1975)).

5. In keeping with an orthographic tradition fashionable among scholars on Cameroon, the orthography "Douala" refers to the town or (coastal) region and "Duala" refers to the people or the language.

6. The treaty between the Germans and the Dualas (of the coast) was in English and a letter written to Queen Victoria in 1841 by the rulers of Duala inviting Britain as "protector" of the territory was in Pidgin English. Both of these are indicative of the British influence on the coast.

7. See Rudin (1938) and Santerre (1969) for details.

8. Translated from "Rapport annuel de governement français sur l'administration sous mandat des territoires du Cameroon pour l'année 1924," p. 20.

9. See Santerre (1969).

10. The exact number of languages spoken in Cameroon is not known for sure. The figures given here are based on Tadadjeu's (1976) estimate (based on Welmer's (1970) and Le Vine (1970)).

11. This is evident from the BEPC and GCE enrollment figures at the Buea Bilingual Grammar School and the Lycee Bilingue d'Application, Yaounde briefly discussed in Chumbow 1971. One explanation for this trend is the complacency of francophones as a result of the dominance of French in the Federation, another is that, there were fewer competent anglophone teachers in these schools during the sixties than francophone teachers--much to the detriment of francophones who had to prepare for

307

the anglophone examination. (See section 2, 4, (b)).

12. Pidgin-English (without any official recognition) also served as the medium of interstate communication for some fraction of the population in the West and South-West parts of the Federation.

13. "Rising generation" refers to the youths, and in this context includes those who had their secondary or university education in Cameroon in the sixties (and benefitted from the measures set-up for implementing English-French bilingualism in the schools. "Descending generation" refers to the older generation, including those who were out of school before bilingualism became government policy.

14. The term bilingualism and bilingual have a restricted semantic scope in the Cameroon context; they almost invariably refer to English-French bilingualism only. Consequently, the term is a misnomer in that the "bilingual" invariably speaks at least one other Cameroon language.

15. Datchoue (1974).

16. Larry Hyman dedicates his Ph.D. thesis on the Phonology of Fe'Fe' to the NUFI and calls the group "la lumiere du peuple Bamileke" (the Light of the Bamileke people). Hyman - 1972.

17. Some Cameroonian scholars who have expressed an opinion in favour of mother tongue education include Bot Ba Njock (1974), Bot Ba Njock, Njougla, Essono and Lemb (1974), Asongwed (1975), Datchoua (1974). Hebga (1976) Mbappe (1974), Mbassi Manga (1973 and 1976), Ngijol Ngijol (1965 and forthcoming), Tadajeu (1975 and 1976), Chumbow (1971, 1974, 1975, and 1978). A few scholars like Marcel Towa and R. Sim have expressed reservations on account of the economic implications (Towa) or on the basis of the unjustifiable assumption that multilingualism slows down the logical activity of the child (R. Sim).

18. This point was raised by the Cameroonian writer, artist, musician, and ethnomusicologist, Francis Bebey (Personal Discussion).

19. A detailed discussion of the potentials of a trilingual policy for Cameroon is provided by Tadadjeu (1975) and an outline procedure of the (relevant) cost account analysis for trilingual language planning is contained in Tadadjeu (1976). While these two papers may not constitute finished policy ground work, they do provide insights that should enhance work on the trilingual policy.

REFERENCES

Afolayan, Adebisi. (1976) "The Six-year Primary
    Project in Western Nigeria," in Ayo Bamgbose
    (editor) Mother Tongue Education: The West
    African Experience, UNESCO Press, Paris.
Asongwed, Tah. (1975) Bilingualism and Bicultural-
    ism in United Cameroon. A myth in Mirth, in
    Cahier de Linguistique d'Ottawa 4: 51-58.
Bot Ba, Njock, Henri, M. (1966) Le probleme lin-
    guistique de Cameroun in Afrique et L'Asie, 73.
Bot Ba, Njock, (ed.). (1974) Les langues africaines
    facteurs de developement, College Libermann.
Bot Ba, Njock, Njougla, Essono, and Lemb. (1974)
    Table ronde, Les langues africaine et l' unite
    nationale, College Libermann 1974: 125-140.
Bokamba, Eyamba and Tlou. (1976) "The Consequences
    of the Language Policies of African States
    vis à vis Education" in Paul Kotey and Haig
    Derthoussikian (editors) Language and Linguis-
    tic Problems in Africa; Hornbeam Press.
Chumbow, B. S. (1971) Le fracais au Cameroun
    Occidental: Interference phonologique dans
    l'apprentissage du francais en milieu pluri-
    lingue. Thesis, Universite Lovanium.
Chumbow, B. S. (1974) "Cameroon and the Bilingual
    Experience." Paper delivered on the occasion
    of the celebration of the advent of the United
    Republic of Cameroon, Champaign-Urbana,
    Illinois, USA.
Chumbow, B. S. (1975) Review of Jean Pierre
    Makouta Mooukou's "Le français en Afrique
    noire" in French Review, October 1975.
Chumbow, B. S. (1978) The Mother Tongue Hypothesis
    in a Multilingual setting, paper presented at
    the 5th International Congress of Applied
    Linguistics, Montreal, Canada.
Datchoua, C. (1974) Les langues locales et le
    dévelopment de la nation in College Libermann
    (ed.) 1974, 79-91.
Eyongetah, T. and Brian, R. (1974) A History of
    Cameroon, Longmans.
Ferguson, C. (1959) Diglossia in Word iv: 325-340.
Fonlon, B. (1969) A Case of Early Bilingualism in
    Abbia, 22.
Greenberg, J. (1966) Languages of Africa, Indiana
    University, Bloomington, Indiana.
Hebga, Meinrad. (1976) L'enseignement des langues
    maternelles dans les establissements privés.
    Douala, College Libermann.
Hyman, L. (1972) A Phonological Study of Fe? Fe?

Bamileke. Studies in African Linguistics, Supplement 4.

Lambert, W., Gardner R., Olton R. and Turnstall, K. (1968) "A Study of the Role of Attitudes and Motivation in second language-learning" in Fishman (ed.) Readings in the Sociology of Language, The Hague, Mouton, 1968.

Le Vine, V. (1970) Cameroon, Tome I. Paris: Les Editions Internationales.

Mbappe, Mbella. (1974) Allocution inaugurale du xle congres de la Societe Linguistique de l'Afrique Occidentale.

Mbassi-Manga, F. (1973) Received Bilingualism and Education in Cameroon, Ms.

Mbassi-Manga, F. (To appear) Langage et communication, Douala, College Libermann.

Ngijol, Ngijol P. (1965) Necessite d'une langue nationale Abbia 7.

Ngijol, Ngijol P. (1976) L'Education et le pluriculturalisme, Douala College Libermann.

Rudin, H. (1938) Germans in the Cameroons 1884-1944. A case study in Modern Imperialism, Yale University Press, 1938 (Reprinted by Archon Books, 1968).

Rapport annuel du gouvernement français dur l'administration sous mandat des territories du Cameroun pour l'année 1924. (Official Report of the French Colonial Administration).

Santerre, R. (1969) Linguistique et Politique au Cameroon, Journal of African Languages 8.3.

Saville, M. and Troike, R. (1971), A handbook of Bilingual Education, Washington, D.C.

Sim, R. (1974) Table ronde: plurilinguisme et developement de l'enfant Camerounais, Douala, College Libermann.

Tadadjeu, Maurice. (1975) Language Planning in Cameroon: Toward a Trilingual Education System. Ohio State University, Working Papers in Linguistics No. 19.

Tadadjeu, Maurice. (1976) "Cost Benefit Analysis and Language Planning in Sub-Saharan Africa" in Paul Kotey and Haig Der Houssikian (Editors) Language and Linguistic Problems of Africa, Hornbeam Press.

Towa, M. (1974) His Contribution on the national Language and national personality at the 1974 Seminar as reported by Tadadjeu (1975).

UNESCO. (1953) The Use of Vernacular Languages in Education Monograph on Fundamental Education, 8. Paris, UNESCO.

Weber, R.   (1970) Linguistics and Reading:
     Washington, D.C. ERIC Clearing House on Lin-
     guistics.
Weinreich, U.   (1953) Languages in Contact: Find-
     ings and Problems. The Hague: Mouton.
Welmers, W.   (1971) Checklist of African Languages
     and Dialect Names, Current Trends in Linguis-
     tics 7.   The Hague, Monton.

11
Educational Reforms in Cameroon: The Case of IPAR

John Kalla Kale
Omer Weyi Yembe

The problem of educational reform in Cameroon like in many other African nations has attracted the attention of national leaders and all those concerned with the business of education during the last two decades. This has been so because the systems of education which most African nations inherited from their colonial pasts have failed to respond to present day socio-economic and cultural exigencies. As delegates pointed out during the conference of African states on the development of education in Africa, held in Addis Ababa in May 1961, the basic educational problem today is how to adapt the different European educational systems existing in the continent to the practical require-ments of Africa. Coombs gives a thorough analysis of this problem when he points out that: "The consequent disparity--taking many forms between educational systems and their environments is the essence of the worldwide crisis in education."[1]

To solve this crisis, to reduce the disparity between the primary school and the rural environment, to stop the rural exodus among youths, to keep the primary school leaver on the land, in brief, to "ruralize" the primary school curriculum are the multiple purposes of the reform project known as IPAR.

In this case study we shall attempt to answer the following questions. What are the main charac-teristics and major consequences of an attempt to adapt or "ruralize" the primary school curriculum to the conditions of rural village life in Cameroon? How can one explain the apparent resistance by many people in Cameroon to this reform effort? Can rele-vant change theories enable an understanding of the various aspects of the reform?

The purposes, major characteristics and consequences of the reform project which this paper sets out to discuss are better understood in the context of the origins, history, and social setting of primary education in Cameroon.[2] The following observation by Katz will very briefly introduce that setting. "Education was something the better part of the community did to others to make them more orderly, moral, and tractable."[3] This observation offers an apt perspective along which to get a telescoped view of the purposes and practice of primary school education in Cameroon from its origins in 1844 to present day. It has always been "the better part of the community" doing something to the others to make them "more orderly, moral, and tractable."

This history of western education in Cameroon can be divided into three major phases, namely, the missionary phase from 1844 to 1910, the colonial phase, from 1910 to 1961 and the post independence phase, from 1961 to present day. This division is useful only for analytical purposes since there was collaboration between church and state in the administration of education.[4]

Eighteen forty-four is considered a great landmark in the history of Cameroon education. To the over 200 ethnic groupings who inhabited the areas of present day Cameroon (lat. 4 degrees N., long. 15 degrees E., east of Nigeria) the establishment of the first primary school in that year by missionaries augured in a new culture. This was the beginning of a cultural change which went beyond the introduction of a tradition of literacy based on formal schooling; henceforth, going to school would divorce the Cameroonian child from agricultural work which supported the traditional society. Indeed, the possession of a certificate or the attainment of literacy would mean a salaried job and a more luxurious modern life.

This pattern of purpose and practice of primary school education which started with the first missionary school in 1844 became interwoven into the school system as evangelisation spread throughout the country. People who acquired even minimal literacy were rewarded with jobs as preachers, pastors, and catechists. The aim of education was therefore to promote christianity but its central purpose was still as Katz lucidly puts it, "something the better part of the community did to others, to make them more orderly, moral, and tractable."[5] All indigenous practices which had no precedent in Christiandom, such as ancestral worship, polygamy,

314

rites of passage, and so on, were labelled backward and primitive. Graduates of the school who were ipso facto Christians, were disuaded from following these practices. This created a cultural gap between the school and the natural and human milieu of pupils.

The words "orderly, moral, and tractable," could not better express the purpose of colonial education in Cameroon. The colonialists were out for political and economic aggrandizement. The purpose of education was therefore to train a local elite to buttress the colonial bureaucratic hierarchy of salaried jobs and administrative power positions. The rural people remained at the bottom of the hierarchy of both this power and reward system. The anxiety for schooling as Calvert (1925) notes was spurred by the desire of getting a European job.

The colonialists used liberal arts curricula which were blueprints of those used in the home countries.[6] No attempt was made to adapt education to the needs of the individual and the community. There was a neglect of training in agriculture, handicrafts, tribal music and dance, folklore, and so on.[7]

Independence for Cameroon as for many other so-called new nations of Africa, meant replacing the colonial administration with a local elite. The early years of independence therefore saw the rapid expansion of schools. The need for trained manpower to man the newly created services was argued with increasing vehemence. The school population grew from 460,000 in 1960/61 to 1,200,000 in 1974/75.[8] At other levels of education the expansion was even more phenomenal. The consequence of this expansion is of interest to this paper.

The immediate consequence of the rapid growth of the school population was that schools at all levels turned out more graduates than the number of available "white collar" jobs in government service, industry, or commerce. Those first hit by the scarcity of "white collar" jobs were the primary school leavers. In 1974/75 there were over 90,000 primary school leavers as against 15,000 secondary and high school graduates.[9] The result was the gravitation of thousands of primary school leavers from the rural areas to the towns where they are faced with a life of squalid urban subsistence. This existence is even made worse by the fact that apart from their literary skills, these youngsters have no other skills which they could use to earn a living.

In view of these phenomena it became only too
apparent that the system of education was in need
of reform. As in many of the so-called developing
nations, the problem of the school leaver was seen
in the large context of the colonial system of
education which as many have argued, does not fit
the exigences of the times.[10]

To solve this crisis, to reduce the disparity
between the primary school and the rural environment, to stop the gravitation of youths from the
rural areas to towns, to keep the primary school
leaver on the land, in brief, to "ruralize" the
primary school curriculum are the multiple purposes
of the reform project we shall now describe.

The following brief history of the primary
school reform will help in the understanding of its
main aspects. The origins of the reform project
which is known as the "IPAR Project" from the name
of the research institute (Institut de Pedagogie
Appliquee a vocation Rurale) set up to direct the
reform, dates back to 1965. In that year an evaluation of the first five-year development plan (1960-
1965) showed an imbalance between the output of
primary schools and job possibilities at that level.
The need to develop agriculture was also highlight-
ed. It was suggested that the primary school be
reformed in order to ensure that primary school
leavers would play a greater role in village life.
In 1967, the government established a research institute to study the best ways of implementing the
reform. This institute (later called IPAR) was
given the elaborate mandate to draw up a new teacher
training curriculum for pre-service training,
organize in-service training along the same lines as
for pre-service training, draw up new primary school
syllabi, and prepare and produce all the instruc-
tional materials for both teacher training and
primary schools.

That year 1967, the Cameroon government, signed
a number of contracts with funding agencies, notably,
the United Nations Educational Scientific and
Cultural Organization (UNESCO). A team of UNESCO
experts arrived in Cameroon in 1968 and along with a
number of Cameroonian educationists started IPAR on
a temporary site.

Between 1967 and 1972, a total of over four
million U.S. dollars had already been spent from
external financing sources and the Cameroon government was already spending over two million U.S.
dollars in annual recurrent expenditure.[11] By 1972
IPAR had a personnel roll of over 103 people. Out

of this, over 83 were researchers or research
assistants, 29 of which were foreigners, 15 UNESCO
experts, 12 Frenchmen, one U.S. Peace Corps volun-
teer, and a German. The presence of these latter
was interpreted by some people as another foreign
imposition.

By 1973, IPAR had prepared basic curriculum
materials for both the primary schools and teacher
training. In fact about 300 had been trained in the
"new philosophy" and were ready to go out into 290
selected experimental schools. New textbooks had
been printed and the experimental phase was about
to begin. That year a seminar was organized to
bring together a cross section of Cameroonian policy-makers, administrators, and educational experts.
This seminar aimed to explain the reform in preparation for the experimental phase. It was at this
point that resistance to the whole reform grew from
murmuring to open and bound opposition.

In fact this opposition became sufficiently
widespread to cause the Ministry of Education to
delay the start of the experimental phase, to the
school year 1975/76. What is therefore reported in
this paper are reactions to events of the pre-
experimental phase of the reform project. In the
following section we shall discuss the relation
between the purposes of the project and the nature
of the above reaction.

What does "ruralization" mean? To what extent
was this objective new? Why did people oppose it?
"Ruralization" in broad terms means the introduction
of curriculum materials and practical work related
to life in the rural areas into the primary school
program. Knowledge and techniques about agriculture,
it was thought, would lead many youngsters to taking
up farming and other agricultural activities after
leaving school. IPAR was to train a new category
of primary school teachers who would teach agriculture and practical work in the school. They would
also work with the villages as extension agricultural workers. This way they would be the link
between the school program and community based
activities. The insertion of primary school leavers
into the rural economy would thereby be facilitated.

The teaching of farm work in Cameroon schools
was not new. The early primary schools encouraged
farm work and many schools still run school gardens.
What was new in the scheme outlined above was the
fact that a comprehensive plan was now laid to
ensure that pupils effectively stayed in the villages to practice agriculture. As far as the policy

317

maker was concerned, this was a formula par excellence, to stem the tide of the rural exodus of the
youth.

But although clearly spelled out, "ruralization" or the IPAR project came to mean different
things to different people, the elite, the rural
folks, and the teachers.

The elite consists of that generation of "white
collar" workers such as civil servants, businessmen,
etc., who owe their rise to power positions to the
fact that they had gone to school. For these
elites, years of schooling had estranged them from
the land. Few of them were anxious to see their
children receive an education different from what
they had received, and worse still an education
which would return their children back to the land
where they themselves had escaped.[12]

The rural folks saw in the innovation, an
attempt to condemn their children to a life of hard-
ship from which only school could save them as it
had done for others, the elite. Wilson succinctly
summarized the African's perception of the role of
education, in the following words:

> . . . bookish education in the three Rs,
> followed by academic secondary and higher edu-
> cation seemed eminently desirable to African
> people themselves for the simple reason that
> it provided a ladder to an altogether different
> world of increased financial and enhanced
> social status.[13]

The above description of the conflicting reactions to the IPAR reforms enable one to observe
the school as an organizational structure surrounded
by powerful societal pressure groups. Here one sees
the Cameroon primary school not only as "vulnerable"
and "subjected to pressures that are incompatible
. . . with its capacity to resist," as Sam D.
Sieber[14] puts it, but really helpless. Both the
elite and the rural folks are fighting to maintain
the status quo. They want the school to remain as
the passport from rural to modern life. But the
powerful central government is there to mandate
changes and the introduction of the "ruralized"
curriculum. Indeed, the school system is part of a
rigid bureaucratic structure. Cameroon has a presidential system of government, power and jurisdiction
descend from the Head of State through the minister
of education to provincial school inspectors, local
school headmasters and primary school teachers.

318

This hierarchical structure explains the nature of the strategy the government used to initiate the reform. It was essentially one that was dictated from the top of the hierarchy to be implemented at the bottom, the local school level. But before describing this, one may ask whether the contemplated reform could have been achieved within the structure of the existing school system? Will this innovation fit into the now well established "regularities" of the existing school culture?

The Cameroon system of education, as has been indicated above has a typically bureaucratic structure. The duties of the primary school teacher, the number of lessons per day, etc. are spelled out in detail. One may therefore inquire as Michael Katz has in Class, Bureaucracy, and Schools, "Must structural changes precede educational change? or is it possible to alter the purposes, biases, and actual functioning of schools without at the same time, changing radically, the structure through which they are organized?"[15]

Katz answers in the negative and explains that organizational structures are not and cannot be neutral. They are interwoven into the basic purposes of the organization. Could the goals of the ruralized curriculum be achieved without changing the basic structure of the school system?

Sarason has pointedly emphasized the futility of attempting to introduce curriculum changes of the type contemplated by the IPAR project without changing the "regularities" especially "programmatic" of the school. He points out that: "Any attempt to change a curriculum independent of changing some characteristic institutional feature runs the risk of partial or complete failure."[16]

So far there is nothing on the literature on the project to show that changes were contemplated in the school year or the school daily timetable, for example, to fit the farming seasons, since the accent of the IPAR innovation is on agriculture. However, the following description of the strategies adopted to introduce the reform may explain, in part, why one could not expect drastic changes in the school system.

In discussing possible approaches for reform, Sieber postulated the following four possible approaches to initiating reform: 1) "rational man strategy, which includes didactic teacher preparation, research reports, and conferences, in short, all forms of one-way communication between the change agent and practitioner;" 2) the "cooperative" strategy, involving two way "communication" between change agent or consultant and school; 3) the "powerless participant" strategy, where influence is provided through legal or bureaucratic channels with direction flowing downwards and evidence of participation flowing upward; and 4) the "status - occupant" strategy, based on a local change agent.[17]

Chin and Benne discuss three of the above strategies in a larger conceptual framework of change seen from the perspective of all the aspects of the American social system. They provide an elaborate description of the strategies of change in America. These strategies are: rational-empirical, normative re-educative, and power coercive.[18] As can be seen, these three strategies bear close resemblances with Sieber's categories. In fact, the third category in both classifications, "powerless participant," and "power coercive" are significant in explaining the creation of the IPAR project.

From what has already been said, one can conclude that the "powerless participant strategy" or the "power coercive strategy" would be preferred by the highly bureaucratic Cameroon educational policy makers. IPAR was therefore established as a division of the Department of Primary Education in the Ministry of Education. Power and authority flow from the Minister to the Director of Primary Education to the Director of IPAR, and so on. As a planning and training institution, IPAR could also be seen as having or exercising some of the attributes of the "rational man strategy" or the "normative re-educative" approach. Albeit, IPAR can more clearly be conceived of as representing a powerful outside change agent. Powerful because it was invested with all the authority of the bureaucracy through the Ministry of Education. From its inception, neither the local teachers and school inspectors nor the local communities were involved in its planning. It is in this sense that it is seen as something from outside the school system.

The following description of the organization and activities of the project will provide more information about the change agency role of IPAR. IPAR, is organized in four main divisions, each headed by an assistant director. The following summary discussion of the activities of each division will help to provide greater insights into the nature of the project.

The first division, the research division is the most important arm of IPAR. It is responsible for planning, programming, budgeting, and preparing major reports and documents for the whole reform project. In the curriculum area, it has already developed new primary school teacher training programs in Mathematics, Language, Environmental studies, and practical work. The major accent in the new textbooks and curriculum materials developed by the research division is on the use of the Cameroon cultural background as the medium for presenting ideas. This is a drastic change from the old textbooks with French or English cultural background.

The second division of IPAR is responsible for production, mainly printing. This press-division edits and publishes manuscripts prepared by the research division. The third and fourth divisions are responsible for teacher training, pre-service and in-service. The service trainees receive diplomas, the highest for primary school teachers, after three years of training from the equivalent of grade eleven.

By 1973, an estimated annual total of 210 trainees were graduating from the pre-service programme and 1,200 from the in-service. In that year there were over 12,000 teachers in the primary schools in Cameroon. More than half were untrained. The estimated need is 20,000 who should either have to be trained in the IPAR pre-service programme or participate in the in-service programme.

In 1974, the major funding agencies who have sponsored the reform sent an evaluation team to review the project. The following major conclusion from the report will give an idea of the stage of development of the project by 1974.

First, it was noted that the reform calendar was running far behind schedule. The reform had been planned in three major phases. An introductory phase, to train teachers and prepare necessary didactic materials. An experimental phase, during which IPAR trainees would start teaching in experimental schools. An implementation phase, beginning in 1976 when all primary schools would be required to implement the new curriculum. By 1974, the experimental phase had not yet been started.

Secondly, the report noted the problem this delay had caused. In effect, the IPAR trained teachers had been posted to teach the traditional curriculum. This was causing quite a stir. The IPAR trainees possessed the highest level of the primary school teachers diploma. They also enjoyed salaries on the highest primary school scale. This put them in a conflict position with the headmasters and the older teachers. Here were younger teachers doing exactly the same work as the older teachers and yet far better paid. We shall return to this point later.

Thirdly, this report questioned the conceptual basis on which the work in the research division of IPAR had been done. Would the new curriculum achieve the objectives of the reform? Apparently the research division had assumed that children processed through the "ruralized" curriculum would "go back to the land." Such a hypothesis was never tested.

The report caused great alarm, especially as it was shown that the tonnage of didactic material being produced did not take note of the cultural environment in which it was going to be used. For example, many lessons required the use of pictures, as many as five or more per lesson. Yet no attempt has been made to check on the problem of storage in the schools.

Finally the report noted the apparent hostility to the IPAR project and the scepticism many people entertained about its possible success. In fact due to this hostility the experimental phase had to be delayed to 1975/76. Up to the time of writing, the experimental phase has not taken off. However, one must return to an analysis of the effects the innovation has had so far on the primary school system, especially on the teachers. What are the perceived consequences of the reform?

A number of change theories could be used to explain the present opposition to the IPAR project. We have already indicated the powerful "saga" the "school" had built in the Cameroon social system. In a largely traditional society practicing a subsistence agriculture, the school came to represent the avenue to a more comfortable modern life. The present school curriculum had thus proved its worth and neither the elite nor the rural folks would want to see things change. For both groups, the school held the promise of a better life for their children. Moreover, teachers, the largest of the elite class have their careers entrenched in the system as "classroom actors" not as agricultural extension workers, the new role the reform aims to give them.

The IPAR innovations could be explained in terms of Kurt Lewin's concept of "unfreezing, changing, refreezing" mechanisms in the adoption of an innovation.[19] At present the IPAR project could be described as passing from the "unfreezing" to the

"changing" stage. Since 1967, information about the
reform has diffused through the school and the
social system. Conflicts between the IPAR trainees
and the old teachers, give evidence of "unfreezing."
The reform is now at a stage where effort is being
made to overcome resistance through activities such
as: pre-service programs, conferences, and so on.
Teachers in the system are adjusting to new role
models provided by the IPAR trainees. One can confidently speculate that by the time the experiment
gets under way, the present "resistance" may be
overcome and the reform will enter fully into the
"changing" stage.

Goodwin Watson's perception of resistance to
change as moving in cyclical stages also offers
another conceptual basis for examining the IPAR
project. He postulates resistance as taking place
in a number of stages: "In the early stage when
only a few pioneers take the reform seriously,
resistance appears massive and undifferentiated."[20]
In the second stage, "forces pro and con become
identifiable," in the third stage, "resistance becomes modified to crush the upstart proposal," in
the fourth, "supporters of the change in power"
and at the fifth, "old adversaries are as few and
as alienated as were the advocates in the first
stage. At this final stage the innovation has been
institutionalized.

Again, one can situate the present stage of
the IPAR project, especially as regards teachers'
attitudes to Watson's second stage. The IPAR
trainees or change agents have all to gain in
supporting the reform against the attitudes of the
old teachers. Also given the fact that the reform
has been initiated by the government, one may not
expect a mobilization of the present resistance.
The ruralized curriculum may, therefore, come to
stay. On the other hand, as Michael Katz (1971)
points out, a bureaucracy may hand down dicta but
the effectiveness of such dicta weaken as they
descend to the base of the hierarchy.

From the above analysis, one may therefore conclude that "ruralization" may well mean nothing more
than new textbooks and curriculum materials, and a
higher pay for IPAR trainees. This expensive project may achieve other objectives except, "get the
youth onto the land," its original purpose. To
achieve the original purpose, a drastic structural
change of the primary school system in Cameroon will
be necessary.

323

In conclusion, this paper aimed to examine the main characteristics and the major consequences of an ongoing planned change of the Cameroon primary school curriculum. The origin of primary education in Cameroon, its development, and the present social unrest caused by unemployment of school leavers provided an introduction to the purpose of the IPAR project. IPAr is a government research institute mandated to produce curriculum materials for primary schools and teacher training. The goal of the new syllabi is to "ruralize" the curriculum so that pupils processed through the system can "remain on the land." After these explanations, we then attempted to systematically describe the main aspects of the reform. Where appropriate, relevant change theories were cited to explain reactions to the reform. The reform is still in its experimental stage, an "unfreezing stage." Finally, we concluded that without a drastic change in the structure of the primary school system, the reform would not achieve its major objectives. Even the strong bureaucratic hierarchy of government, which will ensure and provide for new "technologies" for the school, such as: textbooks and other curriculum materials, will find it hard to change the school day, the school year, and so on. These structural changes will be logically necessary for the application of a "ruralized curriculum" belong to the "saga" of the school. That "sage," the belief in the school as the avenue for upward social climbing, will be defended against any attack by both the peasant and the elite community in Cameroon.

Sarason's assertion that, "the more things change the more they remain the same"[21] may be a fitting prediction of the outcome of the reform project described in this paper.

NOTES

1. P. H. Coombs. The World Educational Crisis. New York: Oxford University Press, 1968.
2. A very lucid summary article on education in Cameroon appears in the New Columbia Encyclopedia, 4th edition, 1975, p. 433.
3. Michael B. Katz. Class Bureaucracy and Schools. New York: Praeger Publishers, 1972, p. 48.
4. See Solomon Neba Shu, "The Collaboration Policy in Cameroon education 1910-1931, Ph.D. thesis, Institute of Education," University of London, 1971, pp. 34-36, for a detailed description of the elements of collaboration between church and state in Cameroon.
5. Katz, op. cit., p. 48.
6. Shu, op. cit., pp. 97-99, says this of the Germanic studies: geography of Germany, history of the German Empire since the Franco-German War of 1870/71. . . ."
7. See, Education in Africa. New York: The Phelps Stokes Fund, p. 18, here, the wholesale transfer of the educational conventions of Europe and America to peoples of Africa, is severely criticized.
8. Cameroon Ministry of Education Statistics, 1974/75.
9. Ibid.
10. See, Opening speech by the Minister of Education, Seminar for Administrative and Political cadres on the Reform of Primary Education, Yaounde, 973, pp. 5-9.
See also, "Discours du Chef de l'Etat lors de la remise des diplômes aux élèves de l'IPAR de Yaounde," le 13 Juin 1970.
11. From, "La Réforme De l'Enseignement au Cameroon," IPAR Yaounde, 1972, pp. 23-24.
12. See, K. G. Robinson, "Toward a new concept of education in developing countries, the Buea experiment," a working paper prepared for the IPAR Buea discussion/action group, Buea, July, 1973, p. 1, mentions the difficulty of convincing graduates of the old school system that a reformed school system will be better.
13. John Wilson. Education and Changing West African Culture. New York: Teachers College, Columbia University, 1963, p. 45.
14. In V. J. Baldridge and T. E. Deal, Managing Change in Educational Organizations. Los Angeles, CA: McCuthan Publishing Corporation, 1975.

15. Katz, op. cit., p. 24.

16. S. B. Sarason. The Culture of the School and the Problem of Change. Boston: Allyn and Bacon, 1974, pp. 68-87.

17. S. D. Sieber, "Organizational influence on innovative roles," in Baldridge and Deal, op. cit., pp. 91-94.

18. R. Chin and Kenneth D. Benne, "General strategies for effecting changes in human systems," in Bennis, et alia, The Planning of Change. New York: Holt, Rinehart & Winston, 1961.

19. Bennis, et alia. op. cit., p. 98.

20. Ibid., p. 488.

21. Sarason, op. cit., p. 2.

BIBLIOGRAPHY

Baldridge, V. J. and T. E. Deal. Managing Change
    in Educational Organizations. Los Angeles,
    CA: McCuthan Publishing Corp., 1975.
Bennis, W. G., et. al. The Planning of Change. New
    York: Holt, Rinehart & Winston, 1961.
Calvert, Albert F. The Cameroons. London: T.
    Werner Laurie Ltd., 1917.
Coombs, P. H. The World Educational Crisis. New
    York: Oxford University Press, 1968.
Katz, Michael B. Class Bureaucracy and Schools.
    New York: Praeger, 1972.
Lallez, Raymond. Une expérience de ruralisation de
    l'enseignement: l'IPAR et la reforme
    camerounaise. Paris: Les Presses de l'Unesco,
    1974.
Levine, Daniel U. and Robert J. Hamighurt. Farewell
    to Schools. Worthington, Ohio: Charles A.
    Jones Publishing Co.
Phelps Stokes Fund. Education in Africa. New
    York: Phelps Stokes Fund.
Robinson, K. G. "Toward a New Concept of Education
    in Developing Countries: The Buea Experiment,"
    Unpublished manuscript, IPAR, Buea, 1973.
Sarason, S. B. The Culture of the School and the
    Social World. Evanston, IL: Northwestern
    University Press, 1967.
Shu, Solomon Neba. "The Collaboration Policy in
    Cameroon Education, 1910-1931," unpublished
    manuscript, IPAR, Buea, 1973.
Teachers College Record, Vol. 37, No. 3, February
    1976.
Unpublished official reports on IPAR, Ministry of
    Education, Yaounde, Cameroon.
Wilson, John. Education and Changing West African
    Culture. New York: Teachers College, Columbia
    University, 1963.

12
The Multiplicity of Times Operating in the Cameroonian Modern Labor Force

Remi Clignet

For a long time, policies of economic development in Africa have been based upon the assumption that local labor markets are monolithic and homogeneous entities subjected to the "laws" of one marketplace. This assumption implies that the rewards that individual workers might derive from their work result from their productivity and that the low income per capita enjoyed by African nations reflect the low educational level of their populations. One of the major contributions of the so called radical American economists has been to explode the underlying myths.[1] Far from being universal, the "laws" of the labor market are contingent upon the processes of segmentation which enhance the differentiation opposing categories of tasks and of wage earners to one another. Indeed there are significant contrasts both in the technical and psychological profile attributed to various occupations and in the characteristics imputed to the wage earners who perform the corresponding activities. Because existing patterns of division of labor lower the specificity of certain roles, their incumbents are deemed to be interchangeable and are hence condemned to enjoy a low occupational stability as well as a low income. In contrast, the scarcity of the skills deemed necessary to perform other industrial or commercial functions enables the relevant categories of wage earners to be more demanding of their employers in terms of the amount and the stability of the economic and social rewards they may claim. Thus, the "laws" underlying the modes of access and of promotion operating in the manual and the non-manual sectors of activity differ from one another. Further, such differences, far from being constant across firms, vary in function of the complexity of economic organizations.

But while the "laws" underlying the functioning
of the labor market are not universal they are not
stable either. The purpose of this chapter is to
stress the variety of times within such "laws"
evolve. More specifically, this chapter aims at
showing the importance of the role played in this
regard by (a) the time of the political economy of
Cameroon as a whole (b) the time of individual
economic organizations (c) the time of individual
workers and (d) the time underlying the interaction
between the characteristice of employers and
employees.

THE HISTORY OF THE CAMEROONIAN POLITICAL ECONOMY

Administrative centralization has enabled
French authorities to impose early on, definite
patterns of division of labor among colonial territories. Thus both Senegal and Dahomey were treated
as pools from which colonial administrations and
employers could draw the educated cadres needed to
occupy middle range positions in the occupational
hierarchy of various areas, whereas a country like
the Ivory Coast was expected to maintain a low
level of educational enrollments in order to mini-
mize the legitimacy of the claims that local job
seekers could make toward their employers both in
the public and private sectors. In contrast to
other French African "possessions," the Cameroon had
the status of a mandate granted by the Société des
Nations to France and was, as such, subjected to
various external controls. This vulnerability to
an international scrutiny had a number of consequences on the functioning of the Cameroonian labor
market. It was more difficult for colonial authorities to control European immigration and this contributed to create tensions in the modes of economic
exploitation chosen by expatriate employers.[2] Similarly, colonial authorities were necessarily
obliged to be more careful in their attempts to
prevent or slow down the processes of elite formation among local populations. Because educational
institutions were both more numerous and more diverse than in many other colonial territories, the
relatively large number of school graduates raised
the spectrum of urban unemployment feared so in-
tensely by colonial authorities. As a result, the
Cameroonian public sector tended to absorb a relatively large number of job seekers. The immigration
of foreign Africans was inhibited but the export of

skilled Cameroonian workers to other parts of French
speaking Africa, encouraged. Last there were few
attempts to eliminate the already existing enterprises of local elites.

To sum up, the pre-World War II period in the
Cameroon is characterized by the development of tensions among various kinds of expatriate economic
concerns, as well as between the most marginal segments of the European population and local elites.
It is also characterized, as elsewhere in Africa,
by the simultaneous development of the primary and
tertiary economic sectors (agriculture and cattle
raising on the one hand, administrative and
commercial services on the other). In this sense,
the picture of the Cameroonian economy invalidates
the model of growth suggested by Colin Clark.
After all, the forces of economic "rationality" are
not always powerful enough to make the growth of a
tertiary sector dependent upon industrialization.[3]

Post-war times in the Cameroon, as elsewhere in
French speaking Africa, mark the systematization of
relations existing between the center and the periphery of the French political and economic
"empire." In educational terms this means that
local schools increased in size and offered their
students a curriculum increasingly analogous to that
existing in metropolitan institutions. In economic
terms, French Governments aimed at financing the
building of a more sophisticated infra-structure
(airports, ports, roads, electrical powerhouses) and
at favoring the development of a local industry.
Such policies could not but enhance the dependence
of Cameroonian taxpayers or consumers upon French
metropolitan banking concerns. Thus, the post war
period marks the blossoming of both construction or
public work concerns and banks or other financial
institutions in Cameroon. In terms of labor laws
and labor mouvements, such a period is characterized by the reluctant adoption on the part of
colonial authorities of a body of measures which
subjected employers and employees alike to opportunities as well as to restrictions analogous to
those confronting their counterparts in the
Metropole. For example, local wage earners became
entitled to receive familial allowances designed to
alleviate the costs attached to the rearing of
children. Similarly, the same wage earners began
to be protected from occupational hazards. At the
same time, labor laws also institutionalized
existing informal patterns of segmentation. Thus,
collective bargaining agreements differed across

331

branches of activity and types of job. Similarly,
the definition of the minimal wages to be distributed by employers varied not only between agricultural
and non-agricultural types of activity but also
across geographic zones and communities with
differing sizes. At the same time, the institu-
tionalization of the relations between the center
and the periphery of the French Empire also generated a parallel segmentation of the local labor
movements. Each Cameroonian labor union was af-
filiated to a metropolitan counterpart which acted
as a broker between the Cameroonian labor force and
the French Government.[4] Last, in political terms,
the most significant negotiations necessarily took
place in Paris but the fragility of the metropolitan
political structures enabled Cameroonian representatives and senators, like their counterparts from
other territories, to often act as mediators and to
use such a position to obtain advantages which
would have been refused to them under other sets of
circumstances.[5]

In short, to argue that the post war period was
characterized by an accentuation of the dependence
of Cameroon on the Metropole would be misleading.
In this case as in others, relationships between
centers and peripheries are not unidirectional. Nor
are they homogeneous since they involve institutions
which may be in conflict with one another. Public
bureaucracies, churches, import/export colonial
firms, political parties, and labor unions did not
necessarily pursue goals that were consistent with
one another.

Finally, the post independence period is
characterized by the opening of the Cameroonian
economy to a number of multinational concerns as
well as by the development of state owned enterprises and the multiplication of small scale
businesses owned by Cameroonian individuals. This
accentuated variability in the organizational
patterns of the local economy has been accompanied
by an increased diversification of the economic
activities themselves. This diversification has
been most visible in the secondary sector with a
profileration of enterprises engaged in the processing of various raw agricultural materials or in
the assembling of raw industrial parts. In other
words, in the Cameroon as in other parts of the
Third World, industrialization has been consecutive
to the development of an administrative and commercial sector.

At the same time, the post independence period has also been characterized by a growing centralization of the political power. This means that new concerns cannot settle in the country as long as they have not reached an agreement with the Government as to their obligations regarding investments taxes or the use of a local labor force. It also means that local labor unions have been obliged to merge into a single entity and that their bargaining power has been severely curtailed by the control that political authorities exert on their initiatives.[6]

In summary, the post independence period is marked by two conflicting trends. On the one hand, the economy is more vulnerable than ever to the vagaries of world markets. On the other hand, the influence of such markets is muted if not transformed by the various measures taken by the Government in order to maximize its impact on employers and employees.

THE TIME OF CAMEROONIAN ECONOMIC ORGANIZATIONS

In the Cameroon as elsewhere, it is possible to differentiate economic organizations in terms of the length of time during which they have been in operation. However, this length of time can be analyzed in the context of two distinctive theoretical frameworks. First, one can assume that firms and enterprises have a life-cycle of their own and that new and old concerns tend to differ from one another in terms of their technological and legal structures as well as in terms of their hiring and promotion policies. In such a perspective, years are considered to be homogeneous and continuous units and contrasts in the behaviors of economic organizations should increase in size as a direct function of their "age."[7]

Second, one can assume that these behaviors are markedly influenced by external historical forces which introduce sharp discontinuities in the pressures and opportunities that employers must take into account in the critical decisions they must take in order to enhance their profits. As an example, it is clear that for a long time, the firms settled in the Cameroon before the war adopted solutions requiring minimal investments and hence hired a large number of workers remunerated at a minimal level.[8] After the war, however some of these firms were obviously considered to be perfect illustrations of the evils caused by colonialism. To the extent that they were keen to continue their operations in the country, they were obliged to change the images they elicited among various segments of the local population and hence to alter drastically their personnel policies. Often enough, such policies may be more egalitarian than those followed by more modern enterprises recently settled in the country and as such less visible.

In short, while the first type of time, labelled sociological time, reflects the strength of factors internal to the dynamics of economic organizations the second one, labelled historical time, corresponds to the dynamics of the external environment and introduces discontinuities in the behaviors of such organizations.

Clearly, there is a marked relationship between the patterns of diffusion of social change across the distinctive regions of the Cameroon and the differential age and structural characteristics of the economic organizations surveyed in 1964 by the local direction de la Statistique.[9] At one extreme of the continuum, the Mungo area is characterized by a relatively large number of older concerns mostly engaged in agricultural activities or in the processing of raw materials. (Tables 12.1 and 12.2). At the other end of the continuum, Douala, the largest and oldest urban center of the nation accommodates 57 percent of the enterprises defined as being modern by Cameroonian authorities. The oldest of these enterprises belong to the tertiary sector and have been more specifically engaged in the export of raw materials toward industrialized nations. Nevertheless, the majority of the concerns located in Douala belong to the secondary sector and include shipyards, garages as well as manufactures specialized in the processing of food or textile fibers and in the production of shoes and clothings. Between these two extremes, there are two additional focal points of economic development. Although initially, colonial authorities moved most administrative services to Yaounde in order to avoid the pressures generated by the land shortage associated with the early development of Douala, they became concerned later on by the concentration of a large number of educated unemployed individuals attracted by the possibilities of finding a job in the public sector of the new capital city. Correspondingly, Yaounde accommodates one-fifth of the Cameroonian modern firms, but one-third of these firms have been created after the second world war and no less

334

TABLE 12.1
Interaction Between Size, Number of Units of a Firm, and Location of its Headquarters (percentage distribution)

Number of Geographical Units in Firm	Fewer than 10		11-25		26-50		Over 50	
	Local	Int'l.	Local	Int'l.	Local	Int'l.	Local	Int'l.
1	84.1	47.9	67.6	61.3	69.4	52.6	59.7	20.0
2	8.7	28.6	17.1	12.9	22.4	21.1	16.9	16.7
More than 2	7.2	28.6	15.2	25.8	8.2	26.3	23.4	63.3
	100.0	100.0	99.9	100.0	100.0	100.0	100.0	100.0
N	(69)	(14)	(105)	(31)	(49)	(19)	(77)	(60)

TABLE 12.2
Location of Firms by Branch of Activity
(percentage distribution)

Branch of Activity	Yaounde	Douala	Nkongsamba	Mungo	Edea	Sanaga	Other	Total	N
Primary[a]	1.1	8.6	0.0	45.6	1.1	11.9	31.6	99.9	92
Processing[b]	25.9	22.2	11.1	27.7	3.9	0.0	9.2	100.0	54
Textile[c]	30.1	60.8	5.9	0.8	0.0	0.8	1.6	100.0	117
Metallurgical[d]	16.0	68.9	10.4	0.0	3.5	0.0	1.2	100.0	37
Construction	33.3	53.0	3.7	3.7	0.0	0.0	1.4	100.1	81
Banks and insurance	17.4	78.3	0.0	0.0	0.0	0.0	4.3	100.0	23
Transport[e]	100.0	0.0	0.0	0.0	0.0	0.0	0.0	100.0	3
Import/export	18.9	55.9	10.0	12.7	0.0	0.0	2.5	100.0	211

[a]Includes forestry and plantations, fishing, and husbandry.
[b]Includes slaughterhouses, food, and tobacco-processing as well as mines.
[c]Includes textile, wood, printing, and chemical industries.
[d]Includes auto repair stations, shipyards, aluminum-processing industries.
[e]The three firms indicated belong to the Camerounian Railroad Company, whose headquarters
   are in Yaounde.

than 60 percent of them after independence. Most of them are geared toward satisfying the needs of the local and national markets. Finally, Edea constitutes an emerging industrial center whose existence results from the construction of an hydroelectric dam and hence from the availability of a cheap source of energy facilitating the processing of aluminum ore.

In summary, the distribution of Cameroonian firms in space as well as in time exemplifies the general patterns of economic development of African countries. Enterprises located in the hinterland tend to be older, to serve a narrower range of functions and indeed no less than 42 percent of the concerns of the primary sector have been created before World War II. In contrast, there is a definite concentration of more diversified industrial and commercial organizations in few cities. Such contrasts are associated with parallel differences in the relative amounts of labor and capital that enter in the activities of these firms and in their legal structures.[10]

First, there tends to be a positive correlation between the size of the labor force and the age of the modern Cameroonian enterprises. The relevant coefficient is .102. Thus, only 41 percent of the concerns settled in Cameroon after independence employ more that 25 workers as opposed to 54 percent of their counterparts created between 1945 and 1960 and 58 percent of those established in the country before the war. Yet, this relationship reflects various phenomena. On the one hand, older firms tend to be larger because they had more time to develop and to expand their activities functionally as well as geographically. As a matter of fact, there is a correlation of .150 between the age of a firm and the number of its geographically distinct production units. On the other hand, older firms tend also to be larger because their modes of activity are uniformly more labor intensive than those of their newer counterparts. This is because technological development has enabled more recent concerns to adopt highly diversified strategies in this regard. Certain employers buy the most sophisticated machinery in Europe and aim at minimizing their dependence upon a large number of unskilled local workers, but other investors import from the western world an equipment which has become obsolete and requires as such a larger labor input.[11] In fact, contrasts in their strategies are accompanied by parallel differences in the

337

profile of their workers engaged in production as opposed to maintenance functions. In the case of the most capital intensive concerns, the status of maintenance workers tends to be higher than that enjoyed by their counterparts located on the production line.[12]

Second, there is a marked relationship between the age of a firm and its legal structures. Thus the systematization of center periphery relationships during the period of time between the end of World War II and independence has been conducive to a proliferation of corporations at the expense of entirely privately owned businesses. Out of the 151 organizations created during such a period, over three quarters have the status of a corporation as opposed to 56 percent of those created before the War and 61 percent of those established after independence. During this later period, Cameroonian authorities have aimed at diversifying the legal base of the local economy. Thus, no less than 58 percent of the 279 small scale privately owned Cameroonian enterprises have been created after independence. Similarly, the systematization of center periphery relationships between the end of the second World War and independence implies that the headquarters of the concerns created during that period are often located in Europe or in other parts of the western World. No less than 40 percent of such concerns have externally located sources of control as opposed to one-fifth of the enterprises which began to operate before the War or after independence. The newest investors are either Cameroonian themselves or have been obliged by local authorities to sever their official ties with the larger entities to which they belonged in order to be more vulnerable to the planning and coordination activities of the Government. Last, the differential legal characteristics of economic organizations with distinctive ages imply parallel variations in the number of their respective European employees. Thus, there is a correlation of .188 between such a number and the age of the concerns defined as modern by the government. In simpler terms, over 70 percent of the firms which began to operate before independence have more than three Europeans on their payroll as against 47 percent of those established after 1960.

To sum up, technological and political developments have modified the organizational profile of Cameroonian economic organizations. Contrasts in such profiles cannot be without effects on the

338

policies they follow as far as the hiring, the training, and the renumeration of their African personnel is concerned.

Clearly, firms with differing ages have distinctive modes of access to existing pools of available job seekers. Because of their location and of the nature of their activities, oldest firms tend to recruit Ewondo and Pahouin individuals. In contrast, the concerns more recently established in the Cameroon take advantage of the increased emigration of Bamileke men toward the major urban centers.[13] Thus, the correlation between the age of modern concerns and the number of their workers who belong to the first ethnic cluster is .159 as opposed to -.119 in the case of the second cluster.

Similarly, large firms with differing ages do not have the same access to a qualified labor force. Thus 23 percent of the large enterprises created before the War have Cameroonian workers who have completed at least the first cycle of post primary studies as opposed to only 6 percent of their counterparts created after independence. In addition, while firms with differing ages do not adopt the same type of on-the-job training programs, the relevant differences vary by sector of activity. In the primary and in the tertiary sector, it is the newest organizations that are most likely to offer these opportunities to their workers. In the secondary sector, conversely, it is the oldest firms which are most prone to provide their wage earners with such facilities. In effect, these differential behaviors result from the fact that there are relative hurdles limiting the relative mobility of workers across economic sectors and that workers themselves are not necessarily similarly attracted toward differing kinds of firms. As a result, employers with differing kinds of experiences in the Cameroonian labor market do not necessarily confront the same scarcities in their search for a trained personnel. In fact, they do not only differ from one another in terms of whether they offer training facilities to their workers but also in terms of the prerequisites they impose for gaining access to the relevant programs as well as of the curriculum of these programs.[14] As a rule, such curricula tend to be more differentiated in the case of the oldest firms.

THE TIME OF CAMEROONIAN INDIVIDUAL WORKERS

In most sociological or economic analyses of
labor markets, age is unduly treated as exclusively
synonymous with the experience that individuals
acquire in the labor force. Such an assumption is
invalid in the context of developing nations because of the high rates of societal changes and
hence of the unavoidable contamination of life
cycle effects by period or cohort effects.[15] Indeed, both the positive and negative effects that
aging might exert on occupational careers are contingent upon changes in the structures of the entire
labor market.

First, disparities between the rates of educational and economic development modify necessarily
the processes of segmentation operating between
manual and non-manual occupational sectors. The
relative scarcity of highly educated individuals
among the cohorts who were seeking jobs before the
end of World War II enabled most of them to enter
the more prestigious white collar occupations which
yielded and continue to yield higher as well as
more stable incomes. Among the individuals over 45
years of age in 1964 who had at least completed
their primary schooling and were present in the
modern Cameroonian labor force, no less than 84
percent were holding non-manual jobs.[16] In contrast, among their counterparts who entered the
labor force between 1958 and 1964 and hence were
under 20 years of age at this later date, the relevant percentage declined to 27 percent. In other
words, the increased output of educational institutions has left educated Cameroonian with only two
options: on the ond hand, they may try to take
advantage of the yet declining solidarity of their
familial groups and remain out of the labor as long
as they do not obtain a position commensurate with
their aspirations.[17] On the other hand, they may
be obliged to adjust their aspirations to the
realities of the market. In short, if educational
currency varies over the life cycle of individuals,
it also varies across cohorts.

Second, while occupational trajectories differ
as between manual and non-manual types of jobs, the
relevant differences vary over time as a function
of the relative rate of development of the various
Cameroonian regions. Thus, the association between
age and number of positions held prior to the current employment follows distinctive curvilinear
patterns by region as well as by type of job

340

(Table 12.3). In overall terms, the low rate of
change characterizing the Cameroonian economy before
the War did not provide the cohorts of workers
entering the labor force at that date with as many
opportunities as those enjoyed by their immediate
successors. In fact, the differential turning
points of the patterns of association between age
and mobility by type of environment and type of job
suggest that there is probably a lag of ten years
or so between the growth of a tertiary urban sector
(which occurred during the war) and the growth of a
rural primary and secondary sector (which did not
occur before 1950). Thus, the percentage of manual
workers living the rural areas who held more than
two jobs since the beginning of their careers begins
to decline for the age groups over 30 years of age
in 1964. In contrast, this decline affects older
segments of the populations who are absorbed by an
urban non-manual labor market.

Further, the differential influence that educational achievement exerts on the occupational
mobility of the two types of worker also varies over
time. Among newcomers to the labor force, this
influence is greater for non-manual than manual wage
earners. In the first case, no less than three
quarters of individuals with a post primary education have held more than two jobs since their entry
in the labor force as opposed to only 5 percent of
their counterparts who did not complete their primary schooling. In the second case, the relevant
percentages are 33 and 9 percent respectively. As
one moves up in the age distribution however, the
effects of educational attainment on mobility becomes more pronounced in the case of manual than of
non-manual workers. In the first case, the proportions of individuals having held more than two jobs
since they began to work ranges between 18 percent
for those who are illiterate and 67 percent for
those who did go beyond primary school. In the
second case, the relevant proportions only range
between 45 and 74 percent. In other words, as we go
back in time, it is clear that the alternatives open
to manual workers were significantly narrower because of the low level of industrialization of the
country. For this reason, manual workers needed
proportionately greater skills to benefit of a
change of occupation.

But if the effects of aging on occupational
trajectories vary over time with societal changes,
they also depend upon the reactions of employers to
such changes. Thus another fallacy of many

341

TABLE 12.3
Influence of Age and of Residence on the Occupational Experience of Manual and Nonmanual Workers

| | Percentage of individuals having held more than two jobs since their entry into the labor market | |
Age	Manual	Nonmanual
15-20		
Rural	2.9	33.1
Urban	18.0	31.3
21-25		
Rural	17.6	52.6
Urban	29.5	42.2
26-30		
Rural	26.4	35.2
Urban	36.3	42.5
31-35		
Rural	22.4	41.7
Urban	35.8	52.8
36-40		
Rural	23.9	50.1
Urban	34.1	70.2
41-45		
Rural	22.9	70.4
Urban	29.7	59.6
Above 45		
Rural	22.4	40.0
Urban	26.7	51.1

sociological and economic analyses of labor markets is to ignore the variability of the meanings attached to overall occupational experiences across types of employment. To be sure, regardless of the specific job he performs, an individual spends the initial years of his career learning occupational patterns, establishing credentials, and preparing himself to move higher in the hierarchy.[18] But while the number of years spent in the labor force and hence age is therefore a predictor of occupational success (as measured in terms of skill level or of earnings), the relationship only holds true within certain limits. The benefits that employers assign to overall experience are necessarily lower whenever a number of significant technological innovations are introduced in an economy. In the Cameroon, these technological innovations are still most significant in the world of industries and hence in the world of blue collar workers.[19] As a result, the image of an older and hence more experienced manual worker conflicts with the image of an individual who, precisely because of his age, is deemed to be rigid and more prone to be fatigued. Thus, the correlation between age (overall occupational experience) and skill level is only .07 for manual workers as opposed to .32 for their non-manual counterparts. Similarly, the correlation between seniority on the present job and skill level is only .18 for the first population but .29 for the second one. Finally, if one takes into consideration the seniority in the firm, the relevant correlations are .11 and .26 respectively. In other words, the principle of diminishing returns begins to operate earlier for blue collar workers. In addition, the consequences attached to various forms of experience are more differentiated in their case.

The same holds true if one considers the patterns of association between these three forms of occupational experience and individual earnings. Among non-manual workers, the correlations between age, seniority on the job, and seniority in the firms on the one hand and their earnings on the other are .231, .161, and .231. Among their manual counterparts, the relevant coefficients are .081, .161, and .191. Further, if one assesses variations in the proportion of individuals earning more than the overall average by type of job, and number of years spent with the present employer, it is clear that the relevant relationship is linear in the case of non-manual workers but curvilinear in the case of their manual counterparts. In this sense, the

343

two categories of workers do not experience similar
kinds of time.

INTERACTION OF FIRMS AND INDIVIDUAL WORKERS
  PROPERTIES OVER TIME

While economic organizations with differing
characteristics are unlikely to attract the same
types of job seekers, and to provide them with
similar kinds of rewards, the relevant contrasts
are not likely to remain stable over time. Both
changes in the composition of the adult Cameroonian
population and in the technological complexity of
the entire economy induce convergences as well as
divergences in the behaviors of the distinctive
types of actors participating in the labor force.[20]
First, internationally based companies always
tend to attract individual wage earners with higher
educational credentials than locally based concerns,
but contrasts between the two types of firms are
significantly more marked among those which settled
in the Cameroon after independence than among those
which began their operations prior to that date.
(Table 12.4)
Secondly, on the whole, the first type of
economic organization offers higher renumeration
than the second one. Yet, differences between the
renumerations that locally and internationally based
concerns offer to their respective manual and non-
manual workers tend to be greater in the case of
newcoming than of well established employers.
(Table 12.5)
Thirdly, however, these differing types of
economic organization do not similarly reward the
educational qualifications of their respective manual and non-manual workers. In the first case, the
educational requirements imposed by internationally
based organizations for gaining access to the top
of the skill hierarchy are relatively independent
of the date of their creation, whereas the newly
created locally based organizations are less demanding in this regard than their well established
counterparts. In short, there are divergences in
the promotion policies followed that internationally
and locally based firms with varying ages adopt
toward their manual workers. Yet, the opposite
pattern is observable in the case of non-manual
workers. The sharp contrasts which characterize the
educational qualifications of the highly skilled
non-manual wage earners attached to international

344

TABLE 12.4
Educational Level of Workers by Selected Characteristics of Firms
(date of foundation and location of headquarters)

	Total Population	Skill Level 4	Skill Levels 5-7
Postindependence			
Local			
Manual	11.5	19.4	24.3
Nonmanual	51.9	56.4	72.2
International			
Manual	21.2	28.5	61.5
Nonmanual	79.3	78.2	70.2
1945 to 1958			
Local			
Manual	14.7	20.2	33.3
Nonmanual	51.8	52.3	85.9
International			
Manual	17.9	28.9	65.6
Nonmanual	70.2	73.8	88.0
Before 1945			
Local			
Manual	12.1	34.9	64.9
Nonmanual	54.8	57.4	66.7
International			
Manual	14.7	19.7	55.5
Nonmanual	64.0	69.9	84.9

Note: Proportion of manual and nonmanual workers
with the equivalent of at least seven years'
formal schooling by skill level and selected
characteristics of firms (date of foundation and
location of headquarters).

TABLE 12.5
Mean Adjusted Annual Income of Workers by Aggregate Training
Score, Age of Firm, and Location of Headquarters
(in thoudands CFA)

Aggregate Training Score	Post-Independence (post 1960)				1965–1959				Before Independence			
	Manual		Nonmanual		Manual		Nonmanual		Manual		Nonmanual	
	Local	Int'l.	Local	Int'l.	Local	Int'l.	Local	Int'l.	Local	Int'l.	Local	Int'l.
0	81.1	103.2	--	--	118.2	125.7	--	--	93.5	120.4	--	--
0.1 to 1.5	110.1	122.4	--	--	120.7	148.5	--	--	105.7	137.1	--	--
1.6 to 6.9	114.0	135.4	175.0	233.3	130.8	184.2	203.8	254.3	121.8	142.4	258.6	275.1
7.0	106.7	135.6	181.0	229.6	123.4	142.6	216.3	300.4	115.8	133.3	265.4	318.0
7.1 to 12.0	146.5	154.3	253.0	315.2	135.2	266.1	261.3	370.2	236.1	171.3	293.5	358.1
Beyond 12.0	*	*	719.2	*	*	*	*	619.2	1427.1	*	929.6	605.1
Percentage of total population earning more than overall average	11.7	41.1	19.2	31.8	26.8	51.7	23.6	41.7	26.8	30.2	36.8	43.2
N	8632	1417	1254	289	4894	3315	528	1342	3211	1713	626	769

*Figures too small to be translated into percentage terms.

and local enterprises created before the war, become hardly significant in the case of firms settled in the Cameroon after independence. In short, there are convergences in the promotion policies they adopt toward this particular segment of the labor force. Alternatively, however, there are over-time convergences in the links that local and international concerns establish between the educational credentials of their blue collar employees and the salaries they are willing to pay them, but over-time divergences in the links that such concerns establish in the case of their white collar labor force. In contrast to international concerns whose salary policies tend to be independent of the date of their creation, their locally based counterparts are more sensitive to the pressures of history. More specifically, the only way for locally based firms created before the war to compensate for the negative image that they tend to project on the labor market and to retain or attract highly qualified manual workers is to reward disproportionately their credentials.

In short, these data suggest that the actual functioning of African labor markets depends not only upon the current bargaining powers of employers and employees but also upon their respective responses to the past practices of their interlocutors. This is because salary negotiations rarely take place in a temporal vacuum.

SUMMARY AND CONCLUSIONS

The purpose of the present chapter has been to show in what sense the Cameroonian labor market reflects the various times experienced by the country as a whole, by employers, and by employees. The stress placed upon time reflects two major preoccupations. On the one hand, much too often, Western social scientists continue, implicitly or explicitly, to adhere to the assumptions made by the forefathers of anthropology and hence to posit that African peoples are not civilized because they have no history.[21] But the point is that much too often it is such social scientists who eliminate arbitrarily the multiple dimensions of time from their analyses. On the other hand, to introduce time dimensions in economic analyses raises the question of determining the extent to which the effects of social change are cumulative and consistent and follow therefore a unilinear pattern. In the case

347

of the Cameroon, we have shown that there are discontinuities in the distinctive behaviors that distinctive types of economic actors adopt toward one another. There are reasons to suspect that such discontinuities characterize as well other developing nations.

1. In contrast to many analysts of development processes who emphasized the significance of individual commitment or of modernity related attitudes and behaviors on the part of African workers, economists such as D. Gordon or M. Reich have shown how the concept of productivity may not reflect as much properties of the objective behaviors displayed by wage earners or other economic actors as qualities imputed to them by individuals who have vested interests to claim that their performances are not satisfactory. For a full exposition of these ideas see for example, D. Gordon, Theories of Poverty and Underemployment (Lexington, Heath, 1972). For a critical review of the literature on modernization as it applies to the industrialization of African countries, see M. Peil, The Ghanaian Factory Worker (Cambridge: Cambridge University Press, 1978).

2. Indeed French colonial authorities have always been quite hesitant about allowing a large number of lower class white migrants into their African colonies. Changes in policies in this regard are indirectly alluded to in S. Tsanga, Le Football Camerounais (Yaounde, 1969).

3. Of course, exceptions to the model suggested by Clark are quite numerous in the case of developing nations, not only in Africa but in Latin America as well. In fact, it could be suggested that the model is only valid with regard to the development of European countries.

4. In this regard it should be remembered that up to quite recently, socialist and nationalist ideologies were highly conflicting. Both Communist and Socialist French parties were in favor of assimilationist policies and argued that any deviation from a centralized jacobinism was a victory for the colonialist forces. There were in fact many hesitations among African political or labor elites as to which strategy would have the highest pay-offs. Under these conditions one can only be surprised by the naivete of the analysis of C. H. Allen, Union-Party Relationships: A Critique of teleguidage Interpretations in R. Sandbrook and R. Cohen, edts. The Development of an African Working Class, Toronto, University of Toronto Press, 1975, pp. 99-128.

5. The presence of representatives of Cameroon in the French Government (Dr. Aujoulat) or in the hierarchy of French National Assembly (Manga Bell

was a vice president) certainly enabled the Cameroon
to obtain some economic "favors" which would have
been difficult to get by other channels. To be
sure, these favors benefited specific interest
groups but their "fall outs" both at the time and
later had necessarily a larger base.

6.   These recent developments are described in
greater details both by V. LeVine The Cameroun
Federal Republique (Ithaca: Cornell University
Press, 1971) and W. Johnson, The Cameroun Federation: Political Integration in a Fragmentary
Society (Princeton: Princeton University Press,
1970).

7.   Thus it is quite important to distinguish
between sociological and historical times in the
analysis of institutions, groups, or individuals.
For an elaboration of this distinction, see C. Levi
Strauss, Anthropologie Structurale (Paris, Plon:
1958).

8.   I will probably remember for ever my
surprise when visiting Africa for the first time in
1952, I observed the total absences of wheel
barrels in a quarry where the stones were transported on the head of the workers. The rationalization used was that "these Africans would not know
how to use a wheel barrel." This ignorance, of
course, justified minimal investments but also low
pay scales.

9.   The data which follow pertain to a very
large segment of the enterprises which were located
in the East Cameroun and used "modern" and government approved accounting systems. For a complete
analysis of these data, see R. Clignet, The
Africanization of the Labor Market (Berkeley:
University of California Press, 1976). For a more
global analysis of the Camerounian economic scene,
see P. Hugon, Analyse du sous développment en Afrique
Noire; L'exemple de l'économie du Cameroun (Paris:
Presses Universitaries de France, 1968). For an
analysis of labor relations in one segment of the
West Cameroun economy, see E. Ardener, et al.,
Plantation and Village in the Cameroons (London:
Oxford University Press, 1960).

10.   These differences contribute of course, to
accentuate disparities in the opportunities enjoyed
by rural as opposed to urban populations and hence
to enhance the complexities of the interdependences
between cities and their hinterlands.

11.   The first solution has often been adopted
by food processing industries while the second

strategy is more often used in the case of textile
and shoe factories.

12. More specifically, maintenance workers are
often highly educated than their counterparts
employed in production lines in the case of construction industries or of the concerns located in
the primary sector. The opposite holds true of
textile and mechanical industries.

13. Indeed the Bamileke living in Douala represented only 16 percent of the total population of
that city in 1947, 26 percent in 1956, but no less
than 33 percent in 1964. See R. Clignet, The
Africanization of the Labor Market, op cit., p. 32.

14. For a general discussion of the distinc-
tions to be introduced between various forms of on
the job training and their economic functions see
L. Thurow, Poverty and Discrimination (Washington:
Brookings Institute, 1969), p. 88. In Africa it is
thus necessary to distinguish such program in terms
of whether they are inter-firms or are only aiming
at developing skills deemed to be necessary for the
sole concern to which workers are attached. In the
same way, some of these programs simply aim at
increasing the number of literate workers whereas
others are only accessible to individuals who have
already achieved a certain level of qualification.

15. For an elaboration of this distinction,
see N. Ryder, "The concept of cohort in the study of
social change," American Sociological Review,
Vol. 30, pp. 840-861.

16. In this analysis, we are of course sup-
posing that transfers between manual and non-manual
jobs have always been and remain infrequent. Such
an assumption tends to be true in the case of the
Cameroon. No less than three quarters of manual
workers began their careers in that sector of
employment as opposed to 56 percent of their non-
manual counterparts.

17. Hence the importance of distinguishing unemployment from deemployment, that is the difficulties encountered by individuals unable or unwilling
to enter the labor market and those unable or
unwilling to remain in such a market. For an
empirical testing of this distinction, see R.
Clignet and J. Sween, "Urban unemployment as a
determinant of political unrest," Canadian Journal
of African Studies, Vol. 3, 1969, pp. 463-488.

18. For an elaboration of this theme, see L.
Thurow, Poverty and Discrimination op cit., p. 181.

19. Indeed while the rationalization of white
collar work is already quite advanced in such

351

sectors as banks and insurance concerns, in the context of highly industrialized countries, this is not so as far as African countries are concerned. In other words, the erosion of non-manual skills is more marked in the first than the second context.

20. For a systematic analysis of the distinction between processes of convergences and divergences, see W. Moore and A. Feldman, "Industrialization and Industrialism: Convergence and differentiation," Vol. II, Transactions of the Fifth World Congress of Sociology; International Sociological Association (Washington, 1962) pp. 151-169.

21. This is a paraphrase of Hegel as quoted by J. Harris, Africans and Their History (New York: New American Library 1972) pp. 13. This argument has been later on amplified by Levi, Bruhl, Durkheim, or even by Gurvitch in his early writings.

The Contributors

J. F. BAYART, Doctorat d'Etat en science
politique (Paris), Research Associate at the
Centre d'Etudes et de Recherches Internationales, Paris, France. Dr. Bayart has
done field work in Cameroon and has contributed
articles on various aspects of Cameroon's
politics in the Revue Française de Science
Politique and in the Revue Française d'Etudes
Politiques Africaines.

SANFORD H. BEDERMAN, Ph.D. (Minnesota), Professor of
Geography at Georgia State University. In
addition to his works on Cameroon which in-
clude The Cameroon Development Corporation:
Partners in National Development, Professor
Bederman has published a number of articles on
urban spatial problems in America, especially
as they relate to the inner city poor. He has
been a recipient of a National Science
Foundation Faculty Fellowship and a Rockefeller
Foundation Research Grant. Professor Bederman
is presently serving as President of the
Southeastern Division of the Association of
American Geographers.

JACQUES BENJAMIN, Doctorat en études politiques
(Paris-Sorbonne), Associate Professor of
Political Science at Simon Fraser University,
British Columbia, Canada. Dr. Benjamin has
carried out field research in Mauritius and
Cameroon and has written extensively on the
politics of these countries. He is the author
of four books on African politics and Canadian
federalism and his major publication on
Cameroon is The West Cameroonians: A Minority
in a Bicommunal Republic.

BONGFEN CHEM-LANGHEE, Ph.D. (British Columbia),
Lecturer in Modern History at the University
of Yaounde, Cameroon. Dr. Chem-Langhee's
research interests are in the mandate and
trusteeship periods of Cameroon history.

REMI CLIGNET, Doctorat de Recherches (Paris-
Sorbonne), Professor of Sociology at Northwestern University. His publications include
The Fortunate Few: A Study of Secondary
Schools and Students in the Ivory Coast;
Many Wives, Many Powers: Authority and Power
in Polygynous Homes; and The Africanization
of the Labor Market as well as numerous
articles in major scholarly journals.

BEBAN SAMMY CHUMBOW, Ph.D. (Indiana), Senior Lecturer
in the Department of Linguistics and Languages,
the University of Ilorin, Nigeria. Dr.
Chumbow has written extensively on the
problem of multilingualism and language
policy in plural states.

MARK W. DeLANCEY, Ph.D. (Indiana), Associate
Professor of Political Science at the University of South Carolina. Dr. DeLancey has
conducted research in Cameroon and Nigeria
and he has taught at the University of Nigeria,
Nsukka. His major publications include A
Bibliography of Cameroon (with Virginia
DeLancey), The United States and World Problems, and articles in various journals such
as the Journal of Modern African Studies and
the Journal of Developing Areas. He is presently conducting research on the national
food policy of Cameroon and writing a book on
the constitution of Nigeria's second republic.

MBU ETONGA, S.J.D. candidate (Yale Law School).
Mr. Etonga received his LL.B. with honors from
the Faculty of Law and Economics, University of
Yaounde, Cameroon, and the LL.M. from Yale
University Law School where he is currently
writing a doctoral dissertation on the legal
implications of the impact of multinational
corporations on the West African economy.

WILLARD R. JOHNSON, Ph.D. (Harvard), Professor of
Political Science, Massachusetts Institute of
Technology and vice-president of the African
Heritage Studies Association. Professor

Johnson is the author of the authoritative
The Cameroon Federation: Political Integration
in a Fragmentary Society.

JOHN KALLA KALE, M.A. (Laval), Research Associate,
Institut Pedagogie Appliqué à vocation rurale
(IPAR), Yaounde. Mr. Kale's research interest
is in the area of educational reform and in
particular the ruralization of primary school
curriculum in Cameroon.

NDIVA KOFELE-KALE, Ph.D. (Northwestern), University
Professor of Comparative/International Politics
and co-Director of the International Studies
Core Project, Governors State University. A
Woodrow Wilson Fellow at Northwestern University, Professor Kofele-Kale has also been the
recipient of research grants from the Ford
Foundation, the American Philosophical Society
and the American Political Science Association.
He has conducted field research in Cameroon
and has been a visiting Scholar at the
University of Michigan. Professor Kofele-
Kale's research on Cameroon political culture
and African leadership have appeared in several
edited books. He has also contributed to such
journals as African Social Research, Civilisa-
tions, Journal of Asian and African Studies,
Journal of Modern African Studies and Social
Action and is the co-author of Comparative
Political Culture and Socialization (1976).

WILFRED A. NDONGKO, Ph.D. (Carleton), Senior
Lecturer, Department of Economics, University
of Calabar, Nigeria. Before joining the
faculty at Calabar, Dr. Ndongko held the
positions of Associate Professor of Economics,
University of Yaounde, 1974-77; Director of
Studies at the Institute of Business Administration, Yaounde, 1975-77. He has also been
an External Examiner (in Economics) JAMB,
Lagos and at the University of Ibadan.
Recipient of research grants from the Ford
Foundation, African-American Scholars Council,
Friedrich-Ebert Foundation and the University
of Calabar Senates Grant Committee. He is the
author of Planning for Economic Development in
a Federal State: The Case of Cameroon 1960-
1971 as well as several articles in scholarly
journals.

MARTIN Z. NJEUMA, Ph.D. (London), Maître de Con-
    ference, Head of the History Department, and
    Dean, Faculty of Arts, University of Yaounde,
    Cameroon. Professor Njeuma has carried out
    field research in Cameroon, Nigeria, and West
    Germany and was a Visiting Professor at the
    University of South Carolina during the 1976-77
    academic year. He has contributed to the Journal
    of African History and is the author of The
    Origins of Pan-Cameroonism and Fulani Hegemony
    in Yola (Old Adamawa) 1808-1902.

FRANK M. STARK, Ph.D. (Northwestern), Assistant
    Professor of Political Science at Concordia
    University, Quebec, Canada. Dr. Stark has
    contributed articles on Cameroon federalism
    in the Canadian Journal of African Studies
    and has recently completed a book length study
    on Cameroon.

OMER WEYI YEMBE, Ed.D. (Columbia), Director of Private
    Education, Ministry of National Education, Yaounde,
    Cameroon. Dr. Yembe has held a number of top
    level administrative positions in the Cameroon
    educational system and is actively involved in
    the school reforms programs under the aegis of
    IPAR.

Name Index

358

359

Subject Index

365

368